W9-BNC-198

DATE DUE

Comparing Theories of Child Development

SECOND EDITION

Comparing Theories
of Child Development

SECOND EDITION

R. MURRAY THOMAS
University of California
Santa Barbara

Wadsworth Publishing Company
Belmont, California
A Division of Wadsworth Inc.

To Shirley

Psychology Editor: Kenneth King
Production Editor: Julia Chitwood, Bookman Productions
Designers: Detta Penna and Hal Lockwood
Copy Editor: Betty Berenson
Illustrator: Nancy Warner
Cover: Hal Lockwood and Wendy Goldberg, Bookman Productions

Printed in the United States of America

6 7 8 9 10— 90

ISBN 0-534-03855-7

Library of Congress Cataloging in Publication Data

Thomas, R. Murray (Robert Murray), 1921-
  Comparing theories of child development.

  Bibliography: p.
  Includes index.
  1. Child psychology. 2. Child development. I. Title.
BF721.T456   1984   155.4'01   84-13015
ISBN 0-534-03855-7

ACKNOWLEDGMENTS

We wish to thank the following for permission to use various excerpts and illustrations.

Alston, W. P. "Comments on Kohlberg's 'From Is to Ought' " in T. Mischel, *Cognitive Development and Epistemology*. New York: Academic, 1971. Used by permission of Academic Press. • Baldwin, A. L. *Theories of Child Development*. New York: Wiley, 1967. Used by permission of John Wiley & Sons, Inc. • Barker, R. G., J. S. Kounin, and H. F. Wright. *Child Behavior and Development*. New York: McGraw-Hill, 1943. Used by permission of McGraw-Hill, Inc. • Freud, S. *An Outline of Psychoanalysis*. London: Hogarth, 1973. Used by permission of Hogarth Press Ltd. • Gesell, A. and F. L. Ilg. *Child Development: An Introduction to the Study of Human Growth*. Excerpts from Part I: "Infant and Child in the Culture of Today" copyright 1949 by Harper & Row, Publishers, Inc. Chart (list) from Part II: "The Child from Five to Ten" copyright 1946 by Arnold Gesell and Frances L. Ilg. Used by permission of Harper & Row, Publishers, Inc. and Hamish Hamilton Ltd. • Havighurst, R. J. *Human Development and Education*. Copyright © 1953 by Longman Inc. Previously published by David McKay Company, Inc. Used by permission of Longman Inc. • Hinde, R. A. *Biological Bases of Human Social Behavior*. New York: McGraw-Hill, 1974. Used by permission of McGraw-Hill, Inc. • Ilg, F. L. and L. B. Ames. *Child Behavior*. Copyright 1955 by Frances L. Ilg and Louise Bates Ames. Used by permission of Harper & Row, Publishers, Inc. and Hamish Hamilton Ltd. • Inhelder, B. and J. Piaget. *The Early Growth of Logic in the Child*. London: Routledge & Kegan Paul, 1964. Used by permission of Harper & Row, Publishers, Inc. and Routledge & Kegan Paul Ltd. • Kohlberg, L. "From Is to Ought" in T. Mischel, *Cognitive Development and Epistemology*. New York: Academic, 1971. Used by permission of Academic Press. • Kohlberg, L. "Moral and Religious Education in the Public Schools: A Developmental View" in T. R. Sizer, *Religion and Public Education*. Copyright © 1967 by Houghton Mifflin Company. Used by permission of Houghton Mifflin Company. • Kohlberg, L. and R. Kramer. "Continuities in Childhood and Adult Moral Development." *Human Development*, Vol. 12 (1969), pp. 93-120. Used by permission of S. Karger AG, Basel, Switzerland. • Lewin K. "The Field Theory Approach to Adolescence." *American Journal of Sociology*, Vol. 44 (1939), pp. 868-896.

Used by permission of The University of Chicago Press. • Maslow, A. H. *The Farther Reaches of Human Nature.* Copyright © 1971 by Bertha G. Maslow. An Esalen Book, used by permission of The Viking Press. • Maslow, A. H. *Toward a Psychology of Being.* © 1968 by Litton Educational Publishing, Inc. Used by permission of D. Van Nostrand Company. • Peters, R. S. "Moral Development: A Plea for Pluralism" in T. Mischel, *Cognitive Development and Epistemology.* New York: Academic, 1971. Used by permission of Academic Press • Skinner, B. F. "Baby in a Box" in B. F. Skinner (ed.), *Cumulative Record: A Selection of Papers, 3d ed.* New York: Appleton-Century-Crofts, 1972. Used by permission of Prentice-Hall, Inc. • Skinner, B. F. *Walden Two.* New York: Macmillan, 1948. Used by permission of Macmillan Publishing Co., Inc. • Thomas, S. M. Drawings and Case Descriptions. Used by permission of Shirley M. Thomas. • Tryon, C. and J. Lilienthal. "Developmental Tasks: I. The Concept and Its Importance" in *Fostering Mental Health in Our Schools.* Copyright © 1950 by the Association for Supervision and Curriculum Development. Used by permission of the Association for Supervision and Curriculum Development. • Vygotsky, L. S. *Thought and Language.* Cambridge, Mass: Massachusetts Institute of Technology, 1962. Used by permission of MIT Press. • Werner, H. and B. Kaplan. *Symbol Formation—An Organismic-Developmental Approach to Language and the Expression of Thought.* New York: Wiley, 1963. Used by permission of Bernard Kaplan.

CONTENTS

CHAPTER NINE   Erikson's Variation of Freud's Theme   233

PART FIVE   *THE GROWTH OF LANGUAGE AND THOUGHT*   257

A search for patterns of development in children's cognitive and verbal skills, and for the mechanisms that bring these patterns about

CHAPTER TEN   Piaget's Cognitive Development Theory   259

CHAPTER ELEVEN   Vygotsky and the Soviet Tradition   304

A search for the way principles of learning explain development

PREFACE

Child development theorists are dissatisfied people. They are not content with existing explanations of how a child grows up, so they search for more adequate explanations. To guide their search, they set up goals at which to aim their efforts, goals that may be either stated or implied. This book's purpose is to identify these goals and to describe the results achieved by more than two dozen theorists in their search.

This text has the same aim in the world of theories that a three-week guided European tour has in the world of travel. I do not pretend in this book to give detailed, in-depth knowledge of any one territory. Instead, I propose to (1) suggest profitable ways to compare theories (Chapters One and Two) and (2) acquaint you with key aspects of a variety of the better known theories (Chapters Three through Sixteen). After reading these chapters, you should be able to study any of the theorists' original writings with greater ease and profit. You will be able to approach the theorists with an understanding of the chief features of their domains, and you will know how the features of each theory compare with those of others.

There are far more theories in the world than a single volume can accommodate. Therefore it has been necessary to select those that are most suitable for our purpose. Each choice has been guided by three criteria, which can be stated as three sets of questions:

1. Has the theory been popular? That is, have many people subscribed to it or at least been acquainted with it?

2. Has the theory been influential? Has it affected people's treatment of children or influenced the beliefs of other theorists?

3. Is the theory representative of a class or family of theories? Theories often fall into groups, with the members of each group

being similar in certain respects and dissimilar in others. Because it is not feasible to include all variants of a particular group, I have chosen only a few theories—in some cases only one—to represent each class. In making this selection I have been influenced not only by the representativeness of a theory but also by my own tastes and interests, including those theories that I feel are more interesting than others.

The fourteen chapters that describe individual theories are organized in seven parts. Each part reflects a key goal pursued by the theorists discussed within that part as they searched for descriptions or explanations of development more adequate than those found in existing theories. I have tried to suggest this key goal by placing under each part title a phrase identifying the sort of search that links together the theorists included in that section.

The final chapter of the book does not describe any theory in detail. Rather, it is an annotated bibliography that can guide you to sources of additional theories that you may find interesting to investigate.

Because this is a revised edition of a book first issued in 1979, I assume that users of the original edition would like to know at the outset what sorts of revisions this second edition contains. One of the most important changes has been the addition of a new chapter on information-processing theory (Chapter Twelve). And at the request of professors using the first edition as a textbook, I have provided two new segments in Chapters Three through Sixteen. The first segment describes each theory's practical applications to child rearing, education, and personal counseling. The second, entitled "Research Challenges," offers a sampling of issues that call for further investigation, with most of the issues cast as unanswered questions that can serve as subjects of further research.

Besides the foregoing changes, substantially more material has been added to a number of chapters, particularly those on Piaget (Chapter Ten), on Vygotsky and other Soviet psychologists (Chapter Eleven), on Skinner's operant conditioning (Chapter Fourteen), and on humanistic theory (Chapter Sixteen). To make room for such additions, two chapters of the first edition have been eliminated: the one on Brown's studies of early language learning and the final chapter describing four "applied" theories. Furthermore, the material that formed a chapter on Wilson's sociobiology has been much condensed and is now combined with the work of other ethologists to make up the last half of Chapter Seven on principles of development. Further minor additions will also be found at various points throughout the book.

If we inspect the origins of the theories discussed, we discover that they display a geographical bias. All originate in the Western world. Their roots are in Western civilization, and they have been nurtured primarily in Europe and North America. To help balance this bias, four of my graduate students who are expert in Oriental languages and cultures joined me in preparing a companion volume entitled *Oriental Theories of Human Development*, which will be published in the near future. This book contains theories extracted from the traditional literature of five Oriental religious traditions (Hinduism, Thai Buddhism, Confucianism, Islam, and Shinto). The theoretical material is supplemented by interviews about human development conducted with more than 100 adherents of each of the religions. The interviews were collected by the research team in India, Thailand, the Republic of China on Taiwan, the Sudan, and Japan.

A note of appreciation is due to both my students and my colleagues at the University of California, Santa Barbara. They have always been helpful in suggesting new sources of further theories and in offering comments that have forced me to improve the clarity and accuracy of what I say and write. I also wish to thank my colleagues in other universities who read this book in manuscript form and offered valuable suggestions for improving its content: Andrew Collins, University of Minnesota; Bernard S. Gorman; Judy Todd; and Eleanor Willemson, Santa Clara University. Appreciation is also expressed to the following, who made valuable suggestions for the revised version: Ronald Mullis, North Dakota State University; Samuel Snyder, North Carolina State University at Raleigh; James Moran, Virginia Polytechnic Institute; Jane Ledingham, University of Ottawa; Richard Newman, State University of New York at Stony Brook; and Billie Housego, University of British Columbia. In addition, I wish to express my appreciation for the wisdom and diligence applied to the production of the new edition by members of the Bookman Productions staff, particularly Julia Chitwood. Finally, a word of thanks is due Ken King, psychology editor at Wadsworth, for his strong support.

STANDARDS OF COMPARISON

Ways of analyzing likenesses and differences among theories

Since this book compares theories of child development, it is reasonable to ask at the outset, Compares theories against what standards? Or, compares them along what dimensions? The two chapters comprising Part One are designed to answer these questions.

Chapter One defines the way such terms as *facts, theory,* and *model* are used throughout the book. It also describes a variety of standards or criteria that people often use to distinguish "good theory" from "bad theory."

Chapter Two looks at theories in a different way. It reviews a range of topics or questions on which a child development theory may focus. These questions are intended as guides to identifying the contents of a theory, that is, as guides to the substantive focus of the theory.

Part One, then, suggests viewpoints from which the theories surveyed in Chapters Three through Sixteen can be analyzed at an introductory or basic level.

Theories, Models, Paradigms, and Such

Many people—parents, teachers, college students—often say, "I don't want a lot of theorizing. I want to know what children are really like. It's the facts of child development I'm interested in."

For such people, "theorizing" means speculating about children in the quiet of a study, producing a kind of armchair philosophy that has little or nothing to do with the way children grow up in the real world. "Facts," they feel, are practical and useful. Facts show how children really develop and why they behave as they do. For these people a book on child development theories is of no value.

The above distinction between "fact" and "theory" is not the one intended in this book. I see the relationship between the two in a different way. I consider facts or data to be either (1) discrete observations and measurements of children and their actions or (2) summaries of such observations and measurements. Here are three typical examples of discrete observations:

> A first-grade teacher poured all of the water from a bowl into a tall drinking glass, then asked six-year-old Anne if the amount of water now in the glass was the same as the amount that had been in the bowl. Anne said there was now more in the glass.

> The parents of thirteen-year-old Martin were upset because, they said, the boy acted "like a sissy." Martin did not like to play with other boys. He wore fancy rings and bracelets. His mother found him in her bedroom putting rouge on his lips and darkening his eyelids with her eye shadow. His father said, "Marty even walks like a girl."

3

> Shortly after supper one evening, seventeen-year-old Linda received a telephone invitation to go to a movie, but she said, "Sorry, Hank, I have to stay in all evening to study chemistry." A few moments later she answered another phone call with, "Okay, Larry, but only for a couple of hours. I'll study till eight o'clock. Then we can go out for a while."

Facts or data can also be in the form of summaries of observations or measurements: the average height of twelve-year-old girls, a list of the reactions of five-year-olds when they first enter kindergarten, the percentage of sixteen-year-olds who have smoked marijuana.

If these are facts, then what is theory? There is no easy, definitive answer to this question because many different meanings for theory are found in writings on philosophy and science. For the purposes of this book, however, I have simplified matters by adopting one definition broad enough to encompass all the different authors that I have included. I define theory as *an explanation of how the facts fit together.* More precisely, I intend the process of theorizing about child development to mean the act of proposing (1) which facts are most important for understanding children and (2) what sorts of relationships among the facts are most significant for producing this understanding. Theory is what makes sense out of facts. Theory gives facts their meaning. Without theory, facts remain a clutter of disorganized specks on the canvas, unconnected spots that form no picture of how and why children grow up as they do.

Thus a book on theories of child development can serve as a practical guide to understanding children, for it describes the underlying structure of different beliefs about what children are like and how children should be treated.

In this opening chapter we focus on four questions that people often ask when they first seriously consider theories of development: (1) What difference does it make which theory you adopt? (2) How does the term *theory* relate to such terms as *model, paradigm, analogue,* and the like? (3) What standards can be used to distinguish good theory from bad theory? (4) Why do scholars develop different theories rather than agree on an existing one?

THE DIFFERENCE YOUR CHOICE OF THEORY CAN MAKE

A theory of child development can be likened to a lens through which we view children and their growth. The theory filters out certain facts and gives a particular pattern to those it lets in. To illustrate the way such filtering operates, let's briefly consider how the incidents of Anne, Martin, and

Linda might be interpreted from the viewpoints of four theories presented later.

These interpretations will, of course, be much simplified since you have not yet had a chance to inspect any of the theories in detail. However, they still illustrate the point that the theory chosen for interpreting facts about children determines the meaning assigned to those facts. When you have read further, you will recognize the complexities the cases of Anne, Martin, and Linda would involve if they were interpreted more completely.

The four theorists whose lenses we peer through are Piaget, Freud, Lewin, and Skinner.

A Piagetian Viewpoint

For more than fifty years a Swiss child psychologist, Jean Piaget, collected facts on how children of different ages solved reasoning problems, express-ed their dreams, made moral judgments, and carried out other mental activities. He proposed that a child's modes of thought form a series of stages of intellectual growth common to all children in all cultures. We might reasonably propose then that Piagetians would interpret the cases of Anne, Martin, and Linda in terms of these stages.

For instance, we would expect an advocate of Piaget's theory to explain that Anne thought there was more water in the tall glass than in the shallow bowl because she had not yet reached the stage at which children understand conservation of volume. By "conservation" we mean that Anne does not yet recognize that the quantity of water remains the same (is "conserved") even though the height and width of the two containers differ.

When we turn to Martin's effeminate behavior, we are on less secure ground in speculating about what a Piagetian would conclude because Piaget focused little if any attention on matters of socially "deviant" behavior. Piaget was more concerned with the thought processes of the typical or average child than with personal-social behavior that differed from a par-ticular society's norms for sex-appropriate actions. However, Piaget did give a good deal of attention to children's moral judgments, to what children considered right and wrong and to how they supported such decisions. Piaget identified a series of stages through which children passed in the development of moral judgment, and we might use these stages for inter-preting what Martin would say in defending the rightness of his wearing lip rouge and eye shadow. In other words, by posing moral-decision questions for Martin to answer, we could estimate the level of reasoning he uses to defend his actions.

When we use a Piagetian lens to view seventeen-year-old Linda's rejection of Hank in favor of Larry, we again receive little direct aid since Piaget did not theorize about sexual attraction and social interaction among adolescents. However, if we put the sexual attraction question aside and limit ourselves to the intellectual companionship aspect of Linda's choice, then we might find some aid in Piagetian theory. We could speculate that Linda may have preferred Larry because her stage of intelligence or mode of thought was more like Larry's than like Hank's. In other words, we would be estimating that youths of similar intellectual levels have a greater affinity for each other than youths of dissimilar levels.

We might also use Piagetian theory in another way to give meaning to the facts about Linda. Since Piaget identified stages of moral judgment that children pass through, we could ask Linda to explain why she thought it was right to reject Hank in favor of Larry. Then we could use her response to estimate her stage of moral judgment.

Let's turn now to a second theorist's perceptions of the same cases.

A Freudian Viewpoint

Toward the end of the nineteenth and the beginning of the twentieth centuries, Sigmund Freud devised a theory of child development based on the childhood recollections of adults that he treated for neuroses in his Vienna, Austria, psychiatric practice. Freud, like Piaget, proposed that children develop through a series of stages. However, instead of concerning himself with children's reasoning skills, Freud focused on *psychosexual* development. He identified steps in personality growth as influenced by children's ways of satisfying sexual drives from one period of childhood to another.

For example, Freud theorized that between the ages of 3 and 5, the typical child views the opposite-sex parent as a desirable love object that he or she wants to possess exclusively. In essence, the boy yearns to possess his mother and the girl her father. However, the child recognizes that she or he has been bested in this competition by the like-sexed parent. In other words, the boy's father has been the victor in the contest for the mother's sexual attention, and the girl's mother has been the victor in the competition for the father's love. To resolve this problem of yearning for the opposite-sex parent, the normal child in Freud's system seeks to acquire the characteristics of the victor. This means that the boy identifies with his father and seeks to adopt his father's traits, the traits of masculinity. In like fashion, the girl identifies with her mother and tries to behave in those feminine ways that apparently have made her mother successfully attractive. This process of identification, then, explains from a Freudian viewpoint why the normal boy develops the characteristics that his society considers masculine and the normal girl develops the characteristics considered feminine.

However, Freudians point out that sometimes the process of resolving the parental love conflict goes awry. The boy may not identify with his father's traits. Instead, he identifies with his mother's characteristics, or perhaps some other twist occurs in the normal process. Consequently the boy adopts feminine characteristics. From a Freudian perspective, we could reasonably assume that such a twist occurred in Martin's case. The boy apparently did not achieve a proper resolution of the conflict he faced in middle childhood, so that in early adolescence he is displaying sexually inappropriate behavior. To find out how this actually happened, Freudians would wish to gather information from the boy's unconscious mind— information collected by means of dream interpretation and by analyzing the free-flowing thoughts that Martin expresses while in a relaxed condition.

We can speculate that Freudians would see Anne's reactions also from a psychosexual viewpoint. Freudians—or at least some Freudians—would interpret Anne's reactions to the bowl and the tall glass in terms of sexual symbols. The meaning of the bowl-and-glass incident, they might say, lies in the unconscious portion of the girl's mind and relates to Anne's concerns about her own drives and the ways they are being satisfied or frustrated. In Freud's view, containers such as bowls and glasses symbolized female sex organs, whereas protruding, projectile-like objects symbolized the male. But exactly how such symbolization might fit into Anne's personality structure in the bowl-and-glass experiment would likely be unclear to psychoanalysts until they collected more information about the girl's feelings and thought processes. This information, intended to reveal the child's unconscious motives, might be gathered through the analyst's listening to Anne's verbalizations while she played with dolls or while she recounted her fantasies.

The case of the high school girl, Linda, might be analyzed in several ways from a Freudian viewpoint. Freudians might explain Linda's behavior in terms of how the characteristics of her two suitors, Hank and Larry, compared with the characteristics of other important males in her life, particularly her father. Did Linda select Larry because he reminded her of her father and was a substitute for him in the girl's affections? Or did Linda reject Hank because he reminded her of her father and she was symbolically striking back at her father whom she resents and wishes to harm? In effect, how is Linda's reaction to the two boys related to the manner in which she has sought to resolve the desire to possess her father—a desire that ostensibly began a decade earlier at the psychosexual stage known generally as the Oedipus stage or, for girls, the Electra stage or Electra conflict? The answer to such questions is not found in the facts of the Larry and Hank incident. Rather, the answer must be sought through the collection of far more information about the nature of Linda's unconscious motives and the manner in which she has interacted with her parents over the past years.

Thus we see that the facts offered earlier about Martin, Anne, and Linda can assume quite different meanings when viewed through the lens of Freudian rather than Piagetian theory.

A Lewinian Viewpoint

A third theorist discussed in this book, Kurt Lewin, made his principal contributions to child development theory during the 1920s and 1930s, first in Germany and then in the United States. One of his favorite ways of viewing child behavior was to plot behavior visually as a map of the child's *life space*. By the term *life space* Lewin meant all the different forces influencing the child's thought processes at the moment the child is making a decision about how to act. These forces are not simply the objects in the child's environment, such as the bowl and glass of water in the case of first-grader Anne. Instead, they include pertinent memories of the past that the child brings to bear on this incident, the child's physical state at this time (such as degree of hunger or fatigue), and whatever the child is perceiving at the moment in the environment. Some of these forces push the child to act one way, and some push her to act another way. The child's final decision results from the stronger collection of forces.

In the incident of Anne and the water containers, a Lewinian would estimate which forces caused the girl to conclude that when the water from the bowl was poured into the tall glass, there was more water.

In the case of Linda, we might expect Lewinians to interpret Linda's choice of Larry over Hank in terms of the psychological forces bearing on the girl at the time of the decision. To illustrate Linda's apparent life space, Lewinians might draw a diagram like that of Figure 1.1. But they would need to gather additional data about Linda in order to determine which forces were influencing her decision at the moment. These factors would be included in the map of her life space at that moment. (For purposes of illustration, I have assumed that we have gathered some of this sort of information in preparing Figure 1.1.) As the diagram suggests, the forces are more favorable to Larry than to Hank.

As for Martin, followers of Lewin could be expected to map out the psychological forces that caused the boy to behave as his parents describe. However, in addition, Lewinians would likely interpret Martin's behavior as a sort of confused groping to understand this new stage of growth he is experiencing, the stage of early adolescence. According to Lewin, adolescence represents a time of movement from one stable period of life (late

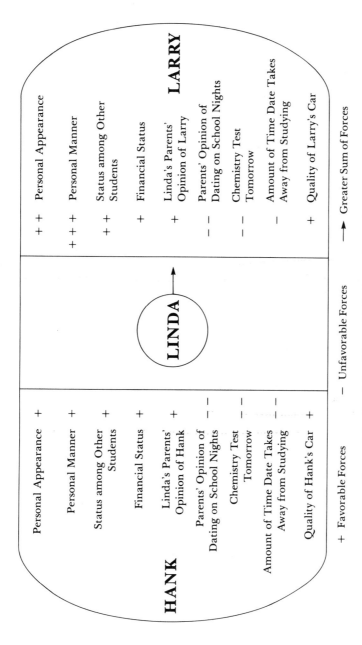

Figure 1.1 Lewinian Map of Life Space in Decision Making

childhood) to another stable period (adulthood) as yet poorly understood by the youth. During the teenage years many puzzling body changes occur, and family and friends alter their expectations of how the boy or girl should behave socially. Lewin proposed that the adolescent feels new emotional tensions and may act in ways considered by parents, and by youths themselves, to be rather odd. So Martin, like adolescents described by Lewin, may be displaying, in his sexually inappropriate behavior, the confusion of a visitor entering a strange land, a poorly mapped domain whose terrain he only vaguely comprehends.

In effect, Lewinian theory casts the data about Anne, Martin, and Linda in a different light than either Piagetian theory or Freudian theory.

A Skinnerian Viewpoint

B. F. Skinner is a contemporary American psychologist who represents a school of thought known as *radical behaviorism*. He believes that it is more profitable to observe the factors in life that seem to influence people's behavior than it is to speculate about what might be in people's minds or personalities. The basic tenets of his system are quite simple. Every time someone acts, the action is followed by a consequence. The nature of this consequence determines whether the person will act in the same way in a similar situation in the future. If the consequence is pleasant and rewarding, then the person will tend to act in the same way in the future. If the consequence is not rewarding, the person will tend to act differently. In essence, according to Skinner, the behaviors we develop as we grow up depend on the consequences that followed those behaviors in the past.

Now let us speculate about how such a theory might enable us to interpret the incidents involving Anne, Martin, and Linda. We may assume that in the past Anne has been rewarded (behaviorists would call it *reinforced* instead of *rewarded*) for concluding that when something is taller, it is larger or bigger in general. Her own experience and other people's remarks have confirmed this conclusion for her. Thus, when she sees the water reach a greater height in the glass than it did in the bowl, she draws the same conclusion that has been reinforced in the past—that there is more of the substance when it is taller. If we wish to change Anne's misconception, we need to arrange the consequences of her behavior so they no longer reinforce her unsophisticated judgment. We would arrange experiments that force her to disconfirm her conclusion about the water containers, and we would also tell her when she is right and wrong. We may even wish to furnish some external reward, such as a toy or candy, for correct conclusions and withhold such reinforcers when she makes errors in judgment. That is, according to Skinnerian theory, we influence Anne's intellectual development by manipulating the consequences of her behavior.

When we consider Martin's behavior from a Skinnerian viewpoint, we conclude that he currently displays feminine ways because when he has done so in the past the consequences have been more satisfying or reinforcing than the consequences following masculine actions he has attempted. Not only does he currently persist in retaining past feminine acts but he can be expected to acquire even more of them in the future if the consequences of doing so are reinforced. The only way to alter his behavior pattern is to manipulate the consequences so that those following feminine acts are nonreinforcing and those following masculine acts are reinforcing or pleasurable.

In like manner we can interpret Linda's preference for Larry rather than Hank in terms of the consequences that have followed the girl's past contacts with the two boys. Apparently her relationship with Larry has been reinforced more strongly than her relationship with Hank. This greater reinforcement accounts for her preference to be with Larry.

So we see that when we view facts of child development through a Skinnerian lens, we achieve different meanings from those we achieved when we used Piagetian, Freudian, or Lewinian theories. Which theory we adopt makes a great difference in what we believe the facts mean and in how we treat children and youths as we seek to promote their optimum development.

Before leaving our four illustrative theorists, I should state explicitly that the interpretations I have offered of the data about Anne, Martin, and Linda are not the only ones that might be drawn from the four theoretical positions. Other interpreters might find other implications in the data. Thus the conclusions I have presented are not *the* correct or definitive analyses; rather they are simply illustrations of meanings that logically could be offered from the four perspectives. Furthermore I obviously have given only a brief glimpse of each theory, just enough to suggest how data can assume quite different meanings when different theories are used for organizing the facts. A more complete examination of each theory is found in later chapters.

THE WORD *THEORY*
AND OTHER TERMS

So far in our discussion we have stayed almost exclusively with the word *theory* in referring to authors' schemes for organizing data. However, in the literature on child development a variety of terms is used, and this is a problem for newcomers to child development theory. The problem is, How do such words as *theory, model, paradigm, analogue,* and *metatheory* relate to each other? Solving the problem would be simple if all writers intended the same meaning for a given term, but such is not the case. One writer will use *theory* and *model* as synonyms; another will not. Before we move further into the analysis of theories, we need to inspect a number of these terms to see how they are used by different theorists.

Of the many words we might consider, I have selected thirteen of the most common to discuss. The first six are used almost synonymously by many writers; they are *theory, model, paradigm, analogy, structure,* and *system.* The seventh is *metatheory,* a term of recent popularity that appears to have spawned a brood of related *meta* words. The last six are typically used for identifying kinds of statements made within a theory; these are *assumption, axiom, postulate, hypothesis, principle,* and *law.*

When we read about theories of child development, we must be alert to the meaning the writer explicitly or implicitly assigns to the word *theory.* For us, a theory will be any statement describing (1) which facts are most important for understanding children and (2) what sorts of relationships among facts are most significant for producing this understanding. Other writers place more restrictions on the term. For example, *theory* can be defined as a "set of statements, including (a) general laws and principles that serve as axioms, (b) other laws, or theorems, that are deducible from the axioms, and (c) definitions of concepts" (Reese & Overton, 1970, p. 117). Skinner on occasion has denied that his explanation of behavior qualifies as theory; and if a very restricted definition of the term is applied, he would appear to be correct in his denial. However, in the broad sense of the word that we have adopted in these pages, Skinner's explanation does indeed qualify as theory (Skinner, 1950).

The word *model* has become increasingly popular in recent decades as a label for theoretical proposals. However, the term has caused some confusion because one writer will use it in a broad sense while another will limit its meaning. In its broad sense, *model* can mean any tentative ideational plan of relationships among variables. At this general level, a model can be a world view (Kuhn, 1962) or a world hypothesis (Pepper, 1942) that suggests something about the basic nature of people or of reality. For example, some child development theories are founded on a machine model in contrast to others founded on a dynamic organism model. That is, one camp of theorists pictures the growing child as a machine that reacts to things done to it by the environment: The child's behavior is primarily a product of the way the environment manipulates it. The other group pictures the child as an active, seeking organism who determines his or her own behavior by internally motivated desires. In a more limited sense writers have used the word *model* to mean, for example, an exclusively mathematical or graphic representation of the way something operates (Suppes, 1969, pp. 10–17). In child development literature, therefore, we should try to decide which of these meanings the writer intends. In the following chapters I will use *model* in the same broad sense as I am using *theory*—as any scheme intended to describe relationships among variables or facts of child development.

Another common term in child development literature is *paradigm* (rhymes with either "dim" or "dime"). Some people use *paradigm* to mean only a very general model (Kuhn, 1962), an overall viewpoint or description of relationships about reality. Others use it to mean either a broad, general picture or as a more specific, more precise description of relationships among variables. In this sense, they equate *paradigm* with *model* and use the terms interchangeably. Again, it is well to determine the way an author intends the term to be used.

Theorists use the term *analogy* or *analogue* when comparing an aspect of growth to something else in order to help explain that aspect of growth. For instance, theorists may say that the mind of the growing child is like an electronic computer, consisting of a finite amount of storage space for ideas and a system for retrieving the ideas when they are needed. Or theorists may liken a highly mobile two-year-old to an inquisitive puppy that noses into everything without any notion of danger or responsibility. Analogies are thus kinds of models, in the sense of one thing representing qualities of something else. In this book, *analogy* or *analogue* will refer to a comparison between child development in a general sense and some other object or system; for example, an analogy would liken stages of growth to steps on a ladder the child ascends as the years pass.

The words *structure* and *system* are considered together for they commonly carry the same meaning. Each identifies the elements that comprise something and describes the way these elements are interrelated. Therefore a theorist's entire complex of beliefs and their interconnections can be called a system. Likewise, one segment of an overall complex of beliefs can be singled out as a separate entity with its own constituent parts and be called a system or subsystem by itself. So we can speak of Piaget's complete set of ideas about child development as his system or theoretical structure, or we can pick one segment of this complex—such as Piaget's explanation of children's play—and view it as a subsystem with its own inner workings (Hall & Lindzey, 1970, pp. 317–318).

Beginning in the 1970s, a host of new *meta* words sprang up in the human development literature: *metatheory, metamemory, metacognition, meta-analysis, metalearning, metaperception, metaprinciples,* and more. This rash of neologisms has caused some confusion since authors often fail to explain how they intend such terms. Furthermore, while there is some consistency of usage, not all authors use a given meta word with the same meaning. In contemporary human development literature *meta* is most often intended to mean "an analysis of" or "knowledge about" the subject to which the meta is prefixed. So in this sense, *metacognition* is knowledge about cognition or, in other words, "thinking about thinking." In like manner, *metamemory* is an awareness of how memory operates, and *metalearning* is the analysis of how learning occurs. Following this same pattern, *metatheory* becomes the analysis of what *theory* is about, how *theory* is developed or used. As a result, what we are doing throughout this book is *metatheory*. It is especially what I am attempting in these first two chapters.

Although most meta terms in child development literature seem to mean "knowledge about" some process, sometimes they are not intended that way. Not long ago I asked an author what he meant by *metatheory* in one of his recent articles. Did he mean "an analysis of" theory? Or, rather, was *metatheory* in this instance an overarching, umbrella theory that encompassed more specific subtheories, as some writers use the term? He said no. On this occasion he used the word to mean a precursor of "true theory," that is, a set of preliminary speculations that would not as yet qualify as tightly knit theory. So, because the meanings for meta terms have not been standardized, it is well to study a theorist's meta words with some care to estimate which meaning she or he is seeking to convey.

Next we turn to six words that refer to types of statements that may be included in a theory. They are *assumption, axiom, postulate, hypothesis, principle,* and *law.* Again, as with the words just discussed, not all writers assign identical meanings to these terms. However, we shall not take time to survey the various uses of each term. Instead we will look at the most widely accepted meaning of each.

One useful way to approach the six terms is to think of their roles within a series of four phases a theorist may go through in creating and refining a model of child development (see Table 1.1). To begin, the theorist accepts certain concepts as true without testing them. These self-evident beliefs are frequently called *assumptions, axioms,* or *postulates.* An axiom or postulate is a formal statement of the conviction on which the theorist's model will be founded. In contrast, an assumption is either informally stated by the theorist or is not stated at all. Sometimes theorists are unaware that they are making certain assumptions until critics point them out.

After establishing a foundation of assumptions and postulates, the theorist erects the superstructure of the model. Typically the model, or at least certain aspects of it, is proposed in only a tentative form because the author is not sure that it represents an accurate picture of the way children develop. The author is saying, in effect, that "it seems likely that children grow up this way and for these reasons." However, she or he is not entirely sure. So to answer questions that are still puzzling about the theory's validity, the theorist composes some "if-then" statements that derive logical-

Table 1.1   Terms and Phases in Theory Building

	Phase 1	Phase 2	Phase 3	Phase 4
	Foundation Convictions	Model Descriptions	Logical Deductions	Conclusions
Products of the Phase:	Axioms Postulates Assumptions	Structure System	Hypotheses	Principles Laws
The Theorist's Behavior:	Accepts certain beliefs as being self-evident.	Defines the parts of the model and their interrelations.	Suggests relationships or outcomes that reasonably might be expected if the model accurately represents the aspect of development it is supposed to describe.	Draws generalizations from evidence collected to test or estimate the accuracy of the model.

Note: Although the process of theory building can thus be described as four sequential steps or phases, in practice a theorist frequently may not move systematically through the sequence. More often than not, theorists appear to shuttle back and forth among the phases, revising here and altering there, to produce a scheme they believe provides a convincing interpretation of the facts.

ly from the model. These yet-to-be-proven statements are usually called *hypotheses*.

One popular way to state a hypothesis is in an if-then form. For example, in Chapter Six we consider a developmental-task theory advocated by an American psychologist named Robert J. Havighurst. The theory proposes that every few years as children grow up, they meet a new set of physical-growth and social-psychological problems or *tasks* they must solve. The theory further contends that if children do not successfully solve a problem at one age level, they will have difficulty in solving tasks at higher age levels in the future. From this general proposal, we create hypotheses to test the validity of Havighurst's notion. As one illustration, we can take the area of emotional development called "giving and receiving affection." Within this area, the preadolescent child is said to face the task of "learning to give as much love as one receives." In early adolescence, the emotional-development task the child is to accomplish is that of "accepting one's self as a worthwhile person, really worthy of love." So we now have a pair of sequential tasks in hand and are thereby able to offer the following hypothesis:

> If, by the end of late childhood, a girl has not learned to give as much love as she receives, then in early adolescence she will not accept herself as a worthwhile person, really worthy of love.

As soon as we define the key terms in this statement (such as *late childhood, as much love, early adolescence, accept herself,* and *worthwhile person*), we are ready to set up an experiment or make observations of adolescents that will test the validity of the hypothesis. In effect, we observe children to decide whether this statement—one aspect of the theory—is true in real life.

A hypothesis or tentative estimate of the real state of affairs is not always in the form of an if-then statement. It can be a simple declarative sentence that only implies the if-then condition. For example, we could rephrase our hypothesis to read:

> A girl who has not learned to give as much love as she receives by the time she reaches the end of late childhood will not accept herself as a worthwhile person, really worthy of love, during her adolescent years.

Or, as another option, the hypothesis can be phrased as a question:

> Will a girl who has not learned by the end of late childhood to give as much love as she receives be able to accept herself as a worthwhile person, really worthy of love, when she is an early adolescent?

Despite the form in which a hypothetical relationship is cast, its status in theory building is the same. It functions as a reasonable, but as yet unproven, idea whose validity needs to be examined.

When the investigators have collected enough evidence to convince themselves that a hypothesized relationship is valid, they may then draw a generalization about it that they call a "principle." Thus we are using the term *principle* to mean a generalization that is accepted as true — not because it seems self-evident but because it is supported by what the theorists believe are sound data. Or if they regard the empirical data and logic behind it as irrefutable, the theorists can accord the generalization a higher status and term it a *law* or *law of nature*.

Finally, in this discussion of terminology, I feel it is useful to make a distinction between *evidence* and *proof*. Perhaps our most basic motive for comparing theories is to discover which of them is "true" or, at least, which parts of them are "valid." We might say that we are seeking proof of the theories. In this search I find it helpful to define the terms *evidence* and *proof* in the following way:

> *Evidence* is a public thing. It consists of the arguments, the logic, the patterns of reasoning, and the facts that bear upon what it treats. This book is intended to present evidence about the theories it includes.
>
> *Proof,* in contrast, is a personal, private thing. It is a conviction that something is true.

The significance of distinguishing between these two concepts is illustrated by arguments that arise over whether a generalization should be labeled an assumption, a hypothesis, or a principle. The arguments seem to arise because the people on the two sides of the debate either (1) have different kinds of evidence at hand or (2) are convinced by different kinds or amounts of evidence. The sort of evidence one person accepts as proof of a theory may not be the same sort that another accepts. A generalization about child growth that I accept as a proven principle or law may be one that you still consider to be a hypothesis.

GOOD THEORY, BAD THEORY

Typically when we compare theories we are interested not only in learning how they are alike or different but also in judging whether one is better than another. To make this judgment, we need to decide what our standards of goodness will be. Everyone does not use the same standards for appraisal. Therefore let's review some of the more common standards people use in differentiating good theory from bad.

We will consider nine popular standards of judgment. These are not necessarily ones you *should* adopt as your own; rather, they are ones you *might* adopt if they seem convincing and if they fit into your own set of values. Further, you will likely discover that they are not all of equal importance to you. You may wish to revise certain ones, eliminate others, and add a few of your own. In this way you will devise your own standards for judging child development theories.

At the beginning of this chapter the term *theory* was defined in a very broad manner. A theory, I proposed, is a description of (1) which facts are most important for understanding children and (2) what sorts of relationships among facts are most significant for producing this understanding. We noted later that some people use *theory* in a more restricted way. They usually restrict the term by adding the sort of criteria described by the nine standards that follow. For instance, some people are unwilling to call a collection of ideas a theory unless the collection is both internally consistent in structure and clearly provides for the generation of testable hypotheses. However, we will use these standards not for deciding what should be called a theory but for deciding how worthwhile or how "good" a theory is.

Standard 1: A theory is better if it accurately reflects the facts of the real world of children.

Some theorists are criticized for producing a model of development that does not accurately represent children. We will consider three reasons why a mismatch may occur between a theory and the facts of child development.

First, a theorist may draw conclusions from a study of only a few children, then improperly apply these conclusions to many children—the error of generalizing beyond the data. This criticism does not apply to the common practice of studying a representative sample of children and then extending the resulting conclusions to the larger population of children accurately reflected by the sample. Indeed, such sampling is involved in virtually all research on development. But it is an error to apply conclusions about a small group to a larger population when there is good reason to believe that the conditions of the two groups are significantly different. For instance, Arnold Gesell (Chapter Five) has been criticized for improperly generalizing conclusions from a study of children who came to his clinic at Yale University. He apparently assumed that the group of children he observed and measured were accurate representatives of nearly all other children. But there is a serious question about whether his conclusions correctly describe child growth in other cultural settings.

Likewise, in the eighteenth century, Jean Jacques Rousseau (Chapter Three) wrote at length about the nature of children, founding his beliefs on three sorts of evidence: (1) his experience as a tutor for several sons of aristocratic European families, (2) some casual observations of French peasant children, and (3) hearsay impressions of the personalities of "noble savages" in primitive cultures. Critics of Rousseau have questioned whether his descriptions of child development, based on such limited data, actually matched the experience of all the children to whom he applied his conclusions (Boyd, 1963; Davidson, 1898).

Second, a theory may not describe children accurately because a researcher who studies one facet of child growth may not be satisfied to limit conclusions to that facet. Instead, in an effort to discover general principles of growth that explain all sorts of behavior, the researcher applies the conclusions to explain other aspects of child growth as well. For example, he or she may measure trends in children's physical growth and then seek to apply the pattern of increases and plateaus in physical growth to other areas of development, such as social or emotional or mental development. But principles governing one aspect of development may not be the same as those governing another, so risk may be involved.

The third cause of conflict between theory and fact may arise from the researcher's faulty memory or inaccurate observation of children. Probably none of us can help being influenced by memories of our own childhood or by our casual impressions of children we have seen and talked with. Unless we are careful to use controlled observing, testing, and measuring of children, we risk allowing distorted observations from the past or from casual impressions to influence the schemes we devise for explaining development.

Standard 2: A theory is better if it is stated in a way that makes it clearly understandable to anyone who is reasonably competent ("reasonably competent" means having a suitable command of language, mathematics, and logical analysis).

More precisely, anyone with reasonable competence should be able to understand: (1) what facets or events in the real world are referred to by each part of the theory, (2) the meaning of terms used in the model, (3) the key assumptions on which the model is founded, and (4) how the explanations and predictions are logically derived from the definitions and assumptions.

This standard may appear simple and straightforward, but in practice it can be quite controversial. If we find that a theory lacks clarity, is it the theorist's fault for being obscure or confused, or is it our own fault for lacking the competence needed to understand the theorist? We usually have a higher regard for a theory whose elements we can readily comprehend.

Standard 3: A theory is better if it not only explains why past events occurred but also accurately predicts future events. Furthermore, it is better if it enables us to make accurate predictions about the specific behaviors of a particular child rather than only speculations about general growth patterns for a group of children.

People who seek to understand children are usually interested in both the past and the future. They look to the past to learn what forces in a child's life caused the child to be the way she or he is today. They look to the future to estimate what the child will probably be like in coming years.

Many theories are better suited to explaining the past than to foretelling the future. And of those that say something of the future, most are better suited to predicting general characteristics of the typical child or of children in general than they are to predicting the specific development characteristics of a particular child. However, those interested in child development — researchers, parents, teachers, physicians — more highly value a theory that produces specific predictions about a given child than one that foretells only general growth directions or yields only estimates of how the average child will turn out. For example, it is my own belief that a behaviorist of the social learning variety (Chapter Fifteen) is better prepared to make predictions about a specific child's verbal development than is a person who founds his or her judgments solely on Werner's theory (Chapter Seven).

Standard 4: A theory is better if it offers practical guidance in solving daily problems of child rearing to people responsible for the welfare of children — parents, teachers, camp counselors, pediatricians, clinical psychologists, juvenile court judges, and so on.

This standard, which is a practical extension of standard 3, is considered by many to be the most important, for they are interested in theory only to the extent that it improves their own skills in understanding and treating the children they meet daily. In contrast, some theorists, and readers of theory, are not particularly concerned with translating ideas into advice on child rearing. Rather, they are searching for basic principles of human growth and behavior; the question of whether these principles will enable people to treat children with greater skill is entirely incidental.

Standard 5: A theory is better if it is internally consistent.

The essence of a theory is its structure, a description of its elements and the way they interact. Theorists choose different ways to display this framework of their beliefs. For example, although all theorists explain their models of development verbally, some supplement their verbal descriptions with mathematical symbols that permit the theory's components to be manipulated according to rules of logic. By quantifying the components, a theorist hopes to gain precision in analyzing and predicting child growth and behavior. Piaget is an example of a theorist who has sought to enhance the clarity of his verbal explanations with such symbols (Piaget, 1950).

Another way to supplement verbal description is through diagrams. For example, if a theory involves two main dimensions that interact (such as the relationship between chronological age and mental growth), then the relationship can be displayed as a simple graph, with age on one axis and mental growth on the other. As illustrated earlier, Lewin used a diagram—a kind of topological map—to show what he conceived to be the relationship among sectors of a child's life space.

Whatever the mode of presentation, however—words, mathematical symbols, or diagrams—the system, according to standard 5, should be internally consistent. A person seeking to understand the system should not have to disregard one segment of a model in order to comprehend another. The parts should all fit together logically.

Standard 6: A theory is better if it is economical in the sense that it is founded on as few unproven assumptions as possible and requires simple mechanisms to explain all the phenomena it encompasses.

This criterion is often referred to as the *law of parsimony, Occam's razor,* or *Morgan's canon,* the latter in recognition of a biologist, Lloyd Morgan, who proposed that if two explanations of a phenomenon fit the facts equally well, it is better in the long run to choose the simpler of the explanations. Note that the purpose of this standard is not to discourage theorists from formulating complex explanations of complex events—indeed, simpler explanations can prove to be inaccurate. Instead it is intended to reduce the establishment of theories with elaborate hypothesized internal mechanisms not well supported by evidence. Frequently the more complicated the theory, the more difficult it is to test, and proponents are left to support it with argument and emotion.

Standard 7: A theory is better if it is falsifiable or disconfirmable.

In scientific circles a theory is generally conceived to be an estimate of the truth rather than a definite statement of the truth. Researchers must test the validity of hypotheses derived from the theory in order to determine to what extent it does indeed explain the facts satisfactorily. Thus if a theory's hypotheses can be tested to determine whether they are true, then the reverse should also obtain—it should be possible to test that a hypothesis is false. Many scientists feel that the validity of a theory should not only be confirmable through logic and the presentation of data, it should also be falsifiable or disconfirmable.

Some theories of child development, however, do not appear to display this characteristic of falsifiability; that is, we cannot conceive of a research result that such a theory is unprepared to answer. The theory is built to explain the negative outcome of an experiment as well as the positive outcome.

We can illustrate the problem of falsifiability with the following example. Imagine that we create a theory of social development in which diet is the prime determinant of a child's social adjustment. We contend that a proper combination of B vitamins is particularly important. The proper combination produces a child who is socially constructive and amiable. The improper combination produces a child who is resentful and commits anti-social acts. Our hypothesis, in this form, becomes falsifiable when we have specified the proper and the improper B-vitamin combinations. Now we can create experiments to determine whether this aspect of the theory is valid or not. But let us add another element to our theory. We will call it the *counterpoise factor* and propose that when it is present, the B-vitamin combinations work in just the opposite way we would normally expect. By adding this factor, we have rendered our theory nonfalsifiable. If someone tries to test our theory and discovers that many children who eat the improper B-vitamin combination are socially well adjusted, we explain that in those children the counterpoise factor has been operating. Thus the theory is nonfalsifiable—it is always "correct."

Many researchers are uncomfortable with a theory that is nonfalsifiable, so they include standard 7 among the criteria they apply for judging the worth of theories. Among the models reviewed in this book, those of Freud, humanistic psychologists, and the Puritans in particular can be criticized as being nonfalsifiable.

Standard 8: A theory is better if it stimulates the creation of new research techniques and the discovery of new knowledge.

This can be called the *fertility criterion*. Some theories have been highly fertile, remarkable for the number of new vistas they have opened and the amount of research they have stimulated. As a review of child development journals will attest, a great proportion of published investigations in the 1960s and 1970s trace their origins to Piaget's writings (Wadsworth, 1971, p. 2). Likewise, Skinnerian behaviorists and social learning theorists have been highly effective motivators of research in recent years. In contrast, the work of Havighurst and other developmental-task advocates has not generated much of a search for new knowledge.

Among researchers, this fertility factor is often regarded as the most valued function of a theory because models of development that stimulate many ideas for research will exert the greatest influence on expanding the world's store of knowledge. Such stimulation can take several forms. Perhaps the simplest form is that which leads to *direct replication studies*— empirical studies on which the original theory was based are repeated by other researchers to determine whether the same empirical outcomes and theoretical conclusions result as those reported by the original theorist. Stimulation also can lead to *hypothesis testing*, where a general principle, which is part of the theory, generates hypotheses that need to be tested on actual children to determine more precisely the conditions under which the principle validly applies. A third form of stimulation is *verification studies*, where research is conducted to discover whether some theoretical proposal is borne out in real life. Verification is typically sought when a theorist's notions seem to conflict with common sense or with some other theorist's well-accepted proposal. A fourth form can be dubbed *population applicability* because the purpose of the research is to discover if an empirical finding or a theoretical conclusion based on one population of children is equally true in other populations, such as among children of different age levels, of different cultures, or of different ability levels. A fifth form is *discrepancy resolution*, referring to research designed to resolve, or at least to expose, what seem to be a theory's internal inconsistencies. A sixth form is *extended theorizing*, when a theorist's ideas stimulate another theorist to create proposals that extend beyond those of the original theorist, with the extended-theorizing resulting in new possibilities for empirical studies.

Standard 9: A good theory is self-satisfying. It explains development in a way that we feel makes good sense.

This might be called the standard of *self-affirmation*. It is a sort of catchall that depends not only on the previous standards but also on emotional and intuitive factors that we cannot readily identify. The operation of these factors is reflected in our saying about a theory, "I just can't believe that's true" or "I can't believe that's the whole story" when we do not know exactly what it is we find dissatisfying about it. Or we may consider a theory valid because "I feel that's right" or "That rings true—it seems to be the way things are."

Among the theories described later in this book, the one type that appears to depend most heavily on self-affirmation factors is humanistic psychology, for it is based on the existentialist's belief that the individual's real world is the one he personally experiences. That is, the feelings and inner experiences of the child are the most important, no matter what sorts of objective factors exist in the world around him. The development of the child's personally sensed *self* is what interests the humanistic psychologist, and this self is known only through introspection. The advocate of humanistic theory, therefore, can comfortably accept a theory because "it feels right" and "makes intuitive sense" without requiring confirmation from outside, "objective" data. On the other hand, a radical behaviorist, although she might informally say she "feels" her theory is true, does not cite this feeling as validating evidence; instead she is compelled by her theoretical position to produce observational or experimental evidence to support the theory.

In the final analysis, of course, all theories depend on self-conviction for their acceptance. And this issue of what makes us satisfied or dissatisfied with a theory brings us to our final question in this chapter.

WHY DO SCHOLARS DEVELOP DIFFERENT THEORIES?

People who are new to investigating theories of development often wonder what influences theorists to propose new models. The most obvious reason is that they are not satisfied with the answers existing theories offer for the questions they believe to be important. Or they may feel that existing theories do not meet the standards they use to judge the worth of a theory. But in addition to these general reasons, we can identify several more specific ones that cause theorists to generate new perspectives on children's growth.

All theorists are affected by the field of knowledge in which they received their principal training. For example, a strong background in biological science can cause a scholar to focus more attention on children's heredity than on their environment in explaining development. In contrast, a strong foundation in sociology may influence a theorist in the opposite direction. As illustrations, the theories of Herbert Spencer and G. Stanley Hall during the late nineteenth century were affected by their study of biology, particularly by their study of Darwin's theory of evolution (Hall, 1904).

Not only do theorists' academic backgrounds influence their explanations of development, but the problems they meet in daily work also funnel their attention toward particular facts and their possible relationships. In the late nineteenth century, the puzzling cases of neurotic patients that Freud met in his psychiatric practice stimulated him to seek explanations that deviated markedly from the neurological theories popular in his day (Chapter Eight). Early in this century, Piaget was working in a psychological testing center in France when he became curious about the thinking processes that caused children to give certain incorrect answers to test questions. This curiosity led him to a lifelong study of the growth of children's thought patterns and to a theory that organized the facts he discovered (Chapter Ten).

The way investigators gather data also influences the conclusions they draw. Skinner distrusted the accuracy of people's reports of their own thought processes so he chose to base his conclusions on objective observations of behavior by an outsider (Chapter Fourteen). However, Charlotte Buhler, a humanistic psychologist, encouraged people to report their feelings, hopes, and ambitions (Chapter Sixteen). Both Piaget and Lawrence Kohlberg presented standard test questions to which children would respond (Chapters Ten and Thirteen). In effect, researchers' sources of information favor their drawing certain types of conclusions and make it unlikely they will draw other types.

One of the most potent forces affecting models devised by experimental psychologists is the appearance of surprising or puzzling results in research they conduct with children. When an experiment turns out in an unexpected way, researchers are faced with the possibility that the existing theory is inaccurate and that changes are called for. This sort of influence has been particularly prominent in the work of such behaviorists as Albert Bandura, Robert Sears, and Howard and Tracy Kendler (Chapter Fifteen).

Finally the personal, nonprofessional concerns of individuals also influence their proposals about development. Rousseau's atypical childhood in eighteenth-century Europe appears to have had a strong effect on the view of child growth he later proposed (Chapter Three). Abraham Maslow's dissatisfaction with the ways behaviorism and psychoanalysis explained his own personality and happenings in his own life played a part in the formulation of his version of humanistic psychology (Chapter Sixteen).

In sum, a variety of factors interact to make theorists dissatisfied with existing explanations of development and to stimulate them to formulate new models. As a result, there are a number of major theories and even more minimodels in existence today, and we can expect many more to appear in the years ahead.

CONCLUSION

Chapter One was designed to accomplish four purposes:

1. Present an initial taste of several quite different theories and suggest how interpreting child behavior from each theory's point of view can result in very different conclusions.

2. Identify some general theoretical terms and the meanings that can be assigned to them.

3. Propose illustrative standards for judging the worth of a theory.

4. Note some of the factors that influence theorists to propose new schemes for interpreting child development.

The material in Chapter One should serve as a useful background for Chapter Two, which suggests a series of questions that can be asked about the contents of theories when different models of child development are being compared.

FOR FURTHER READING

The following publications are useful sources of information about theoretical terminology, criteria for judging the worth of theories, and illustrative appraisals of theories.

Baldwin, A. L. (1967) *Theories of Child Development.* New York: Wiley. Chaps. 1, 2, 19.

Brody, B. A. (1970) *Readings in the Philosophy of Science.* Englewood Cliffs, N.J.: Prentice-Hall. Pp. 252–267.

Developmental Psychology Today. (1983) New York: Random House. Chap. 3.

Hall, C. S., and G. Lindzey. (1970) *Theories of Personality,* 2d ed. New York: Wiley. Chap. 1.

Lerner, R. M. (1976) *Concepts and Theories of Human Development.* Reading, Mass.: Addison-Wesley. Chap. 1.

Marx, M. H. (ed.). (1963) *Theories in Contemporary Psychology.* New York: Macmillan.

Marx, M. H., and F. E. Goodson (eds.). (1976) *Theories in Contemporary Psychology.* New York: Macmillan. (This volume is sufficiently different from the 1963 Marx publication that both are worth inspecting.)

Miller, P. H. (1983) *Theories of Developmental Psychology.* San Francisco: W. H. Freeman. Intro.

Reese, H. W., and W. F. Overton. (1970) "Models of Development and Theories of Development." In L. R. Goulet and Paul B. Baltes, *Life-Span Developmental Psychology.* New York: Academic Press. Pp. 115–145.

Skinner, B. F. (1972) *Cumulative Record: A Selection of Papers,* 3d ed. New York: Appleton-Century-Crofts. (See Skinner's questioning of the need for theory in the Part II selection, "Are Theories of Learning Necessary?")

CHAPTER TWO

The Contents of Child Development Theories

In comparing theories, we need to consider not only the sorts of criteria described in Chapter One but also the content characteristics. By *content* I mean both the aspects of child development on which theorists focus attention and the key philosophical and methodological convictions that undergird the model they propose.

This second chapter introduces a variety of content categories often included in theories. One aim of the chapter is to alert you to questions that child development theories frequently try to answer, so you can decide which of these questions are the most important from your viewpoint. Another aim is to illustrate the fact that not all theorists seek to answer the same questions or accord the same significance to a given question. It is important to recognize this because two theories that at first appear to be in conflict may, in fact, be merely directed at different aspects of child growth. Two ostensibly conflicting viewpoints could even, perhaps, be satisfactorily combined, as J. Dollard and N. E. Miller sought to do with behaviorist and psychoanalytic theories in their book *Personality and Psychotherapy* (1950).

In Chapter Two a number of questions that identify either the content focus of theories or their philosophical and methodological understructure are presented. The questions are organized into thirteen clusters. The names of the clusters and an overall question that encompasses the subquestions in each are given below.

CONTENT CHARACTERISTICS

1. *Scope or range.* What age levels, aspects of development, and human cultures are the objects of the theory?

27

2. *Nature and nurture.* How does heredity compare with environment as a contributor to development?

3. *Direction of development.* What sorts of maturity or what future condition does the infant grow toward?

4. *Continuous versus stepwise change.* Do children grow by imperceptibly small increments or do they periodically move up from one identifiable stage to another?

5. *Original moral condition.* Is the child born moral, immoral, or amoral?

6. *Personality structure.* What are the key components of human personality, and how are these related to each other?

7. *Motivation and the learning process.* What motivates development, and by what process does a child learn?

8. *Individual differences.* How does the theory account for differences in development among children of the same chronological age?

9. *Desirable-undesirable, normal-abnormal.* How does the theory distinguish desirable from undesirable development and normal from abnormal development?

10. *Philosophical origins and assumptions.* From what philosophical viewpoint has the theory arisen, and on what assumptions is it founded?

11. *Investigative methods.* What methods has the theorist used for gathering, analyzing, and validating ideas, and how have these methods influenced the content and structure of the theory?

12. *Appeal for acceptance.* On what sort of appeal does the theorist depend for convincing people of the theory's worth?

13. *Terminology.* What special terms are used in the theory, and how do they relate to similar concepts in other theories?

Before inspecting each of these topics in some detail, we should note three characteristics of this list. First, the topics are not mutually exclusive. They overlap and crisscross. For example, when we discuss Freud's proposed structure for personality development, we necessarily consider as well his growth stages, his idea of the child's original moral condition, and his special terminology. Thus these questions are not separate entities but are simply different angles from which to view the integrated body of a theory.

Second, the list itself is not proposed as *the correct* list of topics for analyzing theories of development. It is just one possible listing, one I have found helpful for directing attention at significant aspects of theories. Other lists, different in content or organized in a different pattern, serve other people just as well.

Third, topics at the beginning of the list are more distinctly developmental than the rest. Within the broad field of psychology, practitioners are traditionally divided into several loosely defined groups: specialists in the clinical treatment of behavior disorders, specialists who compare human behavior with that of animals, specialists in research on learning, and specialists in development. This last group is the one that we are concerned with. Developmental psychologists have a dominant interest in questions about how and why people change with the passing of time or the advancement of age. In our list of thirteen topics, items 1 through 5 are most distinctly concerns of developmentalists. Items 6 through 13 are generally of equal or greater interest to practitioners in other psychological groups. Now let's turn to a more detailed explanation of the topics.

1. Scope or Range   The term *scope* is used here to identify three aspects of a theory: (a) its *age range*—the way the theory marks the beginning and end of the development period; (b) its *variety of aspects*—the number and kinds of facets stressed or included by the theory; and (c) its *cultural range*—the variety of cultures the theory proposes to describe. To discover how a particular theorist treats these matters, we can be guided by the following set of questions:

> **1.1** How are the beginning and end of the development period defined? What characteristics, such as age in years, particular changes in behavior, or changes in growth rate, define this period?

Some of the schemes discussed in later chapters are best labeled *theories of human development* since they propose structures and principles describing the entire life span, from conception to death. Others are more accurately called *theories of child development* because they focus exclusively, or primarily, on the first two decades or so of life. In this book we are concerned only with these initial two decades, regardless of whether the theory being considered extends into adulthood and old age.

Many theories use chronological age as the chief measure of child development periods, with either biological conception or birth marking the lower limit and age 18 or 21 marking the upper limit. Thus the adolescent years are typically included within the span of the term *child development*, although some writers prefer to limit the word *childhood* to the years before puberty—age 12 or 14—and *adolescence* to the years between puberty and adulthood.

Other theorists find chronological age an unsatisfactory dimension in analyzing development (Wohlwill, 1976). They use some other characteristic, such as the attainment of adult height or the emergence of specified adult behaviors, as the indicator that childhood is over. Also their boundary lines for stages of growth throughout the childhood period are set by developmental signs other than years since birth.

Some authors focus their theories on the entire range of childhood and adolescence experiences, whereas others attend to only one segment of this range.

1.2 What aspects of growth or behavior does the theory include or emphasize?

Some models concentrate on a narrow range of behavior. For example, Kohlberg (Chapter Thirteen) concerns himself solely with moral aspects, and humanistic psychologists (Chapter Sixteen) focus chiefly on the development of the self. Other theories are much broader in scope. Havighurst's scheme (Chapter Six) involves physical, emotional, moral, cognitive, and social aspects. Gesell (Chapter Five) also includes a wide range of behaviors and growth characteristics in his studies.

1.3 Does the theory propose to explain child development in all cultures or only in certain ones?

Most theorists want their model to apply to as many children as possible. In effect, they try to produce a universal theory. Their broad-ranging statements imply that they are talking about children in all places and, seemingly, in all times. Such is true of Piaget, Freud, Lewin, Skinner, and many more. Other theorists state that their proposals are intended to describe development within defined cultural or geographic domains. For example, Havighurst has said that his "tasks of development" are ones faced by mid-twentieth-century American boys and girls, particularly those from the middle and upper social classes.

These three facets of a theory's scope help delineate the territory the theorist is trying to map out.

2. Nature and Nurture   Over the decades the most fundamental concern of child development theorists has been the heredity–environment issue. The terminology of the debate has varied from time to time—nature versus nurture, nativism versus cultural relativism, genetics versus social controls, maturation versus learning, innate traits versus acquired characteristics— but the basic issue has been the same: How do inborn factors compare with environmental factors in contributing to a child's development?

As demonstrated throughout most of this book, the question of what causes development is typically cast in one of these heredity–environment forms, thus implying that there are only two sources for the way a child grows up: (1) her inherited nature and (2) the way she is nurtured by parents and others. However, some theorists have proposed other possible causes as well. Before identifying these additional possibilities, we will first inspect the nature–nurture issue since it remains the central concern of most psychologists, biologists, and sociologists when they argue questions of cause. As the debate has progressed over the years, the focal question has shifted somewhat, moving first from *which one* to *how much*, and then subsequently to *in what manner* (Anastasi, 1958). We will inspect each of these in turn.

Which one? In past centuries philosophers seemed to be answering the question, Which causes developmental changes, a child's heredity *or* environment? An example from the environmentalist side of the issue is the proposal of British philosopher John Locke (1632–1704) that at birth a child's mind is a void, an unmarked page or *tabula rasa* on which the contents of the mind are sketched by the child's experiences as he grows up. At the other extreme was Rousseau (1712–1778), who considered the child's inherited "nature" to be the most influential force in determining her steps in development.

The which-one controversy can be simply illustrated as positions on either side of a fence (see Table 2.1). Traditionally the people on the heredity side have been divided into two groups: the *preformationists* and the *predeterminists*.

The distinction between preformationists and predeterminists chiefly concerns how powerful the theorist believes hereditary effects are. Preformationists believe that *all* of an individual's potentials—his or her personality, values, motives, mental abilities, and emotional makeup—exist com-

Table 2.1   The "Which-One" Issue

	Hereditarians	
Environmentalists	*Preformationists*	*Predeterminists*
The child's experiences are preeminent in determining development.	Environment has no influence.	Environment has little influence.

pletely formed within the infant at birth. As the child advances in age, these potentials unfold on a prearranged genetic schedule. Since all significant elements of development are preformed, the particular environment in which the child grows up has no role in determining development. Predeterminists, however, are not so willing to dismiss the influence of a child's physical and social surroundings. They believe environment has some effect. But since they believe a child's genetic schedule is so important, they belong on the heredity side of the controversy along with the preformationists. Rousseau has been credited with formulating the "first definitive predeterministic theory of child development" (Ausubel and Sullivan, 1970, p. 2).

Actually the issue of *which one* — heredity *or* environment — determines development is rather silly since even rudimentary reasoning will show that neither factor can exert influence or even exist without the other. A child's heredity cannot display itself in a condition of nothingness, that is, in a nonenvironment. Nor can a child be spontaneously generated without ancestors, as if springing out of nowhere to be influenced by an environment. Even the most radical environmentalists and hereditarians of the past recognized the necessary existence of both factors, nature and nurture. So the argument actually was not *which one* but *how much*.

How much? During the nineteenth century and through the first half of the twentieth, the nature–nurture issue centered primarily on the question of how much heredity contributed to development in comparison to environment. Graphically the issue can be pictured as a line, with the heredity component above and the environment component below (see Table 2.2). A given theorist's position on the issue can be identified at some point along the line. To illustrate, we cite the famous debate that attracted the attention of American psychologists in the 1920s and 1930s concerning which factor contributed more to a child's intellectual growth, heredity or environment. By statistical methods, B. S. Burks (1928) concluded that heredity deserved 83 percent of the credit for mental ability and environment only 17. Other investigators (Leahy, 1935; Shuttleworth, 1935) also concluded that heredity played the major role, though the proportions they derived were somewhat different. Still other researchers, using a series of studies conducted in the midwestern United States, concluded that the opposite was true, that environment was the stronger factor in determining mental ability (Skeels, 1940; Skodak, 1939). This debate has never been settled, and the main reason may well be that the wrong question — or at least an unprofitable question — was being asked.

Investigations based on the how-much issue have led to conflicting conclusions about the same data and to interpretations of questionable usefulness. As a consequence, in recent decades there has been a strong

Table 2.2   The "How-Much" Issue

	Extreme Hereditarians	Moderates	Extreme Environmentalists
Percentage of Nature's Contribution	95%	50%	5%
Percentage of Nurture's Contribution	5%	50%	95%

movement among people interested in these matters to recast the key question from *how much* to *how* or *in what manner* the factors interact (Anastasi, 1958).

In what manner do nature and nurture interact? A basic tenet of this modern interactionist approach is that nature and nurture are two different dimensions, each operating 100 percent in its role. Although this approach does not really abandon concern with how much, its more important question by far is: How does the interaction of heredity and environment take place in order to produce the observed development of the child? There are a variety of answers to the question, each depending on the point of view of the particular theorist being examined. Since it is our purpose in the present chapter only to outline issues that theories treat and to pose guide questions for use in comparing theories, we will not analyze a wide array of interpretations of interaction here. Rather we will describe briefly only two views in order to illustrate the extent to which ideas about interaction can vary.

According to the first view, heredity defines the boundaries of potential development, and environment determines where, within these boundaries, a child's actual development is realized. "Heredity determines what we can do, and environment what we do do" (Montagu, 1959). Furthermore, it is assumed that the boundaries differ for different characteristics. For certain traits, such as eye color, heredity sets very narrow limits within which environmental forces—such as nutrition—can operate. For other characteristics, such as the cognitive ability to analyze complex abstract relationships, the boundaries set by heredity appear to be wide, allowing considerable room for the operation of such environmental factors as nutrition, instruction, rewards for the child who practices such analysis, and many more.

This interactionist viewpoint also assumes that the potential defined by heredity is manifested differently at different times in the child's life. For example, at puberty a genetically timed ripening occurs for the primary sex characteristics (maturing ova in girls, maturing sperm in boys, and maturing systems for delivering these cells) and such secondary sex characteristics as changes in body shape. Thus puberty produces different potentials from those available when the child was age 2 or 4 or 6.

From this interactionist perspective, the question of how much nature contributes as compared to nurture is no longer of prime interest. Instead we now seek to know (1) how wide are the boundaries set by heredity for various aspects of development—physical traits, cognitive abilities, frustration tolerance, and others; (2) what environmental forces influence the way these aspects manifest themselves in the child's structure and behavior; and (3) how this interaction of inherited potential and environmental forces operates at different stages of the child's growth period.

Some idea of how the complex interrelations of this model differ from the interrelations of the which-one and how-much approaches can be shown in the simplified diagram in Figure 2.1. Three concepts are plotted here:

1. *Genetic influence over different developmental characteristics varies from one characteristic to another.* The three characteristics shown in Figure 2.1 are height, skill at analyzing abstract relationships, and emotional control under stress. The top and bottom of each box represent, respectively, the greatest and least genetic potential that is humanly possible for that characteristic (at a certain age level). The white space in each box represents one hypothetical child's genetic potential for that characteristic.

2. *Heredity establishes boundaries of potential for each characteristic.* In Figure 2.1 the hypothetical upper limit for development—for example, the tallest that child can grow—is the upper dotted line, and the lower limit—the shortest height the child can grow to—is the lower dotted line.

3. *Environmental influences determine where within the boundaries a child's development will manifest itself.* The range within which environment can affect development is shown as the white area between the dotted lines in each characteristic. The letter *F* signifies the level of development a child will exhibit if the environmental influences are very favorable (near the upper limit). The letter *U* signifies the level of development exhibited if environmental conditions are very unfavorable (near the lower limit).

Thus in Figure 2.1 we hypothesize that there is more leeway for the influence of environmental factors in determining a child's emotional con-

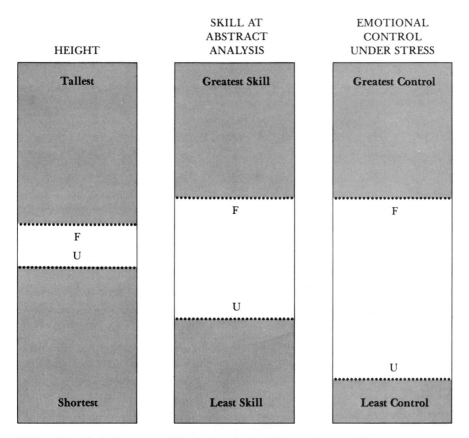

•••• = Hypothesized upper and lower boundaries of inherited potential
F = Development in favorable environment
U = Development in unfavorable environment

Figure 2.1   An Interactionist Viewpoint: In What Manner?

trol than there is in determining either height or skill at abstract analysis. Whether such a hypothesis is true becomes a matter of empirical investigation.

To complete this first analysis of interaction, we need to explain which environmental factors are most potent in determining how genetic potential is realized and how these forces are interrelated. We also need to describe how the interaction may vary at different stages of the child's development.

Although this first interactionist approach does not tell us, as older how-much theories did, what proportion of development is due to heredity and what proportion is due to environment, it still enables us to differentiate between "environmentalists" and "hereditarians." In terms of Figure 2.1, theorists who picture the area between the inherited-potential boundaries as narrow are hereditarians, for they believe the child's genetically designed nature does not permit much manipulation by environmental factors. Theorists who picture the boundaries as widely separated are more environmentalist, for they think environmental influences greatly affect the way development characteristics are manifested.

Let's turn now to the second way of viewing the *in-what-manner* approach to interaction. Some writers consider interaction in terms of how directly heredity influences development (Anastasi, 1958; R. M. Lerner, 1976, pp. 48–83). To illustrate, let us consider three examples of mental development that range from very direct to very indirect hereditary influence.

At the very direct end of the scale is the case of a child suffering from phenylketonuria. This mental defect results from hereditary metabolic dysfunctions that are not significantly improved by changes made in the child's environment—the affected child will remain mentally defective (Anastasi, 1958, p. 198).

Heredity has a less direct influence on mental development in cases of hereditary blindness or deafness. A blind or deaf child who is raised in an environment designed for children with normal sight and hearing will typically display symptoms of retarded mental growth. Although sight and hearing cannot be restored, changes can be made in the environment to compensate for the handicap. A blind child can be given audio-recordings of books and can be taught to read by the braille method; the deaf child can be taught sign language and lip reading. These compensatory measures enable mental development to proceed far more normally.

Our third example from the very indirect end of the scale of hereditary influence concerns social stereotypes. We recognize that genetic endowment has much influence in determining a child's skin color, height, weight, facial features, acuity of senses, and so forth. People within a given culture often associate certain intellectual or personality traits with such physical characteristics. In other words, people often hold social stereotypes. If a child's facial features and her movements are usually viewed in her society as typical of sweet, clever girls, then people will often treat this child as though she were sweet and bright. Since the way people treat a child influences the way that child comes to perceive herself, we can conclude that the child's self-concept—her feeling of adequacy—is at least partially the result of social stereotypes associated with inherited physical characteristics. In effect, if the child perceives herself as clever rather than dull, she may be motivated to display higher levels of mental development than if she believed herself dull. Heredity, in this instance, has influenced mental development in a very indirect manner.

Earlier we said that although theorists who adopt one of these interactionist approaches emphasize the *in-what-manner* or *how* of the nature–nurture interaction, they have not abandoned the question of *how much*. However, they phrase the question in new ways. For instance, when A. Anastasi (1958, p. 206) proposed that it is best to view nature–nurture in terms of a directness-indirectness scale, she added that the more indirectly heredity influences a behavior, "the wider will be the range of variation of possible outcomes." In other words, there is not much room for environment to influence a child's characteristics that most directly depend on genetic factors. Yet environment can very much influence those characteristics that are very indirectly linked to heredity. Thus Anastasi is still posing a how-much question in terms of the amount of variability possible.

What can we say then about modern theorists' position on the heredity–environment issue? Today, most theorists consider themselves interactionists in that they think both nature and nurture are indispensable and work together to produce development. However, this does not mean that the debate has ended—theorists continue to disagree on the conditions of the nature–nurture interaction. Indeed, one of the most incendiary social controversies in American educational circles in recent years centers on the question of whether the genetic endowment of certain racial groups limits their potential mental ability compared to that of other racial groups (Hebb, 1970; Hirsch, 1970; Jensen, 1969, 1973; Layzer, 1974). Since the issues are complex and far from settled, arguments of this type can be expected to continue in the years ahead.

When we analyze theories of development, we can include such guide questions as the following:

2.1 Can the theorist be identified by such traditional labels as *preformationist, predeterminist, interactionist, hereditarian,* or *environmentalist?*

2.2 Does the theorist see some aspects of development as being more constrained by hereditary boundaries than others? For example: Are the inherited-potential boundaries narrower or the heredity connections more direct for skin color than for oral language skills (if, indeed, two such different characteristics can be adequately compared in terms of amounts)?

2.3 Does the theorist see heredity as more constraining for certain growth characteristics at different periods of childhood? For example: Are the inherited-potential boundaries for the development of reading ability different at age 6 than they are at age 12?

2.4 Does the theorist describe the process by which the interaction of nature and nurture takes place?

Earlier I noted that, in contrast to most present-day theorists, some writers have proposed further sources of influence besides heredity and environment. As examples of such proposals, there are the conceptions of a respected developmentalist, T. C. Schneirla, and two beliefs common to many of the world's major religious traditions.

Schneirla (1957) has suggested that a third force affecting development is the growing organism, that is, the child itself. This influence arises from the manner in which the hereditary and environmental factors interact. For example, assume that infant A is born with a genetic structure that predisposes him to a high level of activity. As a result, he sleeps less than most babies. When he is awake he cries for his parents' attention. Although the parents seek to provide the comfort and care their son seems to require, they soon become physically tired and emotionally irritated by his irregular rest habits and demanding activity. Their irritation is reflected in the way they handle the child and in the harshness of their voices when they lose their patience. In their frustration and exhaustion, they increasingly escape by closing the door to the baby's bedroom to "let him cry it out." This treatment serves to heighten, rather than decrease, their son's activity level because the child is stimulated by his emotional distress to make even greater demands on his parents' time and patience. In effect, a cycle of interaction has been established in which the evolving characteristics of the organism—the growing child—become a significant influence—a third force—in determining the way the environment will treat him (R. M. Lerner, 1976, pp. 102–103). Schneirla has concluded, in essence, that "the individual seems to be interactive with itself throughout development, as the processes of each stage open the way for further stimulus-reaction relationships depending on the scope of the intrinsic and extrinsic conditions then prevalent" (1957, p. 86).

We turn now to a pair of additional influences found in concepts of development embedded in many of the world's religions. The pair are *human will* and *supernatural intervention*. In the case of will, the assumption is made that a person's life pattern is not determined entirely by genetic and environmental variables but is influenced as well by the individual's free-will choices and by how hard she tries to implement such choices. This conception of the importance of will appears in such diverse religions as Christianity, Judaism, Islam, Confucianism, Hinduism, and Shintoism, as well as in much of the commonsense or naive psychology of the general public. In the following chapters, the role of human will is illustrated in the cases of Puritan and Rousseauean doctrine in Chapter Three and of commonsense psychology in Chapter Four.

The operation of *supernatural intervention* as a contributor to development is a central element in most if not all religious traditions. Adherents of such traditions believe that a person's developmental fate can be determined to a large degree by the action of destructive supernatural forces (Satan or other evil spirits) and of constructive or salutary powers (God, Allah, Cosmic Energy, or other beneficient spirits). Sometimes the supernatural powers act on their own volition to influence people's lives. In other cases supernatural intercession is solicited by people through prayers, rituals, and offerings. This type of cause is generally given no place in such modern "scientific theories" as those described in Chapters Five through Sixteen. (Nevertheless, proponents of scientific theories may sometimes in their everyday lives display a belief in supernatural influence. Particularly in times of danger, as during a child's illness or a threat to the family's safety, even a scientific developmentalist may appeal to a supreme power to intercede on the developmentalist's behalf.)

3. Direction of Development   The terms *growth* and *development** both imply change, and it has been one of the central concerns of theorists to identify the directions of this change.

A good example of a theory that gives central attention to directions of development is Heinz Werner's (Chapter Seven). Werner identified one direction of growth, for instance, as that from rigidity to flexibility. By this he meant that an infant displays rigid behaviors suited specifically to given situations and does not readily alter these behaviors to suit new conditions. An adolescent's behaviors, however, are more flexible and adapt readily to changed conditions.

Perhaps the easiest way to discover the directions of development assumed within a theory is to ask, How does the child differ from the adult? In Rousseau's view of children, one important direction is from an irrational to a rational person. In the Puritan view, the proper direction is from a naturally sinful person to a consciously moral person.

In our search for the directions described or implied in a theory, we can ask:

3.1 What aspects of behavior or growth (for example, physical growth, cognitive development, social skills) are encompassed by a particular principle or statement of direction?

3.2 What interrelationships, if any, exist between the direction of change of one aspect and that of another? For example: Does attainment of physical maturity come before the attainment of intellectual

---

*Growth is often defined as change in size, development as change in the complexity and functions of the individual. However, both terms may be defined as change in both size and function. It is in this second, more inclusive manner that the terms are used in this book.

maturity? Does the differentiation of behaviors in the young child proceed more rapidly than the integration of various individual actions into smoothly flowing systems of behavior?

4. Continuous Versus Stepwise Change   Usually theories not only define directions of change, they tell whether this change occurs gradually in small increments or dramatically in large periodic increments (steep advances) that are followed by periods of less apparent change (plateaus). Skinner's behaviorism is an example of a theory that pictures growth as occurring in imperceptibly small increments. In contrast, other theories picture growth as shifting from one major step or stage to another. Piaget proposed steps and substeps of cognitive development. Freud identified several major psychosexual stages of growth. Havighurst proposed that children at different points in their life are confronted with particular tasks of growing up and that these tasks form a series of stages in development. In effect, the essence of many theories is found in the sorts of stages postulated and in the way the child's movement from one level to the next is viewed. The controversy about these matters among developmentalists has traditionally been known as the *continuity–discontinuity issue.*

Everyone agrees that development from one day to the next is gradual. No one claims that a twelve-year-old girl is a prepuberal child one week and a full-blown adolescent the next. In this sense growth is continuous and occurs in small increments. The real question, then, is whether, during this process, the child's structure and behavior periodically display symptoms that warrant the label of a new stage of development. Behaviorists such as Skinner answer no to this question; other theorists answer yes. Theorists who answer yes are then obligated to identify the traits of a stage so that, following their theories, we can recognize a new stage when we see one.

Consequently, in analyzing a theorist's position on the continuity–discontinuity issue, we first pose this question:

4.1 Does children's development proceed through a series of small, continuous increments without any dramatic changes or identifiable qualitative plateaus? Or do children develop from one recognizable stage to another?

If the answer to this first query is that children pass through stages, then we can profitably pose several more questions:

4.2 How does the theorist define *stage* or *step* or *period?*

4.3 How many stages are identified in the system, and what are the names and distinguishing characteristics of each stage?

4.4 On what aspects of life or growth do the stages focus? In other words, what dimensions of development do the stages represent? For example: Are these stages of physical growth? Of sexual development? Of socialization? Of moral judgment? Of oral-language development?

4.5 Do the aspects or dimensions have the same importance at all times during childhood? For example: Are physical growth stages more prominent in the early years than they are later in childhood?

Since the matter of whether children are growing up "normally" is of interest to many people—parents, teachers, pediatricians, and children themselves—it is also useful to ask what a theory expects of developmental stages. To begin:

4.6 How are the levels or stages related to chronological age?

Of the proposals discussed in later chapters, that of Gesell's (Chapter Five) is the most specific in correlating age with growth characteristics. Gesell described in rather definite terms what the typical two-year-old is like and how his or her characteristics differ from those of the one-year-old and the three-year-old. The stages described by Piaget, Freud, and Havighurst are less closely tied to specific ages than Gesell's, and Maslow's levels of human needs (Chapter Sixteen) are even less specifically correlated with chronological age than those of Piaget and Freud.

The question of age–stage correlation is not the only one pertinent to the task of judging the normality of a child's growth. For example, a number of questions arise about the universality and invariance of stages.

4.7 Are the stages universal, that is, true for all children in all cultures? Or do children in one culture pass through different stages from those in another? Within a culture, is it possible for a child to skip what has been described as a stage, or must everyone move through the stages in a single defined sequence? If a child can skip a stage or proceed by a different path than some of his peers, why does this deviation occur?

Many theorists consider the stages they describe to be universal— found among all children in all cultures—and their sequence invariant. *Invariant* means that not only are the stages found in all cultures for which we have reports, but the nature of development is such that no other sequence in the pattern of growth stages is possible. Such writers as Piaget (Chapter Ten), Kohlberg (Chapter Sixteen), and Erik Erikson (Chapter Nine) have assumed invariance although this position has been questioned recently by critics (Phillips & Kelly, 1975). Remember, therefore, not only to inquire about a theorist's position but also to consider whether the evidence or line of reasoning used to support that position is convincing.

Three other sets of questions can be asked about how growth rates, fixation at a stage, and regression to an earlier stage may be treated in a theory.

4.8 Does everyone go through the stages at the same pace? If not, why not?

The terms *retarded, normal, advanced,* and *gifted* have traditionally been used to describe children who are growing at particular rates compared to their age mates, regardless of whether growth is viewed as continuous or stepwise. Question 4.8 is directed at whether a theory recognizes such phenomena and, if so, how it accounts for them.

Another question related to the rate of passing through stages is:

4.9 Can a child display typical characteristics of more than one stage at the same time? If so, why does this occur?

Some theorists (Gesell, Havighurst) make little or no mention of this possibility; others accord it considerable attention (Erikson, Piaget, Kohlberg). An example of the simultaneous presence of multiple stages is found in Piaget's subtheory about children's ideas of causality. When Piaget studied what children believe causes certain physical events in the world, he concluded that a child who accounts for cloud movements by saying elves push the clouds is operating on a lower level of thought than a child who says that air currents (rising hot air, descending cool air) move the clouds. Piaget found, however, that while a child may use fantasy beings (elves) to account for certain physical events, the same child may give naturalistic explanations (air currents) to account for others. In effect, the child is operating on two stage levels at the same time (Piaget, 1930).

4.10 Can a child's progress through the stages become arrested or fixated at a particular stage? If so, what causes the fixating? What can be done to release the fixation and stimulate progress to the next stage?

Theorists account for fixation in several ways. Gesell's system, which can be labeled a predeterminist theory, views arrested development as caused by inadequate genetic endowment. Behaviorists feel it results from inadequate stimulus from the environment. Freud's psychoanalysis views it as seated in either too much satisfaction of needs at the present stage of development or too little satisfaction.

4.11 Can a child return to an earlier stage after entering a more advanced one? If so, what causes this *regression* or *retrogression?* What can be done to help the child recover and move ahead once more?

Regression, like fixation, is of particular interest to therapists, whose task it is to assist children whose development seems to be going awry. The most popular explanation, by theorists who recognize the phenomenon of regression, is that a child slips back to an earlier stage of development when the adjustment skills developed at the present stage prove inadequate for coping with current problems. However, some theorists contend that there is no such thing as true regression. The child does not really slip back but just gives the appearance of regressing by adopting a segment of behavior from an earlier time.

Our concern with retardation, fixation, regression, and uneven development can also lead logically to another question:

4.12 If a child experiences growth problems at one stage, how may these problems influence success at subsequent levels? And how can we best deal with such problems?

For most theorists, problems that are not adequately resolved at one stage either will prevent the child from moving on to the next or will make it difficult for the child to adjust to subsequent levels. And most feel that therapy or retraining is required to correct or ameliorate the problems and thus enable the child to continue her or his development. However, not all theories see the issue in this same light. Theories like Gesell's, which see genetic factors as greatly restricting the range within which environmental factors can affect development, do not usually propose therapy or retraining. For instance, Gesell's model of development contains the concept of alternating "good" and "bad" years or phases of growth. This pattern of alternation is seen as a "natural" one, common to virtually all children. So problems at one level of growth are seen as instances of "going through a bad phase" that will naturally pass with time. Patience rather than therapy is needed to wait out the passing of the phase (Ilg & Ames, 1955, pp. 22–24).

In summary, twelve sets of questions have been proposed to guide our inquiry into the way a theorist handles the continuity–discontinuity issue. Although most of the questions are directed at theories that view growth as occurring in steps or stages, a number of them are also useful for understanding nonstage or continuous theories as well. For example, we can ask if a continuous growth model pictures all children as developing along the same route (4.7) and at the same pace (4.8). We can also ask if a child can become fixated (4.10) or can regress (4.11) and how growth problems can be ameliorated (4.12).

5. Original Moral Condition   An issue of greater interest in past centuries than it is today is that of the child's natural moral state. Some theorists either state outright or imply that the child at birth, and by natural inclination, is in a particular moral condition: good (moral), bad (immoral), or neutral (amoral). Rousseau considered children to be innately moral and felt that if they are to remain good, they need to be protected throughout their growing years from the corruptions of an immoral society. The Puritans, in contrast, considered children to be innately immoral and felt that they need a great deal of strict guidance if they are to be saved from the devil. Freudians regard children as innately amoral—that is, without knowledge of right or wrong at birth—but with a capacity to internalize the morals of their social environment so that these values eventually become a part of their personalities, the *superego*. Maslow, as a humanistic psychologist, viewed the child's sense of morals as being partly innate and partly learned.

Therefore, in comparing theories, we may wish to ask:

5.1 What is the original or genetically determined condition of the child: moral, immoral, or amoral? Can the newborn be some mixture of the three, depending on which aspect of development is under consideration?

6. Personality Structure   Most theories of development assume that the child has a psychological system or a sort of mental machinery, which is known by such terms as *personality, mind, intervening variables,* or *cognitive structure*. Usually this system is assumed to contain elements or functions that interact to determine the child's behavior. Part of the task of understanding development, then, consists of identifying these components and the ways they interact over the first two decades of life. Freud's system includes three such key elements: the *id*, the *ego*, and the *superego*. Both the Puritans and Rousseau called the important elements of personality *mental faculties*. Thus, in analyzing a theory, we may wish to ask:

6.1 What are the components of personality or of behavior?

6.2 How do the components interact and change as the child grows up?

7. Motivation and the Learning Process   In the field of psychology, the topics of motivation and learning are often considered separately. However, *motivation* is typically seen as the fuel for learning, the director of the child's attention toward what she will seek to learn. Therefore, since motivation can be viewed as a beginning step or condition in the learning process, we will discuss them together.

Not all theorists use the same terms to identify motivating forces. However, the two most popular terms are *need* and *drive*. These terms are like two sides of a coin, two ways of looking at the same phenomenon. The word *need* implies intake, a void seeking to be filled. *Drive* implies output, pent-up energy searching for a place in which to invest or expend itself. So the need for food is the hunger drive, and the need for drink is the thirst drive. Although there is a tendency for some theorists to favor the term *need* (humanistic psychologists) and others to favor *drive* (behaviorists), in each case the intention is to identify a motivating force that energizes behavior (Hall & Lindzey, 1970, pp. 175–180, 425–436).

In some theories little or no attention is given to describing motivating forces (Gesell, Chapter Five, Kohlberg, Chapter Thirteen). In others, however, motivating forces are at the center of the schemes (the Puritans, Chapter Three; Freud, Chapter Eight; Maslow, Chapter Sixteen).

Furthermore, some theorists conceive of a single general force that activates all behavior. In Freud's early model he called this general force *libido,* an energy arising in a component of the personality called the *id* but utilized by other components of the personality as well to fuel their functions. Freud originally pictured libidinal energy as dominantly a sexual drive. However, in his later years he altered his beliefs and suggested that development and behavior are motivated by the interaction of two contrary drives, a life-promoting force (*libido* from a source termed *eros*) that accounted for constructive events in the personality and a death-directed force *(thanatos)* that accounted for destructive ones (S. Freud, 1938, pp. 5–6).

Many theories of personality and development either explicitly or implicitly differentiate among levels of needs. For example, a commonly postulated basic need from the field of biology is that of self-preservation. But when we observe behavior, we can propose that this basic need is manifested through a variety of more specific needs, such as those for food, for oxygen, for sexual expression, and for succor (the need to be nursed, supported, and consoled) (Hall & Lindzey, 1970, pp. 174–180).

Theorists, then, differ in the number of motivating forces they identify or imply, as well as in the way they name and organize the proposed drives or needs. Therefore we may wish to include in our guide questions the following:

7.1 Does the theorist identify or imply forces that motivate behavior? If so, what are these forces and what are their characteristics?

Not all theorists who propose the existence of various drives or needs agree as to the potency of each. For instance, Freud described his general force, libidinal energy, as being preeminently sexual. An early colleague of Freud's, Alfred Adler (1870–1937), disagreed that the prepotent human drive was sexual. Although he recognized sex as a significant drive, Adler contended that the truly overriding motive in human development was a *will to power,* a striving for superiority. He wrote that "whatever premises all our philosophers and psychologists dream of—self-preservation, pleasure principle, equalization—all these are but vague representations, attempts to express the great upward drive" (Adler, 1930, p. 398).

Maslow's system (Chapter Sixteen) also recognizes differences in the potency of various motivating forces but pictures their operation in a manner different from Freud's or Adler's. Maslow suggested that a person's needs are arranged in a hierarchy, like steps on a ladder, with the lower-step needs requiring fulfillment before the upper-step needs. He relegated such survival needs as those for food, drink, and physical safety to the lower levels of the hierarchy and drives for creative expression and "self-actualization" to the upper levels.

Not only may theorists claim that some needs are more significant than others throughout life, but they may also propose that certain needs are more potent at one stage of development than at another. For instance, a need for physical protection and nurturance is often considered more important during infancy, while a need for sexual expression is considered more demanding following puberty. (See the developmental tasks of Chapter Six.)

From this discussion we can generate another set of guide questions:

7.2 If several motivating forces are identified in the theory, do all of them carry equal power and importance? If not, which are more significant and why? If they differ in potency, do their relative degrees of power change from one growth stage or one age level to another?

Most theorists agree that a child is not only motivated strongly or weakly, but is also motivated toward particular things in the environment. In other words, a motivating force not only has power but also direction. Theorists do not agree, however, about the source or cause of this direction. The question is essentially:

7.3 Which source—the child's inner needs or the environment's stimuli—is more important in determining where the child directs attention?

Theorists such as Piaget and Freud credit inner needs with the greater power to direct attention, while behaviorists consider environmental stimuli to be more powerful. To a substantial degree, this difference of opinion reflects the more basic disagreement about which model each camp of theorists believes best represents human behavior. In Chapter One we noted that some theories of development are founded on the analogy of the machine, while others are based on the analogy of an organism. A machine reacts to things done to it by outside forces. It is "motivated" by environmental stimuli. An organism contains internal driving forces that seek expression in the environment; it is motivated by inner needs that direct its attention to those things in the environment that will likely fulfill the needs.

We noted earlier that motivation or stimulation is commonly considered to be a beginning step in the learning process. Exactly what steps occur after this stimulation is a matter of dispute among theorists. A behaviorist such as Skinner sketches one picture of the process, Piaget quite a different picture, and Lewin still another. Therefore, in analyzing theories, we can suitably ask:

7.4 In this theory, how does motivation fit into the overall picture of the learning process?

7.5 What are the necessary conditions for learning to occur? What elements or mechanisms comprise the learning process, and how do the elements interact?

8. Individual Differences   It is obvious that children of a given age level are not all alike. They differ in many ways. Theories of child development also differ in how they treat this matter of variation. Some theorists—Gesell, for example—give little recognition to the issue of differences. They talk almost exclusively about the typical child, passing over the fact that nearly all children deviate to some degree from the average. Other theories, such as behaviorism and Lewin's topological viewpoint, account more adequately for differences among individuals. Hence, to guide out comparisons among theories, we can ask:

8.1 What sorts of individual differences among children are given attention in the theory?

8.2 How does the theory account for such differences? To what extent do the factors that cause differences arise from heredity or from environment, and how do the causal factors operate or develop?

9. Desirable–Undesirable, Normal–Abnormal   One of the most common, practical questions asked by parents, teachers, and others who deal with children is whether a child's development is normal. Since not everyone defines the term *normal* in the same way, this question can be misleading. In one sense *normal* is used to mean "well adjusted" or "getting along very nicely." In another sense it means that the child's growth is about average for his age, or his behavior is common for his size or grade in school. We encounter problems of communication when these two meanings are mixed. For example, smoking cigarettes is very common among American youths in their upper teens and early twenties, so in this sense smoking is "normal"— that is, typical. But medical evidence suggests that smoking is not desirable, so in the sense of "getting along very nicely," smoking is not normal.

Another term that is often linked or confused with *normal* is *natural.* People usually think of *natural* as being what occurs if we do not consciously try to change things. It is letting Nature take her course. But not everyone agrees that natural growth is desirable or good. In the following chapters, the two theories that are most conspicuously on opposite sides in this debate are the Puritan and Rousseauistic views. The Puritans said that the child is naturally bad, so the task of parents is to combat these natural tendencies. Rousseau said that the child is naturally good and will develop into a paragon of wisdom and virtue if not corrupted by an evil environment.

Other theorists have not concerned themselves with the issues of either normal or natural development. Instead they have either implied or specifically defined the characteristics of desirable or proper development. They have pointed out the desired goals or directions of growth, then assumed that deviations from the path toward the goals are undesirable.

To guide our efforts in sorting out these matters, we can ask:

9.1 Is normal or natural or desirable development defined, or at least implied? If two or more of these terms appear in the theory, are they used synonymously? If not, how are they different from each other?

9.2 Is abnormal, unnatural, or undesirable development identified? If two or more of these terms appear in the theory, are they used synonymously? If not, how do they differ?

9.3 What causes abnormal, unnatural, or undesirable development? What, if anything, can be done to change such development into normal, natural, or desirable growth?

10. Philosophical Origins and Assumptions   No theory is an entirely new creation. Each has its philosophical progenitors, and our understanding of a theory is usually enhanced by our learning something of this ancestry. Our grasp of Maslow's brand of humanistic psychology (Chapter Sixteen) is enriched by our knowing that his proposals, in part, represent his reaction against what he believed were the shortcomings of both psychoanalysis and behaviorism. We can profit from knowing that Erikson's ideas (Chapter Nine) are founded primarily on Freud's teachings but have been influenced as well by methodology and concepts from cultural anthropology.

So we add another pair of queries to our list:

10.1 On what philosophical traditions, beliefs, and assumptions is the theory founded?

10.2 Against what beliefs is the theory reacting?

11. Investigative Methods   There is something of a chicken-and-egg relationship between a theory and its investigative methods. We never know whether (a) the theory's structure has defined the methods used for gathering data or whether (b) the data-collecting methods have dictated the structure of the theory. In any event, models of child development are heavily influenced by the investigative techniques used in producing the data they treat.

For instance, Freud's main method of collecting information was listening to neurotic adults recall incidents from their childhood and from their current dreams. The particular recollections this method evoked clearly influenced the nature of the theory he proposed. The charge that his theory gives a gloomy, disturbed view of human development has been raised by critics who blame his choice of neurotic informants as the cause of the ostensibly pessimistic picture he paints of child growth. Likewise, his dependence on self-reports of memories and dreams as his source of data is compatible with his willingness to fashion an imaginary structure of the "mind" from which these memories and dreams are generated. In contrast, Skinner rejected introspective reports as sources of evidence and depended instead on descriptions of child behavior as recorded by an outside observer. This dedication to observable events is compatible with Skinner's unwillingness to speculate about such hypothetical elements as an unseeable "mind" or such mental components as Freud's id, ego, and superego.

Thus, in analyzing theories, we can ask:

11.1 What investigative methods are used by the theorist?

11.2 How have these methods influenced the form and content of the theory?

12. Appeal for Acceptance   Typically, theorists want others to believe their proposals. To this end they seek to present the sorts of arguments they feel will appeal to the people they want to accept their scheme. For instance, early Puritan writers appealed to their parishioners' faith in the word of God as found in the Bible and on a set of deductions about child rearing that pastors drew from church doctrine. Rousseau sought to convince his readers by means of illustrative anecdotes drawn from his imagination or his experience as a tutor of children of aristocrats. Classical psychoanalysts propose that, in addition to the intuitive good sense their theory makes, a person becomes convinced of its validity by going through the process of psychoanalysis. Experimental psychologists describe their experiments in detail and cast the results in statistical form, with the expectation that anyone who questions the results can carry out the same experiments and see the validity of the conclusions.

Thus different theorists use different approaches in appealing for acceptance of their schemes. Likewise, different consumers of child development theories find some sorts of evidence more convincing than others. Whether you find a particular theory more useful or valid than another depends on how well the theorist's mode of appeal matches the types of evidence you consider most acceptable. Hence we may ask:

12.1 On what sorts of evidence or on what types of appeal does the theory depend to convince people of its worth?

13. Terminology   In the following chapters you will find many terms created or adopted by theorists to describe their ideas of personality structure, growth stages, and growth principles. These include *id, orthogenetic principle, soul, growth gradients, topological maps, formal operations,* and many more. Often the essence of a theorist's position is contained in the terms she uses. If you comprehend the terms, you understand the substance of her beliefs.

If, in our investigation of a theory, we answer the twelve clusters of questions already considered in this chapter, then we will likely have learned the meaning of most or all the key terms in the theory. But in case we have missed any, we can add two final sets of queries:

13.1 Does the theory have a special terminology? If so, what does each term mean?

13.2 Do the terms refer to concepts unique to this theory, or do they identify things for which other theorists have used different words?

CONCLUSION

In Chapter Two, a series of questions has been proposed that can be asked about the contents and philosophical underpinnings of theories we wish to analyze and compare. This list does not include all the questions that could be asked; it contains ones I feel might be of general interest. You may wish to add others that focus on matters of particular importance to you.

In the following chapters separate theories are described. In organizing each chapter I have sought, as far as space permits, to answer the questions posed in Chapter Two. However, none of the chapters is designed as a sequential list of answers to these questions, with topic 1 presented first and topic 13 last. Such a catalogue pattern would make the chapters read too much like catechisms. Therefore each chapter is presented in a form intended to give the essence of the theorist's approach in a logical and interesting fashion. In the process as many of Chapter Two questions are answered as is feasible. Some chapters do not treat certain questions because the theorist or theorists did not ask such questions. In other instances a topic plays such a small part in a particular theory that it was not worth discussing in this introductory level volume.

Now, with the perspectives of Chapters One and Two in mind, we move to the theories themselves, beginning at a point several centuries in the past and then rushing quickly to modern times.

FOR FURTHER READING

You may wish to find additional topics and questions to supplement the list given in this chapter. If so, your most convenient source may be child development textbooks. Chapter titles and topic headings in such books often imply questions the authors believe are important for theorists to answer. Thus an inspection of titles and headings can suggest additional guide questions. Furthermore, under such headings you often find concise answers to the questions as seen from various theorists' points of view.

To aid you in this search, the following list of representative sources is suggested:

Bee, Helen. (1978) *The Developing Child.* New York: Harper & Row.

Crain, William C. (1980) *Theories of Development: Concepts and Applications.* Englewood Cliffs, N. J.: Prentice-Hall.

Dworetsky, John P. (1981) *Introduction to Child Development.* St. Paul: West.

Gordon, Ira J. (1975) *Human Development: A Transactional Perspective.* New York: Harper & Row.

Langer, Jonas. (1969) *Theories of Development.* New York: Holt, Rinehart, & Winston.

Lawton, Joseph T. (1982) *Introduction to Child Development.* Dubuque, Iowa: William C. Brown.

McClinton, Barbara S., and Blanche G. Meier. (1978) *Beginnings: Psychology of Early Childhood.* St. Louis: C. V. Mosby.

Mussen, Paul H., John J. Conger, and J. Kagan. (1980) *Essentials of Child Development and Personality.* New York: Harper & Row.

Papalia, Diane E., and Sally W. Olds. (1981) *Human Development.* New York: McGraw-Hill.

Pinkunas, Justin. (1976) *Human Development: An Emergent Science.* New York: McGraw-Hill.

Yussen, Steven R., and John W. Santrock. (1982) *Child Development: An Introduction.* Dubuque, Iowa: William C. Brown.

TRACES FROM THE PAST

A search for the child's original nature and for ways to react to such a nature

Theories of child development are not unique to the twentieth century. People have always had beliefs about how children develop. Sometimes these convictions were held in common by a certain segment of society. Other times they were views expressed by a single author and subsequently adopted by people who found the author's argument convincing. Three sets of such beliefs are considered in Part Two.

The initial two sets, reviewed in Chapter Three, illustrate contrasting patterns of conviction that have exerted significant influence in Europe and North America in recent centuries. The first of this pair traces its origin to such Protestant writers as John Calvin (1509–1564) and John Knox (1505–1572). The second is based mainly on the writings of the Swiss fomenter of social protest, Jean Jacques Rousseau (1712–1778). Since vestiges of both viewpoints are found in modern society, an understanding of the basic elements of each is of use today.

The third of the sets, summarized in Chapter Four, is called *commonsense* or *naive* psychology since it consists of a cluster of ideas that most people hold about how children develop. According to such psychologists as Fritz Heider, this cluster is not just a disorganized conglomeration of opinions; it has an identifiable underlying pattern that warrants its being labeled a theory of child development.

As a preparation for Chapters Three and Four, we will profit from a brief preview of the origins of the three theories that make up Part Two.

The Puritans' Sinful and Obstinate Child

In the 1530s Calvin, a Swiss theologian, followed Martin Luther's (1483–1546) lead and launched his own movement of protest against the church of

Rome. The Protestant doctrines preached by Calvin and the Scotsman Knox became the founding principles for Presbyterianism in Scotland and for Puritanism in England and in colonial America.

At the core of Calvin's doctrine was a conception of human nature that pictured the newborn child as a sinner, possessed by motives to do evil. The task of parents and teachers was to discover ways to dissuade children from this naturally evil bent and make them worthy to enter heaven for life after death. Thus the Calvinist conception of child development represents a search for proper ways of reacting to children's sinful and obstinate nature.

The Puritan view was particularly strong in New England from the seventeenth to the nineteenth centuries; then its popularity waned. However, Puritan concepts of child development did not entirely disappear. Elements of the doctrine can be found today in the words and deeds of many adults. As a result, the beliefs contained in Puritan theory are not just historical curiosities. Understanding them is useful for bringing to light the religious and cultural origins of the strict child-rearing practices found today in some homes and schoolrooms.

Rousseau's Moral and Curious Child

In 1762 the Swiss social philosopher Rousseau published two books that made him famous. *The Social Contract* made him an idol among the instigators of the French Revolution, and *Emile* established him as a forebear of the nineteenth- and twentieth-century theorists who have written on early childhood education.

In contrast to the Puritans, Rousseau proposed in *Emile* that children are born morally good. Children will naturally do the right thing unless misled by a corrupt social environment. So Rousseau's description of child development is the result of his search for ways of guiding children's growth so they remain true to their natural inclinations. Elements of Rousseau's beliefs are found today in the writings of such theorists as Piaget (Chapter Ten) and Maria Montessori (Montessori, 1967) and in books on "discovery methods" in teaching science.

Heider's Analysis of Commonsense Theory

The collection of ideas that most people hold about how children develop is usually called *common sense*. Heider, an American psychologist, proposed that this collection is not simply a scattering of beliefs but rather is founded on an intuitive theoretical framework that can be analyzed and described.

Principal elements of this framework, as depicted by Heider, form the commonsense model of development presented in Chapter Four.

Since the term *common sense* has different meanings for different people, it is important at the outset to clarify our definition of it.

In ancient Greece, Aristotle proposed that there were five external senses—sight, hearing, taste, smell, and touch—plus a common sense, located in the heart, which served as the coordinating center for the other five. Remnants of this belief are still found in our language in such statements as, "She learned it by heart." Later philosophers relocated the common sense in the brain, where the Puritans and Rousseau thought it resided. However, in Chapter Four the term *common sense* is not used with this meaning.

For many people, common sense refers to convictions held by a person because the truth of such beliefs is self-evident. If we need no special training or special instruments to arrive at a conclusion about something we see or hear or smell, then we usually say our conclusion is "just common sense." We believe that anyone in his "right mind" would come to the same conclusion. In Chapter Four, this sort of common sense—self-evident conclusions—is part of what we intend.

For the other part of our meaning, common sense is equated with the term *popular opinion*. To some people common sense means an idea that everybody, or nearly everybody, subscribes to, whether it is obvious or not. In our culture, for example, the fact that the earth is a sphere is common sense today, though that "fact" is not obvious to the eye. Nor was that "fact" common sense at the time of Columbus.

Thus in Chapter Four the phrase "a commonsense view of child development" identifies those beliefs shared by a large proportion of society—with many of the beliefs being self-evident conclusions.

Although at first this definition of commonsense theory may appear uncomplicated, we will see, when we analyze specific beliefs, that people do not all agree on what they believe about children's growth and development. Differences of opinion are especially apparent in large, complex modern societies in which scholars have both the time and desire to speculate and conduct research about the nature of humanity. These thinkers come up with ideas that sometimes conflict with the common sense of the populace. But as the novel ideas are communicated, many people become convinced of their validity and join this new school of thought. Such splintering of common sense into different camps can be expected to occur more frequently in societies that are blessed, or burdened, not only with the leisure time for speculation but also with highly penetrating mass communication devices—

television, radio, newspapers, magazines, and books. Smaller, more isolated and cohesive societies subscribe to a more commonly accepted set of convictions about children than do larger, more disparate ones. Therefore, as we consider one version of commonsense theory, there may be a problem of consensus.

Furthermore, the common sense outlined in Chapter Four applies chiefly to societies that have evolved from European roots. How closely this version represents common sense in traditional African, Asian, Native American, and Pacific Island cultures is not known.

Another aspect of naive psychology that deserves attention was described by an American developmental psychologist, A. L. Baldwin (1967, p. 38):

> It is important to realize . . . that naive psychology is not a stated theory but a body of beliefs about human behavior. Only the systematic description of naive psychology gives it the look of a theory.

Thus we are interested not just in the commonsense beliefs themselves but in the systematic way they are analyzed. However, we may ask whether such everyday beliefs about children deserve a chapter in a book on formal theories. Aren't naive assumptions too ordinary to warrant serious discussion? There are at least four reasons why they are not and why they do indeed deserve attention.

First, commonsense psychology is the sort that all of us use, either entirely or to a great degree, in dealing with children during the routine of daily living. A study of the structure and content of naive notions of development should help us analyze the strengths and weaknesses of such notions. As a result, we may be able to alter at least some of the least defensible aspects of our commonsense opinions and perhaps substitute more valid ones.

Second, the analysis of common sense can help us understand the nature of more formal theories of development because those theories often include many commonsense assumptions. After we observe the way psychologists such as Heider analyze naive beliefs, we will be better prepared to recognize the naive-psychology aspects of other theories we study.

Third, formal theories, in a sense, are often the reactions of theorists against naive-psychology notions that they believe are in error. Thus, when we recognize the commonsense ideas theorists are reacting against, we are better equipped to understand the formal theories.

Fourth, an inspection of commonsense theory can help us gain some perspective about the historical roots of beliefs widely held in our society today. For example, when we learn about the old faculty-psychology concept of the human soul or personality, as depicted in Chapter Three, we recognize that today's commonsense acceptance of belief in imagination, reasoning, and the will are holdovers from that supposedly discredited concept.

For these reasons, then, a chapter on naive psychology is of value in a modern-day book on theories of development.

The Puritans' Sinful Child and Rousseau's Moral Child

In order to expedite the comparison of Puritan theories and those of Rousseau, Chapter Three is organized in a series of sections, each treating a particular aspect of development. Then within each section the two viewpoints toward that aspect are described, first the Puritans' and then Rousseau's. The topic sequence is (1) the theories' published sources, (2) the basic premises and their consequences, (3) the human personality—structure and function, (4) the stages of development, (5) the importance of instruction, (6) individual differences, (7) practical applications, (8) research challenges, (9) the Puritan view: an assessment, and (10) Rousseau's view: an assessment.

THE THEORIES' PUBLISHED SOURCES

Of the two theoretical positions, the published sources of Rousseau's proposals are far easier to locate since they represent the products of a single author who expressed his ideas in a limited number of books, essays, and letters. In contrast, the Puritan view of child development must be pieced together from records found in a wide variety of places.

Sources of Puritan Beliefs

No Puritan author apparently ever collected early Protestant thoughts about child nature and organized them into a systematic description of the Puritan child development theory of colonial America. Hence we have to search through the writings of Protestant leaders to extract from them the Puritan picture of the child.*

The picture offered in the following pages is composed primarily of gleanings from a variety of seventeenth- and eighteenth-century Protestant writings, including those of such prominent theologians as Jonathan Edwards, John Cotton, Cotton Mather, Samuel Sewall, and Benjamin Wadsworth. But perhaps the most interesting of the sources is *The New England Primer,* a tiny volume hardly longer or broader than a young child's hand. Between 1687 and the mid-1800s, six million copies of the *Primer* were sold, an average of 40,000 a year in a then sparsely settled America (Morison, 1936, p. 79). During the 1700s it was *the* schoolbook for children of Protestant families, and during the 1800s it was still widely used in conjunction with other texts (Ford, 1962, p. 19). It is unlikely that parents, pastors, and schoolmasters would have permitted such heavy dependence on a textbook if it did not represent their idea of the truth. So it seems safe to assume that the view of child nature reflected in the *Primer* is a fair representation of the beliefs held by a major segment of the population.

Sources of Rousseau's Beliefs

To an eighteenth-century Europe that widely believed that children were innately bad, Jean Jacques Rousseau declared, "All things are good as they come out of the hands of their Creator, but everything degenerates in the hands of man" (Rousseau, 1773, vol. 1, p. 1).

This statement opened the novel *Emile,* published in France in 1762 when Rousseau, at age 50, was already widely known for his essays on social philosophy and for his recent, highly popular novel, *The New Héloise.* As noted earlier, *Emile* appeared the same year as *The Social Contract,* an anti-monarchy volume that would later make the author a favorite among the activists of the French Revolution.

Emile, though in the form of a novel, was actually what its subtitle explained: "A Treatise of Education." In the treatise, Rousseau described the chief elements of a proper education for the sons of economically well-to-do European families. But his advice appears to have been intended for parents of children in other strata of European society as well. The description of the rearing of Emile from birth to adulthood implies a theory

---

*The terms *Puritan, Calvinist,* and *Protestant* are used interchangeably throughout Chapter Three, with the understanding that Calvinism is intended to mean "Calvinism of colonial times" and Protestant refers to "an early Calvinist form of Protestant belief." I recognize that modern Calvinists would not necessarily hold all the beliefs reviewed in Chapter Three, and that all forms of Protestantism, today or in the past, would not include all the views described in this chapter.

of child development, a theory that has exerted significant influence on generations of authors, educators, and parents in diverse parts of the world.

Rousseau's novel did not dwell exclusively on the education of boys. In the closing sections he discussed as well the proper training for the model girl, Sophia, who "must be endowed with every qualification suitable to her species and sex in order to act her part in the natural and moral system" (Rousseau, 1773, vol. 1, p. 6).

Although the major part of Rousseau's conception of child growth was presented in *Emile*, he produced a number of other works that extended—and in minor ways conflicted with—the picture of children given in *Emile*. The view of Rousseau's theory offered here is drawn from these works.*

Over the two centuries since the publication of *Emile*, readers of Rousseau have debated the question of whether the ideas the book espouses were really new. Critics have claimed that most of Rousseau's key concepts are found in the writings of authors from Plato to Locke (Patterson, 1971, pp. 12–13). Rousseau's supporters have held that most of the ideas were actually his own, and certainly the pattern they formed in his hands was new. But whether or not he originated the ideas, his supporters and critics alike agree that his writings strongly influenced people's views of children.

Whereas Puritan theory was founded chiefly on the Protestant Bible and on religious leaders' interpretations of what the Bible intended for human development, the main influences behind Rousseau's theory seem to have been four: memories of his own childhood, his experience tutoring boys of aristocratic families, his reading in philosophy and in books on "primitive peoples," and his casual observations of European peasant children.

In regard to his childhood, he wrote in his *Confessions:* "If ever child received a sound and reasonable education, it was I" (Boyd, 1963, p. 13). This education of which he boasted was a most erratic one. His mother had died shortly after his birth, so until later childhood he was raised mainly by his father, a sometime watchmaker and dancing teacher with romantic ideas he passed on to his son. Jean Jacques learned to read by age 6, starting with romantic novels his mother had left him. At age 7 he began reading philosophy and history. When the boy entered early adolescence, his father ran off from Geneva to escape punishment for breaking the law, and Jean Jacques was schooled by relatives. He then was apprenticed to an engraver, but soon quit the trade and moved from one job to another. Finally, he attached himself to upper-class families as a secretary or tutor. This childhood,

---

*These additional writings include a portion of *The New Héloise*, parts of *The Confessions*, his *Memoir on the Education of the Prince of Wurttemberg's InfantDaughter*,and *Letters to the Abbé M. on the Education of a Boy* (Boyd, 1962).

unfettered by formal schooling or a strict home life, seems to have become his model for that of Emile.

In his writings on child development and education, Rousseau emphasized that parents should spend much time in supervising their children's development if a tutor cannot be provided to do the job. But in his own life, Rousseau did not take fatherhood so seriously. He never married but lived many years with a young woman of servant status who bore him five children, all of whom Rousseau promptly sent off to foundling homes, despite the tears of their mother. Thus at no time did Rousseau apply to his own offspring the advice he offered other parents. In describing the proper development of the girl Sophia in the novel *Emile,* Rousseau apparently drew at least some traits from the woman who bore his own children. She was devoted and loyal, but apparently a bit simpleminded. She seems to have satisfied Rousseau's needs without causing trouble over the other romantic attachments he established during their years together (Davidson, 1898).

A third influence on Rousseau's views was the books he read about the native peoples of the Americas, the South Seas, Africa, and Asia. The books were written either by adventurers who had visited these lands or by authors who imagined what such places might be like. While some writers deplored the state of the "primitive peoples," others praised the "noble savages' " way of life. Rousseau admired certain traits of these fabled people so much that he sought to have Emile emulate their naivete and their close bond with nature.

The fourth main influence on Rousseau's theory was his observations of the European peasants' child-rearing practices in villages he frequented throughout his life. Although he did not approve of certain crudities of the common folk, he considered some of their practices laudable (such as breast-feeding infants) and incorporated them into his own recommendations on child rearing.

From such a background Rousseau fashioned his theory of child nature.

THE BASIC PREMISES AND THEIR CONSEQUENCES

Differences between theories of development often arise chiefly from differences in the philosophical assumptions on which the theories are erected. This fact is dramatically illustrated in the case of the theories of the Puritans and those of Rousseau.

Puritan Premises

Three key assumptions undergirded the Puritan view: (1) children are born evil, bound to sin if not guided away from their natural state; (2) children are born without knowledge, meaning that they are not sufficiently aware of sinfulness or of how to lead a good life; and (3) children are born with a capacity to learn. The first of these assumptions was founded on religious doctrine, the second and third apparently on common sense.

The role of education in the home, church, and school was to redirect children from their natural inclinations so they might be saved from an eternity in hell after death. Salvation was not guaranteed to people who learned to live a good life because salvation was a gift of God, not earned by humans through good works in the world. But Puritans believed that striving to lead the kind of life that would please God could open the channel to salvation. Leading a good life improved one's chances of receiving God's grace.

Most crucial to the Puritan doctrine was the idea that the sin of disobedience to God that Adam and Eve committed when they ate the forbidden fruit in the Garden of Eden was a sin carried down through all generations. Each newborn child was the recipient of this original sin and would be condemned to hell after death if not redeemed. The *New England Primer* introduced children to the first letter of the alphabet with a verse that made this premise clear (1836, p. 11):

A = In *A*dam's fall we sinned all.

The result of this innate sin was that children's natural motivation was to behave in evil ways that would please the devil. The child would naturally frolic "and take delight among young folk who spend their days in joy and mirth" (*Primer*, 1836, p. 57). Children would pass the time in idleness, disobey parents and others in authority, lie and curse and steal, ignore their studies and play truant from school, hate others, fight with brothers and sisters and schoolmates, refuse to pray or attend church, not read the Bible, fail to abide by the Ten Commandments, and refuse to accept or follow Christ (*Primer*, 1836, pp. 10–64). Such behavior as this signified to the Puritan the expected, natural course of development.

Thus children were urged not to follow their natural inclinations but instead to prepare themselves properly for "life after death." In Calvinism, as in so many other denominations, the years between earthly birth and death are only a trial period. They are a time of testing and of preparation for eternal life in the "great beyond." To avoid an afterlife of eternal misery in hell, children need to adopt the goals of the good child. The good child is one who keeps himself engaged in profitable tasks and does not idle away his time, obeys his superiors, does not lie or swear or steal, studies hard in school, forgives his enemies, speaks well of others and treats them with kindness, reads the Bible and prays regularly, attends church, abides by the Ten Commandments, loves Christ, and accepts Christ as his redeemer from sin. In this way, the Puritans defined the desired course of child development.

Rousseau's Premises

The most basic assumption on which Rousseau based his proposals has already been mentioned—children are innately good and any shortcomings they develop while growing up are the result of an unfavorable environment. As a consequence, the task of parents and teachers is to protect young children from such evil environmental influences until the children are sufficiently mature to protect themselves.

Three further assumptions undergirding Rousseau's theory are of particular importance today. They are his beliefs in *critical periods, discovery learning,* and *permissiveness.* The term *critical periods* identifies the belief that in child rearing, as in the blacksmith trade, one should strike while the iron is hot. Striking too soon or too late will ruin the product. Those who subscribe to a belief in critical periods say that before a child can profit from environmental influences—from instruction or experience—she must have attained a particular degree of internal maturation. That a child needs a certain amount of readiness or "growing up" before learning is not new. We waste our time if we try teaching a two-week-old infant to walk or a one-year-old child to read books. However, there is more to the critical-periods concept than this. There is also the question of when is the optimal time to provide experiences for each activity—walking, reading, analyzing concepts of algebra, engaging in sexual relations, and so forth. Furthermore, if we miss this optimum time, if we wait too long to begin the experiences, will the child fail to develop adequately? In other words, is there both a lower and an upper age limit for the optimal—or even the possible—period in which environmental forces can interact with maturational preparation to produce development? These issues engage the active attention of researchers today, just as the matter of maturational readiness did Rousseau two centuries ago (R. M. Lerner, 1976, pp. 98–100).

Rousseau's concern, however, was not with the problem of parents' waiting too long before teaching children, and thus passing over the critical period for learning a particular skill. Rather, he was concerned about the parents' making the error of trying to teach too soon or of furnishing the wrong experiences and thus irreparably damaging the child for the future. Rousseau felt that each dimension of development (physical, mental, social, moral) flowered at a particular time, and he felt it important to protect the child's growth schedule to ensure that each dimension flowered in nature's intended way.

Linked to the matter of critical periods was Rousseau's belief in what is known today as *discovery learning.* In recent decades, educators have expressed strong convictions about the value of stimulating children to discover the operating principles of their physical and social worlds rather than memorizing principles given them by parents and teachers. These ideas of discovery or inquiry learning are not new but were advocated by Rousseau in *Emile* and illustrated by detailed examples of how to carry them out in practice.

Another current issue that has been partly credited to, or blamed on, Rousseau is that of *permissiveness* in child rearing. Rousseau's prime tenet was that children are born naturally good and will develop into models of wisdom and virtue if permitted to follow nature's way and not driven off the track by the meddling of a corrupt society. In modern times there have been various interpretations of Rousseau's permissiveness, and at least one of the more popular interpretations is clearly wrong. It is the interpretation that nature's proper course involves letting children do as they wish in all things, indulging them at every turn. But this is not what Rousseau intended. He believed that it is the mature adult's responsibility to analyze nature's way, as he himself did in *Emile,* and, on the basis of this analysis, manipulate the child's experiences so they suit the sequence of critical periods he pictured as comprising desirable development. Thus, within structured limits of opportunity that were devised by an adult, the child was permitted to grow the natural way. This was the Rousseauistic version of permissiveness.

THE HUMAN PERSONALITY— STRUCTURE AND FUNCTION

Neither the Calvinists nor Rousseau created the theory of human intellect— faculty psychology—to which they subscribed in common. They inherited it from the medieval theologians Albertus Magnus (1193?–1280) and Thomas Aquinas (1225–1274) and the philosopher-psychologists of the Renaissance who refined the theory. Among Protestants it was altered slightly to accommodate certain of their own beliefs, but in the main faculty psychology was believed in and taught. Puritan sermons also abound in allusions to this model of the mind, thus attesting to the general understanding of it on the part of both the theologians and their parishioners (P. Miller, 1963, pp. 242–244). Although it is here oversimplified, this model was accepted as obvious truth by the followers of Luther, Calvin, and Knox and apparently by Rousseau as well.

We can best explain the nature of the *mind* or *soul* from the faculty psychologist's point of view if we consider what occurs in a child's mental apparatus as he encounters a barking dog. The first part of the child's thought-and-action system that is activated is the set of *external senses,* the five senses Aristotle identified: sight, hearing, touch, taste, and smell. The noisy dog produces on the eye and ear a replica or image of the animal's visage and sound. Each image, the *phantasm* or *species* of the observed object, is then picked up from the eye and ear by *animal spirits,* the powers that convey information through the nerves from one organ to another (see Figure 3.1). The animal spirits deliver the dog phantasms to a chamber in the center of the brain labeled the *common sense;* this is the place in which phantasms from all the senses are collected, apprehended, and distinguished from one another. The common sense is an *internal sense* or *faculty*—"faculty" meaning a power, capacity, or function of the mind.

Within the common sense, the phantasms of sight and sound are identified as belonging to the species dog, specifically a barking dog that is showing its teeth and not wagging its tail. The common sense passes the results of its interpretation to a forward chamber of the brain where the faculty of *imagination* (sometimes called the *fancy* or *phantasy*) judges and compares phantasms with each other, retains them when the object (the dog in this instance) is no longer present, and renders them more vivid. The imagination compares the dog image with remembered images from the past and judges it to be unfriendly and perhaps dangerous. This judgment by the imagination is next relayed to the faculty of *memory* at the rear of the brain to be stored for future reference.

At the same time, somewhere above the common sense, the faculty of *reason* or *understanding* calls before it phantasms either from imagination or from memory. Reason judges whether the phantasms are true or false, desirable or undesirable, good or evil. Phantasms of past dogs (drawn from memory) and the present dog (drawn from imagination) are analyzed by reason, which concludes that the present animal might attack, particularly if the child should run as if afraid. Reason determines that the wisest behavior is to walk past the dog cautiously, without a show of fear, while keeping a wary eye on the beast.

This conclusion about wise action is conveyed from reason by animal spirits along the nerves to the faculty of the *will,* which resides in the heart. The role of the will is to accept the images of wise behavior from reason and

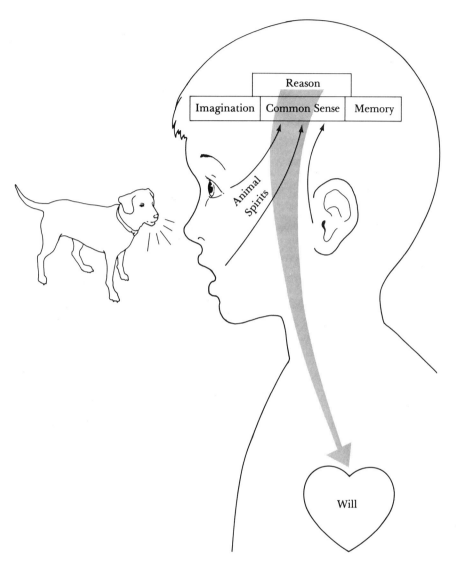

Figure 3.1   Faculties of the Mind

to command suitable emotions (usually called *affections* or *passions*) in the heart to activate appropriate muscles to carry out reason's decision. This entire process, from the instant the child first sees the dog until his will orders his feet to walk, requires just a moment or two, and we see him hesitate only briefly when he meets the dog, before he walks by the animal as if not afraid, all the time willing his emotion of fear to be tempered with courage and caution (P. Miller, 1963, pp. 240–242).

This system of human thought and action was called the *soul* by both Renaissance philosophers and Calvinists. The soul, in contrast to the body, is not transmitted through heredity. Rather it is individually "created by God of nothing, immediately infused into the body (at birth) as the proper form thereof, by which man is, liveth, is sensible, moveth, understandeth, willeth, and is affected" (John Norton in P. Miller, 1963, p. 240). The human soul in this view is a unitary object, but, like God, it forms a trinity consisting of a *vegetative* soul, a *sensible* soul, and a *rational* soul. The vegetative soul has the powers of nourishing and propagating, two characteristics that people share with the earth's plant life. The sensible soul has not only powers of nourishing and propagating but also additional equipment possessed by animals—external senses and animal spirits, as well as the interior senses of common sense, imagination, memory, the passions or emotions, and the musculature *(sinews)* that makes motion possible. But it is the rational soul, the highest in the trinity, which distinguishes humans from the earth's other living things. The rational soul contains all the powers of the other two, plus the faculties of reason and will.

It was the fate of this rational soul that sorely concerned Puritan parents in their child-rearing practices, for the soul was immortal and continued after death through eternity, condemned to misery in hell or blessed with happiness in heaven. As in life, the soul after death was a sensitive being. The American theologian Jonathan Edwards (1703–1758) told his parishioners, "An unbodied spirit may be as capable of love and hatred, joy and sorrow, hope or fear, or other affections, as one that is united to a body" (Simonson, 1970, p. 163).

This doctrine of the human mind or personality to which the Puritans and Rousseau subscribed had many other aspects as well. For instance, an important additional faculty was the *conscience*, defined as the awareness of distinctions between good and evil, between right and wrong. Puritans held that conscience was inborn, so young children—even though they lacked much experience in the world—could not excuse misdemeanors by saying they did not know any better. As Edwards pointed out (Smith, 1959, p. 207):

> Conscience naturally gives men an apprehension of right and wrong, and suggests the relation there is between right and wrong and retribution; the Spirit of God assists men's consciences to do this in a greater degree, helps conscience against the stupefying influence of worldly objects and their lusts.

In the case of conscience, as in many other matters, Puritan thinkers struggled with the nature–nurture issue. How much of the child's character and faculties is innate or God-given, and how much is due to instruction and experience? It was agreed that children normally were born with all their faculties, or mental chambers. But the contents of the chambers, such as imagination and memory, were not filled until the child had experiences or instruction. For Puritans, the activation and development of faculties depended on two factors as children grew to maturity: (1) God's grace in endowing the child with a particular level of different faculties or abilities—a child might have a special "bent" that could be developed—and (2) influences in the child's daily life at home, in school and church, and in the community. Although the conscience or knowledge of right from wrong was considered to be innate, Puritans did not hesitate to nourish it with threats, moralizing, and the whip.

Another faculty, *intuition*, apparently did not depend on instruction for its development. A person searched for this inner "sixth sense" through meditation, prayer, and introspection. Edwards regarded intuition as the instigator of the "great awakening" of religious conversion that Puritans so valued. He preached that conversion did not consist of a person's acting in a pious manner or even in doing good works but rather it was an overwhelming and immediate sense of God's reality (Simonson, 1970, p. 13). From an early age, children were urged to seek out this sense.

These, then, are the general outlines of the structure and function of the human soul or mind in Puritan times, although as Samuel Willard in his colonial period volume the *Compleat Body* admitted: "Our knowledge of the nature of our own Souls, is very shallow and confused" (P. Miller, 1963, p. 244).

THE STAGES OF DEVELOPMENT

The stages through which children develop to maturity were not specified clearly in Puritan doctrine, although they were described in sequence and in considerable detail by Rousseau in *Emile*.

The Puritan Pattern of Stages

Although Puritan writers did not leave us a well-defined description of the levels of development through which children progress, we are able to propose four stages by considering the ways children and youths were treated at different age levels and by analyzing the expectations held for them.

Infancy: Birth to Age 1½ or 2   This was the time when babies were completely dependent on adults to meet their physical needs. The period ended with the child's being able to walk alone and say a few meaningful words in communicating with others. Early in this stage, the parents had the infant baptized; the child was officially named and blessed by the church and was pledged to a Christian life by his or her parents. This pledge by the infant's guardians was necessary because a baby's faculties of reason and of will were obviously not yet developed enough for the infant to make such a decision.

Early Childhood: Age 2 to Age 5–7   During these years the child became increasingly mobile and learned to communicate in a basic manner. Young children were expected, as an early leader of American congregationalism, John Cotton (1584–1652), wrote, to "spend much time in pastime and play, for their bodyes are too weak to labour, and their minds to study are too shallow . . . even the first seven years are spent in pastime, and God looks not much at it" (Morgan, 1956, pp. 28–29). Though Cotton chose seven years as the upper limit for this stage of idleness, in many households children were put to useful work, at least part-time, at age 5 or 6.

During these years, children were to begin their indoctrination into Christian duty and the dangers of a sinful life. Learning at this early age was expected to be rote, with little or no comprehension of subtle meanings or interpretations since the faculty of reason was as yet undeveloped. Martin Luther had suggested that it was all right to deal with the complexities of ideas when preaching to "scholars or wise men," but "with the young, keep always to one form, and teach them first of all these articles, namely, the Ten Commandments, the Belief, the Lord's Prayer, etc., according to the text, word for word, so that they may repeat them and learn them by heart" (Eby, 1971, p. 89).

Later Childhood: Age 5–7 to Age 11–14   At this stage children were to engage in useful work around the home and to attend school, if one was available. The most essential skill was that of reading, with computation and writing close behind. Mothers would begin their daughters on sewing, cooking, and housekeeping early in this period. Fathers or older brothers would supervise boys in masculine pursuits around the farm, shop, or home. Boys also changed their long dresses, called "coats," for pants that fastened just under the knees. At least once a week parents were expected to assess each child's progress in Biblical learning and make new assignments.

The two chief purposes behind all this activity were apparently to ensure that children had constructive tasks to keep them from devilry and to establish early the habit of diligence. As John Cotton warned in the early 1700s, "Idleness in youth is scarcely healed without a scar in age" (Morgan, 1956, p. 29).

During these years the faculties of common sense and imagination were quickened, memory was being filled, and reason and will were maturing.

Youth: Age 11–14 to Age 18–21 or Economic Independence

This was often called the "age of reason," for the faculties of understanding and will were now thought to be relatively mature, at least mature enough for the teenager to be considered a rational, responsible being. It was at this time that the youth typically joined the church, consciously fulfilling the baptismal pledge parents had expressed at infancy.

At the outset of this stage, the youth was expected to heed his or her calling. A *calling* in colonial times was of several types. First, the youth accepted God's call to a Christian life, as evidenced by achieving membership in the church. *Calling* also meant that the adolescent identified the vocation for which she or he was fitted by God. On the basis of this identification, a boy accepted an apprenticeship or, for a chosen few, an opportunity to attend Latin grammar school and enroll at Harvard or Yale, usually to become a minister. Even though a girl's calling was always to be a housekeeper, she, like her brothers, might be sent at puberty to service in someone else's home. Apprentices always lived with their masters and typically served in the master's home and shop for seven to ten years, until the boy reached age 21 and the girl age 18. E. S. Morgan, a modern writer on Puritan times, suggests that (1956, p. 38):

> Psychologically this separation of parents and children may have had a sound foundation. The child left home just at the time when parental discipline caused increasing friction, just at the time when a child begins to assert his independence. By allowing a strange master to take over the disciplinary function, the parent could meet the child upon a plane of affection and friendliness. At the same time the child would be taught good behavior by someone who would not forgive him any mischief out of affection for his person.

Since the faculties of the soul by this age were well developed, the youth was expected to go beyond the rote memorization of theological material. Now he should be able to argue subtleties of meaning and identify the best reasoned among several interpretations. He was also expected to display a strong will, to act on what his reason told him was right. When all this had occurred, childhood was past.

Rousseau's Pattern of Stages

The beliefs Rousseau held about growth stages are quite clear since he organized the novel *Emile* into a sequence of sections, each representing a more advanced stage in the growing child's life. Significant characteristics of the stages are summarized in the following paragraphs.

Infancy: Birth to Age 2   This was the critical period for establishing physical health and sharp senses. In Rousseau's opinion, newborn infants have vague feelings of pleasure and pain but no real *sentiments* (definite feelings about things), and during infancy they develop no ideas. They do, however, sense things in their environment and begin to store in memory the impressions of these sensations.

The goal of this stage was to produce a healthy young animal with keen senses of sight, hearing, touch, taste, and smell. Rousseau felt that nature intended the infant to be breast-fed by its own mother and not turned over to a nurse, as was the practice in many upper-class European households of the day, so he stressed the virtues of mothers feeding their own offspring. Rousseau also believed that nature did not intend children to be fettered by heavy, tight clothing. With great conviction but little evidence, he contended that in countries where infants have the freedom of loose clothing, "the people are tall, robust, and well proportioned" (1773, vol. 1, p. 16). But where infants are confined in swaddling clothes, the nations "swarm with hunch-backed, crooked-legged, lame, rickety, and deformed persons of every kind" (1773, vol. 1, p. 16).

The purpose of these suggestions about food and clothing was not to indulge infants and maximize their comfort but rather to ensure that they were raised in nature's way. And often, as Rousseau interpreted it, this way was harsh indeed. For example, he suggested putting babies by gradual stages into extreme physical conditions so as to "harden their bodies to the intemperance of the seasons, climates, and elements; to hunger, thirst and fatigue" (1773, vol. 1, pp. 24–25).

The period of infancy ended when the baby was weaned, took her first steps, and mastered some rudimentary speech.

Young Childhood: Age 2 to Age 12   This was the critical period for developing physical strength and agility and for storing up sensations. Throughout this stage, children—like the "noble savages" whom Rousseau admired from accounts he had read of "primitive peoples"—learn through direct experience related to daily needs and interests. They should also be taught to make useful objects, such as toys and simple science mechanisms, with their hands.

Like his contemporaries, Rousseau assumed that the mind consists of faculties or functions that emerge at different times during childhood. He wrote that "of all our faculties, the senses are perfected the first; these therefore are the first we should cultivate; they are, nevertheless, the only ones that are usually forgotten or the most neglected" (1773, vol. 1, p. 217). In order to sharpen the senses and store up sensations, children, he felt, were best reared in the countryside, in a pastoral setting undisturbed by the evil influences of city life and the child's own peers. Emile is not even around other children until he reaches the mid-teens.

Children's mentors during these years should place them in situations that exercise the body and senses. The method of instruction should be what Rousseau labeled *negative teaching*. Rather than teaching what is right (which is *positive teaching*), the wise tutor or parent protects the child from instruction in such improper things as rote or stock answers, clever repartee, or religious doctrine. Negative teaching consists "neither in teaching virtue or truth; but in guarding the heart from vice. . . . Exercise the child's corporal organs, senses, and faculties as much as you please; but keep his intellectual ones inactive as long as possible" (1773, vol. 1, pp. 126–127).

With such treatment, children would arrive at age 12 as honest youth—agile, keen of sight and hearing, animated, but socially naive.

Pubescence or Later Childhood: Age 12 to Age 15   This was the critical period for developing the first phases of reasoning. During these three years, children no longer operate mainly on the sensations they collect, but begin to develop real ideas. Rousseau, like the Puritans, believed that sense impressions are carried to a processing center in the brain called the *common sense*. During pubescence this sense matures. It not only processes impressions from the external senses but its impressions are "partly internal, being called *perceptions* or *ideas*. It is the number of these ideas that limits the extent of our knowledge; it is their perspicuity that determines the clearness of the understanding; and it is the art of comparing them with each other that is called human reason" (1773, vol. 1, pp. 275–276).

In his treatment of the source of ideas, Rousseau adopted a position on an old issue that continues to be of great importance to psychologists and philosophers today. It is the question of whether ideas are built up entirely of people's experiences or are partly determined by human nature. That is, are there genetically determined ideas or, at least, genetically determined cognitive functions? Rousseau would say that indeed there are, and they begin to show themselves during pubescence.

The first stage of reasoning that Rousseau said manifests itself during pubescence is called *sensitive* or *puerile* reason. It consists only of forming "simple ideas from the concurrence of various sensations" (1773, vol. 1, p. 276). Children put together sensations they receive at a given moment and draw some simple conclusions. These ideas are committed to memory.

Later, in adolescence, children advance to the age of *true* human reasoning, which consists of "forming complex ideas from the concurrence of many simple ideas" (1773, vol. 1, p. 276). (In Chapter 10 we will see that there are parallels between Rousseau's observations about reasoning and Piaget's.)

Pubescence was the period for stimulating the faculty of *curiosity*. Prior to this stage the child's motivation—his seeking behavior—was seated in a drive to achieve a sort of hedonistic happiness. This drive stimulated the child's seeking to exerise his body and senses. But during pubescence, the child starts to display significant intellectual curiosity that become his "chief spring of action" (1773, vol. 1, p. 294). Rousseau's recommendations about how to take advantage of curiosity sound much like the suggestions about discovery learning or inquiry teaching today:

> Direct the attention of your pupil to the phenomena of nature, and you will soon awaken his curiosity; but to keep that curiosity alive, you must be in no haste to satisfy it. Put questions to him adapted to his capacity, and leave him to resolve them. Let him take nothing on trust from his (tutor), but on his own comprehension and convictions; he should not learn, but invent the sciences. If ever you substitute authority in the place of argument, he will reason no longer; he will be ever afterwards bandied like a shuttle-cock between the opinions of others (1773, vol. 1, p. 296).

Rousseau would have tutors teach children to read and write, prior to pubescence, only those sorts of communications needed to fulfill the child's daily wants: "Children, when taught to read, learn that only; they never think; they gain no information; all their learning consists in words" (1773, vol. 1, p. 296). However, by the time of pubescence, he felt, children could comprehend ideas and not simply store up impressions. So they could begin reading about places and times distant from their own.

With such a regime, Emile arrived at the close of pubescence knowing only how to reason about the physical world he had been observing for more than a decade. "He knows not even the name of history, nor what is meant by metaphysics and morality. . . . He is ill qualified to generalize his ideas or form abstract nothings of things. . . . Emile is laborious, temperate, patient, resolute, and bold" (1773, vol. 1, p. 389).

Adolescence: Age 15 to Age 25   This was the critical period for becoming socialized and developing true morality. In Rousseau's scheme, the rise of powerful sexual passions in adolescence was accompanied by the flowering of the faculty of *imagination*, which stimulated social and moral (ethical) development, and the formation of the *conscience*. At this time the faculty of the *will* also asserted itself in yearnings for greater independence.

Rousseau believed that youths become socialized and consciously moral when they are able to imagine themselves in the shoes of people who are suffering. So the task of parents and tutors was to introduce the adolescent to such suffering, but not through direct observation of human misery and vice since overexposure to suffering could cause the youth to become callous rather than humane:

> I would show him mankind at a distance, in other times and other places; so that he might be a spectator of the scene without having it in his power to become an actor. This is the proper time to introduce history. . . . There he will behold mankind, not as their accomplice or accuser, but as their impartial judge (1773, vol. 2, 59–60).

The ethical feeling that developed during these years was not, however, solely a product of the adolescent's experiences. Part of it arose in her soul as "an innate principle of justice and goodness; by which . . . we approve or condemn the actions of ourselves and others; to this principle it is that I give the appellation *conscience*" (1773, vol. 2, p. 172). Although conscience, in Rousseau's view, was inborn, it could be dulled or heightened by social experiences.

Finally, there is the most obvious developmental change of adolescence, the maturation of sexual functions, or as Rousseau called them, the *passions*. He believed that children, prior to adolescence, should be protected from situations that might stimulate sexual ideas. But once puberty arrived, the youth's questions should be answered truthfully, without fables or evasion. Later, during the closing years of adolescence, it was the tutor's or parent's responsibility to help the youth select a mate.

Thus by the time properly raised youth reached their mid-twenties, they commanded all the physical, intellectual, social, and moral virtues anyone could desire and were ready for marriage. At this time the development of the child was complete.

THE IMPORTANCE OF INSTRUCTION

Although both the Puritans and Rousseau believed that children should receive instruction from their earliest years, they disagreed with each other on what sort of instruction this should be.

Puritan Teaching

Since, in the Puritan view, children's fates depended so heavily on their being taught to combat their innate wickedness, it was important that those who cared about them should get about the business of providing suitable instruction as soon as possible. Puritans believed that both evil and ignorance could be overcome through education. To combat Satan's influence, parents were urged to begin instructing infants as soon as they were able to understand anything. But, assuming that young children had but limited capacities for learning, Puritan leaders suggested that instruction should, like putting a liquid into a narrow-mouthed container, be poured into them "but by drops" (Morgan, 1956, p. 53). In the early years, this instruction was to be casual and informal, with the parent "often speaking to them of good things, now a little and then a little, line upon line, precept upon precept, little and often, as they are able to receive" (Cotton Mather in Morgan, 1956, pp. 53–54).

The sort of learning that would lead to salvation was the mastery of truths about God's plan as revealed in the Bible. In their earliest years children were expected to memorize these truths as told to them by their parents or siblings. But as their capacities increased, they were to learn to read the Bible by themselves so that, in keeping with Protestant doctrine, they might be their own priest and communicate directly with the Lord and the Lord's written word. In 1647 this conviction that every child should learn to read was used to support a law compelling every sizable community to establish a school so as to foil the scheme of "that old deluder, Satan, to keep men from the knowledge of the scriptures" (Vaughn, 1972, p. 237).

To enable children to combat their natural evil inclinations, it was necessary for parents and teachers to generate in them a strong motivation to pursue disciplined, constructive lives. Important tools for generating such motivation were threats of dire consequences, moderated somewhat by expressions of love. Puritan children were not so much enticed into good behavior by promises of rewards, now or in the hereafter, as they were frightened out of bad behavior by prospects of the fires of hell. In the *Primer* and in such sermons as Jonathan Edwards's "Sinners in the Hands of an Angry God," children and youth met far more threats of death and misery than promises of happiness and heaven. In the list of phrases intended to drill children on the letters of the alphabet, the *Primer* included these illustrations of the use of *L* and *U* (1836, pp. 15–16).

L = *L*iars will have their part in the lake which burns with fire and brimstone.
U = *U*pon the wicked, God will rain a horrible tempest.

Martin Luther had written that "children should be educated not only to fear their parents, but to feel that God will be angry with them if they do *not* fear their parents" (Eby, 1971, pp. 25–27).

Always in conflict with the picture of the innately wicked child who deserved harsh treatment was the Puritan parents' feelings of love and affection for their children. Parents' fear of letting their hearts overrule their reason was apparently a prime motivator of the common practice in New England of sending children out at age 8 or 12 or 14 to be raised in someone else's home, "even when there was no apparent educational or economic advantage involved.... I suggest that Puritan parents did not trust themselves with their own children, that they were afraid of spoiling them with too great affection" (Peter Laslett in Rutman, 1970, p. 44).

When direct instruction, admonition, and threats of dire consequences failed to keep a child on the path of righteousness, Puritans turned to corporal punishment. Luther, in an essay deploring the general use of harsh teaching methods in schools, admitted, "Nevertheless, the child needs the discipline of the rod; but it must be tempered with admonition, and directed to his improvement; for without this, he will never come to any good, but will be ruined, soul and body" (Eby, 1971, p. 32).

These sentiments, first voiced in Europe, were later echoed in the American colonies by such Calvinists as Cotton Mather, who entitled one of his sermons "Better Whipt, than Damn'd" (Morgan, 1956, p. 58). Although the rod appeared often in both homes and schoolrooms, it was generally applied as a last resort. Morgan, in his modern monograph on the Puritan family, concluded that the ministers who wrote and spoke on the subject of instruction "almost always counselled their readers and listeners to win children to holiness by kindness rather than to force them to it by severity" (Morgan, 1956, p. 58).

In sum, the purpose of instruction was to direct children away from their evil inclinations and toward God's way. Instruction consisted of giving information and advice, of relating fables and verses containing moral lessons, and of teaching children to read so they might derive truth directly from the Bible. Motivation to pursue this learning was encouraged by threats of an eternity in hell, by promises that the best chance for salvation came from leading a Christian life, and ultimately by a sound whipping with a birch rod.

Rousseau's Teaching

As described earlier, Rousseau's theory of instruction was founded on convictions about child development that led to three main principles:

1. The realms of learning should be introduced in the proper sequence, with physical development first, mental development second, and social development third. Since the child's nature is suited to this order, deviating from the order will lead to unfortunate results.

2. The years of early and middle childhood should feature *negative teaching,* which consists of placing a child in a controlled environment, that is, an environment arranged to stimulate the child's curiosity in a given direction while protecting the child from influences that could distort development at this point in life.

3. Direct instruction about the world beyond the child's direct daily experience should be postponed until late childhood and adolescence, that is, until the child already has developed a strong and agile body, quick senses, a curious mind, a firm grasp of principles underlying the natural phenomena met in daily life, and a resulting sense of self-confidence from having successfully mastered the tasks of development up to this point.

INDIVIDUAL DIFFERENCES

In Puritan and Rousseau's theory alike, differences among individual children who are the same age result from both innate and environmental factors, with the environmental influences the more important.

The Puritan View

In Puritan doctrine all children are born alike in their inclination to evil. However, children innately differ from each other in their bent for a vocation or for a mission or *calling* in life. Girls' inner voices generally call them to different missions than do boys', so inborn sex differences in personality are also assumed in Puritan theory.

However, innate factors are not as important in accounting for differences as are two other factors—environmental forces and supernatural intervention. The main agents of environmental influence are parents, religious leaders, the Bible, teachers, relatives, and peers. As for supernatural intervention, two competing sources of supernatural influence work to control the directon of the child's development: the Trinity (consisting of God, Christ, and the Holy Spirit), which can intervene at any time, either to remove impediments in the child's path toward righteous living or to correct some deviant characteristic of the child, and Satan, who may mar children physically or mentally and may lure them into sin by casting worldly temptations and evil companions in the paths of their daily lives.

A further force affecting development is that of *human will,* meaning the individual's own determination or power of decision. In Puritan belief, will is a product of both heredity and environment. Some people may be born with a stronger will than others, that is, with greater ability than others to carry out a plan of action against opposing forces. But perhaps even more important for strengthening a child's will are such environmental influences as sermons, catechisms, prayers, Bible reading, parental advice, and punishment.

Rousseau's View

In his theorizing, Rousseau implied that nature's clock runs at the same pace for everyone. Each boy and girl reaches early childhood at age 2, enters pubescence at age 12, and adolescence at age 15. However, the condition of the child at each of these stages will be influenced by the sorts of experiences she or he has. Consequently there will be marked differences among children in physical strength and agility, in the acuity of their senses, in the contents of their memories, and in their moral and social traits.

However, it is not only the environment that accounts for variations among children of the same age. Rousseau proposed as well that children can be originally endowed with different capabilities. He suggested that tutors and parents give the young child many chances to investigate science, art, and music so that "by exciting his curiosity and training its tendency, we may be enabled to study his taste, inclinations and propensities" (1773, vol. 1, p. 367). Nevertheless, the most powerful cause of individual differences, he felt, was the quality of the growing child's environment.

Had Rousseau lived in the late twentieth century, he would have been a prime target of women's rights advocates, for he considered women intellectually inferior to men and properly subservient to them:

> Woman is framed particularly for the delight and pleasure of man. . . . His merit consists in his power; he pleases her only because he is possessed of strength. This is not the law of love, I grant you; but it is that of nature, antecedent to love itself (1773, vol. 3, p. 7).

The stages outlined for the growth of boys are the same for girls, however. In fact, "Till the age of puberty, there is little apparent difference between the sexes in children" (1773, vol. 3, p. 25). But there should be a different emphasis in the upbringing of the two. For young boys, stress should be placed on gaining strength, but for girls the stress should be on charm. After puberty, girls should not be expected to master the same intellectual material as boys. The young woman's concerns are not "abstract and speculative truths, principles and axioms of sciences. Their studies ought to be all practical; it is their business to apply the principles discovered by man. . . . Woman, honor thy chief; it is he that labors for thee, he that earns thy bread, he that nourishes thee; this is man!" (1773, vol. 3, pp. 71–72, 191).

PRACTICAL APPLICATIONS

When the theories of Rousseau and of the Puritans are appraised for their specificity in furnishing guidance to people engaged in rearing children, both theories deserve rather high marks. Each of them distinguishes clearly between desirable and undesirable goals of development so that parents can judge whether a child is growing up properly. Furthermore, for each major stage in the child's development, both theories propose child-raising practices deemed suitable at that stage, with Rousseau's definition of stages and his proposals for child treatment being a good deal more detailed than the Puritans'. In particular, Rousseau included lifelike examples of what to do and what not to do in raising children, thereby providing models for parents to follow.

In addition to the two theories' proposals for general child rearing, they also offer suggestions for the conduct of schooling. The contents of the *New England Primer* show the way moral education from a Puritan viewpoint can be incorporated into learning materials. The *Primer's* contents also reflect instructional methods recommended by Puritans, as illustrated in the verse used for teaching children the letter *F*—"The idle *Fool* is whipt at school" (1836, p. 13). As for Rousseau, his formula for teaching school-age children includes recommendations about what subject matter should be in the curriculum at different age levels and what teaching methods are appropriate at successive stages of development. *Emile* also gives examples of how to apply Rousseau's notions of critical periods for learning, of discovery learning, and of ways to manipulate the instructional environment in order to interest the child in pursuing suitable learning activities.

In summary, while both theories are practical in the sense of providing child-rearing suggestions that are easily understood and can be implemented in daily life, there is a serious question about whether certain of the suggestions will foster desirable child development or, on the contrary, will result in unfortunate developmental outcomes. Examples of questionable practices are the Puritans' burdening the child with guilt through harsh threats and punishment and Rousseau's isolating the child from peers until adolescence as a means of promoting social development.

RESEARCH CHALLENGES

For at least three reasons, researchers have rarely if ever turned in modern times to the theories of the Puritans or Rousseau for questions to investigate.

First, some of the issues raised by these two theories are no longer identified with the Puritans or Rousseau but appear today under different names or within other theories. For instance, Rousseau's notion of waiting until a child has entered a particular growth stage before we try to teach her or him certain things is found today under such titles as *maturation* in Piaget's theory (Chapter 10) and as the *teachable moment* in Havighurst's (Chapter 6).

Second, scientific research techniques available today are not well suited for investigating some aspects of these models. Two cases in point are the Puritan contention that the child is innately evil and Rousseau's proposal that the child is innately good. Likewise, researchers lack proper methods for investigating such Puritan beliefs as life after death, a Satanic force that influences development, and the effect of prayer on child growth.

Third, the field of human development, like many other disciplines, is marked by waves of interest in different theories at different times. Methodological behaviorism was popular in the United States in the 1920s and 1930s; then Skinner's radical behaviorism in the 1940s and 1950s essentially replaced early behaviorism. In the latter 1960s and throughout the 1970s social learning theory overshadowed the behavioristic approach, and subsequently information-processing theory has grown rapidly in popularity. Furthermore, the enthusiasm for Freudian psychoanalysis in the 1930s and 1940s diminished greatly over the following decades. Such trends in interest may vary not only from time to time but also from place to place. Piaget's work was widely known and respected in Europe from the latter 1920s and into the 1950s but did not become popular in North America until the 1960s. These waves of interest are activated by various agents in the child development community—by professors in universities who direct their students' attention toward the professors' favorite models, by editors of journals and books who prefer one theoretical approach over another, and by research-funding agencies that give preference to particular theories. Puritan theory—or indeed, any theory deriving from a religious base—and Rousseau's beliefs have not been popular among such people in recent times.

THE PURITAN VIEW: AN ASSESSMENT

Although the Puritan period has passed, there are still vestiges of the Puritans' conception of child development in European and American societies, Catholic as well as Protestant. Some Christian denominations continue to subscribe to many of their tenets. Far more people accept only certain of the beliefs, such as that the child tends to be innately bad, that idleness in later childhood is dangerous, and that children are incapable of rational thought and behavior until after puberty. People still try to "scare the devil out" of children and attribute a youth's irresponsible behavior to his "losing his faculties."

Nevertheless, the Puritan view has greatly decreased in popularity over the past centuries. This decrease is the result of several forces. One is the advancement of science, which has produced new theories of human nature and new standards for the kind of evidence needed to establish a proposal as "truth." Darwin's theory of evolution struck a blow at the concept of the rational soul by proposing that humans were not so distinctly different from animals as church doctrine had supposed. Freud struck a further blow at the concept of the importance of reasoning powers in the governance of behavior by postulating that much of our behavior is motivated by unconscious forces. The growth of experimental psychology, with its rules of evidence adopted from the field of physics, has stimulated more and more people to doubt the validity of a model of child nature based on such sources of data as divine revelation and on "blind faith" in the word of theologians of a given sect.

The Puritans' view of the child, in addition to suffering attacks from the scientific community, also lost adherents during the eighteenth and nineteenth centuries to the rising humanist movement. The humanists or humanitarians objected to what they considered the harsh treatment of children, treatment defended on the grounds of Protestant doctrine.

People who wish to defend Puritan theory and practice can marshal arguments on their side also. Some students of colonial times suggest that in most Puritan homes kindness prevailed, and fear was used as a child control device only to protect children from harm, either in this world or in the one beyond (Martin Luther in Eby, 1971, pp. 33, 153; Morgan, 1956, p. 58). Furthermore, defenders of the Puritan position can point to the increasing rates of delinquency and a supposed lack of socially acceptable goals among today's adolescent population, and can ask whether these modern social problems are perhaps a result of the abandonment of Puritan views of child raising. Also, when the faculty conception of mental operations is criticized as naive or unscientific, defenders may ask whether modern theorists have not simply renamed the faculties without offering any better evidence of their nature—renaming them with such terms as *id* and *ego* (as did Freud) or *intervening variables* (as have certain behaviorists). Thus arguments about the Puritan position are not yet settled to everyone's satisfaction.

To complete this brief assessment of Puritan theory, recall the nine appraisal standards from Chapter One and use them to judge the worth of Puritan views. As we make this appraisal, you should recognize immediately that it is not simply a matter of applying the criteria and arriving at an objective judgment with which everyone will agree. Rather, this sort of assessment involves a large amount of personal opinion. It is not a revelation of universal truth but simply an estimate on the part of the one doing the judging. In this case it is my own estimate, reflecting the kind of evidence I think bears on each standard and the kind of values I use to weight each piece of evidence. Consequently the following appraisal is for your consideration, not necessarily for your acceptance. Which of the conclusions you accept, which you wish to revise, and which you choose to reject completely depends on your own values, on the evidence you think bears on the issues, and on the weights you apply to the evidence.

The standards are displayed in the form of nine rating scales. Such a system is easily read but oversimplified. To solve the problem of oversimplification would require several pages of detail on the line of reasoning and the evidence that led to the conclusions. But since space limitations do not permit a detailed clarification for every theory in this book, the explanation for each rating is limited to a few comments. You may find it useful to prepare a rating sheet of your own and list the reasons you would cite to support your judgments.

On each of the accompanying scales, the X indicates where, in my opinion, Puritan theory should be rated for each particular standard.

Puritan theory is rated highest on item 4 because the theory does indeed give clear advice to parents on how to raise children. However, if this standard read "Gives proper guidance for child rearing," I would have rated it low, because I disagree with the basic tenet that children are naturally evil. This brings us to the relatively low rating on item 1. I think the evidence supporting the concept of children's innate sinful strivings is not convincing. It consists of a few biblical passages and "divine revelations" reported by clerics of past centuries. However, I believe that some of the assumptions about children found in the Puritans' ideas of stages of development are accurate, so I marked item 1 overall as slightly below "moderately well."

The moderate ratings for items 2 and 5 are based on my impression that, while the main lines of Puritan theory are clear and consistent, there remain significant areas of confusion elsewhere. Such confusion seems

Puritan Theory

How well do I think the theory meets the standards?

The Standards	Very Well	Moderately Well	Very Poorly
1. Reflects the real world of children		X	
2. Is clearly understandable		X	
3. Explains the past and predicts the future	X		X
4. Guides child rearing	X		
5. Is internally consistent		X	
6. Is economical		X	
7. Is falsifiable			X
8. Stimulates new discoveries			X
9. Is self-satisfying		X	

inevitable when a model of child nature and development is founded on so many assumptions whose validity cannot be checked empirically but must be accepted on the word of an authority or on doctrine divinely revealed to a select few. An example of such an area of confusion is the issue of whether God, in choosing which people will go to heaven, will really include such considerations of whether or not a child has lived a good Christian life on earth. Another is the issue of what happens to the infant who dies before having had a chance to live much of a life at all, good or bad. Such clouded issues and inconsistencies in Puritan doctrine did, however, furnish ministers with a seemingly endless source of topics for their sermons.

Items 7 and 8 have very low markings because so much of Puritan theory is founded on "revealed truths" whose validity cannot be tested. The theory is essentially nonfalsifiable and does not stimulate the generation of testable hypotheses that might result in new discoveries. Furthermore, the theory is not very economical—it offers some rather complex explanations (for example, its structure of the soul)—to account for phenomena that might be explained with fewer untested assumptions. Of course, it can be argued from another viewpont that the theory is quite simple in that when we ask why certain types of child growth take place, a Puritan cleric could respond, "It's God's will" or "It is the Lord's plan."

Item 3 gets both a high and a low mark. The high mark indicates that if you accept Puritan assumptions about innate sin and life after death, then the theory does explain accurately what has happened in the child's past (she has inherited Adam and Eve's sin) and does predict fairly well what will occur in the future (she will go either to heaven or to hell, depending on whether she receives God's grace). But if you do not accept these assumptions, then you mark item 3 at the low point, for the theory does not explain the past development of a child or predict her future development, except along the rather general growth lines suggested by the development stages.

This brings us to item 9. Because of the reservations I have expressed about Puritan theory, plus my intuitive sense of children's basic natures, I do not find the Puritan view self-satisfying. Other people who seriously study children's growth would probably rank Puritan theory equally low, as suggested by the fact that Puritan doctrine is no longer in the mainstream of theories of child development. Nevertheless, certain elements of the Puritan view are still very much alive, particularly in the commonsense psychology we will meet in Chapter Four. Understanding Puritan beliefs helps explain some of the roots of current theories and some of the beliefs against which other theorists have reacted.

ROUSSEAU'S VIEW: AN ASSESSMENT

In appraising the strengths and weaknesses of Rousseau's theory of child development, I will use the same method used in assessing the Puritan viewpoint. Rousseau's theory is first rated according to my estimates on each evaluation standard; then some explanation for the ratings is given. Again, you may wish to prepare your own rating sheet and appraise Rousseau's view of children according to your own criteria.

Rousseau's theory is rated highest on item 8 because he exerted such a strong influence on nineteenth- and twentieth-century educational practice. Four distinguished educational innovators who owed much to Rousseau's *Emile* were Johann Heinrich Pestalozzi (1746–1827), Friedrich Froebel (1782–1852), Johann Friedrich Herbart (1776–1841), and Maria Montessori (1870–1952). Pestalozzi, a Swiss, refined Rousseau's basic teaching methods and made them work in a practical manner in the classroom (Heafford, 1967). Froebel, a German, launched the kindergarten movement. He used Rousseau's predeterminist concepts as the foundation for learning activities for young children, and his influence is still apparent in kindergartens today, particularly in Europe (Froebel, 1889; Kilpatrick, 1916). Herbart, a German interested in the education of older children, analyzed the ways ideas of the mind are built up, and then translated his analysis into classroom teaching methods. Montessori, an Italian physician, based her system of teaching the mentally retarded partly on Rousseau's principles, then extended her scheme to include an instructional program for normal children as well.

Rousseau's Theory

How well do I think the theory meets the standards?

The Standards	Very Well	Moderately Well	Very Poorly
1. Refects the real world of children		X	
2. Is clearly understandable	X		
3. Explains the past and predicts the future	Specifically X	Accurately X	
4. Guides child rearing	Specifically X	Accurately X	
5. Is internally consistent		X	
6. Is economical		X	
7. Is falsifiable	X		
8. Stimulates new discoveries	X		
9. Is self-satisfying		X	

Various writers on the history of education have credited Rousseau with being the father of other movements as well—of manual training, of modern pedagogy, and of the discovery method in science (Boyd, 1963, pp. 296–350; Davidson, 1898, pp. 211–244). In short, when Rousseau's work is judged by its effect on subsequent educators, he comes off with high marks.

As a guide to child rearing, Rousseau's theory gets two different marks, one for the number and specificity of his suggestions and the other for the likely accuracy of the suggestions. I gave a high rating for the fact that he offers many specific illustrations in *Emile* of ways his principles of child raising could be implemented. However, since I believe the content of some of his suggestions is highly questionable, I gave him only a moderate rating on the accuracy of his recommendations. In particular, I think he is wrong about how children are most effectively socialized, that is, how they develop the skills of getting along with their peers. Rousseau isolated Emile from other children until the boy was an adolescent, then proposed that, as a teenager, he would immediately display all of the admirable skills in human relations that would make him recognized by his peers as their natural leader. It is unlikely, however, that any serious observer of developing children would accept such a proposition. Most early childhood education today is based on quite an opposite belief. An important role assigned to nursery schools and kindergartens is that of offering children guided opportunities for learning the skills of getting along with their peers. This proposition that children profit from social practice seems more convincing than Rousseau's belief in the value of isolation from peers in childhood as a means of socializing the child.

The two ratings on item 3 are given for similar reasons. Rousseau's predictions of a child's future as a result of different child-raising practices are relatively specific. Likewise, Rousseau also claimed he could view a child's present behavior and appearance and offer confident estimates about the treatment the child received in the past. Thus, on specificity I rated his theory rather highly. But the accuracy of his explanations and predictions can be questioned in some instances. The most obvious is that of socialization. Another is his prediction about the effect of tight infant clothing on ultimate physical stature and fitness. With such reservations, I judged his accuracy to be moderate.

I rated Rousseau's description of his scheme (item 2), the theory's internal consistency (item 5), and the economy of its explanations (item 6) rather highly. Of these three, the economy rating (item 6) may be the most controversial. Rousseau does not propose an elaborate explanatory mechanism when a simpler one might suffice. His framework of development, for example, is not unduly complex: He explains the sequence of critical development periods simply as "nature's way," and he explains that distortions of development are the result of parents' misunderstanding the treatment each stage requires for natural development. On the other hand, if we wish to ask why the critical periods arise in such a sequence or why discovery learning is superior to indoctrination, then we find that Rousseau does not offer much of an answer. His scheme is too simple to answer such *why* questions. Thus his theory is economical for answering questions about how certain child-raising practices are suited to each of his proposed growth stages, but not why the stages appear in such an order.

In regard to item 1, Rousseau's picture of childhood in *Emile* and other writings represents the real world of children only moderately well. I believe he was correct in reacting against the view that children are born naturally sinful, but I question his proposal that they are born naturally moral and will do right if left to their own inclinations. In his practical suggestions, he moderated this position somewhat by suggesting that the freedom allowed children not be boundless but have defined limits, and this moderated position appears to me to make sense. I agree with Rousseau's suggestion that it is desirable to give children many opportunities to exercise their bodies, to practice using their senses, and to draw conclusions from their observations of nature. But I question how realistic he is in concluding that exposing infants to inclement weather and pain promotes their optimum development by inuring them to hardships in the early months of life. Furthermore, present-day observations of girls' behavior and tests of their abilities cast serious doubts on Rousseau's contention that girls are inferior to boys intellectually. Rousseau's sketch of childhood, therefore, seems only partially realistic.

Item 7 focuses on the issue of whether the theory is falsifiable. Is it possible to perform experiments or observations that test the validity of Rousseau's scheme? To a considerable extent, I believe it is. If we were to conduct careful observations of children, following their development under different environmental conditions over a period of years, we could test Rousseau's contentions about (1) the effect of tight clothing, (2) the influence of interactions with peers throughout childhood on the ultimate social skills adolescents display, and (3) the effectiveness of negative teaching compared to direct instruction for achieving learning goals. Also, since modern-day scientists have devised ways to investigate the concept of critical periods in development, the critical-period aspect of Rousseau's system can be tested as well (Schneirla & Rosenblatt, 1963; Scott, 1963). Although Rousseau's basic tenet that children are born naturally moral is perhaps the most difficult of his ideas to test, it is conceivable that this belief is falsifiable as well. For example, comparisons could be made of young children's moral judgments both within a given culture and across cultures that hold different moral value standards.

Finally, there is item 9, whether Rousseau's system overall is self-satisfying or not. To me his theory is at least moderately self-satisfying, particularly as seen in its cultural environment. Despite the aspects I have criticized as shortcomings, Rousseau did have some convincing insights not widely held in his day. These contributions include (1) his insistence that children are not simply undersized adults but are different in quality of mind and in needs, (2) his emphasis on the importance of firsthand experience as the most basic foundation of learning in childhood, (3) his desire to allow children the freedom to exercise their bodies and explore their environment, (4) his suggestion that children profit from constructing useful objects with their hands, and (5) his technique of questioning and of arranging experiences that lead children to draw their own conclusions about what they observe.

For students of child development, some knowledge of Rousseau's ideas is useful since his work is an important source of the ideas currently found in several modern theories, particularly theories on teaching young children.

FOR FURTHER READING

Boyd, William. (1963) *The Educational Theory of Jean Jacques Rousseau.* New York: Russell & Russell. A description and critique of Rousseau's viewpoint.

Boyd, William (ed. and trans.). (1962) *The Minor Educational Writings of Jean Jacques Rousseau.* New York: Columbia University Press. A collection of segments on education other than from *Emile.*

Greven, Philip. (1977) *The Protestant Temperament: Patterns of Child Rearing, Religious Experience, and the Self in Early America.* New York: Knopf.

Miller, Perry. (1963) *The New England Mind: The Seventeenth Century.* Cambridge, Mass.: Harvard University Press.

Morgan, Edmund S. (1956) *The Puritan Family.* Boston: Trustees of the Public Library.

New England Primer, The. (Any edition.) This beginning reader for children of colonial times reflects Puritan views of child nature, the goals of desirable development, and ways of directing children's behavior.

Rousseau, Jean Jacques. *Emile; or, A Treatise of Education.* The novel is available in its original French version and in several English translations.

CHAPTER FOUR

Commonsense Attribution Theory

We could adopt any of several ways to construct a commonsense theory of development. We might conduct a poll, asking a sample of people to answer questions about children. We might collect folklore, proverbs, and traditional sorts of advice about child raising, and then search for the pattern of concepts that underlies them. We might observe adults as they interact with children or as they talk about children and then estimate what theory of child nature is implied in such action and talk. We might analyze laws relating to children, on the assumption that laws reflect a common set of beliefs for a society. Or we could use all of these approaches. However, due to space limitations, in this chapter we will use only two: an analysis of typical daily talk and an inspection of a few key laws that relate to children.

For the analysis of talk, we will use as a guide the work of Fritz Heider (born 1896), a German who moved to the faculty of the University of Kansas, where he dedicated himself to tracing the framework of naive psychology, which undergirds the way most of us conduct our lives. The principles Heider derived were described in his book, *The Psychology of Interpersonal Relations* (1958). However, since his description focuses primarily on the adult, the mature personality, and not on the child, it is necessary to extend his treatment to show how commonsense psychology views a child's developmental changes from one age level to the next. In making this modest extension, we will depend not only on people's everyday language but also on civil and criminal laws commonly found in modern American communities.

It is important to realize that this chapter is designed only to suggest some of the main lines of naive theory and to illustrate the way a theorist such as Heider identifies such lines. The material included falls far short of describing the complexity of Heider's analysis.

The present-day derivative of Heider's naive psychology is called *attribution theory*, meaning a theory that seeks to explain how and why people attribute human behavior to particular causes. Using the term *attribution* to distinguish this theory from others may seem a bit odd since essentially all theories of human development or of personality *attribute* human thought and action to those factors the theorists regard as the most potent causes. Freudians attribute much of development to the ways the child's inner drives interact with such agents of the environment as parents. Behaviorists attribute development to the way the consequences of the child's present actions will influence actions when she or he faces similar situations in the future. However, even though all theorists attribute, it is the particular line of theorizing set off by Heider that is typically referred to as attribution theory, so I am using the term *commonsense attribution theory* to identify the model of development built on Heider's proposals.

THE CAUSES OF HUMAN ACTION

A key question that commonsense psychology seeks to answer is: Why do people act as they do? When this question is translated into child development terms it becomes: How and why does the pattern of a child's behavior change as he or she grows up?

In answer to the first question, Heider's analysis of daily language tells us that three factors determine whether or not a person carries out a given act. Two of these factors are inside the person: *personal power* (Can he do it?) and *effort* or motivation (Will he try to do it?). The third factor, which can be called *task difficulty*, is outside the person and is composed of all the forces in the environment that influence the accomplishment of the act.

From this perspective of personal power, effort, and task difficulty, we can define the study of child development as an investigation of the changes that occur in a child's power and efforts between the time of birth and the end of adolescence, that is, the changes as they relate to the different environments with which the child interacts over these years. We will analyze the three factors to illustrate how they can be used to explain human behavior at different age levels.

To suggest the flavor of the raw materials from which such a view of child psychology is constructed, I have prefaced the analysis with a fictitious conversation, a typical chat about children that might be overheard in many American neighborhoods. Phrases from this conversation will be used later to illustrate the assumptions or convictions about child behavior that under-lie people's daily interactions according to commonsense theory.

Talk About Children—Grist for the Commonsense Psychologist's Mill

Mr. Young and Mrs. Campbell meet at the market.

Mr. Young: What do you think of the kids' third-grade teacher? I think she's expecting too much of them. My son Freddie says hardly anyone in the class can do the math. Have you seen the problems she gives?

Mrs. Campbell: Yes, Doris brings work home every day. But luckily she seems to get it done all right without my help.

Mr. Young: She must be pretty smart.

Mrs. Campbell: It's not just that. She works hard at it, too. I guess having to compete with her twelve-year-old brother has caused her to try hard. He's good in physical activities but kind of average in school work, so she seems to want to show that she's good with her brain. She tries to get her recognition that way.

Mr. Young: Oh, yes, your son. I saw in the paper that he's on the football team.

Mrs. Campbell: Well, he's crazy about sports. But getting on the team isn't much of a distinction. Nearly every boy who showed up was put in uniform.

Mr. Young: But isn't he some kind of a star?

Mrs. Campbell: Well, for the first couple of weeks he was the starting quarterback. He's quick and he throws the ball well. But then he had a streak of bad luck. He hurt his ankle, and that put him out for over a week. And since then the coach hasn't given him a fair chance to show what he can do. The poor kid's spending every game on the bench.

Mr. Young: That's too bad. Say, I see you didn't bring your baby with you.

Mrs. Campbell: No, I left Doris with him at home.

Mr. Young: Really? Aren't you afraid to leave a nine-year-old in charge of such a small baby?

Mrs. Campbell: Oh, no. Doris is very good at it, and she likes it.

Mr. Young: Well, that's brave. I don't think I'd let my daughter Charlene try that, even at fourteen. It's not that Charlene can't do it. It's just that she's always thinking of something else—mostly boys and loud music. Well, I'd better pay for my groceries and get going. I left Charlene out in the car. She's fiddling with all the gadgets, pretending she's driving. She just can't wait till she's sixteen to get a driver's license.

With this conversation in mind, let's turn to the three main components of action. First we consider personal power, then effort or motivation, and finally environmental forces.

"Can Do"—The Factor of Personal Power

In daily conversation, the commonsense notion of personal power is reflected in the use of the terms *can* and *cannot* ("Hardly anyone in the class can do the math," "It's not that Charlene can't do it"). Personal power has several components. The most important of these is *ability*. Others that exert a minor influence are *attitudes, social status,* and such *temporary personal conditions* as fatigue.

During a typical day, a typical teenager uses many specific skills or abilities in performing tasks. However, in commonsense psychology, these abilities are not all discrete and unconnected. Instead, they seem to fall into two categories: physical and mental. And it is not uncommon for people to believe that a youth can have one level of ability in the physical realm and another in the mental. For example, it appears to surprise no one that a twelve-year-old boy might be a fine football player but not much of a scholar, or that his nine-year-old sister might be the opposite. But it seems less common for people to see that within either category a youth's subabilities may vary. In short, people seem to think that mental ability is all-encompassing, a unitary skill or aptitude that covers all intellectual task performance. So Mr. Young, on hearing of Doris's skill in mathematics, concludes that Doris must be smart in general. Mrs. Campbell, too, reflects this idea of an all-encompassing intelligence by saying that Doris is "good with her brain." This belief that abilities are divided into physical and mental realms that are each unitary rather than composed of discrete subskills has important implications for the way children are treated in school and at home. And although widely accepted, the belief is somewhat at odds with empirical evidence (Thomas & Thomas, 1965, pp. 4–10, 386–388, 425–428).

As people try to understand and predict their own and others' behavior, they are interested in knowing whether a person's ability is high, medium, or low. It is therefore useful for us to examine three kinds of information on which this judgment is based.

The first clue to ability level is the proportion of other people who can perform the task or tasks we have in mind. Specifically, if only a few people can perform the task, then any individual who does so is credited with having high ability. The main cause of success is thought to reside in the individual's personal power, and consequently that individual is accorded respect. But if nearly everyone can perform the task, then we conclude that it was easy, and those people who perform it successfully are not credited with much ability. In fact, the cause of success is not attributed to the person at all but to the environment. We believe the individual succeeded because environmental factors were in his or her favor.

A second important factor in judging ability is a knowledge of the people who have already performed the task. This matter is far more significant for assessing ability in childhood and adolescence than in the adult years because children's physical and mental skills increase noticeably with age, while adult skills are thought to be stable until the declining years. So in naive psychology we seek to learn the ages of the people with whom a given child is being compared. It is considered fairest to compare the child with age peers — often age-mates of the same sex. However, it is frequently useful to compare the child with older or younger children as well. A young child who performs as well as an average child several years older is credited with high ability and is labeled gifted, bright, or even genius. An older child who performs no better than an average child several years younger is said to be retarded, deficient, or handicapped.

A third sort of information that tells us about ability level is the amount of effort exerted to perform a task. The child who succeeds with ease is credited with greater ability than the one who has to struggle and strain to accomplish the same job.

As for whether or not people feel a person can perform a task at all, we noted earlier the tendency people often have to feel that a child who is apt at one physical (or mental) task will also be apt at other physical (or mental) activities. This belief in a high correlation among subabilities within a broad category enables people to predict whether a person can or cannot perform a task not actually tried before. Such was the case when Mr. Young stated that fourteen-year-old Charlene could care for a baby even though the girl has never done so. Mr. Young's opinion was apparently based on his knowledge that Charlene had succeeded in other physical and mental tasks as well as her age-mates who did care for babies. So Charlene could do the things necessary for child care. The girl's problem, in her father's eyes, lay not in a lack of ability ("It's not that Charlene can't do it") but in a lack of motivation ("She's always thinking of something else").

Although abilities are the most important constituents of personal power, several other elements affect power in lesser degrees. Three of these are attitudes, social status, and temporary personal conditions.

Attitudes, in the sense intended here, reflect the individual's estimate of how able she is to do tasks. If she feels generally incapable, she is said to be pessimistic, feel inferior, have a poor self-concept, lack confidence, have low self-esteem, or be shy. If she feels she can succeed, she is described as optimistic, confident, having a good self-concept, and displaying a positive approach. So a person's power is not only based on true ability, but is influenced by attitudes that determine how well ability and effort can be marshaled.

Social status affects personal power when it influences the attitude the individual has toward accomplishing a task. If she has the status of team leader, she can give directions to team members with the conviction that her directions will be followed. A boy who, along with his classmates, recognizes that he is from a lower social-class background may fare poorly at the class party because he lacks the confidence to try his social skills around others whose manners, clothes and speech differ from his own.

Temporary conditions, such as fatigue and illness, influence how a person performs on a given occasion, but these conditions do not decrease the true ability attributed to that individual.

To close this brief look at commonsense notions of personal power, we note three of the most significant assumptions underlying naive psychology's view of child development:

1. Abilities are considered rather permanent attributes of an individual. They do not change over the short term.

2. Abilities increase, sometimes regularly and sometimes in spurts, over the period of childhood and adolescence. To a great extent, the study of child development is the study of the manner in which abilities increase. A child described as a "problem learner" in school is usually one whose abilities are not increasing at the rate considered desirable.

3. Abilities are determined by both heredity ("His good memory is from his mother's side of the family") and environment ("It took a lot of practice for her to pronounce French properly"). However, the proportion that each of these two sources contributes to various abilities and the manner in which the two interact are not clear.

"Try to"—The Factor of Effort

Not only must children have the personal power or ability to perform, they must also want to do it. So "can" and "try" are both necessary for action. Neither is sufficient alone. Doris, for example, was not only smart, she also worked hard.

The factor of trying, which psychologists usually call *motivation*, has two aspects: *direction* and *amount*. Direction refers to what the person is trying to do. It is often called her *intention*. Amount refers to how hard she tries and is called *exertion* or *intensity of effort*. Mr. Young's remarks about Charlene suggested that the girl would probably not look after a baby's needs seriously. On the other hand, it seems clear that Charlene intends to drive a car when she is permitted to do so, for she spends time in a car pretending to drive.

We noted earlier that in naive psychology abilities are expected to increase regularly with age. Effort is also expected to change in predictable ways as the child grows older. For one thing, the child's attention span, the time dedicated to a given task, is expected to lengthen with age. As a youth matures, his or her interests are supposed to settle down and not jump from one thing to another all the time. Also, the child is expected to expend greater effort as he grows up, to give his best and not be a quitter.

Compared to the other two factors of action, personal power and task difficulty, trying is considered to be more under the conscious control of the individual. Consequently, when an individual fails because of an apparent lack of trying, she is more liable to be blamed than if her failure were based on either a lack of ability or a task that was too difficult. Commonsense psychology thus holds the child personally responsible for laziness, for quitting a job before it is completed, or for daydreaming instead of working. In contrast, a child is usually not blamed for being mentally retarded or physically handicapped.

The concept of motivation is crucial in daily social interaction as we try to understand and predict others' behavior. The matter of motivation constantly arises in such queries as: "What's he up to?" "What does she want?" and "What's he after?" To a great extent, the way we react to others is based on the objectives we think they are trying to reach rather than simply on their overt actions at the moment. Commonsense psychology gives a larger role to this matter of predicting others' motives than do most of the other theories we will be considering.

Task Difficulty—The Role of the Environment

The last of the three factors that determine action is the environment. This factor can be labeled *task difficulty*. At any given moment, it consists only of those aspects of the environment that influence, either favorably or unfavorably, whether the child can accomplish a task he is attempting.

According to Heider, a person's efforts to understand the facts, principles, and laws by which the environment operates are motivated by the desire to "establish himself in a stable world in which the future can be anticipated and controlled" (Heider, 1958, p. 91). Thus what we wish to learn about the environment are those stable, permanent conditions that influence task difficulty. However, predictions based on understanding such conditions sometimes turn out wrong because of unexpected influences. It is not always clear where the blame or credit for these influences should be placed, on the person or on the environment, but usually we do not attribute them to the person, particularly if we like the person. These surprising or unpredicted happenings are usually accounted for by chance, opportunity, luck, fate, or the breaks. Mrs. Campbell felt such temporary, unpredictable influences accounted for her son's losing his quarterback position: He had "a streak of bad luck" in the form of an injury and the coach's later overlooking him on the bench. The boy's loss of position has not lessened his ability in his mother's eyes. She feels he still can play well even though he no longer has the chance to show it in a game.

By following Heider's general line of reasoning about environmental influences, we can suggest two additional assumptions people make about development:

1. The difficulty of a task is judged by the number of children or youths of a given age level who can accomplish it and by the effort expended to carry out the task.

2. Environmental conditions are divided into two general categories: (a) those that are stable and operate in a predictable manner and (b) unexpected occurrences, which are usually called "opportunity," "chance," or "luck." In an effort to make life more predictable, people try to increase their command of conditions in category a and decrease the number of conditions in b.

Our analysis of task difficulty leads us to generate the following rule of thumb for child rearing: People who are in charge of children will best serve the children's welfare by adjusting the difficulty of tasks to the gradually increasing level of ability the children attain as they grow up.

IMPLICATIONS FOR THE TREATMENT OF CHILDREN

From naive psychology's three factors that account for action, we can draw several implications about child rearing to guide adults' treatment of children. For instance, if we want to help a child complete a task at which she is currently failing, we first need to estimate which of the three factors— ability, task difficulty, or effort—is causing the failure. Then we can try to remedy the faulty condition of the identified factor.

If we think the child is striving as well as she is able and that her ability cannot be improved very readily, then we logically should attempt to reduce the difficulty of the task so she can succeed. To reduce the task's difficulty level, we can either do part of the task ourselves or break it down into smaller steps she can manage. However, in many cases we either cannot or do not wish to simplify the task. Then we may concentrate on improving the child's ability through training. In other cases we may conclude that the child's abilities are sufficient, that she either has not focused on the task (direction of motivation) or has not tried hard enough. So we try to convince the child that the task is something she really wants to do. We might try logic, cajoling, promises of rewards, or threats of punishment to motivate her to action (Heider, 1958, p. 123).

If this line of reasoning appears too obvious to be worth analyzing, it is not surprising. It's all common sense.

CHILDREN'S INTERPRETATIONS OF THEIR OWN BEHAVIOR

So far we have looked only at ways adults use commonsense psychology in explaining children's behavior. But equally important, or perhaps even more important, is children's use of commonsense psychology as a foundation for their own attitudes and behavior. One child may consistently avoid engaging in new experiences because he has a very low regard for his ability or personal power in relation to virtually all unfamiliar tasks. People perceive him as being "painfully shy" because of his "negative self-concept," his "low level of self-esteem and self-efficacy," or his "general feelings of inferiority." Another child may be willing to try some tasks but unwilling to try others. She may account for this difference by contending that some of the tasks are easy but others are too hard, or else she may attribute the difference to the factor of motivation: "I like to do these things, but those others don't interest me." Still a third child appears to have unflagging confidence in his personal power so that he eagerly takes on any new task and then attributes any failures to not having tried hard enough the first time (Weiner, 1974).

The importance of understanding a child's system of attributions lies in the observation that people do not behave on the basis of reality but rather act on the basis of their perceptions of reality. That is, they act on their attributions. Thus what stimulates a child to try a task is not the *objective fact* that she can succeed; instead, it is her *belief* that she can do it. Hence, from this view of human development, an important measure of a child's or youth's personal maturity is how closely his or her pattern of attributions fits conditions of the real world. This measure is reflected in the question, How accurately can an individual predict the outcome of a task performance when he or she really tries (exerts strong effort) to accomplish the task? The child who predicts more accurately—that is, who correctly estimates the relation of personal power to the difficulty level of tasks—is regarded as the more mature.

PRIVILEGE AND RESPONSIBILITY

Like other theories of development, the commonsense theory depicts child growth in terms of stages. The three most general stages are *infancy, childhood,* and *adolescence.* The borders between them are distinguished by relatively sudden physiological and psychological changes. An infant or baby crosses the border into childhood when he becomes "more of a real person" through learning to walk and talk around age 1½ or 2. The child crosses the border into adolescence or teenage status when sexual functions mature and such secondary sex characteristics as voice change, a spurt in height, body hair, and changes in skin texture show up around ages 12 to 15.

Paralleling these marks of physical maturation are a series of changes in privilege and responsibility that society regards as suitable for the growing child. Consequently one way to analyze directions or stages of development from a commonsense perspective is to do so in terms of the sorts of privileges and responsibilities that are added at different age levels.

The phrase *growth in privileges* here means increased opportunities to engage in a wider variety of activities, particularly activities the child considers desirable. In other words, she can do more things that she would like to do. *Growth in responsibility* means that the child incurs the obligation to carry out, under her own initiative or supervision, additional tasks that society considers proper, constructive, and desirable. In naive psychology, responsibility is composed of what Heider has called *ought forces* (1958, pp. 218–243). These are attitudes regarding the duties people fulfill that are shared widely by a community. Such duties are necessary for providing individuals with a stable, predictable social environment in which to live, in the same way that "man can operate in the physical environment only when physical laws hold" (Heider, 1958, p. 229).

As suggested by the folk saying, "With each privilege you incur a responsibility," common sense conceives privilege and responsibility to be the opposite ends of a balance scale. Throughout a child's development, his increasing abilities enable him to do more things by himself, so he gradually is permitted by his society to carry out a greater variety of actions and make more decisions on his own. But as privileges are gained by the child, society, primarily in the form of parents and teachers, adds oughts or duties. Much of the conflict between children and adults during the first two decades of life comes from (1) children wanting more privileges at an early age and (2) adults seeking to postpone the privileges or to impose responsibilities before the child wants them.

Since the most commonly agreed upon gauge of developmental level is chronological age, society uses age for defining when children's abilities (and sense of responsibility) are sufficient to permit them to try certain tasks or make certain decisions. Some of these age expectations are in the form of custom, such as the custom in certain Christian churches of having children gain church membership at around age 12. Other expectations are formalized as laws and regulations. By inspecting these laws, we can see what the common sense of the day considers to be proper steps or stages of development. For example, the stage of early childhood is typically distinguished from later childhood by school entrance laws. In the United States children are both permitted and obligated to attend school around age 5 or 6. Such formal laws reflect commonsense perceptions of steps in development; less formal regulations, such as the school's curriculum guidelines, delineate substages within the major steps. For instance, it is common in American schools to focus kindergarten activities on broadening the children's experience with their physical and social world and not on formally teaching them reading, writing, or arithmetic. But when children enter first grade at age 6 or so, they are expected to begin reading, writing, and formally analyzing quantitative concepts.

Criminal law reflects the commonsense belief that children before puberty are not yet reasonable or responsible beings, and even after puberty they are not considered to be entirely reasonable. The California penal code states that children under age 14 are not capable of committing actual crimes unless there is "clear proof that at the time of committing the act charged against them, they knew its wrongfulness." So the excuse that "she didn't know what she was doing" is sufficient for not prosecuting a child as a "reasonable" adult would be prosecuted. Between ages 14 and 17, youths are still considered only partially responsible beings, so that when they commit unlawful acts they are labeled delinquents rather than criminals and are processed through special juvenile courts. Furthermore, many states prohibit the public press from publishing the names of youths under age 18 who are involved in crimes, under the belief that prior to 18 an adolescent is still not fully responsible and does not deserve public blame and shame.

The number of laws, both civil and criminal, that use age 18 as the cutting point for various privileges and responsibilities suggests that common sense today defines the period of childhood and adolescence as extending from birth through age 17, even though in American society many youths are still not economically independent of their parents by age 18. There is a general expectation, or hope, that all youths will graduate from high school, and this usually occurs around age 18. In recent years the legal voting age was lowered from 21 to 18. One result of this was to make the voting age more closely coincide with the age at which boys acquire the privilege or obligation to fight and die for their country (age 17—voluntary enlistment; age 18—registering for conscription).

In effect, laws and customs reflect common notions of steps in development, with each step representing a point at which abilities and children's acceptance of ought forces are sufficient for them to be accorded new privileges and responsibilities. However, reaching the designated age for taking a step is not a guarantee that a privilege or responsibility will actually be provided. Other measures of development are also used. Before a child is considered ready for first grade, for example, he is tested or observed to determine whether he has the abilities needed to succeed at typical first-grade tasks. And Mr. Young's daughter, Charlene, is not guaranteed a driver's license at age 16. The girl's driving skill and knowledge of traffic laws will also be tested, and she will be denied a license until she has proven her skill. On the other hand, privileges are sometimes given before the minimum age level is reached. An adolescent who is slightly underage but who can prove her driving skill and a compelling need to drive (such as to provide the family income) may be given a driver's license before age 16. In sum, age is the main criterion of developmental sufficiency in commonsense psychology, but other criteria are also used to accommodate individual differences in children's ability.

Thus commonsense psychology proposes (1) generalizations that describe the average child and (2) minor amendments that describe children who deviate from the average. And these conclusions that form a society's naive view of development are found in the customs, regulations, and laws that apply to life in the home, in the school, and in the wider community.

PRACTICAL APPLICATIONS

When the word *practical* is defined as "something firmly tied to the realities of daily living," then commonsense attribution theory by its very nature is indeed practical since it represents the framework of assumptions that underlie the way people in everyday life account for how and why children develop as they do. Furthermore, when *practical* is defined as "something useful in the solution of daily problems," commonsense theory again qualifies as practical for it explains the system of reasoning people employ as they interpret children's behavior. For example, if we know from commonsense theory about the interaction that most people assume exists among ability, task difficulty, and trying hard, we are better prepared to understand the structure of parents' reasoning as we hear them explain why their child is or is not developing satisfactorily.

Another practical function of commonsense theory is its potential usefulness in revealing to us the structure of our own unstated assumptions about children's growth. As a consequence of such self-revelation, we may newly recognize certain of our underlying beliefs which, when carefully analyzed, prove to be contradictory or perhaps inconsistent with research evidence. Armed with this increased awareness, we may be able to devise a more logical version of attribution theory, a version that properly fits with our personal system of values and the available facts about children's growth.

RESEARCH CHALLENGES

In two major ways, commonsense psychology has served to generate empirical research and theorizing.

First, the line of analysis initiated by Heider has been further advanced by such psychologists as E. E. Jones and R. E. Nisbett (1971), H. H. Kelley (1973, pp. 107–128), and B. Weiner (1972, 1974). Their studies, however, have treated the ways people account for general behavior rather than the developmental aspects of behavior. As a result, there are at least two varieties of research questions yet to be answered from a developmental perspective. The first variety is reflected in the question, What principles of cause do people use in accounting for behavior at any and all age levels, and what principles are used in accounting for behavior at one stage of life in contrast to another stage? In other words, do people attribute the behavior of a three-year-old to the same set of causal factors as they do the behavior of a twenty-year-old or an eighty-year-old? And if not, why not? The second set of questions concerns the ways children at different age levels attribute cause. For example, (1) what are the factors children and youths at different stages of development use in accounting for people's behavior, (2) to what extent are these causal attributions the same for all children at a given age level, (3) to what extent do children's attributions differ between one culture and another, and (4) what are the apparent reasons behind the likenesses and differences in these attributions?

To some extent, questions from this second set have been studied by researchers from perspectives other than that of commonsense theory. An example is the theoretical viewpoint proposed by Piaget (1948), who analyzed explanations of social causality offered by children of different age levels. Yet a host of research questions about such matters still remain to be answered.

Second, naive psychology provides research challenges in its serving as an explanation against which the results of empirical studies can be judged. When observations of children's behavior and development are not easily interpreted by commonsense psychology, the researcher may be stimulated to devise a new basis for analysis—that is, a new theoretical explanation— that better fits the observed facts. Thus an important stimulus behind the creation of many, if not all, new theories has been the conflict the theorist has noted between observed facts and the commonsense way of explaining those facts. Such was true when Freud, in his role as a neurologist, recognized that his patients' symptoms did not make sense in terms of the popular neurological theory of his day. The same was true when Piaget sought to explain from the viewpoint of current common sense why children gave certain wrong answers on intelligence tests. Commonsense theory, then, may play some part in the generation of most research questions. When studies of children yield puzzling results, researchers propose alternative theories to explain the results and then conduct further studies to test these alternatives.

NAIVE PSYCHOLOGY: AN ASSESSMENT

The appraisal of commonsense theory is also based on the nine evaluation standards used previously. My estimates of how well naive theory meets the standards are given as marks on the nine scales; then my explanations for the ratings are given. Again, because your value system or your weighing of the evidence may differ from mine, you may well arrive at a different pattern of ratings and may wish to prepare your own rating sheet.

The logic behind my ratings may be easier to follow if we begin with item 5, the degree of internal consistency in the theory. There is necessarily considerable consistency among the assumptions on which people conduct their everyday treatment of children. Otherwise child rearing would be far more chaotic than it is. However, as Heider has pointed out, one can also criticize naive theory and its sources of data for "the many contradictions that are to be found in this body of material, such as antithetical proverbs or contradictions in a person's interpretation of even simple events" (1958, p.5). Which is the proper guide to child raising: "A little love and kindness goes a long way" or "Spare the rod and spoil the child"? How does a teacher reconcile the contradictions in his observation that "she really doesn't have the ability to do it, but she tries so hard that she is able to overachieve"? In

Naive Theory

How well do I think the theory meets the standards?

The Standards	Very Well	Moderately Well	Very Poorly
1. Reflects the real world of children		X	
2. Is clearly understandable		X	
3. Explains the past and predicts the future		X	
4. Guides child rearing		X	
5. Is internally consistent		X	
6. Is economical		X	
7. Is falsifiable		X	
8. Stimulates new discoveries	X		
9. Is self-satisfying		X	

judging item 5, then, the substantial consistencies in naive theory are balanced against what seem to be a substantial number of contradictions, and the theory is rated in the upper portion of the moderately well segment.

There are at least two ways of looking at item 2, regarding the clarity of naive theory. First, naive psychology is not some scientist's creation. It is the set of assumptions upon which people base their treatment of children. So a first way of viewing the issue of clarity in item 2 is reflected in the question, Are the assumptions about children that comprise common sense clearly understood and agreed upon within a given society? I believe the answer to this is that the contents of commonsense psychology are only moderately clear. People in a society have different assumptions about what makes sense in terms of child development. Even within a given person's set of assumptions there are contradictions, as illustrated in the discussion of internal consistency. However, there is considerable clarity about many aspects of naive psychology. If there were not, we would have far more conflict in our society than we do.

A second way to look at the clarity issue is illustrated by the question, Have psychologists who analyze naive theory clearly described all of its characteristics? Heider made a good start toward clarifying the structure of commonsense views, writers such as Baldwin (1967) extended Heider's general system to focus it more distinctly on childhood, and a large body of literature has grown up over the past two decades to expand attribution theory still further (Worchel & Cooper, 1979). However, much of the comtemporary literature focuses on adults rather than on children so that many aspects of children's use of naive psychology remain to be investigated.

Therefore, from both points of view—from people's understanding and agreeing upon the nature of commonsense beliefs and from psychologists' descriptions of the underlying structure—I have estimated that naive theory is only moderately clear.

Now to item 1: Does naive theory accurately describe the real world of childhood and adolescence? I believe that to a great extent it does. As Heider has observed, "The ordinary person has a great and profound understanding of himself and of other people which, though unformulated or only vaguely conceived, enables him to interact with others in more or less adaptive ways. . . . Intuitive knowledge may be remarkably penetrating and can go a long way toward the understanding of human behavior" (1958, p. 2). However, there are, at the same time, some notably unrealistic aspects to commonsense views. One of the most obvious is the tendency for people to attribute happenings in a child's development or behavior to a single cause. A careful analysis of events illustrates that an event results from multiple causes, with some causes exerting more influence than others. Past arguments about whether nature or nurture caused a particular development exemplify this commonsense tendency to attribute a happening to a single cause. Baldwin has written that "in many ways this feature of naive theory is its most insidious error and creeps most easily into attempts to develop a better, more scientific theory of human behavior" (1967, p. 75).

There are numerous other aspects of naive theory that bring into question its accuracy in describing children. For example, studies in recent decades of intellectual abilities have furnished a mass of evidence that contradicts the commonsense notion that the level of ability in one subarea of mental life will be the same in all other subareas. As a consequence, psychologists have moved increasingly away from a single general intelligence test that yields one overall intelligence quotient and have moved instead toward the use of multiple-factor tests that yield separate scores for each of several types of mental skills (Guilford, 1967; M. L. Harris & C. H. Harris, 1971). Likewise, studies of children's reading readiness contradict the belief that the time when all children are ready to begin reading is when they enter first grade (Durkin, 1976).

Thus, balancing the strengths of naive theory against its weaknesses in terms of describing children realistically, I rated the theory in the upper portion of the moderately well segment.

Related to a realistic view of children are item 3 (explaining the past, predicting the future) and item 4 (guides child-rearing practices). Since naive theory is better prepared to explain past events than to predict future ones, it cannot achieve a top rating for its ability to guide child rearing. As Baldwin has pointed out, the theory's weakness in predicting the future behavior of children rests to a great extent on two of its prominent characteristics. First, it does not specify all of the conditions or causes that interact to bring about an event or an aspect of development. For this reason, if the cause it does identify is not the most powerful of those actually operating, then the prediction will be in error.

Second, naive theory assumes that the child has a free will. The issue of free will is an old one in philosophy, one that has never been resolved satisfactorily. The concept of free will is usually discussed in connection with the contrasting or contrary concept of *determinism,* which has long been a basic tenet of the physical sciences or what is known as the *scientific method.* Determinism is a belief that everything that happens has been absolutely set or established by preceding conditions and could not have turned out any other way. In effect, if you know all the causal factors, you can make an exact, error-free prediction of what will happen. In contrast, the concept of free will holds that determinism may be true for strictly physical phenomena, such as thunderstorms and the growth of violets, but events that involve human decisions are influenced as well by the individual's freedom to make a choice. In effect, in human events a knowledge of preceding conditions or causal factors enables us to estimate likely outcomes, but we still must consider the individual's free will. The issue of determinism versus free will is a complex one. Here we will simply recognize that the idea of free will poses problems for naive theory when the theory is used as the basis for predicting future child behavior. No matter how much is known about causal conditions in a child's life, if the child has freedom of choice, errorless predictions of future development or behavior are not possible. This fact limits the value of naive theory for child-rearing purposes. When we treat a child a given way, we never know for sure how the child will interpret our actions and choose to respond.

Therefore, even though naive theory contains a lot of folk truths that, over the generations, have enabled people to guide children's development with some measure of success, it also has shortcomings that limit the accuracy of its predictions and child-guidance suggestions. Hence I rate naive theory in the moderate range for items 3 and 4.

Item 6 was difficult to mark because in some ways naive theory is too economical. That is, it makes what appear to be simplistic assumptions about aspects of development that seem to require more complex explanations. You may recall from Chapter One that Morgan's canon states: A theory is better if it is economical in the sense that it is founded on as few unproven assumptions as possible and requires rather simple mechanisms to explain all the phenomena encompassed by the theory. Naive theory violates this standard by failing in some ways to provide the simple mechanisms and in other ways to explain all the phenomena. In failing to fulfill the attribute of simplicity, naive theory may be too complex—for example, it still accepts certain assumptions about the divisions of the mind held over from faculty psychology. In failing to fulfill the attribute of explaining all the phenomena, naive theory may be too simple or simplistic.

Let us consider this charge of oversimplification in more detail. Baldwin (1967, pp. 64–70) has illustrated this problem with examples focusing on matters of perception and intentional action. He points out that the assumption is made in naive psychology that everyone perceives things in the same way. In other words, the child's perceptual equipment is like a television camera, recording sight and sound the way "they really are." And everyone's camera records events in the same way. (This assumption underlies the practice in courts of having witnesses describe what they perceived so the judge and jury can determine what "really" happened.) But today a growing body of research suggests that perception is far more complex than naive theory would suppose. In effect, naive theory neglects the complexities of the phenomenon and proposes an overly simple picture of what apparently occurs.

Baldwin charges that, in like manner, common sense fails to explain adequately the relationship between a person's intention and his actions. This objection leads us to the traditional philosophical issue of *teleology*. In a teleological explanation, the main cause of an event is found in the future rather than in the past or present. Instead of specifying the past and present conditions that have caused a young child to speak a few words, the teleological approach identifies some future purpose of outcome that has "caused" the speech behavior. For example, a child learns to speak because she now will be able to communicate her wants more adequately. Or, adolescents seek sexual mates out of a need to reproduce and thus preserve the human species for the future. Although this line of logic may at first appear reasonable, it is not in keeping with basic rules traditionally followed in the natural sciences. In the natural sciences, a cause does not appear in the future, that is, a cause does not appear before its effect. Thus, for people who want child development theory to adhere to the tenets of biological and physical sciences, the teleological aspects of naive theory are an embarrassment, just as are the beliefs in free will and single causal factors.

There are, of course, theorists who say that human behavior follows different laws (at least to some degree) from those governing nonhuman events. For these theorists, including the humanistic psychologists (Chapter Sixteen), teleological causation and free will are not objectionable features of commonsense psychology.

In terms of its economy of explanation, then, naive theory oversimplifies certain aspects of development, thus violating part of item 6, and I have rated it only moderately well.

As for item 7, falsifiability, parts of the theory are testable or disconfirmable, and other parts are not. Although many research studies conducted over the past century on child development represent successful efforts to test the validity of commonsense views, some important aspects of the theory have not as yet appeared testable or falsifiable. These aspects have depended for their confirmation on personal opinion or faith. Two examples of such aspects are the concepts of free will and teleological causation. Balancing these positive and negative factors against each other, I rated item 7 in the moderately well range of the scale.

The highest rating has been given to item 8 in recognition of the great fertility of commonsense beliefs for stimulating new discoveries. As mentioned earlier, in the last analysis, all new theories and new research have resulted from people's dissatisfaction with commonsense answers or from people's attempts to defend naive theory in the face of attacks on it. Furthermore, the sort of analysis of commonsense theory carried out by Heider and his disciples has itself led to the growing body of research called *attribution theory*.

Finally, naive theory is, overall, moderately self-satisfying (item 9). Although much of my own treatment of children is based on commonsense notions, in many ways this common sense fails to answer my child development questions adequately and I am left discontented with naive theory. This discontent serves as a sufficient stimulus for learning what more formal theories, such as the ones in the following chapters, offer.

FOR FURTHER READING

Baldwin, Alfred L. (1967) *Theories of Child Development.* New York: Wiley. Baldwin reviews Heider's general theory to show the implications it holds for child development; he offers a detailed critique of naive theory and its relation to scientific method and other theories of development.

Heider, Fritz. (1958) *The Psychology of Interpersonal Relations.* New York: Wiley. Heider describes what he conceives to be the theoretical framework on which people's commonsense psychology is founded.

Worchel, Stephen, and Joel Cooper. (1979) *Understanding Social Psychology.* Homewood, Ill.: Dorsey Press. Chapter 5 reviews findings in attribution theory.

PART THREE

DEVELOPMENTAL MILESTONES, DIRECTIONS, AND PRINCIPLES

A search for childhood's typical steps of growth, directions of growth, and principles of development

The chief goal of some theorists has been to chart the steps or stages through which children advance as the years pass. The question guiding these efforts has been, What are children's characteristics at different age levels in physical, mental, social, emotional, and other realms? Other theorists have concentrated more on identifying general directions of growth and principles of development, an endeavor guided by two questions: A child advances in what directions, that is, advances from what condition as an infant toward what new condition as an adult? And what generalizations or principles best describe the process of change that children experience as they grow up?

The first two chapters in Part Three illustrate theories emphasizing milestones. The third chapter depicts theories emphasizing directions and principles of development.

Descriptions of Developmental Milestones

G. Stanley Hall, with the publication in 1891 of his study entitled "The Contents of Children's Minds on Entering School," is credited with starting a tradition that dominated child development investigation in America during the first half of the twentieth century. This is the tradition of measuring and observing groups of children and then summarizing the results in the form of averages for different age levels. Studies of this type have focused on a wide array of children's characteristics, ranging from measurements of height and weight, through the testing of mental and physical skills, to observations of social relations, sleep habits, and outbursts of anger. The number of such published studies from around the world runs into many thousands. They have been called *normative, descriptive* investigations because they describe the normal, in the sense of average, status of children on specified characteristics at different age levels. The summarized results of these studies typically are labeled *descriptive norms* or *age norms.*

The theorist who best exemplifies the normative-descriptive school of child development is Arnold Gesell, a physician and child psychologist who studied under Hall at Clark University before setting up a clinic at Yale University to conduct descriptive research on children. Gesell's apparent intention was to chart with as great care and thoroughness as possible children's characteristics at each age level in a great many facets of their lives. A brief review of Gesell's work is given in Chapter Five.

A second approach to describing milestones on the road to maturity is illustrated in Chapter Six. The approach, known as *developmental-task theory,* grew in the 1930s and 1940s in the United States within the progressive education movement that dominated the educational thought of that era. Like Gesell, leaders of the developmental-task approach tried to identify the typical steps in development at different age periods in many aspects of growth—physical, intellectual, social, and emotional. But, unlike Gesell, developmental-task adherents did not systematically measure, test, and observe children who were chosen as typical representatives. Rather, they based their growth stages on data drawn from a great variety of sources: empirical studies like those from Gesell's clinic, anthropological and sociological investigations, observations by teachers of children in school, commonsense ideas about child raising, and others. Furthermore, whereas Gesell was most interested in describing what children are like at different age levels, the developmental-task theorists were more interested in speculating about what children are trying to accomplish during each successive age period. The term *developmental task* was created to reflect the theorists' conviction that growth should be viewed as the child's seeking to achieve new goals or perform new tasks at each new stage of development.

In sum, Gesell endeavored to describe what children are like. Advocates of the developmental-task approach not only wished to describe what children are like at each phase of growth, they also sought to infer from these descriptions the sorts of goals they felt children were pursuing or the needs they were seeking to fulfill by their behavior.

The tradition of normative-descriptive studies in which Gesell played such an important role continues to be very active today. Likewise, although the peak of developmental-task theorizing was reached in the 1940s, the movement continues to exert a significant influence on curriculum development in schools and on child development textbooks.

Directions and Principles of Development

Chapter Seven is divided into two sections. The first reviews general principles and directions of development as proposed by two psychologists, Kurt Lewin and Heinz Werner. The second summarizes principles of development advanced by ethologists, that is, by researchers who base most of their theorizing on studies of animals and then try to apply their principles to the interpretation of human development as well. As a backdrop against which to view Chapter Seven the following paragraphs offer a brief description of the origins of the two psychologists and of the field of ethology.

Lewin's topological psychology and Werner's orthogenetic model are considered together because the authors of these two theories have several things in common.

Both sought to identify general principles or patterns of development, principles that would be valid for *all* aspects of growth—cognitive, physical, emotional, and social. Neither proposed an overall system of growth stages, although both identified steps of development for certain specific phenomena that they investigated, such as stages of play behavior (Lewin) and language use (Werner). Both conducted and stimulated innovative empirical research on children.

Furthermore, Lewin and Werner came from a European holistic or Gestalt background, which emphasizes the development of the child as a whole, integrated organism. This holistic view, typical of European theorists in many scientific disciplines, contrasts with the British associationism from which behaviorism partially derived. Associationism represents a tradition that conceives of development as proceeding by small, additive increments that gradually accumulate to form the personality or to form a child's repertoire of acts. But to the holistic or field theorist, a new stimulus or experience does not simply add a new element to a child's store of actions or knowledge, leaving the previous elements undisturbed. Instead, each new experience alters the relationship of many or all the existing elements that have made up the personality to this point, so the patterning of the whole personality is influenced.

The holistic or field-theory concept of personality development is sometimes explained by the use of an example from astronomy. Assume that a new planet the size of Saturn is added to the solar system between Earth and Mars. This addition does not simply place a new speck of light in the sky of earthlings and martians, its gravitational pull influences the paths of all planets in the solar system, having more effect on the closer planets than on the distant ones. So with the entire pattern of the solar system altered, the system itself becomes something new. In the realm of psychology, holistic or Gestalt (a German word meaning "configuration") theorists propose that a similar thing occurs in the development of a child's personality each time the child encounters new experiences or each time an internal change is triggered by the child's genetic structure. In Chapter Seven we will see that the field-theory concept is part of the systems proposed by Lewin and Werner.

Finally, Lewin and Werner are also alike in their having left Germany in mid-career, emigrating to the United States to escape the rising Nazi regime. Lewin (whose name is pronounced either in its original German as La-*veen* or in its Americanized version as *Lou*-in) came to the United States in 1932 and spent the next decade and a half as a university professor, mostly at the University of Iowa and the Massachusetts Institute of Technology. Werner (pronounced either *Ver*-ner or *Wer*-ner) came to America and established his child development research center at Clark University in Massachusetts.

Of the two theorists, Lewin has had the broader influence on the field of psychology. One example of this influence in the area of child behavior is the development of ecological psychology, a theoretical position described briefly in Chapter Seven.

The second major section of Chapter Seven identifies contributions to child development theory from ethology, which is the relatively new research discipline concerned with comparative studies of animal species. The aim of ethologists has been to discover two sorts of growth principles, those governing development within a single species and those governing development in many species, including humans. As a scientific pursuit, ethology is an outgrowth of Charles Darwin's theory of evolution, the notion that all species of living things are biologically linked together in a network of creatures that have evolved over millions of years from a common ancestry. Darwinians thus assume that certain characteristics of development should be common to all beings within the network.

The discipline of ethology owes much of its origin in the 1930s to a pair of Europeans. One is the Austrian Konrad Z. Lorenz (born 1903), who was awarded the Nobel Prize in physiology in 1973, the year he assumed the directorship of the department for animal sociology in the Austrian Academy of Science. The other is the Dutch Nikolaas Tinbergen (born 1907), who spent most of his professorial life at Oxford University in England. Lorenz is perhaps best known for describing the phenomenon of *imprinting,* which is the propensity of a newborn animal to attach itself emotionally to the first being it encounters as a nurturing guardian, such as a mother. This imprinting attachment was demonstrated by Lorenz when he persuaded a family of goslings to follow him as their nurturing guardian.

Since the 1930s ethological research has burgeoned, but mainly as the study of nonhuman species. As a result, the question is often asked, Why use studies of animals to elucidate the development of humans? Why not simply study humans directly? A typical answer is that provided by R. A. Hinde in *Biological Bases of Human Social Behaviour:*

> Understanding human behaviour involves problems infinitely more diffi-
> cult than landing a man on the moon or unravelling the structure of
> complex molecules. . . . If we are to tackle them, we must use every source
> of evidence available to us. Studies of animals are one such source. Some-
> times such studies are useful to the extent that animals resemble man, and
> sometimes they help just because animals are different and permit the
> study of issues in a simplified, isolated, or exaggerated form. They may
> assist us in understanding the behaviour of man not only through factual
> comparison between animal and man, but also by helping us to refine the
> categories and concepts used in the description and explanation of be-
> haviour and social structure. But the use of animals involves dangers: it is
> so easy to make rash generalizations, to slip from firm fact to flight of fancy,
> to select examples to fit preconceptions. Studies of animals must therefore
> be used circumspectly, and the limitations of their usefulness specified
> (1974, p. xiii).

CHAPTER FIVE

Gesell's Growth Gradients

An early stage in the development of any natural science is that of describing phenomena and putting the descriptions into some sort of order. In the field of child development in America, such a task of describing and ordering was done over the first half of this century by Arnold Gesell and his colleagues at the Yale University School of Medicine.

Gesell was born in 1880 in Wisconsin, where he was educated and eventually took a college degree in teaching before earning a Ph.D. in psychology at Clark University in Massachusetts in 1906. In 1911 Gesell was appointed to the Yale faculty as an assistant professor of education. At the same time he established the Clinic of Child Development, which he directed during the next thirty-seven years. While at Yale he earned a doctorate in medicine (1915), and his clinic was attached to the school of medicine. After Gesell's retirement, several of his co-workers set up a private institution near Yale in New Haven, naming it the Gesell Institute of Child Development. Gesell served as a consultant to the clinic from 1950 through 1958. He died in 1961, but the work of his clinic has continued since that time.

Throughout his professional years Gesell pursued the task of describing the observable changes in child growth and behavior from birth to adolescence. Although his principal concern was with development after birth, he also conducted studies on prenatal growth stages.* In our review of the theoretical themes that dominated his investigations, we will consider the

---

*The following sample of titles of books he authored suggests the range of his interests: *The Normal Child and Primary Education* in 1912, *Guidance of Mental Growth in Infant and Child* in 1930, *An Atlas of Infant Behavior* in 1934, *The Embryology of Behavior* in 1945, *The Child from 5 to 10* in 1946, *Youth: The Years from 10 to 16* in 1956.

following: (1) the aspects of development on which Gesell focused, (2) the primacy of genetic determinants, (3) cycles of behavior, (4) his manner of accounting for individual differences, (5) practical applications, and (6) research challenges.

ASPECTS OF DEVELOPMENT

The work of Gesell and his colleagues consisted mainly of studying children brought to their clinic from families in New England of varying socioeconomic status. The number of children studied as representative of children in general was not specified in such key volumes as Gesell and Frances Ilg's *Child Development* (1949), nor were other characteristics of the group defined except in such broad terms as: "The nursery school children have in general been above an average level in intelligence. The parents of all these children have assisted us with a high order of cooperation" (Gesell & Ilg, 1949, pp. xx). The results reported in *Child Development* were based not only on studies of the New England children but also on data about "a special group of fourteen Swedish infants . . . studied by Dr. Ilg in 1936–37 while she was in residence in Stockholm" (Gesell & Ilg, 1949, p. xx).

To carry out their studies, Gesell and his staff created an array of tests, measuring procedures, and techniques of observation that would enable them to describe children's status precisely in a wide range of growth areas. The research team gathered information about children in the clinic, and also interviewed parents to learn about the children's behavior at home. These data enabled the staff to describe the steps or *gradients of growth* for the typical child at each age level. The array of developmental aspects for which Gesell identified *maturity traits* and *gradients of growth* were categorized into the following ten major areas, with several minor divisions under each major category (Gesell & Ilg, 1949, p. 69):

1. Motor characteristics
   a. Bodily activity
   b. Eyes and hands

2. Personal hygiene
   a. Eating
   b. Sleeping
   c. Elimination
   d. Bathing and dressing
   e. Health and somatic complaints
   f. Tensional outlets

3. Emotional expression
  a. Affective attitudes
  b. Crying and related behaviors
  c. Assertion and anger

4. Fears and dreams

5. Self and sex

6. Interpersonal relations
  a. Mother–child
  b. Child–child
  c. Groupings in play

7. Play and pastimes
  a. General interests
  b. Reading
  c. Music, radio, and cinema

8. School life
  a. Adjustment to school
  b. Classroom demeanor
  c. Reading
  d. Writing
  e. Arithmetic

9. Ethical sense
  a. Blaming and alibiing
  b. Response to direction, punishment, praise
  c. Responsiveness to reason
  d. Sense of good and bad
  e. Truth and property

10. Philosophic outlook
  a. Time
  b. Space
  c. Language and thought
  d. War
  e. Death
  f. Deity

An inspection of this extensive list shows that Gesell adopted a multifaceted view of children rather than concentrating on one or two aspects of growth. And the fact that the topics cover growth areas that are of daily concern to parents and teachers helps account for the popularity of his books in the mid-twentieth century. When a mother worried about whether a particular kind of behavior was typical or "normal" for her child, she could turn to one of Gesell's volumes for an answer. The writing style of the most widely read books was adjusted to the reading tastes of parents. The volumes were not composed of statistical tables, showing the frequency of certain behaviors or of the number of children above and below the average at a given level. Instead, Gesell and his staff digested the statistics and turned them into specific statements of what a child was like at a given age. For example, here are typical descriptions of an aspect of behavior—children's fears—for ages 5 and 6 from a volume by two of Gesell's closest co-workers, Frances L. Ilg and Louise B. Ames.

> *5-year-olds:* Not a fearful age. More visual fears than others. Less fear of animals, bad people, bogeymen. Concrete, down-to-earth fears: bodily harm, falling, dogs. The dark. That mother will not return.
>
> *6-year-olds:* Very fearful. Especially auditory fears: doorbell, telephone, static, ugly voice tones, flushing of toilet, insect and bird noises. Fear of supernatural: ghosts, witches. Fear that someone is hiding under the bed. Fear of the elements: fire, water, thunder, lightning. Fear of sleeping alone in a room or of being only one on a floor of a house (1955, pp. 172–173).

Thus the main body of books issued from the Gesell clinic was composed of such "typical traits and growth trends of each age . . . summarized in a 'Behavior Profile' " (Gesell & Ilg, 1949, p. 2). In addition, Gesell and his co-workers expressed three important convictions that warrant our attention: (1) that development is primarily a product of genetic factors, (2) that better and worse years alternate systematically in child growth, and (3) that there is a clear correlation between a child's body type and personality. These are the matters to which we now turn.

THE PRIMACY OF GENETIC DETERMINANTS

In the heredity–environment controversy, Gesell is clearly a predeterminist. In his opinion, changes in children's structure and behavior are chiefly the result of their genetic endowment. The genes set the schedule by which the child's characteristics emerge over the first two decades of life, and the social and physical environments have little effect on these characteristics.

In light of this belief in the primacy of genetic determination, it is hardly surprising that Gesell and his staff saw as the most important mission in the field of child development that of cataloguing the physical and mental characteristics at each age level. This catalogue of average, normal characteristics could inform parents, teachers, and pediatricians of the traits they might expect to see unfold with each year of growth.

CYCLES OF BEHAVIOR

The Yale group also identified each year of development as either better or worse. They proposed that the better and worse phases appear in recurring cycles and are essentially the same for all children, or for nearly all. The term *better stage* was applied to any year in which the child appears to be in good adjustment or in good balance, both within himself and with the people in his world. The term *worse stage* was given to years during which the child is unhappy and confused within himself and at odds with his social and physical environments. Ilg and Ames termed these cycles "an alternation of stages of equilibrium and disequilibrium" (1955, p. 91).

As Table 5.1 shows, the first cycle of alternating better and worse ages begins at year 2 and ends at 5. The next cycle starts at 5 and lasts until age 10. Then a third cycle begins and continues through age 16.

Since the Gesell group envisioned the characteristics of the better and worse years to be determined by internal maturational factors, their advice to parents and teachers concerning what to do about the worse years was basically to be patient and wait until the inevitable bad times passed. Therapy, which Freudians might suggest, or retraining, which behaviorists would recommend, was not proposed. "We can try to smooth over the child's 'worse' stages. . . . But if we can accept . . . these extremes . . . as necessary parts of growth, and not blame them on somebody (teacher, other parent, neighbor, child himself), we will be looking at things realistically" (Ilg & Ames, 1955, p. 17).

INDIVIDUAL DIFFERENCES

When a system like Gesell's is described, with children at each age level depicted as so much alike in so many ways, the question of individual differences among age peers comes up. In acknowledging the existence of exceptions to their descriptions of typical characteristics, Gesell and his colleagues inserted in their writings such comments as:

> The prevalence of significant variations [is] recognized at every turn (Gesell & Ilg, 1949, pp. 1–2).

> Any description of age levels such as that which we have just given you is a gross oversimplification. When we describe characteristic behavior for any age, we do not mean that all children of that age will behave just that way all of the time (Ilg & Ames, 1955, pp. 22–23).

Table 5.1 Alternation of Stages of Equilibrium and Disequilibrium in Child Behavior

Stages of Child Behavior				
First Cycle	*Second Cycle*	*Third Cycle*		
Age	*Age*	*Age*	*General Personality Trends*	*Quality of the Age*
2	5	10	Smooth, consolidated	Better
2½	5½–6	11	Breaking up	Worse
3	6½	12	Rounded, balanced	Better
3½	7	13	Inwardized	Worse
4	8	14	Vigorous, expansive	Better
4½	9	15	Inwardized-outwardized, troubled, "neurotic"	Worse
5	10	16	Smooth, consolidated	Better

Table adapted from Ilg and Ames, 1955, p. 22.

Seldom is more specific mention made in these writings, particularly in books written before 1950, of deviations from the typical traits. In one of the later volumes (1955), Ilg and Ames did give somewhat more recognition to individual differences by first describing typical traits and then describing two or three types of children that were deviations from or variations of these traits. In addition, the authors offered suggestions about what might be done to aid the deviant make a better adjustment. As an example, the following is part of the authors' discussion of eating behavior:

> Some children live to eat. They are the round, often plump children. They are rarely feeding problems. But there are others who rarely think of eating. They are the small, petite, or even scrawny children. Hunger may come often to them but it is usually sharp and shortlived. These children do better on small, frequent meals, even five or six a day. . . . They gain weight very slowly but are active and healthy, more healthy, often, than the larger robust children (Ilg & Ames, 1955, p. 91).

This passage illustrates three characteristics frequently found in publications emanating from the Gesell Institute. First, any differences among children at a given age are described in terms of two or three types of children, in this case the plump and the petite or scrawny, with the implication that all children fit into either the basic category for their age or into one of the deviant groups. Second, little or no attempt is made to suggest any environmental factors that might have contributed to a child's becoming one of these types, the implication being that children are naturally that way because of their genetic structure. Third, when advice is offered about what can be done for children whose type deviates from the average, the advice does not derive from principles inherent in Gesell's theory. Rather, the advice either qualifies as common sense or derives more logically from studies or theories of other workers in the field of child behavior.

In view of the dominant role the Gesell group has assigned to heredity in all aspects of development, it is easy to understand why they turned to William Sheldon's theory of *somatotypes* to account for personality differences among children. In Sheldon's opinion, there are three basic body types among people, or at least three tendencies. He labeled these the endomorph, the mesomorph, and the ectomorph (Sheldon, 1940, 1942).

The person who is predominantly *endomorphic* tends to be fat, soft, and round. Sheldon proposed that this body build is accompanied by a personality type that displays a love of comfort and relaxation, of food, of the company of other people, and of affection.

The *mesomorph* has big bones and heavy muscles. This type loves vigorous muscular activity and is assertive, wishing to dominate others in social situations.

The *ectomorph* is thin, fragile, poorly muscled. This personality is restrained, inhibited, oversensitive, seeks concealment, and avoids social contact.

Although Sheldon agreed that few people are entirely one of these body types, he claimed that everyone tends toward one or the other. Ilg and Ames, subscribing to the Sheldon position, have stated that at each age level individual personality differences among children can be accounted for to a considerable degree by the children's body builds, which, in turn, have been determined by their genes. The authors have allowed some room for the influence of the environment, however, by adding: "All of this does not mean that human behavior is *entirely* determined by hereditary factors. What it does mean is that the body structure provides the raw material out of which personality is formed" (Ilg & Ames, 1955, p. 55). Nevertheless, despite this passing notice of environmental factors, the dominant theme throughout all of the Gesell Institute work is that the prime factor in shaping development both for the average child and for types deviating from the average is the child's genetically set maturation schedule.

PRACTICAL APPLICATIONS

Gesell's work and that of similar investigators have furnished standards in many aspects of development against which children may be compared to discover if a child's growth is progressing normally. The popularity of books containing descriptive norms demonstrates that such studies have been highly practical in the sense of being easy for the general public to use in understanding development. For example, methods of assessing the growth levels of babies submitted for adoption and of children applying for entrance to kindergartens continue to be founded on standards established by Gesell and his followers.

However, there have been complaints that too often the normative standards have been applied to children in naive, unwise ways. Critics have charged that when researchers publish only the average score achieved at a certain age level on such characteristics as height, intelligence, or social behavior, there is a danger that people using such norms will believe that their child should be *at the average* if she is to be considered "normal." The danger arises from three factors: (1) lack of data about deviations from the average, (2) lack of information about how the measured characteristic relates to other characteristics, and (3) equating *average* with *desirable* and thereby inferring that any deviation from the average is undesirable. By analyzing this trio of factors, we can devise a policy for using normative data that averts this danger.

Deviations from the Average

The problem with knowing only average scores is that very few children score exactly on the average. Most children score somewhere above or below average. Thus, if we are to interpret an individual child's score wisely, we can profit from knowing how closely the bulk of the children cluster around the average. For example, if an eight-year-old boy earns a score of 96 on a test of verbal ability and we know that the average for this age is 100, we will be better equipped to interpret the significance of the boy's score if we know how far other children's scores range above and below 100. If we learn that only 15 percent of eight-year-olds in the original standardization sample scored at or below 96 (thus leaving 85 percent scoring above our child), our concern will be different than if, in contrast, we discover that 43 percent scored at or below 96 (leaving only 57 percent scoring better than our child). In the first instance, our child is "well below average" but in the second he is "right around average."

Therefore knowing how much the majority of children's scores range above and below the average helps us judge whether or not to be concerned about a particular child's development.

Relations Among Characteristics

A second helpful sort of information about normative data is the relationship among selected variables. For instance, in comparing a girl's weight to that reported for other girls her age, it is useful to have norms that report not only average weight by age, but also report weight as it relates to height and skeletal type. A girl who is taller than average and has larger than average bone structure can reasonably be heavier than the average girl her age.

Hence, normative data reported in a form that shows how one variable relates to other pertinent variables provide a better basis for assessing child growth than do data that focus only on an isolated variable.

Normal versus Desirable

Of course, knowing the extent of group deviations from the average and knowing relations among variables can only alert us to how a child compares to age-mates. It still does not tell whether the child's development is satisfactory. A child who is *abnormal*, in the sense of deviating from the average, is not necessarily growing up improperly. To draw a conclusion about how satisfactory a child's growth pattern is, we also need a definition of *desirable development* from the point of view of the family or culture in which the child is raised. In the dominant culture of North America, as well as in much of Europe and in Japan, parents usually approve of children who are precocious in such behaviors as learning to walk, talk, read, do mathematical computation, and play a musical instrument. Being thus deviant (markedly above average) in such characteristics is interpreted as very desirable. But a child's precocity in sexual activity is not considered desirable in these same cultures. A child who is average or even somewhat below average in sexual activity is judged more acceptable.

In contrast to this value of intellectual development are attitudes in certain traditional Pacific Island societies where displays of intellectual precocity are frowned upon. In such cultures a child who displays average intellectual skills is approved of more than one who appears ahead of the group.

In summary, then, I am suggesting that descriptive norms based on studies of large groups of children at successive age levels can alert parents, teachers, and physicians to the way a given child's development compares with that of other children. But the norms themselves do not tell whether a child's growth pattern is to be admired or deplored. To judge how suitable such a pattern is, we need to know the way desirable growth is defined by the child's parents and by the surrounding society.

RESEARCH CHALLENGES

Frequently research opportunities stimulated by a theorist's work arise from critics' observing that the data compiled by the theorist are incomplete or faulty. Such a source of research ideas can be illustrated with three criticisms made of Gesell's work: (1) that he drew generalizations about all children on the basis of a very limited sample of children, (2) that he slighted the matter of individual differences among children of the same age, and (3) that he relegated children to a few types on the basis of one or two variables rather than considering the patterning of many variables that make up the attributes of an individual child. Let us now speculate about the additional research needs implied by such criticisms.

The main question behind the complaint about Gesell's sampling procedure is, If children were studied from cultures and ethnic groups other than those in the vicinity of New Haven, Connecticut, would the average measurements resulting from such studies be the same as those reported by Gesell? The obvious way to answer this question is to conduct similar studies with children in other places. The research technique, then, would be to do more of the same, but among different populations. And, indeed, a great host of studies of this sort have been carried out by other researchers. Furthermore, the results of these studies have been compared to show the extent to which groups of children of the same age in different settings are, on the average, similar to and different from each other. And many more investigations of the same sort can be expected in the future.

The second criticism is that Gesell overlooked individual differences among children by centering attention almost exclusively on the average child at each age level. Therefore what is needed is additional research that reports the ways children vary from the average. And over recent decades, this has been done. Researchers have systematically reported the kinds and extent of variation among children. And theorists have been challenged to explain why these variations have occurred—why some children have scored above the average and others have scored below.

The third criticism is that Gesell and his colleagues tended to place children in a few types on the basis of one or two characteristics; then they implied that the children in each type-category were essentially alike on significant personality characteristics. For example, thin and wiry children were all assumed to have similar personalities that contrasted with the type of personality exhibited by husky, strong children. But even commonsense observation suggests that relegating children to a few types is simplistic and does violence to the actual patterns of variation that children display. The research challenge here, then, is to devise ways of combining the assessments of children on many characteristics so that we have a more sophisticated picture of an individual child compared with others. This matter of trying to understand the complex patterning of attributes of an individual child is particularly important for parents, teachers, pediatritions, and club leaders who do not want to treat all children alike but wish to vary their treatment of children in ways best suited to the needs of each individual child. The concern for not categorizing children into a few types has stimulated researchers to adopt such statistical techniques as factor analysis, which is a method of estimating the extent to which one aspect of children's development is correlated with other aspects. This effort has been much aided by advances in computer technology, making possible the rapid, accurate computation required to determine relationships among multiple measurements of child characteristics.

So we recognize that shortcomings in descriptive studies have motivated subsequent researchers to design studies that obviate these shortcomings and produce increasingly sophisticated descriptions of child development.

GESELL'S CONTRIBUTIONS: AN ASSESSMENT

In keeping with the system of assessment used in previous chapters, I first rate Gesell's work on nine scales based on the appraisal standards suggested in Chapter 1.

My ratings of Gesell's work may appear to form a strange pattern since I have given his approach high marks on five of the nine criteria, yet have judged his theory overall as not very satisfying. To explain these conclusions, let's consider first the high ratings. With few exceptions, his beliefs are described (item 2) quite clearly. Also, with the exception of his position on the extent of and causes of individual differences among children of the same age, his proposals are internally consistent (item 5).

His work is also falsifiable (item 7). His growth gradients and descriptions of behavior by age levels are the result of empirical findings, and their accuracy can be checked empirically. Likewise, the validity of the concept of better and worse years can readily be determined by a researcher who prepares careful definitions of *better* and *worse* behavior or adjustment and then observes children of different age levels to see how well the hypothesis about better and worse years holds up. In a similar manner, the proposed

Gesell's Theory

How well do I think the theory meets the standards?

The Standards	Very Well	Moderately Well	Very Poorly
1. Reflects the real world of children		X	
2. Is clearly understandable	X		
3. Explains the past and predicts the future	Specifically X	Accurately X	
4. Guides child rearing	Specifically X	Accurately X	
5. Is internally consistent	X		
6. Is economical		Simplistic X	
7. Is falsifiable	X		
8. Stimulates new discoveries		X	
9. Is self-satisfying			X

correlation between body build and personality characteristics is amenable to empirical testing.

Item 8 gets a rather high rating in recognition of the influence Gesell's work has exerted on other researchers in the field of development. During the years of his greatest productivity, he devised a variety of testing and observation procedures, particularly for use with very young children, which have been admired for their precision and ingenuity. His procedures have become part of commonly used scales for judging development over the first year or so of life. Not only are his research methods still used in normative studies, but much of what he learned about the early years of growth continues to be respected today. Burton L. White, a Harvard University authority on infancy, wrote in 1971, "In this country, the most widely utilized source of information on the behavior of the human infant is probably the work of Arnold Gesell" (White, 1971, p. 7).

The rating on item 6 for the degree of economy Gesell's system displays represents a compromise between (1) his extremely simple, and in that sense economical, explanation of the causes of development and (2) the oversimplicity of the explanation. Although Gesell did not devise an unduly elaborate array of untested assumptions on which to erect his explanations, he did ignore a mass of research evidence that suggested environmental influences were far more important than his system recognized. As E. Zigler has commented:

> It is difficult to refer to [Gesell's scheme] as a theory. It appears rather to be a grand view having but a single construct, maturation. . . . Within such a framework, no other choice exists than to make the norms discovered through empirical investigations into explanatory devices . . . [so that] explanation is thus reduced to a labeling process. . . . The vacuousness and conceptual inadequacy of such a procedure has frequently been noted (1963, pp. 359–360).

In effect, the system is not overly complex, so it appears economical. In reality, however, it is unconvincingly simplistic. So I have rated it rather low on item 6.

On item 1, concerning how well a theory reflects the real world of children, Gesell deserves credit as an empiricist for founding his beliefs on observations of actual children, not imagined ones. He did not speculate about what children might be like or should be like. However, his penchant for reducing his observations to convenient averages or statements concerning typical characteristics at each age level distorted the picture of the real world of children. At any age level, and on any dimension of development, there are marked variations among children. For example, studies of reading ability among American schoolchildren have shown that in the fifth grade of elementary school (ages 10–11), the most apt pupils will read as well as the average tenth-grade student in high school, while the least adept will read no better than the average first grader in primary school (Thomas & Thomas, 1965, pp. 304–309). Most pupils will fall between these two extremes, with the greater number near the fifth-grade average. Gesell's reporting of only averages, or at best his noting of subtypes of children who deviate from the average, gives an unrealistic picture of the growth status of many children at every age level.

Besides the problems of Gesell's reporting only typical characteristics of children, there is also a question of how accurately his developmental norms represent children in general. The question concerns both the number and the cultural background of the children on whom he based the norms. The exact number of boys and girls studied in the clinic is not specified in Gesell's major publications, but the total at each age level apparently was no more than a few dozen. Furthermore, the children studied were from New England families interested enough in Gesell's research to bring their children to the clinic periodically for testing and observation. This method of sampling might well bias the results since there might be systematic differences between these families and those that did not participate in the clinic's studies. Indeed, Gesell pointed out that the preschool children in his group were above average in intelligence. Thus there is reason to doubt that the typical behaviors recorded for this sample, even when supplemented by observations of fourteen Swedish infants, give a realistic picture of children from other geographic and cultural settings.

Of course, this question about the representativeness of the sample is really not a serious issue when viewed from Gesell's predeterminist perspective. Since he believed that development depends heavily on heredity rather than environment, he could reason that it is unnecessary to choose children from different cultural environments—environment has little influence. It is necessary only to observe enough children to convince yourself that you have included the few major genetic types that make up the population. Thus Gesell was willing to generalize his observations to all children. But because I agree with those researchers who state that environment does exert an important influence on development, I have concluded that Gesell's sampling procedures were inadequate.

By balancing Gesell's admirable care in studying real children against his practice of describing only typical behaviors of a sample of New England children, I decided to rate his scheme only moderately realistic (item 1).

Both item 3 (explains past, predicts future) and item 4 (guides child rearing) are given two marks. The first mark in each case is for the degree of specificity of Gesell's system. In his system a child's past development is explained as the result of the natural unfolding of the preset genetic pattern. A child's future growth is described in terms of the typical characteristics of the age in which we are interested. Gesell's guides to child-rearing practices are equally definite. Basically we should let nature take its course. If the child's current development seems unsatisfactory, it is because the child is in one of the worse years, and patience on the part of adults is required until the stage passes. For such specificity Gesell's system rates high marks.

However, in terms of the accuracy of his explanations of the past, predictions for the future, and child-raising recommendations, he is rated further down the scales. I disagree with his practice of limiting his attention to "average" or "typical" behavior for an age group. Probably no child is average or typical in every way. Each child has a pattern of characteristics that makes up his individuality. Group averages are of limited use in explaining a child's past, predicting his future status, and suggesting what should be done to guide his development. The faith that researchers during the first half of the twentieth century placed in the value of normative group studies that yielded average scores (called *nomothetic* studies) has decreased in recent decades. More attention has been given recently to devising methods of investigating the growth of the individual child (called *idiographic* studies), particularly for purposes of prediction and child-rearing guidance.

Not only do I question Gesell's heavy dependence on typical behaviors, but I also question his crediting the environment with such a meager role in shaping development. In later chapters we will inspect the work of theorists who marshal evidence and a line of reasoning that suggest that environmental factors are extremely important in fashioning child growth, and much of this evidence I find convincing. (In particular see Lewin and Barker in Chapter Seven, Vygotsky in Chapter 11, and the behaviorists in Part Six.) Gesell's neglect of children's physical and social surroundings reduces the accuracy of his explanations of the child's past, predictions of her future, and recommendations for guiding her upbringing. For these reasons I have marked items 3 and 4 in the low to moderate range for accuracy.

Finally, I judge Gesell's system overall to be in the low to moderate range in terms of being self-satisfying (item 9). I respect his practice of making careful firsthand investigations of children and his devising techniques for carrying out such studies. However, these contributions do not sufficiently compensate for his overdependence on maturation and his overconcentration on "typical" behavior to warrant a higher rating.

FOR FURTHER READING

Gesell, Arnold, and Frances L. Ilg. (1949) *Child Development: An Introduction to the Study of Human Growth.* New York: Harper & Row. This volume contains the most complete, systematic summaries of typical developmental characteristics by age levels that have been drawn from the research of the Gesell group.

Ilg, Frances L., and Louise B. Ames. (1955) *The Gesell Institute's Child Behavior.* New York: Dell. Two of Gesell's closest co-workers offer the results of the institute's studies in a popular form intended particularly for parents and teachers.

CHAPTER SIX

Havighurst's Developmental Tasks

According to the developmental-task theory, the process of living, from birth to death, consists of an individual's working her way from one stage of development to the next by solving problems that are met at each stage. These problems, common to virtually everyone in a particular culture, are life's *developmental tasks*. If a person is successful in achieving each task, she is happy and receives the approval of her society. This success builds a good foundation for accomplishing later tasks. If the individual fails with a task, she feels unhappy, society does not approve, and she faces difficulty with later tasks (Havighurst, 1953, p. 2).

Examples of developmental tasks at the first stage of life, infancy, are learning to walk and learning to talk. Examples from middle childhood are learning the physical skills necessary for ordinary games and developing the fundamental skills of reading, writing, and calculating. Examples from later adolescence are achieving emotional independence from parents and preparing for an occupation.

The developmental-task theory is not the product of a single theorist. The basic idea underlying the scheme and the identification of important tasks began in the 1930s and evolved during the 1940s among groups of child psychologists and educators who played leading roles in the Progressive Education Association in the United States.* The theory was subsequently cast in its most systematic and extensive form by Robert J. Havighurst in his 1953 volume entitled *Human Development and Education*

---

*Havighurst (1953, pp. 328–333) credits the following people with contributions to the developmental-task concept: Frankwood Williams, Lawrence K. Frank, Carolyn Zachry, Erik Erikson, Fritz Redl, Caroline Tryon, Jesse Lilienthal, Stephen M. Corey, Peter Blos, Daniel Prescott, Evelyn Duvall, and Reuben Hill.

and by Carolyn Tryon and Jesse Lilienthal in two chapters of their 1950 work *Fostering Mental Health in Our Schools*. The picture of the theory sketched in the following pages is based mainly on these two sources.

Although the developmental-task model found its greatest popularity in the 1940s and 1950s in the field of education, it has continued to influence ·child psychologists and educators and has periodically stimulated the publication of new books in Europe and America founded on the concept.

The following brief overview of the theory treats five topics: (1) characteristics of tasks, (2) timing of tasks, (3) evidence to support the theory, (4) practical applications, and (5) research challenges.

CHARACTERISTICS OF TASKS

The term *developmental task* was apparently coined in the 1930s by people prominent in the Progressive Education Association. It was adopted and popularized by Havighurst in the 1940s and 1950s because, in discussions of adolescent development, he said he had "seen so much misunderstanding result from the use of the equivocal term 'needs' as a central concept" (1953, p. 330). He felt that the new term *developmental tasks* better described what young people were attempting to do as they grew up. According to Havighurst, the developmental tasks of life are pursuits that:

> constitute a healthy and satisfactory growth in our society. They are those things a person must learn if he is to be judged and to judge himself to be a reasonably happy and successful person. A developmental task is a task which arises at or about a certain period in the life of the individual, successful achievement of which leads to his happiness and to success with later tasks, while failure leads to unhappiness in the individual, disapproval by society, and difficulty with later tasks (1953, p. 2).

What are the tasks at different age levels? How many are there? Havighurst said that the number is somewhat arbitrary. It depends both on the way a person chooses to specify them and also on the particular society the person is talking about. For instance, the task of learning independent locomotion can be seen either as a single complex task composed of subactivities (creeping, walking, trotting, running, hopping, jumping) or as six different small tasks.

Some tasks arise mainly from the biological nature of humans and thus will be found in all human societies. Their form is essentially the same in all cultures. Other tasks derive their characteristics from the unique cultural patterns of a given society; these either exist in different forms in different societies or else are found in some cultures but not in others. A task like learning to walk, which depends primarily on genetically determined growth factors, is essentially the same in all societies and arises at about the same time in a child's life. However, the task of selecting and preparing for an occupation is a complex one in highly industrialized societies that are characterized by much specialization and division of labor, while in nonindustrialized societies in which nearly everyone is a farmer or hunter or fisher, the task of choosing a vocation is perhaps simpler and is achieved at a younger age than in the industrialized society. Furthermore, the tasks of learning to read and write, which are so important in highly literate cultures, do not even exist in preliterate ones.

Consequently, lists of developmental tasks will not be the same for all cultures, and the items in the lists identifying a culture's tasks will be determined to some degree by the personal value systems of the people who prepare them. Havighurst admitted that the description of tasks he produced was "based on American democratic values seen from a middle-class point of view, with some attempt at pointing out the variations for lower-class and upper-class Americans" (1953, p. 26).

Havighurst felt that, in applying the developmental-task approach to children's education, it is most useful to define six to ten tasks at each stage of development. One such application is shown in Table 6.1, which was adapted from a table by Tryon and Lilienthal. The chart contains ten general categories or types of tasks. These categories are listed in the far-left column. To find the specific tasks in each category at each age level, look to the right of the category name.

For example, consider the first category, that of the child's achieving an appropriate dependence-independence pattern in growth. In the second column from the left, we find two specific tasks the infant faces in this category: (1) establishing one's self as a very dependent being and (2) beginning the establishment of self-awareness. For children at the stage of early adolescence (fifth column), we find one task described in this category, that of establishing one's independence from adults in all areas of behavior. In a similar manner we can find the specific tasks for each growth stage in any of the ten task categories.

Just as the number of tasks is somewhat arbitrary, so also are the stages through which an individual's development is traced. Tryon and Lilienthal identified five stages from birth to around age 20. Havighurst, however, divided the entire life span into six stages: (1) infancy and early childhood (birth through age 5), (2) middle childhood (ages 6 through 12), (3) adolescence (ages 13 through 17), (4) early adulthood (ages 18 through 30), (5) middle age (ages 31 through 54), and (6) later maturity (ages 55 and beyond).

No matter how the stages are defined in terms of age levels, tasks at each stage arise from three sources: (1) the biological structure and function of the individual, (2) the particular society or culture in which the individual lives, and (3) the personal values and aspirations of the individual. Havighurst called these the biological, the cultural, and the psychological bases of development. Three examples of biologically based tasks are: (1) learning to control the elimination of one's bodily wastes, (2) learning to accept one's physical sex changes in adolescence, and (3) learning to behave appropriately toward the opposite sex. Three tasks originating mainly from the pressures of society are: (1) learning to read and write, (2) learning to respect other people's property, and (3) accepting the responsibility to do one's share of the work in group projects. Two tasks arising in later adolescence chiefly from the personal values and motives of the individual are: (1) selecting an occupation and (2) establishing one's philosophical or religious convictions.

To guide people who wish to analyze the anatomy of each task for themselves, Havighurst recommended a series of questions that fall under five categories: task definition, biological basis, psychological basis, cultural basis, and educational implications. Specifically, he recommended that we try to answer these queries about a given task.

Nature of the task: How is it defined?

Biological basis: What can the biological sciences tell us about this task? How is a person's physical maturation related to achieving it? How do individual biological differences influence achievement of the task?

Psychological basis: What can psychology tell us about the task? How is the person's mental development related to it? How do the values and aspirations of the individual influence her or his achievement of the task? How is the task related to individual mental and personality differences? How can success or failure in accomplishing the task influence personality?

Cultural basis: What can sociology and social anthropology tell us about the task? How does the task vary from one culture to another? How is the task defined in the upper, middle, and lower social classes?

Educational implications: What are the responsibilities of general education for helping children and youth accomplish this task? How well are these responsibilities now being met? How might the educational system do a better job of helping young people achieve the task? (Havighurst, 1953, p. 17)

Table 6.1 The Tasks of Five Stages of Development in Ten Categories of Behavior

	Infancy (Birth to 1 or 2)	Early Childhood (2–3 to 5–6–7)	Late Childhood (5–6–7 to Pubescence)	Early Adolescence (Pubescence to Puberty)	Late Adolescence (Puberty to Early Maturity)
I Achieving appropriate dependence-independence pattern	1. Establishing oneself as very dependent being 2. Beginning to establish self-awareness	1. Adjusting to less attention; becoming independent physically (while remaining dependent emotionally)	1. Freeing oneself from primary identification with adults	1. Beginning to establish independence from adults in all behavior areas	1. Establishing oneself as independent individual in an adult manner
II Achieving appropriate giving-receiving pattern of affection	1. Developing a feeling for affection	1. Developing ability to give affection 2. Learning to share affection	1. Learning to give as much love as one receives; forming friendships with peers	1. Accepting oneself as worthwhile person, worthy of love	1. Building strong mutual affectional bond with possible marriage partner
III Relating to changing social groups*	1. Becoming aware of the alive vs. the inanimate, the familiar vs. the unfamiliar 2. Developing rudimentary social interaction	1. Beginning to develop ability to interact with agemates 2. Adjusting to family expectations for child as member of the social unit	1. Clarifying adult world vs. child's world 2. Establishing peer grouping and learning to belong	1. Behaving according to shifting peer code	1. Adopting adult-patterned social values by learning new peer code

IV Developing a conscience	1. Beginning to adjust to expectations of others	1. Developing ability to take directions, to be obedient in presence of authority 2. Developing ability to be obedient in absence of authority (conscience substitutes for)	1. Learning more rules; developing true morality	1. Learning to verbalize contradictions in moral codes, discrepancies between principle and practice; resolving these problems responsibly
V Learning one's psycho-socio-biological sex role		1. Learning to identify with adult male and female roles	1. Beginning to identify with same-sex social contemporaries	1. Strong identification with one's own sex 2. Learning one's role in heterosexual relationships
				1. Exploring possibilities for future mate; acquiring "desirability" 2. Choosing an occupation 3. Preparing for future role as responsible citizen

*Tryon and Lilienthal, 1950, pp. 77–89. We have not dealt with the developmental tasks of relating to "secondary" social groups. As the child grows and develops, he or she must relate to groups other than the family and peers — to school, community, nation, world. There are not yet sufficient data to enable us to delineate the specific developmental tasks in this area.

Table 6.1 The Tasks of Five Stages of Development in Ten Categories of Behavior (continued)

	Infancy (Birth to 1 or 2)	Early Childhood (2–3 to 5–6–7)	Late Childhood (5–6–7 to Pubescence)	Early Adolescence (Pubescence to Puberty)	Late Adolescence (Puberty to Early Maturity)
VI Accepting and adjusting to a changing body	1. Adjusting to adult feeding demands 2. Adjusting to adult cleanliness demands 3. Adjusting to adult attitudes toward genital manipulation	1. Adjusting to expectations based on improving muscular abilities 2. Developing sex modesty		1. Reorganizing self concept in the face of significant bodily changes 2. Accepting one's appearance	1. Learning appropriate outlets for sexual drives
VII Managing a changing body and learning new motor patterns	1. Developing physiological equilibrium 2. Developing eye–hand coordination 3. Establishing satisfactory rest–activity rhythm	1. Developing large muscle control 2. Learning to coordinate large and small muscles	1. Improving skill in use of small muscles	1. Controlling and using "new" body	

VIII Learning to understand and control the physical world	1. Exploring the physical world	1. Meeting adult restrictions on exploration and manipulation of expanding environment	1. Learning more realistic ways of studying and controlling physical world	1. Reaching one's potential level of reasoning
IX Developing an appropriate symbol system and conceptual abilities	1. Developing preverbal communication 2. Developing verbal communication 3. Rudimentary concept formation	1. Improving one's use of the symbol system 2. Great elaboration of concept pattern	1. Learning to use language to exchange ideas or to influence 2. Beginning to understand causal relationships 3. Making finer conceptual distinctions; thinking reflectively	1. Using language to express and clarify more complex concepts 2. Moving from the concrete to the abstract; applying general principles to the particular
X Relating oneself to the cosmos		1. Developing a rudimentary notion of one's place in the cosmos	1. Developing a scientific approach	1. Formulating a workable belief and value system

To learn how Havighurst himself used these questions as guidelines for the complex job of delineating tasks, see his *Human Development and Education* in which he offers detailed analyses of the key tasks he identified for six periods of the life span.

THE TIMING OF TASKS

For any theory involving stages of development, an important question to ask is, How crucial is it that a child pass through a stage at the time designated as normal or usual? In other words, are there critical stages? In his theory, Havighurst differentiated between two general categories of tasks: ones that arise only at a particular time and must be completed at that time and ones that are continuing tasks whose fulfillment the individual works on for many years. In the first category are such tasks as learning to walk and talk, learning how to eliminate bodily wastes in an acceptable manner, and selecting a vocation. In the second category are such long-term, recurrent tasks as learning to participate as a responsible citizen and learning a feminine or masculine role. These recurrent tasks, however, have substages that are to be completed at given times in the child's and adolescent's development.

According to Havighurst, it is critical that the child pursue and succeed with most, if not all, tasks at the time designated for them. To support this opinion, he cited studies of children "who were denied human companionship during their first few years of life and therefore did not learn to talk" (1953, p. 3). He suggested that such cases furnish at least some evidence that if the task of learning to talk is not accomplished during the second year of life, it may never be accomplished successfully. Hence the second year of life is seen as the critical period for achieving initial speaking skill. Furthermore, failure with a task during its critical period causes difficulties in performing later tasks related to the one that was failed. Failure in learning to talk, for example, will prevent the child from learning to read and write and from understanding many concepts normal to children at later stages of growth.

The model for this concept of timing tasks was drawn by Havighurst from evidence about the biological development of humans, particularly development in the prenatal, embryonic stage. In the embryo, the organ that does not arise at its proper time not only damages its own chance of developing but "endangers the whole hierarchy of organs" (1953, p. 3). Havighurst then extended this generalization to all of the bio-socio-psychological tasks treated in his scheme. "If the task is not achieved at the proper time it will not be achieved well, and failure in this task will cause partial or complete failure in the achievement of other tasks yet to come" (Havighurst, 1953, p. 3).

EVIDENCE TO SUPPORT THE TASK THEORY

Adherents of the developmental-task concept of child growth base most of their theorizing on normative studies and on their own casual observations of children and adolescents. Also, Havighurst acknowledged that the psychoanalytic ideas of Erik Erikson influenced the sorts of tasks he defined regarding the development of a self-concept in the early years of growth. And, as noted, Havighurst found it convenient to derive growth principles from biological studies and then to extend these principles to encompass social and psychological development as well. However, he regarded this extension more as a plausible hypothesis than a description of absolute truth.

In an effort to test the hypothesis that biological growth principles could be extended to other areas, he and his colleagues conducted a study of fifteen boys and fifteen girls in a small American town over a period of six years. The children were age 10 when the study began and age 16 when it was completed. To make the study broad in scope, the researchers used a variety of assessment techniques, including interviews with pupils and their parents, sociometric tests, projective tests (the Rorschach, Thematic-Apperception, and sentence-completion tests), observational reports by teachers and other adults, essays and checklists from the pupils, tests of aptitude and intelligence, ratings of personality, and measurements of physical growth.

The five developmental tasks on which the study focused were: (1) learning an appropriate sex role, (2) achieving emotional independence from parents and other adults, (3) developing a conscience and a set of values, (4) getting along with age-mates, and (5) developing intellectual skills.

At the end of the study, the researchers concluded that, in general, success with one task was correlated with success in others, although the amount of relationship varied with the types of tasks. For example, there was a high relationship between getting along with age-mates and developing a scale of values. However, the relationships were only moderately high for other tasks, such as learning an appropriate sex role (which correlated only r = .61 between ages 10 and 13). In most cases success with a task at one age would be followed by good performance on the task at later ages although the relationships were not so strict as to "rule out any possibility of improvement on the part of a poor performer as he grows older" (Havighurst, 1953, pp. 290, 325–326).

The research team also found some evidence to support the concept of compensation. A child might make up for poor performance on one task by good performance on another. However, such children seemed to be exceptions to the general rule, so that "the number of people who are using good achievement in one task to compensate for poor achievement in another must be quite small" (Havighurst, 1953, p. 322).

This investigation of the developmental-task theory, conducted with a very small sample of children, is apparently the most intensive and best controlled study designed to test the theory. Thus belief in the theory remains grounded mainly in normative studies—what the average child is like at different age levels—and in the logic or reasonableness of the scheme.

PRACTICAL APPLICATIONS

Applications of developmental-task theory have been of several kinds. One has been in the form of efforts to improve school curricula and out-of-school programs for children. As curriculum planners have sought to suit schoolwork to pupils' needs, they have assessed how well the subject matter and activities of the current curriculum match the developmental tasks identified for children at different age levels. In this way improvements have been made in parts of the course of study that apparently had not previously contributed toward the achievement of important tasks (Tryon & Lilienthal, 1950). Leaders in charge of extracurricular and out-of-school programs for young people have also used task analysis in selecting activities to be included in their programs.

As a further type of application, authors of child development textbooks in both America and Europe have described childhood from a developmental-task perspective (see, for example, Bernard, 1970; Hurlock, 1968; Muller, 1969; Travers, 1977). Their assumption has been that an understanding of tasks children are attempting to accomplish will help parents and teachers to be more patient with such attempts and to provide activities that help the young succeed in their endeavors.

In addition, researchers working in particular fields have adopted the notion of developmental tasks as a productive way to approach their specialized realms of interest. An example is A. Godin's (1971) proposed sequence of five developmental tasks in Christian education. The first task consists of the child's discovering Jesus at the center of God's plan in history, an accomplishment that becomes possible only when the child's *historical con-*

sciousness is awakened around age 12 or 13. Second is the task of comprehending that Jesus was not simply a historical figure but is a continuing symbol of God's present-day actions. In Godin's opinion, this comprehension first becomes possible around age 13. Godin's third task is that of the child's gradually abandoning a magical view of religion in middle adolescence and replacing it with true faith in God's plan. Fourth is the task of progressively leaving behind the notion that moral behavior earns favors from God. This notion is replaced by the adolescent's growing desire to do good works because they are an expression of humanism, without expecting God to provide gifts in proportion to the works performed. The fifth task, to be met in later adolescence and early adulthood, is that of freeing one's Christian beliefs from the parental images of mother and father. Then, on the foundation of these five tasks, Godin constructs Christian educational practices that depart markedly from the typical teaching strategies found in religious education programs.

A second example of applying the developmental-task concept outside the realm of Havighurst's model appears in E. M. Duvall's book *Family Development* (1971) in which she organizes her presentation around developmental tasks of the family. Duvall's model is founded on the premise that families grow through predictable stages that can be analyzed in terms of the development of both the individual family members and the family as a unit.

In summary, some applications of the developmental-task approach have involved using the original sets of tasks from Havighurst and his colleagues as the bases for educational and child-rearing practices. Other applications, such as Godin's and Duvall's, have consisted of creating entirely different tasks and then basing analyses and educational practices on this new set.

RESEARCH CHALLENGES

Like other models of child development, developmental-task theory has generated questions as yet unanswered, questions that therefore can serve as research topics. These questions fall into two categories.

In the first are issues already investigated empirically by Havighurst and his colleagues but in so limited a way that their answers are far from complete. These questions call for additional research that employs larger samples of children, a greater variety of developmental tasks, and perhaps more adequate assessment techniques. The following examples illustrate items in this first category: To what extent does success or failure with one task influence success or failure with others, both at the present time and in the future? To what extent can a child compensate for failure in one task area by striving to succeed in another area?

In the second category are issues still not studied empirically by those who formulated the theory. For instance, what criteria should be used for judging which tasks are significant in a specified culture at different stages of development? And when these criteria are used for establishing tasks in various cultures, what likenesses and differences appear among the tasks for one culture and those for another? Furthermore, why do such likenesses and differences occur? When you observe a given behavior, how do you know which tasks are being pursued by means of that behavior? (For example, on what task is an adolescent boy working when he helps a friend study a chapter entitled "Human Sexuality"?) In what specific activities can children most profitably engage at different stages of growth to succeed with their developmental tasks?

These are some typical research challenges derived from Havighurst's developmental-task model.

DEVELOPMENTAL-TASK THEORY: AN ASSESSMENT

In keeping with the mode of assessment used in previous chapters, I will use the nine assessment standards described in Chapter One to appraise developmental-task theory.

I have rated developmental-task theory high on item 1 because Havighurst offers a realistic picture of the cultural group to which he restricted his particular list of tasks. That is, his list is intended to represent the developmental tasks of mid-twentieth-century, middle-class, American children and youths. My observations of such children suggest that Havighurst's claim that these young people are seeking to accomplish his list of tasks is reasonable.

I have also rated the developmental-task system high for its clarity of explanation (item 2) and its internal consistency (item 5). Likewise, the theory appears to fulfill the criterion of economy (item 6), for it does not require a large number of untested assumptions as its foundation when a smaller number would suffice. While it is not unduly complex, neither is it overly simplified, as I feel Gesell's system is. Havighurst has gone to considerable length to analyze for each task the biological, social, and personal-psychological roots from which he proposes the tasks have grown.

On items 3 (explains past, predicts future) and 4 (guides child rearing) I have rated the theory in the moderately well range. It does, in a general way, predict the future for a child by describing tasks that seem common to all children in a given culture. Thus it suggests on what areas of life children at different stages will be focusing attention. Likewise, if a child seems maladjusted at a particular stage, developmental-task theory suggests what tasks were possibly not achieved adequately in the past and are thus causing difficulties with present tasks. However, the theory is more a way of describing behavior, of telling what children are like in their interests and concerns at different age periods, than a way of explaining why a child is behaving in a particular manner at the present time. In short, the theory is more descriptive than explanatory, as is Gesell's system. If you ask how biological factors interact with environmental factors to yield a particular behavior, developmental-task theory does not provide a clear answer.

Developmental-task Theory

How well do I think the theory meets the standards?

The Standards	Very Well	Moderately Well	Very Poorly
1. Reflects the real world of children	X		
2. Is clearly understandable	X		
3. Explains the past and predicts the future		X	
4. Guides child rearing		X	
5. Is internally consistent	X		
6. Is economical	X		
7. Is falsifiable		X	
8. Stimulates new discoveries			X
9. Is self-satisfying		X	

In terms of child rearing, the theory tells what sorts of problems children may be expected to face while growing up, but it does not offer much useful advice to parents and teachers about how to promote successful achievement of the tasks. The most useful implications for child rearing to be drawn from developmental-task theory seem to be that (1) we should recognize the nature of children's tasks at each age period and provide opportunities for them to practice solutions of the tasks, (2) we should be patient with children's attempts to solve the problems inherent in the tasks, and (3) we should furnish them information and training in skills that can promote accomplishment of the tasks.

As for item 7, the theory appears to be only moderately falsifiable. Some of its key hypotheses are testable, as was demonstrated in Havighurst's study of how satisfactory accomplishment of earlier tasks seems to influence the achievement of later ones. However, other aspects of the theory are not falsifiable. For example, how can we determine what the proper number of tasks and grouping of tasks should be for a given culture? Or, how do we identify with confidence which task or combination of tasks is being pursued in a specified segment of behavior, such as in a girl's agreeing to stay home and wash clothes for her mother rather than going to a movie with her friends? Identifying the tasks that are ostensibly motivating a particular series of actions or developmental changes involves a large measure of personal opinion. Testing the validity of personal interpretations made in matching tasks with behaviors would seem to be, in many cases at least, impossible. In this sense, then, developmental-task theory does not appear to be falsifiable, and the theory is rated moderately low on this scale.

In terms of item 8 (the fertility of the theory for stimulating new discoveries), the developmental-task approach has a mixed record. As noted earlier, the theory has been fertile in the sense of providing a useful scheme for revising school curricula and for offering parents and teachers another way of looking at children's developmental needs. However, relatively little research has been stimulated by developmental-task concepts. When compared to Freud's psychoanalysis or Piaget's cognitive theory, the developmental-task approach ranks very poorly on this score, and it is here rated low for that reason.

Finally, how self-satisfying is the theory (item 9)? It is limited in terms of its capability to explain rather than just describe behavior. And it is not precise in identifying tasks and matching them to segments of behavior. Furthermore, it has not opened new vistas for investigation; or at least few researchers have seen it as a fertile source of new discoveries. Despite these limitations, though, the developmental-task perspective is useful for interpreting children's behavior. The idea that children are struggling to achieve the goals implied in the tasks makes sense to me. Balancing these shortcomings of the theory against its usefulness as a way of viewing children, I have rated it as moderately self-satisfying.

FOR FURTHER READING

Bernard, Harold W. (1970) *Human Development in Western Culture*. Boston: Allyn & Bacon. A child development book featuring developmental tasks at each stage of growth, infancy through adolescence.

Havighurst, Robert J. (1953) *Human Development and Education*. New York: Longmans, Green. The most complete analysis of the developmental-task approach available.

Principles of Development: Lewin, Werner, and Ethologists

The theorists described in Chapter Seven share a common aim, that of identifying general principles by which development proceeds, with the principles intended to form the developmental framework not only of humans but of nonhuman creatures as well. The first half of the chapter features principles and directions of development proposed by two German-American psychologists, Kurt Lewin and Heinz Werner. The second half illustrates concepts and generalizations offered by ethologists to account for the way the genetic characteristics of the human species promote survival and development for individual members of the species.

CONTRIBUTIONS OF LEWIN AND WERNER: A COMPARISON

In describing the key characteristics of Lewin's and Werner's theoretical schemes, we begin with (1) a brief note about the general nature of each man's work and then continue with (2) a comparison of the growth principles they proposed, (3) their beliefs about stages of development, (4) Lewin's scheme for analyzing decisions, (5) practical applications of the two theorists' work, (6) research challenges deriving from their models, and (7) an assessment of their contributions.

Lewin and Werner: The Nature of Their Work

Although Kurt Lewin (1890–1947) spent much of his professional life studying children, he was not strictly a child psychologist. He was more of a general theorist, applying his schemes to the realms of social and industrial psychology as well as to child development. His focus on children was most evident during the 1920s in Germany and during the 1930s in America at the University of Iowa.

Alfred L. Baldwin, a prominent American developmental psychologist, (1967, p. 87) has written that it is more accurate to speak of the "Lewinian approach" rather than the "Lewinian theory" because Lewin never presented a clearly structured description of his view of child development. He never wrote a book that gave a systematic picture of child behavior. Thus, in order to understand how he conceived child growth, we must gather from his scattered writings the key elements of his viewpoint and piece together his interpretation of child behavior. Such a gleaning process has provided the material for this chapter.

Lewin produced a number of notable innovations in the field of development. Among them was his adaptation of topological concepts and diagrams to explain human behavior. *Topology* is a type of geometry that gives special attention to the relationships among spaces, especially to the distance between one space and another and to the barriers between the two. Lewin's psychological version of topology enabled him to draw maps of both (1) a child's developmental condition at different points between birth and adulthood, which illustrate principles of development, and (2) the forces that cause a child to act the way she does at a given moment. These maps served Lewin as adjuncts to his verbal explanations of behavior.

Heinz Werner (1890–1964) adopted the term *orthogenetic theory* to describe his self-imposed mission of discovering the correct *(ortho)* principles and processes of development *(genetic)* from infancy to adulthood. In pursuing his mission, first in Germany and then at Clark University in America, Werner carried out an extensive series of experiments, many of them focusing on children's perception and language use. From these experiments he was able not only to derive support for the general growth principles he sought but also to identify specific phenomena of perception and language use that have since been added to the body of knowledge in these particular subfields of psychology.

PRINCIPLES OF DEVELOPMENT: LEWIN AND WERNER

Lewin's View

To understand Lewin's scheme, we must first learn what he meant by four of his favorite terms: *life space, fact, region,* and *boundary.*

A child's *life space* in Lewin's system consists of all the facts that influence the child's behavior at a given time. In this system a *fact* is not an objectively verifiable observation from the "real world." Instead, a fact is any element within the child's psychological environment that affects the child's behavior or thought; this includes both forces of which the child is unaware and elements the child accepts as real or true. If a second-grade boy believes his teacher dislikes him, while actually the teacher likes him well enough, then the child's impression that "I'm not liked" is still a fact within his life space. This misconception or illusion influences the child's behavior as much as if it were objectively true.

To illustrate the sorts of elements or facts that make up a child's life space, let us consider the second-grade boy during the arithmetic period just before noon on the last day of October. We can estimate many of the facts that are influencing his performance on this lesson, which concerns the metric system. One fact, of course, is the child's impression that the teacher dislikes him. Another is the child's physical condition—the boy ate only a doughnut for breakfast and is now hungry. Also, he missed school last week as the result of a cold, so he missed the week's lessons on weights and measures. However, over the past months he has done well in arithmetic and considers himself a good arithmetic student. Another fact is the child's knowledge that this afternoon the second-grade class will have a Halloween party and each child will wear a costume. His costume is in his locker waiting to be put on during lunch period. These, then, are some of the forces or facts in the boy's life space as he faces the lesson on measuring with meters and centimeters.

Based on this illustration, we can identify several important characteristics of the facts of life space. First, the facts can originate from various sources. The child's hunger, which disturbs his concentration on the arithmetic lesson, originates from a physiological condition. In contrast, his desire to have the teacher like him, along with his fear that the teacher actually does not, influences the boy to try to obey the teacher's instructions, but also causes him to hesitate to ask questions because this might suggest to the teacher that he does not entirely understand what the teacher wants the pupils to do. These feelings toward the teacher are not founded in physiological needs but in social needs—those of being liked and approved of.

Furthermore, some of the facts are from the past, some from the present, and some from the future. The boy's opinion of himself as good at arithmetic is based on his past successes with arithmetic assignments. The teacher's explanation of measuring with meters is in the present. And the child's plans for the upcoming Halloween party, which distract him from the measuring lesson, center on the future.

In speaking of the way past events affect present behavior, Lewin was careful to distinguish between his own approach and that of such historically focused theories as psychoanalysis. In the traditional Freudian model, the sources of a youth's or adult's psychological disorder lie in the past. To the psychoanalyst, therefore, the patient's dreams or free-flowing stream of memories is a means of digging into the patient's past to learn what incidents caused the present-day neurotic symptoms. A Lewinian, however, is not interested in such historical material. Although Lewinians agree that past experiences can influence an individual's present actions, they are concerned only with the vestiges of those experiences as they exist in the form of memory traces in the present-day life space. They are not concerned with the nature of the original incidents. Consequently, Lewinians seek to learn about present feelings, attitudes, and knowledge rather than past experiences that may have historical links with these present-day facts in the individual's life space.

Some people have mistakenly equated Lewin's concept of life space with the *phenomenal self* of humanistic psychology, which we will meet in Chapter Sixteen. To humanistic psychologists, the phenomenal self is the "I" or "me" of which each person is aware. In contrast, life space consists not only of these conscious aspects but also of all the forces of which the individual is unaware, forces that, nonetheless, influence the way the individual acts. In the case of the second-grader, it is likely that traces of the illness he suffered last week remain within his system and will affect how well he completes the arithmetic assignment. A lingering infection, together with inadequate nourishment from the doughnut breakfast, can reduce his ability to concentrate on the lesson. These physiological facts are significant influences that do not fall within the definition of the humanists' phenomenal self but are still part of the boy's life space.

The contents of life space differ also from the objectively observed environment of the behaviorist. As we will see in Part Six, the behaviorist is interested in those aspects of the "objective, observable or measurable environment" that serve as stimuli to the child. The Lewinian, on the other hand, is not so concerned with the objective "real world" as with the child's perceptions. In the Lewinian view, the child does not act on the basis of objective reality but on the basis of what the child perceives is true, whether this perception is the same as "objective reality" or is an illusion or hallucination (Lewin, 1942, p. 217).

When the child's life space is thus constructed from a Lewinian viewpoint, we recognize that its contents are an amalgam of both nature and nurture. The second-grader's success on the measurement lesson depends partly on his genetic endowment (the neurological structure of his sense organs and brain) and partly on his experiences with his environment (last year's arithmetic lessons as well as last week's absence from school). Lewin did not seek to make distinctions concerning which source contributes more to a child's life space, heredity or environment—he apparently saw both sources merging to produce the life-space contents.

Two other terms needed to understand Lewin's concept of child development are *region* and *boundary*. A *region*, in the most frequent way Lewin used the word, is an element or a fact within the child's life space. Two aspects of regions are of particular importance. One is the *relationship* among two or more regions—they may be closely connected or distant. The other is the nature of the *boundaries* between regions. A boundary may be weak, permitting one region to influence the other quite easily, or it may be strong, serving as an effective barrier to the influence of adjacent regions.

With these definitions in mind, we can inspect Lewin's growth principles, that is, the principles governing the way the child develops into an adult. Lewin proposed that as the child develops, five sorts of changes occur in the life space. The growing child becomes more *differentiated*, the boundaries between regions become more *rigid*, the space *expands*, regions increase in *complexity of organization,* and behavior becomes more *realistic* (Barker, Dembo, & Lewin, 1943, pp. 441–442). We will look at each of these principles and try to clarify their meanings.

Differentiation   The first principle of development states that as a child grows older, her life space becomes more differentiated (Figure 7.1). This means that regions increase in number and in specificity of function. Dif-

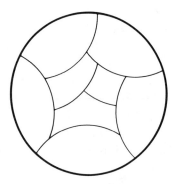

Young child: few regions
with weak boundaries

Adult: many regions
with rigid boundaries

Figure 7.1   Life-Space Structure of the Young Child and the Adult
(Adapted from Kounin, 1943, p. 181)

ferentiation occurs as a result of the child's increased experiences in the world and her increased capacity to perceive differences between one situation and another. For example, as an infant, the child grasps a crayon in a single grip, fingers tightly curled around it, and her only uses of the crayon are to wave it about and put the end into her mouth. But by age 6 she can hold the crayon in several different grips and can manipulate it in many ways, even coloring in such varied shapes as those of a dog, a star, and a triangle. Likewise, in the realm of language, the very young child uses the word *go* to include a wide variety of activities. The older child can differentiate these activities into an array of related concepts such as "let's go," "he went," "shall we go," "if we go," "they are still going," and many more.

Rigidification   The second development principle states that as the child grows up, the boundaries between regions become stronger so that one region is increasingly less influenced by adjacent ones (Figure 7.1).

The phenomenon of rigidification was conceived by Lewin in terms of *tension* arising within a region that is in a state of need. Lewin used the physiological need for food as the model for what he believed happened in other regions of the life space. When hunger arises, tension builds up and motivates the individual to action. In the young child, the tension from the hunger region spreads easily to other regions, influencing others aspects of the life space. But in an older youth, the boundaries between one region and another are greater so that the hunger tension can be expected to exert less influence over other aspects of the life space. With the food analogy in mind, Lewin postulated that other sorts of needs or hungers arise in other regions—such as needs for the approval of other people or for novel and interesting experiences.

To test these ideas about the spread of tension over region boundaries, several of Lewin's disciples conducted a series of experiments that involved children drawing simple outline sketches of animals such as cats, turtles, and rabbits. Each animal was considered to represent a different subregion in the child's life space. The experimenters sought to determine how many copies a child would produce of a given animal before the need in that region was satiated and the tension generated by the need dissipated. They also attempted to judge how much of the tension developed in one region (cat drawings) would spread to another (turtle drawings) and influence the child's attention or interest in the second region.

In one such experiment, a colleague of Lewin's, Joseph Kounin, hypothesized that rigidity increased with chronological age, whereas differentiation increased with mental age (Figure 7.2). To test his hypothesis, Kounin tried the animal-drawing activities with a group of mentally normal children and also with a group of mentally retarded adults whose measured

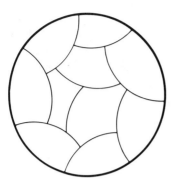

Ten-year-old of normal
intelligence: few regions
with weak boundaries

Retarded adult **with mental**
age of 10: **few regions**
with rigid boundaries

Figure 7.2   Life-Space Structure of the Normal Child and the Mentally
Retarded Adult (Adapted from Kounin, 1943, p. 181)

intellectual maturity was the same as the children's. The experiment confirmed the rigidity hypothesis. The feebleminded adults drew a new animal (turtle) for almost as long as they had the original one (cat). But the normal children, after drawing cats until satiated, drew turtles for a much shorter time. Kounin interpreted this to mean that the boundaries between regions in the adults were stronger or more rigid than those in the children. For the children, the satiation from drawing turtles passed more readily into the region of cats and reduced the children's interest in drawing cats (Kounin, 1943, pp. 194–196). Lewin used the term *co-satiation* to describe this process of the satisfaction (or boredom) of one region reducing the amount of activity needed to satiate the need of another region.

Expansion   As a third principle of development, Lewin stated that the life space of the child enlarges in terms of both time and space as the years pass. Furthermore, the child gains access to an increasing number of regions in his life space as he grows older.

Space expansion occurs for a number of reasons. Physically, the child grows larger, stronger, and more agile, able to coordinate individual movements into complex activities that permit the child to move into more environments and accomplish more tasks. Intellectually she improves her knowledge of the environment and her problem-solving strategies so that she sees more ways to take advantage of more opportunities. Socially, she becomes more responsible, so that those in control of society permit her to engage in more activities under her own supervision. The older youth is allowed to drive a car, stay out late at night, and enter places of entertainment not open to children.

Time expansion occurs because the child has memories of the past and gains access to skills—such as reading and a growing concept of historical time—that extend his vision to include what happened decades and centuries ago. Likewise, the growing child achieves an increasing grasp of the future. He improves his ability to imagine, expect, hope for, and plan what may take place months and years ahead.

Organized Interdependence   According to this interdependence principle, regions of the life space, including segments of the child's behavior, become increasingly interlinked as the child grows older. On the surface this generalization appears to conflict with the principle of rigidification. If the boundaries between regions become stronger with age, doesn't this produce greater independence rather than interdependence of regions? Lewin sought to meet this objection by differentiating between *simple interdependence* and *organizational interdependence*. Simple interdependence is represented by weak boundaries between regions so that the tension or satiation of one region affects adjacent ones. Such simple interdependence decreases as the child grows up. In contrast, organizational interdependence consists of the arrangement of different regions into hierarchical systems or sequences of actions designed to accomplish a more distant or more complex goal. Whereas a one-year-old child has difficulty picking up a small ball and throwing it in a desired direction, a ten-year-old can scoop a baseball into a glove while on the run, can snatch the ball from the glove with the other hand, and can throw it accurately to another child a good distance away. In effect, the ten-year-old can coordinate a sequence of behaviors and regions in her life space to accomplish the goal of putting out a base runner. This is organizational interdependence. In the realm of nonphysical activity, such organization of life-space regions is exhibited in complex intellectual operations—in the child's acts of decoding puzzles, analyzing a diagram of how to build a model airplane, or in creating a drama to be enacted by his or her classmates.

Realism   Finally, normal growth is evidenced by an increase in realism. This is the development of distinctions between levels of reality, between (1) what might be or we wish to be or we imagine could be and (2) what things really are to us. As Baldwin has explained:

> Where realism is high, the boundaries between regions are relatively rigid;
> goals are not reached merely by wishing or imagining but only by behavior

that conforms to some rules. It probably represents the child's acquiring the concept of an objective world external to himself (1967, p. 121).

In summary, then, Lewin saw development as movement toward greater differentiation of life space, toward more rigid boundaries between regions, toward expanded time and space, toward better organized interdependence of activities and regions, and toward greater realism.

Werner's Principles of Development

Poets and theorists alike adopt observations from one aspect of life to explain phenomena in another aspect. The poet Martin Tupper did this when he wrote that the friendship of a child is a "jewel worth a world of pains." Heinz Werner did it when he proposed that the growth of the child's intellect followed the same pattern as (1) the biological evolution of organisms and (2) the development of a society from a primitive state to an advanced condition.

The general features of Werner's plan were not new. They dated back to the recapitulation theory of zoologists of the nineteenth century. This theory, known to biology students as *ontogeny recapitulates phylogeny*, suggests that the evolutionary stages through which species develop (phylogeny) are paralleled by stages in the development of the individual animal or human (ontogeny). This notion had been proposed occasionally by natural scientists and philosophers in earlier centuries, but it acquired its greatest appeal after Darwin traced the steps through which the human species apparently evolved from simpler forms of life over eons of time. Zoologists also observed that the fetal development of more advanced animals and of humans progressed from a single fertilized cell (which might represent a single-celled, simple organism) through many stages that simulated the mature states of increasingly complex organisms or animals. In A. Sidgwick's words, "the developmental history of the individual appears to be a short and simplified repetition, or in a certain sense a recapitulation, of the course of development of the species" (1959, p. 268).

The British philosopher Herbert Spencer (1820–1903) was not content to have the recapitulation theory apply only to biological development. He extended it as well to both psychological and sociological phenomena. In Spencer's opinion, the child developed intellectually from a primitive to an advanced condition. Likewise, primitive societies, he said, represented early stages of the social evolution that eventually produced advanced societies.

In America in the 1890s and early 1900s the chief protagonist of the recapitulation theory in child development was G. Stanley Hall (1904), president and professor of psychology at Clark University. During the early decades of the twentieth century the recapitulation theory fell into disrepute as the result of criticism by biologists, psychologists, and sociologists. By the 1930s and 1940s, developmentalists generally no longer accepted the discredited view that the growing child lives through the same developmental stages as the species but at a highly accelerated pace.

When Werner arrived at Clark University from Germany a half century after Hall had begun his work there, Werner's own views of development looked curiously like a modern version of the recapitulation theory. But Werner pointed out that the similarities were superficial and that he was not espousing Spencer's and Hall's position (Werner, 1961, pp. 24–25). In order to make clear the distinctions he had to offer, let us first consider some of the similarities between Spencer's and Werner's views and then inspect in greater detail the nature of Werner's scheme.

Spencer had defined three basic principles of evolution that he felt applied to all things in the world—to materials organic and inorganic, to psychological growth, and to societies. He proposed that as something develops, it becomes increasingly differentiated in parts and functions, better integrated in the way the parts work together, and more segregated. By segregation, he meant that each part attained more individualized qualities that distinguished it from other parts as time passed (Royce, 1959, p. 392). (Spencer's three principles are not unlike Lewin's principles of differentiation, organized interdependence, and rigidification.)

Just as Spencer sought to identify general principles of evolution, so Werner, with a strong background in both biology and anthropology, set for himself the task of identifying the principles that proper development (orthogenesis) follows in the realms of biological and intellectual growth, with special emphasis on the area of human perception. Werner's studies led him to this general conclusion:

> We assume that organisms are naturally directed toward a series of transformations—reflecting a tendency to move from a state of relative globality and undifferentiatedness towards states of increasing differentiation and hierarchic integration. It is this tendency, formulated as "the orthogenetic principle," which serves for us to characterize development as distinct from other types of change over time (Werner & Kaplan, 1963, p. 7).

Does Werner's subscribing to such a view mean that he believed in the recapitulation theory? Werner said that it does not:

> There exist certain similarities between developmental series. These similarities, for instance between the child's mentality and that of primitive

man, cannot be reduced to conform with any law of recapitulation. It is the very fact of development itself, in so far as it implies a change from generalized to more specialized forms, which gives the false impression of a recapitulation and occasions certain parallel phenomena in two related genetic series. For all practical purposes one may speak of a principle of parallelism: development in mental life follows certain general and formal rules whether it concerns the individual or the species. Such a principle implies that, apart from general and formal similarities, there do exist material differences in the comparable phenomena (1961, pp. 24–25).

Werner's Directiveness Assumption   As implied in Werner's terms *naturally directed* and *tendency,* he believed that it is the nature of the species to grow in the direction of "some preordained end." Werner and his colleague Bernard Kaplan called this belief the *directiveness assumption* and explained that they did not intend directiveness to mean "conscious effort toward an end, so-called 'subjective teleology.' Directiveness in the sense of 'objective teleology' is an observable characteristic of organismic behavior irrespective of any consciousness of ends on the part of the organism" (Werner & Kaplan, 1963, pp. 5–6).

In the concept of directiveness Werner expressed his vision of the human being being activated by a drive to survive and to master his fate. People, compared to other living things, are particularly advanced in their skill of adapting to various environments, a skill that depends to a great extent on the use of symbols that represent objects and ideas—symbols that can be manipulated into new configurations, recorded for later use, and sent from one place to another. Werner and Kaplan wrote:

> Man, destined to conquer the world through knowing, starts out with confusion, disorientation, and chaos, which he struggles to overcome. . . . Man lives constantly in a world of becoming rather than in a world of being. Now it is our contention that in order to build a truly human universe, that is, a world that is known rather than merely reacted to, man requires a new tool, the symbol (Werner & Kaplan, 1963, p. 5).

So it was that Werner pictured development as movement toward greater differentiation, improved integration of the differentiated parts, and ever clearer understanding of the world, an understanding that depended to a large extent on the use of symbols.

In addition to sketching these general outlines of development, Werner embellished the orthogenetic principle with subterms and subaspects. For instance, he used the phrase *syncretic to discrete* in speaking of the child's progressing from an undifferentiated to a differentiated being. *Syncresis* refers to global actions or concepts, in which terms a child acts or perceives things early in life. As the child grows up, these general actions or ideas separate out into more discrete, identifiably different constituent parts. For example, a one-year-old infant's attempts to pick up a pencil are marked by a single gross movement of arm and body and hand, but a ten-year-old's attempts show far more differentiation of parts. The body does not move at all; only the arm and hand move. The wrist bends, and the thumb and forefinger easily grasp the pencil in a pincer movement that does not require the rest of the fingers. In addition, the ten-year-old's grasp can be altered to accommodate different objects, such as a tennis ball, a pebble, a worm, a hammer, and a wet orange seed. Differentiation of parts of the arm and hand makes such accommodation possible.

Syncresis that develops into greater discreteness is seen in intellectual growth as well. The young child displays *holophrasis* in his speech. That is, the child uses one word to represent an entire situation or series of actions that an older youth would describe in a variety of words that more completely delineate the elements of the situation. For example, the two-year-old may say "Go car" to encompass the request that the adolescent might express as, "If Dad's driving to town this morning, I'd like to go along."

Although Werner believed that development proceeds from the syncretic to the discrete, he did not propose that the adult loses the ability to perceive in a syncretic manner. For example, an adult can grasp the general impression of a room she enters, or can take in the general panorama of a mountain landscape in addition to analyzing it discretely, part by part. Furthermore, as Baldwin has explained:

> Syncresis is primitive, in the sense that it is characteristic of children and primitive man and of perception under conditions of impoverished input, but it is not, per se, maladaptive, disordered, or incompatible with the more discrete varieties of perception that characterize everyday adult life (1967, p. 502).

Articulation, Flexibility, and Stability   Not only does development move toward discreteness, but the parts become increasingly articulated. This factor of *articulation* is like Lewin's organized interdependence. As the child grows older, the increasingly differentiated aspects of physical and mental life are arranged into hierarchies and interlinked sequences that permit complex thoughts and actions. The young child who wishes to ride in the car with his or her father cannot smoothly string together a series of interdependent thoughts that take into consideration past and future conditions, as can the teenager who might say, "If Dad's driving to town this morning, I'd like to go along and take my skis to be fixed. And since Caroline got to take Linda last time, I think it's my turn to take friends—like Frank and Ted, or at least Frank, if he doesn't have to work today."

As another orthogenetic subprinciple, Werner proposed that development moves from a state of rigidity toward greater flexibility. On first consideration, this principle appears in conflict with Lewin's concept of rigidification. Does Werner say children become less rigid and Lewin claim they become more rigid as they grow older? Closer inspection of their definitions shows that the answer is no. They really are not in conflict, for the two theorists used *rigid* in quite different ways. Whereas Lewin coined *rigidification* to identify an increasing discreteness of life-space regions (stronger barriers between regions), Werner used *rigid* to indicate the young child's inability to adapt present concepts or skills to suit new environmental demands. To Werner, the older child is more flexible, more sensitive to subtle changes in surroundings, and better prepared to select from a repertoire of behaviors those that can adequately handle these changes. The older child not only draws from a broader repertoire of ideas and actions but is better prepared to alter existing ideas and skills to meet new demands. For instance, when a young child plays the game of checkers, he typically conceives of a very limited number of ways to move the discs, and he cannot predict very well what influence a present move may have on subsequent moves. In contrast, the older, more experienced child plays a more flexible game. She can readily conceive of several possible present moves and can more accurately foresee the likely consequences for future moves. She is also assisted by her greater ability to imagine her opponent's responses to her moves.

Another direction of orthogenetic growth in Werner's model is from instability toward stability. This characteristic is readily illustrated in the area of children's interests and attention. The young child's interests and concentration are labile, shifting easily from one thing to another. But by the time he reaches adolescence, he is able to concentrate longer on one thing, he can conceive of long-term goals to pursue, and his interests become increasingly stable.

Finally, Werner believed that the passing years allow the child to differentiate more clearly between self and the world. The infant at first fails to distinguish self from non-self. And when she begins to do so, she perhaps feels that satisfying things are self and nonsatisfying ones are non-self. So the oppositeness or separateness of self and the world "is relatively lacking in early childhood and increases with age. . . . The fundamental nature of the 'self:world' polarity is particularly evident under those circumstances where it breaks down, for example, in pathology," with *pathology* referring to such states of confused identity as schizophrenia (Wapner & Werner, 1965, p. 10).

Thus, as the foregoing examples illustrate, Werner believed that it is the nature of humans to develop physically and psychologically toward increased (1) differentiation of parts and their functions, (2) integration of individual parts to form complex behaviors and intricate thought patterns, (3) flexibility in adapting actions and thoughts to changing environmental conditions, (4) stability of interest and intention, and (5) distinctions between self and the world.

STAGES OF DEVELOPMENT: LEWIN AND WERNER

Lewin's Analysis

Although Lewin considered the identification of growth *principles* more important than the description of growth *stages,* he did give attention to stages in two different ways. First, he acknowledged the popularly recognized growth periods, such as infancy, early childhood, and adolescence. Second, he identified phases through which children pass in several specific areas of their lives, such as the areas of play and of drawing activities. We can illustrate the way he applied topology to such matters by describing some examples of his work.

General Growth Periods   Lewin mentioned general growth periods in his essays and research reports and occasionally dedicated an essay to explaining how a given period could be analyzed by means of topological diagrams. He used two kinds of topological diagrams to illustrate his concepts of the differences between general stages of development. For instance, when he wrote about adolescence, he described it as a stage of instability, a time of locomotion from one stable period (late childhood) to another stable but as yet poorly comprehended stage (adulthood). Lewin believed that the adolescent's life space was forced into a labile, fluid state by the puzzling bodily changes brought on by puberty, by the youth's growing intellect, and by the new opportunities for social freedom offered by society. To compound his problems, the teenager in the modern Western world is not quite sure about how much freedom he really has or wants. In short, after late childhood, the terrain ahead is poorly mapped in the youth's mind. The "cognitively unstructured character" of the new situation causes the adolescent to be shy, sensitive, or aggressive. Emotional tensions arise from the conflict between the various attitudes, values, and styles of life of the period being left

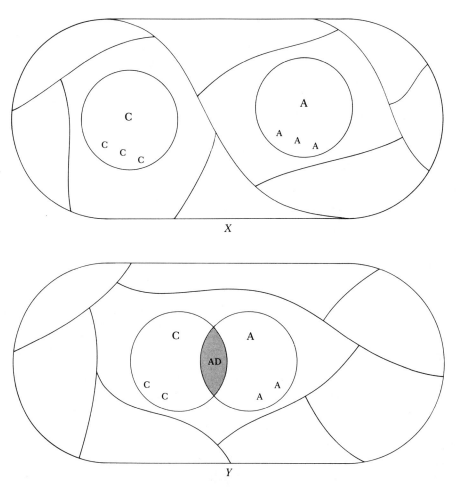

Figure 7.3   Society's Structure for Children, Adolescents, and Adults
(After Lewin, 1939, p. 882)

(childhood) and the one vaguely seen ahead (adulthood). The youth is apt to take extreme attitudes in politics or social behavior and to shift positions radically. He is like an emigrant to a new culture—the sociologist's *marginal man*—living with both old and new cultures but not completely accepted by either. Lewin illustrated this aspect of adolescence by the sorts of diagrams shown in Figure 7.3.

While Figure 7.3 represents the relationships among groups in society, Figure 7.4 represents the shift within the life space of the individual as she or he passes from the clearly defined regions and boundaries of childhood through the shifting, vague regions of adolescence, and into the clearly delineated life space of mature adulthood.

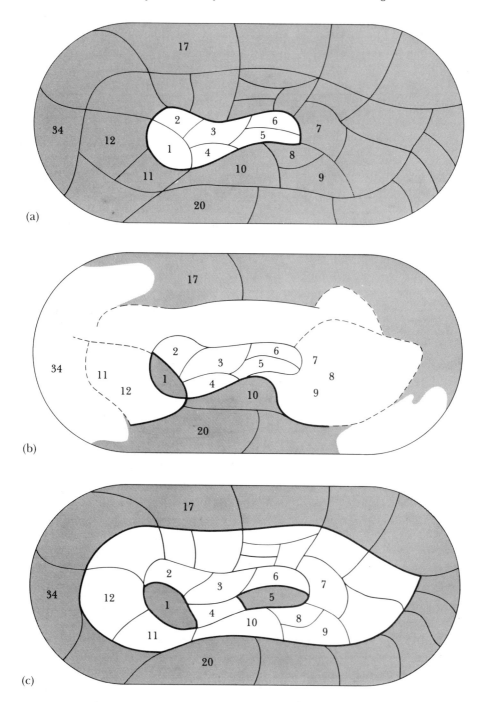

(a)

(b)

(c)

Figure 7.4 Space of Free Movement of the Child, Adolescent, and Adult (After Lewin, 1939, pp. 875, 877)

As the upper (*X*) diagram in Figure 7.3 shows, the world of the child (C) is distinct from the world of the adult (A). Individual children (c, c, c) and adults (a, a, a) know their roles clearly. As the lower (*Y*) diagram shows, the adolescent (AD) is caught as the marginal man between the two worlds and thus does not clearly know his role or the "rules of the game."

In Figure 7.4a, the child's space of free movement is shown by white regions, which are clearly separated by rigid boundaries from the adult space (shaded). Regions 1–6 represent such activities as getting into the movies at half price and belonging to the Boy Scouts or Girl Scouts. For the adolescent (shown in Figure 7.4b), the space of free movement is not well defined in many instances. For some activities the expectations are clear. The adolescent can no longer get into the movies at half price (region 1), nor can he yet vote or buy alcoholic beverages (10), but he does acquire new privileges (7–9, 11–12), such as a driver's license, a chance to stay out late at night, and freedom to smoke, although even these are not guaranteed. The adult space (Figure 7.4c) includes far more regions, regions that are clearly defined. However, some activities are prohibited, such as half-fare movies (1) and certain childish acts (5). Prohibited also are such activities as killing people (20) and entering occupations for which she or he is unprepared (17, 34).

Growth Stages in a Specific Realm of Life   In an experiment entitled "Frustration and Regression," Lewin and his co-workers studied thirty children, ages 2 to 5, in free play with a variety of toys (Barker, Dembo, & Lewin, 1943). Each child was observed as the child played alone with the toys in a room. Later, a transparent screen was lowered in the middle of the room, separating the child from the most attractive toys, while the experimenters observed the child now playing with the remaining, less appealing ones. This experimental arrangement enabled the researchers to note two things: (1) the level of constructiveness of play before and after the screen was lowered and (2) the extent to which the level of the child's play was influenced by separation from the more appealing toys.

From the experiment, the research team concluded that play with toys like trucks, dolls, and a playhouse can be divided into at least eight levels of constructiveness, levels that are correlated with age. They also concluded that after the children experienced the frustration of the barrier being lowered, they regressed to a lower level of constructiveness during the subsequent play period (Barker, Dembo, & Lewin, 1943, pp. 452–456). The nature of these levels of constructiveness can be illustrated by the following three examples:

Level 2: The toys are superficially examined. Example: The child sits on the floor and picks up the truck.

Level 5: More complicated, elaborate manipulation. Example: Truck and trailer unloaded, detached, pulled in circles, reattached, detached, reattached, pulled in circles.

Level 7: Dramatic meaning given to play by composing a story involving a larger setting than the experimental room. Example: "Here's a car truck, and it's going out fishing, so we have to take the trailer off. First, we have to go to the gas station. Toot, toot." Gets gas, goes back for trailer and fishing pole, and attaches a motor boat to the truck and trailer. "Hummmm! There he goes" (Barker, Dembo, & Lewin, 1943, pp. 449–450).

In this way Lewin and his associates identified stages of development for specific realms of child behavior. However, the task of specifying such stages was not pursued for its own value but was incidental to the researchers' investigating theoretical issues of greater interest to them. For instance, in the play experiment the primary concern was the nature of children's reactions to frustration, and the play-constructiveness hierarchy was devised as a necessary instrument for measuring hypothesized regression following frustration.

Werner's Analysis

Like Lewin, Werner's main concern was with identifying growth principles or directions rather than spelling out the nature of growth stages. However, Werner did not entirely neglect the matter of stages. To understand his position, we can cast the opposite sides of the continuity–discontinuity argument as a pair of questions: Do new forms of development emerge gradually and continuously out of old forms, so that there are no discernible steps or stages? Or do novel forms spring up to replace the old, producing discontinuous steps or levels? In Werner's opinion, both of these processes occur. The general movement of development is continuous and unbroken, but periodically, along this growth incline, steps are seen. "On the one side, the orthogenetic principle in *overall terms* . . . necessarily implies continuity. On the other hand, concrete forms and operations, novel functions and structures 'emerge,' and in this respect changes are discontinuous" (Werner & Kaplan, 1963, pp. 7–8).

However, in Werner's system, when a new form of behavior or thought replaces an earlier one, the earlier form is not lost. It is simply subordinated to the newer form. In a sense, it is put on a back shelf to be retrieved if needed. Under ordinary circumstances the growing child uses the newer, more advanced behavior pattern. However, under special internal or external circumstances the old, discarded patterns may come to the fore again. Samples of such internal circumstances are dream states, pathological conditions, or intoxication by certain drugs. Unusual external conditions most often take the form of difficult or novel tasks. In facing a novel task, the child frequently returns to a more primitive mode of functioning before progressing toward "full-fledged higher operations; we may refer to this tendency as a manifestation of the *genetic principle of spirality*" (Werner & Kaplan, 1963, p. 8).

In a number of subrealms of development, Werner identified growth stages. However, unlike Gesell, he did not attach specific age designations to the stages. We can illustrate the way he treated such growth steps by citing those he proposed for two sorts of communication—gesture and speech. For example, when a child gives a close representation (by gesture) of the shape or use or (by speech) of the sound of an object she sees, a low level of communication is involved. As she matures, her reference to the object becomes less and less a direct representation. The symbols eventually used will typically have no apparent similarity to the objects they represent at all. This developmental trend was labeled *distancing* by Werner (Werner & Kaplan, 1963, pp. 82–83).

In summary, Werner identified stages in various realms of behavior. However, he did not formulate these into a single system, as did Piaget, nor did he specify ages when the typical child would be in each stage.

Lewin's Analysis of Decisions

Lewin used topology not only to illustrate growth principles and the nature of developmental stages but also to explain why a child acts in a particular way at a given moment. To do this, he first assumed that children's behavior is goal-directed. A child acts in order to achieve a goal that will satisfy a felt need. Achieving the goal, however, is not always easy, for the child may be caught between two incompatible needs at the same time. Or there may be physical, social, or psychological barriers to be overcome or bypassed before the goal is reached. Consequently, at any given moment, the child's life space consists of a variety of regions or elements, each exerting a particular amount of force in a given direction. The final decision about how to act is determined by which of these forces proves most powerful.

To illustrate the manner in which decision-making situations have been charted by Lewinians, let's examine the simple problem of a child's being faced with two desirable alternatives—a kindergarten girl is attracted by both the doll-play corner and the easel-painting corner of the classroom. As

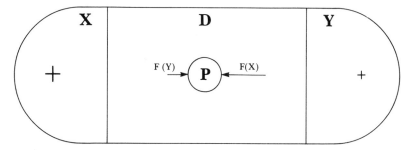

Figure 7.5   Choosing between Two Attractive Alternatives

Figure 7.5 shows, the situation can be diagrammed as three life-space regions. Region X is the doll-play corner, region Y the easel-painting corner, and region D the decision-making condition in which the girl finds herself. She is symbolized by the circled P (for "person") in region D. Lewin adopted the term *valence* from the physical sciences to represent the psychological power or strength of a region or fact in the life space. A positive valence attracts the child toward that region, while a negative valence repels the child. The plus (+) signs in regions X and Y represent their valence values. The heavier and larger plus in region X shows that playing with a doll has a stronger attraction for the girl, so we can expect her to resolve the problem by going to the doll corner. The arrows pointing at the child (P) suggest the comparative power of the forces toward X and Y. The force toward X—shown as the long arrow F(X)—is stronger than the force toward Y—the short arrow F(Y).

Although the kindergarten example illustrates how decision situations can be charted, it does not show how more complex decisions are diagramed. A more complex step is shown in Figure 7.6, which introduces barriers (region B_A) into the life space. Figure 7.6 represents the problem of a boy, Harry, who is trying to decide which of two girls to invite to the high school dance. He likes both of them, so both are represented by positive valences (regions A and B). But he finds Betty (region B) more attractive than Ann (region A), partly because his friend Bart has dated Betty and found her to be a lot of fun. Bart though is probably going to ask Betty to the dance. Consequently, Harry faces the likelihood that he will alienate his friend Bart if he tries to date the more attractive Betty. This fear of alienation serves as a psychological barrier (region B_A) to his asking Betty to the dance. The barrier, therefore, is exerting a force on Harry opposite to that of the positive valence of Betty. This barrier force, which represents Bart's interest in Betty, is symbolized by the $F(B_A)$ arrow and functions in two ways. It enhances Betty's attractiveness, making her a prize particularly worth win-

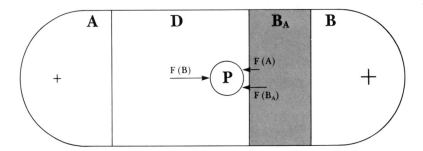

Figure 7.6   The Function of a Barrier in Decision Making

ning, but at the same time it threatens the friendship with Bart. In the end, Harry resolves the problem by asking Ann to the dance because the combined forces in Ann's direction, F(A) and F(B$_A$), overpower the single strong force, F(B), in Betty's direction. Thus Harry prefers Betty, partly because she is hard to get, but chooses Ann because the psychological price of getting Betty is too high.

Of course, most of life's decisions are not as simple as those pictured in our two examples. At any moment of decision there are multiple attractions and barriers exerting force on an individual. To diagram the life space under these conditions requires far more complex topological maps than those of Figures 7.5 and 7.6. Lewinians, in their theorizing, have produced many varieties of diagrams, each intended to elucidate a particular sort of decision or to propose new hypotheses.*

It is also important to recognize the connection between Lewin's view of decision making and his principles of development. As the child grows up and her life space changes, her decision-making mechanism is altered in ways described by these principles. For example, a seven-year-old boy and a seventeen-year-old boy who are ostensibly facing the same decision are actually facing quite different decisions because their life spaces are so different. Let us assume that in the case of each boy there is a girl at school who has invited him to visit her after school. She tells him the street on which she lives, a street more than a mile from his own home, but forgets to give him the house number. When the boy gets home after school, he must decide whether to visit the girl and, if he does, by what means of transportation. If we recall Lewin's main principles of development, we can estimate significant ways in which the seven-year-old's and the seventeen-year-old's life spaces will differ. Because the seventeen-year-old's life space is more

*A sampling of Lewinian maps is found in Baldwin's third chapter (1967).

expansive in space and time, he can be expected to see more realistic possibilities for modes of transportation to the girl's home than the seven-year-old: he can walk, or drive the family car, or use his bicycle or his skateboard. He is also more likely to perceive possible ways of finding the girl's house number. Thus his life-space regions of transportation possibilities and of finding his destination are more *differentiated* than those of the seven-year-old.

Let us also assume that when each boy was age 5, he became separated from his mother during a shopping trip, and for more than an hour had feared being abandoned. Now, as each boy faces this current decision, we may speculate that the seven-year-old is more likely to be influenced by this fear from the past than is the seventeen-year-old; the boundaries between subregions (the past and present incidents) are more *rigid* in the seventeen-year-old and he is more *realistic* in estimating consequences than is the younger boy. Finally, we might expect that the older boy would coordinate his activities in arriving at the decision and carrying it out more effectively than the younger one because he has become more adept at *organizing* the complex of regions that compose his life space.

In short, the decision-making process is influenced by developmental differences that affect the structure of a child's space, as conceived in Lewinian theory.

PRACTICAL APPLICATIONS

When the word *practical* is used to mean "guidance in solving problems of child rearing and education," then the principles of development proposed by Lewin and Werner hardly qualify as practical. The principles may help parents and teachers a bit in interpreting the behavior of children at different age levels, but knowing and accepting the principles is unlikely to help adults decide how to treat children. The same is true of Lewin's model of decision making. As an ex post facto explanation of why a child decided to act in a certain way, his model can be of some intellectual interest. But it does not enable us to predict how a child will act, because, even if the model is a true representation of decision making, we typically lack knowledge of the factors in the child's life space that bear on a particular decision. And even if we were able to discover all the factors, we might still be ignorant of their relative valences and their powers for influencing the decision.

In effect, both Lewin's and Werner's principles are of some use to people who speculate about the general directions in which development moves, but the principles seem of little value in the daily work of parents, teachers, physicians, and youth-group leaders.

RESEARCH CHALLENGES

Perhaps the most noteworthy line of research spawned in recent decades out of Lewin's theorizing has been the series of studies in *ecological psychology*. Apparently the theoretical notion behind this sort of research was Lewin's idea of life space, his belief that a child's behavior at any moment is not simply a result of the child's psychological history. Rather, the child's life space is composed of both the present remnants of his or her developmental history and significant sociophysical forces now in the child's immediate environment. In the hands of ecological psychologists, Lewin's notion took a strong environmental turn, emphasizing the growing child's surroundings. Here is the way the movement developed.

After Lewin's death in 1947, two of his colleagues, Roger W. Barker and H. F. Wright, made it their mission at the University of Kansas to investigate the role of environmental forces in a child's life space. Noting that in biology the term *ecology* refers to the interrelationship between a plant or animal and its environment, Barker and Wright borrowed the term to describe their way of studying how children's surroundings affect their behavior and development.

The most basic conviction behind ecological theory is that a child's behavior patterns and personality are, to a great extent, fashioned by the environments the child inhabits. The task of an ecological theorist is to describe the anatomy and operating principles of such environments.

Barker has noted that traditional psychology shows ways in which people differ from each other but fails to trace the great variations in thought, feeling, and action that an individual child experiences during a typical day. Furthermore, according to Barker, a large proportion of this variation within a single child's life can be accounted for by the environments or *behavior settings* through which the child commonly moves. In effect, ecological theorists contend that we can account for a great deal of a child's behavior if we know her current environment.

For example, we can predict that if a typical teenager is in church, she will not shout, but if she is at a basketball game, she will shout loud and long. We can predict that if she is in the middle of an ice-skating rink, she will not be sitting reading a book, but if she is home in bed at nine o'clock, she may very well be reading. If she is walking to the drug store, we can predict that she will not be walking in line, but if she is in the school band in the Fourth of July parade, she will be carefully keeping in line and in step with her companions.

Components of Behavior Settings

To move ecological theory beyond these commonsense observations, Barker and his colleagues have identified and labeled a variety of components of behavior settings. Consequently, the nature of a child's significant surroundings can be analyzed more systematically. For example, ecological psychologists have proposed that a behavior setting (such as a history class or a dinner party) is composed of two main elements: (1) typical ways people act (called *standing patterns of behavior*) and (2) the *milieu,* which is made up of two components. The first component is *physical things*—desks and wall maps in history class, the dining table and silverware at the dinner party. The second is *time boundaries*—a forty-five-minute class period, a two-hour dinner party. The milieu is said to be circumjacent to (that is, it encompasses) the behavior of the people in the setting. These terms have been created by ecological theorists to help organize their observations of the environments in which children grow up.

Ecological psychology is not simply an intellectual pastime—it has proven to be a useful tool for answering practical questions. One of the most detailed applications of the approach has been the analysis of the way small and large high schools can differ in how they influence adolescents' development. During an investigation in several schools in the midwestern United States, Barker and his colleagues accurately predicted that students of smaller high schools engage in a wider variety of activities, assume more responsibility, hold more extracurricular positions of importance, and are more highly motivated to take active part in voluntary activities than students in larger schools. These discoveries led Barker and his co-workers to conclude that:

> The educational process . . . thrives on participation, enthusiasm, and responsibility. Our findings and our theory posit a negative relationship between school size and individual student participation. What seems to happen is that as schools get larger and (their behavior) settings more heavily populated, more of the students are less needed; they become superfluous, redundant. . . . A school should be small enough that students are not redundant (Barker et al., 1970, p. 42).

In this way, ecological theory has contributed to the literature on child psychology and furnished suggestions about how behavior settings might be arranged to promote children's more satisfactory development.

The case of Lewin brings up the question of whether research challenges credited to a theorist truly derive from the theory itself or, instead, are more a result of the theorist's research inventiveness than a logical outcome of the theory. For instance, K. W. Spence, a leading behaviorist in the field of learning, has written that:

> Lewin employs very fragmentary parts or subsystems of topology. As for the formal system of dynamics, it remains thus far closeted . . . in Lewin's

mind. Like so many of these field theorists, Lewin sets up a most attractive program for theory. Taken in conjunction with his interesting experiments the illusion is nicely created that there is some connection between them (1963, p. 168).

When Lewin was at the University of Iowa, the group that worked with him produced an influential series of developmental research studies. But, as Spence has suggested, it remains a matter of debate as to whether such productivity was generated chiefly by Lewin's theorizing or by his experimental ingenuity and the sorts of enthusiastic colleagues and students he attracted.

In recent years, other than among ecological psychologists, few if any development studies appear to trace their origins to Lewinian theory. Yet among Lewin's theoretical proposals there are still questions to be answered for anyone interested in pursuing them. For example, in relation to our comments about practical applications, what methods can be used to discover which life-space factors influence a child's decision making at various stages of development? To what extent are children at different age levels conscious of the factors affecting their decisions? And how do the consequences of a decision made today alter the child's life space and affect decisions in the future?

Werner's Research Methodology

Werner, like Lewin, not only proposed general growth principles but also produced a good deal of empirical research and stimulated others to do the same. Again like Lewin, he interpreted the results of his research as support for his growth principles. But there is a question of whether his growth-principle theorizing generated the empirical studies or he merely used the theory to interpret studies that actually derived more from his ingenuity at contriving experiments on perception. An example of his investigative methodology is found in his studies of children's perceptions of language. In one kind of experiment, a nonsense word was inserted into each of a series of sentences. The child's task was to analyze the sentences to determine which familiar English word might properly substitute for the nonsense word. Here is one such series (Baldwin, 1967, p. 511):

1. You can't fill anything with a *contavish.*
2. The more you take out of a *contavish,* the larger it gets.
3. Before the house is finished, the walls must have *contavishes.*
4. You can't feel or touch a *contavish.*

5. A bottle has only one *contavish*.

6. John fell in a *contavish* in the road.

The experimenter asked children of different age levels to insert a single word that would fit reasonably into each sentence in the series; they also asked the children to explain how and why they arrived at the answers they gave. By analyzing children's responses, Werner and his staff were able to identify sorts of thinking that appeared to follow orthogenetic principles.

For example, some children thought of a word that would make sense in the first sentence—such as *smile* or *space*. However, they considered this a final solution, applicable to all the rest of the sentences, rather than as a tentative or trial word that had to be tested in all six sentences before it could be accepted as the proper solution. When they came to subsequent sentences, these children either blindly inserted their first word or engaged in specious logic to force the fit, such as, "People are happy that the walls are all up, so they smile at their new house." This is the argument they used to defend the use of *smile* in sentence 3. Werner found that younger children more often stayed with their first guess, while older children more often considered their first try as a tentative estimate that might need adjusting or eliminating as later sentences were faced. The researchers interpreted this trend as support for the orthogenetic direction of growth from the rigid to the flexible.

Other patterns of answers that children offered seemed, in Werner's opinion, to illustrate the principle of greater differentiation as the child got older. For example, some children could not conceive that the key word for which they were searching could assume different meanings in different sentences. Furthermore, some of the younger elementary school children in the experiment felt that the word they were hunting for had the meaning of the entire sentence. This is the phenomenon of holophrasis mentioned earlier. For these children *contavishes* meant "having something in the walls when the house is finished." Or a *contavish* was "a bottle with something in it." The older children were far more capable of differentiating the word's meaning according to its context and also of seeing the word as a unit by itself—as part of the sentence and not as the conveyor of the entire meaning of the sentence.

In these ways and in a variety of others, Werner used the results of such experiments to support and illustrate orthogenetic theory. In addition, his experiments provided data for use by other psychologists and suggested new phenomena for Werner and his colleagues to investigate and to integrate into orthogenetic psychology.

LEWIN'S AND WERNER'S THEORIES:
AN ASSESSMENT

In evaluating the two theories along the nine dimensions introduced in Chapter One, I will first consider Lewin's views and then Werner's. So that the comparison of the two theories can be readily grasped, ratings of both theories are plotted on the same chart, with the letter *L* indicating the rating for Lewin and *W* for Werner.

Lewin's Work

The interest of child psychologists in Lewinian theory reached a peak in the late 1930s and in the 1940s when the works of Lewin and his associates were first being published. Since then, the influence of topological child psychology has declined. Today it is represented by a few key concepts that have entered the general body of theory and by works of certain of Lewin's followers who have evolved their own variants of his approach.

The rather high mark on item 1 (reflects the real world of children) is based principally on my belief that one of Lewin's lasting contributions was his emphasis on the complexity of forces exerted on the individual child to determine behavior at a given moment. The terms *life space* and *psychological field* have been accepted into the child psychologist's general vocabulary in recognition of this. The emphasis is in contrast to the simplistic notion that a single, isolated stimulus causes an individual's response. Furthermore, Lewinian theory has high potential for explaining individual differences among children the same age since it proposes that the combination of facts comprising one child's life space differs from that of another. As further evidence of the real life foundations of Lewinian theory, we should note that he and his colleagues did not merely speculate about what children might be like; they conducted an extensive series of experiments and observational studies of children's actual behavior.

However, there still remains some question about how truly the topological maps of life space are reflections of the real operation of children's development dynamics. This question about the validity of the theory has caused me to mark item 1 somewhat short of the highest rating. The issues that lie behind this question are discussed in the following paragraphs.

The high rating on item 8 (stimulates new discoveries) is based on Lewin's being credited with generating a large amount of innovative research on children. Lewin had a talent not only for developing his own research proposals but also for motivating students and colleagues to carry out novel studies. Reports of these investigations typically have included descriptions of the empirical results and interpretations of what the results mean from a topological-psychological viewpoint. However, as noted earlier, there are psychologists who would question whether it is Lewin's theory or Lewin the man that deserves credit for such a high rating.

The comments about the questionable relationship between the theory and the experiments brings us to the matters of clarity of description (item 2) and internal consistency (item 5) of Lewin's system. I would agree with those psychologists who value Lewin's topological diagrams as a means of illustrating the dynamics of his conception of life space. The maps are helpful supplements to the verbal descriptions of concepts that most theorists use to explain their systems. Likewise, the empirical studies of children that Lewin used as the raw material for his theorizing function as real life bridges

Lewin's and Werner's Theories

How well do I think the theory meets the standards?

The Standards	Very Well	Moderately Well	Very Poorly
1. Reflects the real world of children	W L		
2. Is clearly understandable	W	L	
3. Explains the past and predicts the future			LW
4. Guides child rearing			LW
5. Is internally consistent	W	L	
6. Is economical	W	L	
7. Is falsifiable			WL
8. Stimulates new discoveries	L	W	
9. Is self-satisfying		LW	

between his abstract ideas and his readers' own ways of looking at children. These, then, are factors in favor of marking Lewinian theory high on clarity.

However, at the same time, there is the kind of confusion noted by Spence. Lewin has been criticized for not presenting his theory in a single book or essay, for not showing how all the parts fit together consistently. He drew ideas from various "hard science" disciplines but did not define his concepts clearly enough or use them consistently (such as the concept of "region") so as to make them clearly understandable to a large number of his readers. Furthermore, the elements of life space are not sufficiently accessible to observation or measurement to permit scientists to determine their composition and power. Thus Lewinians have frequently needed to turn to illustrative anecdotes, like the ones I created about the kindergarten girl and the high school dance, to convince their audience of the validity of their theory. To arrive at a rating on item 2, I matched the positive factors against the negative ones and decided the theory overall was only moderately clear.

This same evidence bears on the theory's internal consistency (item 5). As Baldwin has observed:

> Field theorists share a common approach to problems and much of the same terminology, but they have not exerted much effort to build a coherent total theory of a mechanism that governs human behavior. . . . Lewinian investigators often use some commonsense term as the starting point for research, without being too concerned about how the concepts will eventually fit others in the theory. They seem to have a faith that if individual problems are carefully investigated and analyzed, the working hypotheses will eventually fit together (1967, p. 142).

For these reasons, I have given Lewinian theory only a moderate score for its internal consistency.

Again for the same reasons—and particularly for inconsistencies in the coordination among such concepts as regions and barriers—I have rated the theory only moderate in its economy of explanation (item 6).

On falsifiability (item 7) the theory deserves a low mark. If we wish to test the validity of a model of development, the terms it employs can be dealt with most readily if they have unequivocal definitions tied closely to observable events in the world. Furthermore, the connections hypothesized between terms or concepts need to be clear enough so that we are not likely to arrive at alternative or, in particular, at conflicting conclusions from our observations of child behavior. Lewinian concepts in many instances are not characterized by such clarity. It is true that Lewin's group have conducted controlled experiments and have carefully observed children in their natural habitats. These sources of data have been useful in estimating the validity of theoretical concepts.

However, Lewinian studies have also depended on phenomenological introspection by the subjects who participate in the experiments and by the researchers themselves. Such testimonial data furnish less secure bases for testing the theory's validity than does more objective, publicly observable child behavior, at least in the opinion of those who follow the research tradition of the physical sciences. It is not clear today how we can determine the accuracy or profitability of conceiving of an individual's life space as consisting of regions separated by barriers, with each region involving tensions or needs. How can we test this conception?

Lewin's system appears weak also in its ability to explain the past and predict the future (item 3) and guide child rearing (item 4). The very concept of life space as a highly complex field whose regions and forces shift each moment has contributed to the weakness of the theory in predicting and guiding a specific child's development. If we are to forecast how a child will act, we need to know what regions are currently active and how the forces among regions are patterned. If this idea of life space is an accurate representation of a child's psychological environment, then in the present imprecise state of psychological measurement, it is not possible to produce the data we need to make predictions. Our methods of assessing the types and powers of goals, needs, barriers, abilities, fears, fatigue, and the rest of the facts of life space are simply too primitive to furnish the information required for either predicting or guiding child development. In addition, our capacity to explain past behavior from a Lewinian viewpoint is nearly as inadequate. It is true that after Harry has asked Ann to the dance, we can safely conclude that the forces in her favor were greater than those in favor of Betty. But we still cannot specify all the regions of Harry's life space at the time he arrived at his decision, nor can we identify the amount and direction of force exerted by any given region. These problems of Lewinian theory with decision making have helped stimulate social psychologists over the past three decades to propose other ways of explaining the dynamics under-lying decisions.

What, then, should be the overall rating for Lewin's system in terms of being self-satisfying (item 9)? On the credit side, Lewin opened new perspec-tives on development by adopting ideas from mathematics and physics. This adaptation helped stimulate a significant amount of novel empirical re-search with children. In addition, Lewin's diagrams have helped people visualize his postulated psychological forces and, consequently, understand his proposals more easily. Furthermore, the general growth principles he proposed—differentiation, rigidification, expansion, organized inter-dependence, and realism—have furnished developmentalists with ways to view the trends in change from infancy to adulthood.

On the debit side, the key concepts of the theory are a mixture of commonsense ideas and more precisely defined theoretical constructs. The theory is somewhat segmented, with gaps and inconsistencies among the parts, and the elements of life space are not sufficiently accessible to appraisal to permit researchers to determine their composition or power. In sum, the Lewinian theory is only moderately self-satisfying.

We might note that an appraisal of Lewin's theory like this would not likely distress him very much, for he did not consider his scheme a finished product. He saw theorizing as a continuing process or strategy for guiding investigation, not as a completed structure depicting the true anatomy of development. When viewed from this perspective, Lewin's theorizing apparently did fulfill his expectations.

Werner's Work

I find that Werner's theory is clear (item 2) and internally consistent (item 5), so I give these the highest marks. The theory is also economical (item 6), in the sense that it does not propose a complicated set of concepts when a simpler set will do. Werner's general growth principles are few in number, and he applies them in a reasonable manner to explain the results of his experiments.

Furthermore, Werner's theory appears to closely reflect the real world of children, a result of his carrying on a continuing series of empirical studies of children's language and perceptual behavior (item 1). Thus I rate him highly on this scale.

I believe Werner also deserves a rather high rating on item 8 (stimulates new discoveries). In books written by developmentalists, his name appears often, attesting to other authors' recognition of his contributions. Further-more, he developed such research tools as the series of sentences containing a nonsense word and techniques for testing perception, all of which have added to experimenters' arsenal of investigative methods. Also, students of Werner such as Seymour Wapner and Jonas Langer have contributed signif-icantly to the field of development using orthogenetic theory.

However, items 3 (explains past, predicts future) and 4 (guides child rearing) are a different matter. Only in a most general sense do Werner's contributions enable us to predict a child's future development or explain the child's past growth. And they offer little or no advice about how to raise a child. This is not surprising, for Werner's goal was to discover general developmental principles, not techniques for guiding the treatment of individual children. Thus I have rated the theory low on these items.

In terms of falsifiability (item 7), orthogenetic theory seems to me to rank low in the moderately well range. Whenever a theory is composed of general principles of development whose application depends to a considerable degree upon personal interpretation, then it is difficult to conceive of tests that would show unequivocably whether the theory is true or false. Such is the case with orthogenetic theory. It is not difficult for advocates of the theory to cite instances of behavior that can serve as evidence that the principles are true. But at the same time, people who are critical of the theory can take the same instances and, by interpreting them differently, claim that the principles are false or in need of some revision.

For example, a mother brings her five-year-old daughter to kindergarten on the first day of school. As they enter the room, the daughter dashes immediately to a rocking horse, while the mother pauses to gaze about the entire room. A critic of orthogenetic theory might cite this incident as evidence that Werner's syncretic-to-discrete principle does not explain such behavior. If behavior progresses from the syncretic to the discrete (from the undifferentiated or global to the differentiated or specific), then why did the girl focus immediately on the rocking horse and her mother look generally around the room? A supporter of Werner's theory, however, might suggest that this is the wrong interpretation of the incident. In the first place, the supporter might say that moving from the undifferentiated to the discrete in visual perception is a momentary developmental trend—the person first sees the whole, then the parts that comprise it, all in a moment or two. So just seeing the mother's and daughter's gross actions does not tell us that they failed to perceive in a syncretic-to-discrete manner, nor does it tell us that the daughter's move in perception from syncretic to discrete occurred as rapidly as her mother's. Furthermore, a defender of orthogenetic theory might say that the incident in the kindergarten could be instead an example of the rigidity-to-flexibility principle. The child's running to the rocking horse might suggest less flexibility of behavior than the mother's looking around the room to observe many possibilities for interesting activities.

Regardless of whether an advocate would argue the case in this way, the point is that general principles that allow considerable leeway for personal interpretation make it difficult to test a theory in order to determine its validity. Of course, Werner and his followers did derive hypotheses from the theory and conduct studies to test these hypotheses, thereby helping estimate the validity of the theory's general principles. And these studies were a step in the right direction. However, I believe that the theory's form is as yet in a state that makes it weak in terms of falsifiability.

Finally, there is the question of how self-satisfying (item 9) Werner's theory is overall. For me, his identification of general growth principles and his convincing examples and experimental demonstrations of them are valuable. The principles help me comprehend general lines of development. Furthermore, his studies of language and perception, along with the research techniques devised to conduct these studies, are positive contributions. However, when I seek aid in understanding the past and predicting the future of individual children in order to be better prepared to guide their development, I find little or no help from Werner. Providing such information was not his mission. So overall, I find the results of orthogenetic theory just moderately self-satisfying.

ETHOLOGISTS' CONTRIBUTIONS

As defined earlier, ethology is the comparative study of animal species, including humans. People in the field of child development turn to such studies to discover aspects of ethological theory and research that may prove of value in explaining child growth and behavior. In the following pages, we first consider theoretical assumptions underlying ethological investigations and then inspect four examples of how the results of animal studies may assist us in understanding child development.

A Foundation of Neo-Darwinism

As indicated in the introduction to Part Three, ethologists base their work on Charles Darwin's theory of evolution. It is impossible to understand their position unless we first recognize assumptions they hold in common. So in the following discussion I will review in an elementary fashion a number of the assumptions, asking your forebearance if the review is unduly reminiscent of a class in high school biology.

At the outset it is important to establish the definitions of two terms: *species* and *population*. A *species* is a collection of individual organisms capable of interbreeding under natural conditions. The phrase *natural conditions* is an essential part of this definition for it requires that we establish separate species categories for two organisms that can be induced to mate under experimental conditions but that do not interbreed in a natural setting. Hence, lions and tigers form two separate species, even though they can be successfully interbred in captivity (Wilson, 1975, pp. 8–9).

A *population* is a set of organisms of the same species occupying a clearly delimited geographical area at the same time. Thus a single hill of ants is not an entire population—a population in this case is all the colonies of ants of the same species in that particular area. Or a population can comprise all the indigenous people living in a cluster of interlinked islands of the South Seas.

With these definitions of species and population in mind, let's turn to five propositions that our theorists appear to subscribe to as underlying assumptions.

1. *Species reproduction.*   For humans, as well as for all other species that require two parents as the source of reproduction, a new member of the species is conceived when a sperm cell from the male combines with an ovum from the female. This combination produces a new cell that immediately divides. The resulting pair of cells also divide, and this process of dividing to produce increasing numbers of cells continues over and over. Each step in the sequence creates cells of slightly different properties, cells capable of specialized functions, until finally they represent a fully constructed new member of the species, including such variegated, coordinated parts as heart and spleen, throat and lungs, skin and hair, eyes and brain.

2. *The genetic plan.*   The architectural design for this new fish or fowl or human is provided by thousands of genes carried by chromo-somes contained in the sperm cell of the father and in the ovum of the mother. In humans the chromosomes total forty-six, with twenty-three contributed by the female and twenty-three by the male.

   The inherited genes determine both (1) the border limits within which development normally can occur and (2) potentialities for variation within these limits. By *border limits* I mean the identifying features of the species, the common elements that all normal indi-viduals in the species share. As a simple example, humans normally are born with two eyes in front of the head, one on each side of the upper bridge of the nose. In contrast, rabbits and frogs are normally born with eyes farther to the side of the head. By *potentialities for variation* I mean that within these limits particular gene combina-tions determine some variation of the general characteristic. So eye color and acuity of sight can vary from one normal child to another, depending on the specific mix of genes received.

   The connection between a gene and a given characteristic, —such as skin color, intelligence, or competitiveness,—is not a sim-ple one. A chromosome does not merely contain a skin color gene or competitiveness gene that by itself determines the hue of the person's skin or the degree of competitiveness. Rather, the inherited foundation of such characteristics is determined by a number of genes located at various places among the chromosomes. Within the same family, one child will inherit a different mix of genes than his siblings, except in the case of identical (monozygotic) twins. Hence it is obviously not only the variations in the environment that cause differences among children in the same family, but also variations in the combination of genes received by each child.

3. *The network of species.* Ethologists subscribe to Darwin's proposition that none of the species, human or otherwise, is a separate creation, unrelated to the others. Rather, all species are links in a network of living things. The network extends from the simplest one-celled organisms—or from even more primitive stages of matter—to the most mature, advanced species, that of the human being.

4. *The natural purpose.* If there is a natural purpose to life, a goal toward which all living things are driven by their nature, then that is *survival*. In its most basic sense, this is not the survival of the individual organism, since all individuals die. Nor is it even the survival of the species, for species are eliminated or altered with the passing of time. Rather, the basic aim seems to be the survival of the genes, which are the carriers of life itself (Wilson, 1975, pp. 3–4).

5. *Natural selection.* Living things obviously do not develop in a vacuum. They develop in environments that can vary in temperature, humidity, oxygen content, food supply, type of predator, and the like. Only those species survive and thrive that are well suited to changes that occur in their environments. Those poorly suited to environmental changes die off. This is the process of natural selection, the survival of the fittest. Such a point of view, refined since Darwin published his theory of evolution in 1859, is the new Darwinism that undergirds much of the work conducted today on the biological origins of human behavior, and thus is the foundation for the origins of child development.

With these observations about the theory of evolution as a background, we turn now to four examples of how animal studies can be applied to the understanding of children.

Four Propositions from Ethological Studies

Contributions that ethology makes to the understanding of child development are illustrated below in the form of four propositions—on the concepts of bonding, altruism, social intelligence, and dominant/submissive behavior. A *proposition,* as the term is used here, is a generalization from the study of animals that may apply as well to humans and, as such, may explain some aspect of child development.

Proposition 1: Bonding. In the earliest hours and days of life a strong mutual emotional attachment or bond occurs between the newborn and an immediate nurturing adult. This bond tends to continue over the following years, even in the face of harsh treatment of the child by the adult.

No newborn creature from species in the upper levels of the animal kingdom is able to fend for itself. In order to survive, all neonates require the aid of at least one nurturing adult until they mature enough to find their own food and shelter and to protect themselves from predators, illness, and accident. An early mutual emotional attachment helps ensure that a specific adult assumes the responsibility for each newborn and that the newborn identifies a particular adult as the one to whom she has a right to turn in time of need. This attachment increases the likelihood that the newborn will survive and will later produce offspring of her own. As interpreted from the perspective of Darwinian theory, within each animal species those genetic lineages that have fostered a strong reciprocal emotional bond between an offspring and a parent at the outset of the newborn's life have survived better than genetic lines that have not. As a consequence, over succeeding generations the gene strains that have fostered bonding have become widespread throughout the species, making bonding a "natural" developmental characteristic of the species.

The notion of early parent-offspring bonding, first generated from observations of nonhumans, stimulated a Britisher, John Bowlby (1969, 1980), to try to determine whether the generalization about bonding was also true for humans. Following Bowlby's lead, M. H. Klaus and J. H. Kennell (1976) have shown that there appears to be a critically sensitive period for bonding during the first few hours following birth. During this period, readiness to establish emotional attachment seems particularly strong. Comparisons between a group of mothers who had close contact with their newborns during the first few hours and a group who did not showed that the close-contact mothers in subsequent months displayed more fondling behavior and eye contact with their infants than did the other group of mothers. Bowlby's research and similar evidence have since affected infant-care routines in hospitals by influencing growing numbers of hospital personnel to have mothers spend more time with their babies in the hours and days immediately after birth.

The bonding example illustrates the process through which ethology can influence child-raising practices. First, a generalization about development is drawn from observations of nonhuman species. Next, the generalization is tested out in laboratory experiments and field studies of humans. If the generalization appears supported by the research on humans, then child-development specialists recommend child-rearing techniques that incorporate the new knowledge.

Proposition 2: Altruism. The greater the genetic similarity between two individuals, such as two children, the greater the degree of altruism they will display toward each other.

This proposition is an extension to humans of a kinship theory that zoologists have recently built from studies of altruistic (self-sacrificing) behavior among insects—ants, bees, wasps, and termites—that differ in the extent of their sociality (Alexander & Sherman, 1977; Hamilton, 1964; Trivers & Hare, 1976; Wilson, 1975).

In this kinship theory, an act is called "altruistic" if it benefits another organism while harming the organism performing the act. And to make *benefit* and *harm* easy to measure objectively, benefit and harm are assessed in terms of the reproductive success of an organism, that is, the organism's success in producing its own offspring. An act is thus altruistic if it harms the individual's chances of producing its own offspring while aiding another organism in producing and maintaining its own. At this point the line of reasoning will not make sense unless we recall that within neo-Darwinism the goal of nature is not the survival of the individual but the survival of the genetic line. And in some cases in which organisms are struggling against difficult environmental circumstances, a self-sacrificing act will better ensure that the organism's genetic line, as carried by a close relative of the individual, will prosper than if each individual behaved entirely selfishly without regard for the welfare of others. When the males of the tribe array themselves in the front line of defense against dangerous predators, each of them is reducing his chances of personal survival and reproductive success more than if he tried to escape on his own, leaving the females and young at the mercy of the predators. But this cooperative, altruistic act helps maximize the chance that the large proportion of his genes, which are also carried by the close relatives he is defending, will survive through future generations.

This general line of logic suggests why natural selection over the centuries has encouraged the development of altruistic behavior by promoting the survival and reproduction of genes particularly conducive to such acts. However, in such a general form, the logic does not help us specify the conditions under which an altruistic act rather than a selfish act can be expected. And it is here that zoologists' recent work on kinship theory may offer some help. Scientists have now devised formulas for estimating under what conditions natural selection will favor genes conducive to altruistic acts. The formulas include two main factors: (1) the degree of genetic relatedness of the two organisms concerned (that is, the proportion of genes common to the two individuals) and (2) the comparative cost and benefit to the organism carrying out the act and to the recipient of the act. As R. L. Trivers and H. Hare have put it:

> For natural selection to favor an altruistic act directed at a relative, the benefit of the act times the altruist's r (degree of relatedness) to the relative must be greater than the cost of the act (1976, p. 249).

In other words, the theory proposes that, through the evolutionary process, genes have been selected that encourage an organism to engage in more self-sacrificing behavior for the benefit of close relatives than for distant relatives. But in all instances, altruism has limits. The individual will bear a higher personal cost for the sake of closely related individuals, but when the cost becomes so high that it exceeds the product of (a) the benefit to the relative times (b) the degree of relatedness, then the actor can be expected to behave selfishly rather than altruistically.

Such, then, is the general direction of reasoning and the beginnings of specifying conditions in kinship theory as based on and tested in altruistic-versus-selfish behavior among social insects. But what might this all have to do with child development? It provides some hypotheses about the bases and conditions of altruism in humans. It suggests some lines of inquiry for investigating such hypotheses as proposition 2, the hypothesis that natural selection for the human species has operated in such a way as to genetically predispose children to display more altruism toward others who are closely related to them than toward people more distantly related. The proposition implies such questions as the following:

1. To what extent do children exhibit self-sacrificing behavior toward members of their family because the children have been taught to do so, and to what extent is such behavior a result of genetic predisposition?

2. A common ideal of social democracy is to have children treat other people on the basis of each person's individual behavior rather than a person's membership in some subgroup of society (a family, tribal, religious, ethnic, or socioeconomic subgroup). Does this

mean that in order to achieve the ideal, those people in charge of child rearing must counteract a natural (genetically based) propensity of children to behave more altruistically toward people who are closely related to them than toward people with whom they have fewer genes in common?

These are some of the generalizations from ethological studies that generate research challenges for the field of child development.

Proposition 3: Social Intelligence. The majority of problems people face in daily living are ones involving interactions with other people. The ability to solve these problems can be labeled "social intelligence." Such ability is not accurately assessed by means of traditional intelligence tests but, rather, requires different appraisal techniques, ones that directly confront the individual with social-interaction problems.

Throughout the twentieth century, the most popular way of formally appraising a person's problem-solving ability has been by means of intelligence tests that consist of oral or printed questions. This line of appraisal began in France with the work of Alfred Binet during the first decade of the century, and the tradition continues strong today. However, a number of critics, including Jean Piaget, have charged that such tests tell only whether a respondent gives an acceptable answer; they do not reveal the thought processes involved in arriving at the answer. Hence Piaget and others have created different techniques for assessing human mental abilities, techniques that involve a tester posing problem situations for a child and then observing how the child's thought processes operate as she or he seeks a solution.

But studies by ethologists have called into question the suitability of both traditional intelligence measures and Piaget's problem-solving tasks. The question has arisen from ethologists' observations of animals during the animals' daily living routines in their natural habitats. What constitutes intelligent behavior in such real life social environments may be rather different from the things measured by typical intelligence tests. In particular, the kinds of problems that appear on intelligence tests are seldom ones involving decisions about how to act in social situations, nor does the contrived laboratory setting in which intelligence tests are typically administered include the same sorts of forces that can affect people's decisions in social settings. So ethological studies have helped alert psychologists to the limitations of both Binet-type and Piaget-type measures of intelligence, thus stimulating the search for better ways of formally assessing children's development in solving problems met in the social intercourse of real life.

Proposition 4: Dominance/Submission. A genetic line best survives if individuals from the line's gene pool are organized socially in such a way that the most capable members are in positions of leadership and control, while members who are less powerful, less inventive, or less talented accept subservient positions.

This proposition derives from neo-Darwinism via the following line of logic. The *gene pool* of a population consists of all varieties of genes possessed by the members of that population. Each new member of the population is constructed from one particular combination of genes from that pool. This means that not all members born into the population have the same characteristics, nor are all combinations of genes that compose individuals equally suited for promoting survival. Furthermore, the genetic line thrives best when individuals of the species do not live isolated from each other, solving the problems of survival alone. Instead, the lineage thrives when its members are organized as a social system that exhibits a division of labor and power, and the inherited differences among individuals in the system equip members better for some roles than for others. As the generations pass, the greater the effectiveness of the social system in fostering survival, the greater will be the survival rate of those members who carry genes that fit them well for that system. That is, more of the fittest members will survive and pass on their socially suitable genes to future generations. Through this process, newborns of the species are increasingly equipped with genetic tendencies that in the past have supported the social organization that has become the norm for the given species, whether it be ants, sharks, bees, baboons, or dogs.

Among the range of social characteristics that ethologists trace to such genetic foundations is the dominant/submissive behavior noted among animals in the upper reaches of the evolutionary system, particularly among primates. The dominance/submission hierarchy is defined in animal societies by the way power and privilege are apportioned among the members, especially in matters of access to mates, to food, to desirable resting spots, and the like. Some animals rather readily assume submissive roles, displaying their submission by such ritualistic postures as rolling onto their backs and exposing their bellies or lowering their heads and cowering. Others do not so easily submit but, instead, challenge rivals for positions of dominance. Yet, once the less powerful are intimidated by threats or defeated in combat, they accept a subservient role, permitting the group to get on with daily living under stable social conditions.

Studies of dominance/submission patterns in animals have stimulated similar studies with children. As a consequence, a growing body of knowledge has accrued about the unstated rules children follow for regulating relationships in childhood groups and about the effectiveness of the adjustment strategies they attempt, such as physical attack and defense, teasing, name-calling and casting insults, verbal threats, escape, gifts of appeasement, weeping, joining forces with peers to gain strength in numbers, and so on. Such studies have shown that in the early stages of a group's formation, as at the beginning of the school year, conflicts are frequent until dominant members prove themselves and the losers in the struggle accept positions lower in the social hierarchy. Thereupon, conflicts diminish dramatically and the work of the group moves ahead more peaceably (Savin-Williams, 1976; Sherif, 1966; Strayer & Strayer, 1976).

Programmed Learning Potential

In summary, explanations of child development and behavior from an ethologist's perspective place far more emphasis on biological factors than on current environmental factors. For instance, a Harvard University ethologist, Edward O. Wilson, writing on human nature, states his conviction that genetic factors play a dominant role in determining what an individual will learn:

> The learning potential of each species appears to be fully programmed by the structure of its brain, the sequence of release of its hormones, and, ultimately, its genes. Each animal species is "prepared" to learn certain stimuli, barred from learning others, and neutral with respect to still others. . . . So the human brain is not a tabula rasa, a clean slate on which experience draws intricate pictures with lines and dots. It is more accurately described as an autonomous decision-making instrument, an alert scanner of the environment that approaches certain kinds of choices and not others in the first place, then innately leans toward one option as opposed to others and urges the body into action according to a flexible schedule that shifts automatically and gradually from infancy into old age (1978, pp. 67, 69).

PRACTICAL APPLICATIONS AND RESEARCH CHALLENGES

I have combined applications and research challenges here because the practical applications of ethology to child development take the form of suggestions for research studies. The purpose of such studies is to discover the extent to which generalizations derived from observing nonhuman species can validly be applied to interpreting children's growth and behavior. In addition to the propositions from ethology mentioned above, let's consider several more in the form of questions that demonstrate the broad range of child development research topics that can be generated from ethological theory.

Wilson (1978, p. 99) has written, "Are human beings innately aggressive? . . . The answer . . . is yes." But in disagreement with Wilson, there are those who contend that aggressivity, although widespread, is the result of living conditions that precipitate conflict and competition and is not the result of an inborn human tendency. From this difference of opinion a variety of research questions can be evoked. For instance, in what ways can children's environments be arranged to eliminate aggressive behavior at successive stages of growth? And if aggressivity cannot be eliminated, what child-rearing practices can be used to channel it into constructive acts (ones aiding other people in fulfilling their needs) rather than destructive acts (ones frustrating others' need-fulfillment attempts)? To what extent do models of aggression the child observes in the family, in school, and on television influence the amount and type of aggression the child exhibits at different age levels?

Wilson (1978, p. 128) has further observed, "Women as a group are less assertive and physically aggressive." Is this true of children of all ages? Or is it simply that boys and girls are equally assertive but use different techniques for expressing assertiveness? And if this is so, to what extent are the differences innate and to what extent the result of cultural influences? More precisely, how can child-rearing practices alter possible sex differences in assertiveness?

As for sexual behavior, to what extent are preferences for heterosexual versus homosexual activities inborn? How do different models of sexual behavior in a child's environment influence the child's sex preferences and activities at different age levels? In terms of vocations, are there certain roles for which females are innately better suited than males, and vice versa?

To what extent are a child's competitive/cooperative and introversive/extroversive actions a result of a genetic tendency to behave in such a manner? How much room is there for environmental forces at different age levels to alter the course of such traits or tendencies?

Is there any truth in beliefs of the past that antisocial acts of children and youths are based, at least partly, on "a bad blood line" or "bad seed"? Or, in more modern parlance, are there actually "psychopathic personalities," meaning people whose underlying genetic endowment so predisposes them to antisocial acts that efforts to teach them prosocial behavior are destined to fail?

How much are children from a given population (such as an inbred tribal or ethnic group) genetically predestined to display one pattern of social behavior (such as a tendency to settle disputes by reasoning) than another (a tendency to settle disputes by physical violence)?

These questions and far more that derive from ethological investigations provide an extensive source of research opportunities for the field of child development.

ETHOLOGICAL THEORY: AN ASSESSMENT

In explaining my reasons for the ratings on the accompanying chart, I begin with items awarded high marks and then consider ones with lower ratings.

Item 1, concerning how closely the theory reflects the real world, is divided into two subscales, the first focusing on ethologists' main source of data—nonhuman species—and the second focusing on the chief subject of this book—children. I rated ethological theory high on item 1a because each concept in the major ethologists' writings is profusely illustrated with examples from field studies of a broad variety of species. However, many sociologists and social psychologists would probably give item 1a a lower rating because they believe ethologists credit genes with too great a role in determining individuals' psychological characteristics and groups' social patterns. Although ethologists do not ignore the place of learning in personal traits and social organization, they do see genetic structure as setting narrower boundary lines within which learning can take place than many social scientists would likely accept. The strong genetic preference exhibited by typical ethologists is reflected in Wilson's contention that what evolves in human development is a set of genetically based capacities to learn certain things rather than others with a certain degree of ease:

> Pavlov was simply wrong when he postulated that "any natural phenomenon chosen at will may be converted into conditioned stimuli." Only small parts of the brain represent a tabula rasa; this is true even for human beings. The remainder is more like an exposed negative, waiting to be dipped into developer fluid (1975, p. 156).

While ethologists may be criticized for taking a position toward the hereditarian camp in nature–nurture controversies, when more data have been compiled it may turn out that they are correct, or nearly so. In any event, I have given them the benefit of such doubts in marking item 1a on the basis of the wide range of field studies with which they have buttressed their theoretical generalizations and principles of development.

Ethological Theory

How well do I think the theory meets the standards?

The Standards	Very Well	Moderately Well	Very Poorly
1. Reflects the real world of:			
1a. Nonhuman species	X		
1b. Children			X
2. Is clearly understandable	X		
3. Explains the past and predicts the future		X	
4. Guides child rearing			X
5. Is internally consistent	X		
6. Is economical	X		
7. Is falsifiable		X	
8. Stimulates new discoveries	Potential X		Actual X
9. Is self-satisfying		X	

In judging the theory's clarity (item 2), internal consistency (item 5), and economy of explanation (item 6), I have concluded that the main books and articles on ethology available to the public are clearly written and contain ample illustrative descriptions of behavior among many species (see, for example, Eibl-Eibesfeldt, 1975; Hinde, 1974; Lorenz, 1977; Wilson, 1975, 1978). Likewise, neo-Darwinism as expressed in ethological theories does not seem encumbered with more concepts than the minimum needed to explain the phenomena ethologists discuss.

The ratings on items 1b and 4 (children's real world and guidance for child rearing) are rather low since most ethological studies have not dealt directly with children's lives. J. Bowlby's work in the 1950s and 1960s has been the most direct application of ethological theory to studies of children (Bowlby, 1969, 1973, 1980).

Items 3 and 7 (explains past and predicts future; is falsifiable) can conveniently be considered together for they share a common weakness. The weakness is that ethological theory, at its present stage of development, is composed of a set of broad concepts and principles intended to explain the evolution of all psychological and social behavior in all species; but as yet the theory is not sufficiently detailed and precise to produce an unequivocal description of any population's past development or future evolution. The theory does not provide the information needed to judge specifically the genetically set limits or potentialities for various aspects of human development. Nor does the theory elucidate the way different environmental influences complement the genetic pattern to produce the characteristics individual humans display at various stages of growth. Ethology is still at the stage of a natural history, with theorists observing social behavior in one or two species, proposing concepts that could explain such behavior, then extending the application of these concepts by "logical reasoning" to other species without rigorously testing the validity of this extension. As Wilson has pointed out in discussing the subrealm of ethology known as sociobiology:

> The greatest snare in sociobiological reasoning is the ease with which it is conducted. Whereas the physical sciences deal with precise results that are usually difficult to explain, sociobiology has imprecise results that can be too easily explained by many different schemes (1975, p. 28).

The cure for this shortcoming, Wilson says, lies in adopting methods of "strong inference." This means deriving alternative hypotheses from the theory, creating crucial experiments or field observations that will reveal which of the competing hypotheses is the most tenable, and then accepting or revising the theory's concepts in light of these test results (Wilson, 1975, p. 28). Until ethological models reach this stage of methodology, they will continue to be nonfalsifiable and will furnish inconclusive explanations of past and future.

On item 8, I have marked ethological theory for both its actual and its potential value in stimulating new discoveries. As demonstrated in the discussion of research challenges, ethological theory has great potential for stimulating new discoveries in child development. However, so far the direct applications of ethological findings to child development research have been quite limited.

For the final assessment standard—how satisfying ethological theory is from a child development perspective—I have marked ethology in the moderate range to reflect a counterbalancing between (1) the strengths of the theorists' line of reasoning about species in general and (2) a lack of conclusiveness that surfaces when they apply this reasoning to explain complex human behavior. In particular, I would like the kind of detailed extension of the theory that would account for why children develop psychologically and socially the way they do during the first two decades of life.

FOR FURTHER READING

About Lewin and Werner:

Baldwin, Alfred L. (1967) *Theories of Child Development*. New York: Wiley. A detailed description and critique of Lewin's topological psychology is presented in Chapters 3 and 4 and of Werner's orthogenetic theory in Chapter 17.

Lewin, Kurt. (1936) *Principles of Topological Psychology*. New York: McGraw-Hill. An early statement of Lewin's general viewpoint.

Werner, Heinz. (1961) *Comparative Psychology of Mental Development*. Rev. ed. New York: Science Editions. An early statement of orthogenetic theory.

About Ethological Theory:

Eibl-Eibesfeldt, Irenaus. (1975) *Ethology: The Biology of Behavior*. 2d ed. New York: Holt, Rinehart & Winston.

Hinde, Robert A. (1974) *Biological Bases of Human Social Behavior*. New York: McGraw-Hill.

Lorenz, Konrad Z. (1977) *Behind the Mirror: A Search for a Natural History of Human Knowledge*. New York: Harcourt Brace Jovanovich.

Tinbergen, Nikolaas. (1973) *The Animal in Its World: Explorations of an Ethologist 1932–1972*. Cambridge, Mass.: Harvard University Press.

Wilson, Edward O. (1978) *On Human Nature*. Cambridge, Mass.: Harvard University Press.

PART FOUR

THE PSYCHOANALYTIC TRADITION

A search for developmental causes and cures of neuroses

From the viewpoint of the general public, the most unsettling theory of child development proposed during the past century has been Sigmund Freud's psychoanalysis. In the late 1800s and throughout the 1900s many people were shocked by Freud's contention that sexual motives—with sex interpreted in a broad sense—underlie much if not all human behavior. More shocking still is the notion of infantile sexuality. To the lay public and medical profession of the late 1800s and early 1900s, the idea that little children have sensuous thoughts that are important determinants of their personal and social adjustment is clearly a distortion of the truth at the hands of a dirty-minded neurotic (S. Freud, 1917, pp. 323–325, 1938, p. 9; Hartmann, 1959, p. 11).

Not as morally shocking but no less disturbing personally was Freud's suggestion that much of the time we do not consciously know why we act the way we do. Instead of behaving as rational beings, we are driven and manipulated by primitive urges and by traumas from our past that reside in what Freud called our *unconscious mind.* In the sixteenth century, Copernicus had already insulted humanity by suggesting that the earth is not the center of the universe. Darwin had carried the insult further by proposing that humans are descendents of lower forms of life and therefore not the divine, unique beings that they had led themselves to believe. Now Freud pushed insult another step by contending that a person's conscious mind was neither master of his fate nor captain of his soul; instead, each person was a victim of unconscious drives.

However, over the years since Freud first put forth his theory, he has gained a substantial following of believers. His work, and the revisions of it by later generations, now represents a major branch of psychology. Indeed, many of his key ideas have nearly achieved the status of common sense. For these reasons, the psychoanalytic tradition deserves a prominent place in a survey of theories of child development.

Chapter Eight presents central concepts of the theory as Freud himself devised them. The chapter ends with a brief description of contributions subsequently made by Freud's third daughter, Anna, specifically concerning the childhood portion of the overall theory.

Chapter Nine illustrates a major extension of psychoanalysis by a disciple of Freud, Erik Erikson. Of the various revised versions of psychoanalysis fashioned during the twentieth century, Erikson's has been the most significant for the field of child development, particularly for the years of adolescence.

CHAPTER EIGHT

Sigmund Freud's Psychoanalysis

Often we will best understand how a theorist arrived at a model of development if we recognize the sequence of experiences that were instrumental in guiding the direction of his theorizing. Since this seems particularly true in the case of psychoanalysis, let's begin the account of Freud's model by looking briefly at the medical puzzles that stimulated him to speculate about the nature of children and the forces that determine their development.

Sigmund Freud (1856–1939) was an Austrian neurologist who, early in his career of private medical practice in Vienna, encountered some very perplexing cases. Patients came to him with a variety of ailments, such as paralysis of the hand or aches or blurred vision, which could not be explained by traditional physiological knowledge. Although the patients' symptoms suggested that nerve tissue had been damaged, examination showed the nervous system to be intact.

How could people suffer such ailments without any organic impairment of the nervous system? While Freud was pondering this problem, he learned about the work that Jean Charcot was conducting on hypnotism in Paris. Charcot had shown that under a hypnotic spell people could be told that they would have one or another bodily symptom after they awakened from the hypnotic state, but would not remember the cause of this symptom. They would not recall that they had received a suggestion under hypnosis. And, indeed, after coming out of hypnosis, they did exhibit the suggested symptoms, such as paralysis of a leg, numbness of the skin, or deafness. Charcot, in addition, was able to use hypnosis to relieve people of certain symptoms. Under hypnosis, patients were told that they no longer suffered the ailment that had brought them to the clinic. Upon awakening, at least some of these patients had lost the symptom of which had they complained (S. Freud, 1910, p. 21).

Freud's interest in Charcot's experiments was so great that he spent the year 1885–1886 in Paris studying the methods and effects of hypnosis. At the same time, he asked questions that might explain these curious phenomena: What relation might there be between the strange cases Freud faced in his medical practice and the cases Charcot exhibited in his clinic? How must human personality be structured and how must mind be related to body in order to cause such things to occur (S. Freud, 1910, pp. 16–22)?

To answer to these queries, Freud, over the next several decades, developed his psychoanalytic theory of personality. Included in the theory is a conception of child development that has exerted significant influence over a number of areas of child psychology today—child psychiatry, counseling children and adolescents, nursery school teaching methods, and research in child development. Certain concepts from Freudian theory have now been generally accepted by psychologists, educators, and social workers, and even by those who reject most of psychoanalytic theory. In effect, Freud's views have had a decided influence on people concerned with raising children.

Psychoanalytic theory in its entirety is quite complex. Not only does it have many ramifications but adherents of psychoanalysis often disagree with each other on important issues. Freud himself altered the theory in major ways on several occasions. For these reasons, the following discussion presents only a simplified sketch of the theory's main elements.

The early part of the chapter is divided into descriptions of (1) levels of consciousness, (2) the apparatus of mental life, (3) psychosexual stages of child development, and (4) the development of consciousness and ego strength. After these, there are (5) a brief review of some contributions to psychoanalytic theory and practice by Anna Freud, (6) practical applications, (7) research challenges, and (8) an assessment of the theory.

LEVELS OF CONSCIOUSNESS

Early in the process of formulating his theory, Freud proposed that each person has an *unconscious* aspect of mind in addition to the conscious aspect of which the individual is aware. By *unconscious* Freud meant a sort of mental receptacle for ideas, a receptacle from which the individual cannot recall ideas at will. These ideas, of which we are unaware, influence our actions just as much as if they were conscious. In effect, much of what we do arises from unconscious motivation (S. Freud, 1923, p. 4).

The concept of an unconscious state of mind was not entirely new in the field of philosophy. An occasional theorist over the centuries had postulated such an aspect. However, it was Freud who elaborated the concept and assigned it a central role in behavior.

By proposing the unconscious, Freud was able to account for otherwise unexplainable disorders suffered by his patients. He hypothesized that a person who faces a distressing, unsolved problem in daily life will find the problem psychologically painful. So the individual's personality, to escape this pain of unresolved conflicts, automatically resolves the problem by pushing the distressing thoughts out of consciousness. The patient actively "forgets" the matter. But Freud believed that such forgotten material does not leave the mind. Instead, it is only relegated to an unconscious condition—in other words, it is "repressed"—to keep the sufferer unaware of its existence and, consequently, enable the person to feel more at peace. But the problem, now unconscious, continues to agitate, and it expresses itself in devious ways. One mode of expression can be a bodily ailment, such as a headache or paralysis of some part of the body. So it was that Freud concluded that the strange symptoms displayed by his patients were caused by unresolved mental conflicts that seethed insistently in their unconscious minds. Not only were these bodily disorders, which he called *conversion hysteria symptoms,* the consequence of repressed mental conflicts but so, Freud believed, was the entire array of neurotic symptoms, an array including phobias, obsessions, compulsions, and anxieties.

To alleviate such symptoms—in effect, to cure the neuroses—Freud proposed that the repressed conflict, which had originated in a problem of development earlier in the patient's life, had to be brought into consciousness. The patient had to recognize the origin of the difficulties and verbally relive the original conflict situation, but now by working out the conflict in a constructive, emotionally satisfying manner and thus being cured of the neuroses.

In order to make his therapeutic scheme work, Freud had to devise a process for uncovering the unconscious conflicts and presenting them so that patients would accept the conflicts as true and deserving of serious attention. Early in his career Freud tried different means for uncovering unconscious conflicts. He began with hypnosis but, as he later reported, "I soon came to dislike hypnosis, for it was a temperamental and . . . mystical ally" (Freud, 1910, p. 22). Hence he gave it up in favor of free association and dream interpretation.

The process of *free association* consists of encouraging the patient to relax, usually on a couch, and to describe free-flowing thoughts without editing them. The analyst listens to hours of such narration in order to locate underlying themes of conflict that are hints or symbols of hidden problems. By using the process of relaxed, free association, the therapist is assuming that "the repressed wishful impulse . . . is on the look-out for an opportunity of being activated, and when that happens it succeeds in sending into consciousness a disguised and unrecognizable substitute for what had been repressed" (Freud, 1910, p. 27). It is the analyst's task to unmask the significant elements of the patient's narration and reveal them for what they really are in the individual's past development.

In a like manner, Freud used *dream interpretation* as a window, albeit murky and distorted, for viewing the contents of the unconscious. He believed that during sleep, a censor force, which seeks to prevent unconscious conflicts from entering consciousness, is not as alert as during waking life. So dreams, in Freud's scheme, are products of the person's trying to satisfy wishes and solve problems during sleep. The dream serves as an audiovisual symbol of unconscious urges pressing for expression into consciousness. The analyst is skilled in interpreting dreams in a way that reveals the nature and source of the patient's unconscious conflicts (Freud, 1900).

The significance of Freud's reliance on free association and dream interpretation is twofold. First, both techniques were tools crucial to the conduct of his system of therapy. Second, and more important for our present purposes, they served almost exclusively as the sources of data about childhood on which he erected his model of development. Rather than spending his time directly observing children in the process of their development, Freud spent endless hours listening to adult neurotics produce memories of childhood. On these memories, extracted from free associations and dreams, he built his picture of sexual growth.

In addition to introducing a view of the mind as consisting of both conscious and unconscious aspects, Freud also distinguished two levels of unconsciousness. One level, he said, contains those ideas that are not in consciousness at the moment, that are latent. We can recall them, "bring them to mind," if we choose, even though it may take a bit of effort. This first level Freud labeled the *preconscious*. The second level contains the truly repressed ideas, those held down purposely by the personality's resistance forces because allowing them to enter consciousness would be too painful for the conscious personality to face. This second level, deeper and less accessible than the preconscious, is the *true* or prototype unconscious in the Freudian scheme. In a sense, then, the preconscious is a shadow zone between the open, bright conscious and the closed, dark unconscious (Freud, 1923, pp. 4–5). A person has thoughts or ideas at each of these levels.

THE PSYCHIC APPARATUS

The levels of consciousness serve as a sort of three-tiered arena in which a person's psychic life takes place. Within the psychical arena, the three main functionaries that compete and cooperate to produce this performance were conceived by Freud to be the *id,* the *ego,* and the *superego.* In the course of a child's development, these three do not appear simultaneously. The id comes first—it is already present at birth. The ego develops out of the growing infant's efforts to satisfy needs through transactions with the environment. Some years later the superego develops as an internal representative of the rules and values of the environment.

The way the development of the id, ego, and superego becomes intertwined with stages of the child's psychosexual growth is rather complex. In order to make this development easier to grasp, I will divide the explanation into two parts. The first, which comprises this section on the psychic apparatus, treats the nature and functions of the id, ego, and superego. The second, in the next section, describes their relation to the psychosexual growth stages that Freud proposed.

As a preface to these matters, we need to recognize that all behavior, physical and psychological, needs energy to activate it. In psychoanalytic theory the sources of all energy are the instincts, with *instinct* defined as an inborn factor that gives force and direction to psychological activities. For at least three decades Freud experimented with various conceptions of instincts. Then in 1920 he settled on a basic pair of motivating forces—the *life* and *death* instincts—which he thought vied for expression and supremacy in directing psychic behavior throughout a person's life span. The influence of the life instinct is reflected in constructive acts, in acts of love and altruism. The influence of the death instinct is displayed in destructive acts, in hate and in aggression. Freud applied the word *libido* to the psychic energy deriving from the life instinct, but he coined no parallel term for the energy emitting from the death instinct (Freud, 1920).

From the viewpoint of the instincts, the process of living consists of a continual competition between the opposing life and death forces—love against hate, life preservation against self-destruction. Often a mode of behaving represents a fusion of the two, as when aggression against a threatening enemy (motivated by the death instinct) preserves one's life and promotes one's welfare (which is the objective of the life instinct). Although throughout childhood and well into adult life the evidences of the life instinct appear to be the more prominent, the ultimate victory obviously goes to the opposing force, when, at life's close, the organism loses all animation and returns to the passive inorganic state that is the ultimate aim of the death instinct.

Now that we have the pair of basic instinctual energy sources in mind, we turn to the psychic apparatus through which the forces are invested or expended. In psychoanalytic theory, the personality of the newborn consists of a single operating component called the *id*. It is at the unconscious level and "contains everything that is inherited, that is present at birth, that is laid down in the constitution—above all, therefore, the instincts" (Freud, 1938, p. 2). It is within this id that libido builds up as a sort of pressure, searching for expression. Seen another way, libidinal energy arising from the id assumes the form of *needs* that demand fulfillment. The expenditure or release of libido is experienced by the infant as pleasure. The blocking of libidinal release is experienced as pain. So the id operates on the *pleasure principle*, which says: "Get as much pleasure as possible as soon as possible without regard for anyone else or anything else in the world." In its converse form the principle becomes: Avoid as much pain as possible.

Hence psychoanalysis pictures the newborn baby as all id, seeking only to satisfy its needs for food, for drink, for warmth, for elimination of body wastes, for freedom from skin irritants, and for affection, affection in the sense of being cuddled by its mother or mother substitute. The newborn's awareness of its condition and of the world is ostensibly very fuzzy. Freudians suppose that a baby does not distinguish among objects in its environment, nor does it recognize a difference between itself and other people or things. The newborn is aware only of discomfort or pain, which signals unfulfilled needs that require attention. The only observable methods the infant has for reacting to these pain or tension signals are crying, mouthing, and randomly moving its arms and legs.

But as time passes and the infant's experience with the world increases, more precise awareness of the environment begins to develop. The earliest level of awareness results in the *primary process,* which is the baby's act of creating in its memory an image of an object that will fulfill a need. For example, when the newborn feels hunger pangs, he automatically cries until someone feeds him. The food reduces the tension of hunger, and the baby experiences pleasure. As days pass, this cycle of hunger, feeding, and tension reduction is played over and over, so that gradually the taste, smell, feel, and sight of the food and of the feeder (usually the mother) are stored as images in the baby's memory. As a result, the infant, by means of the primary process, can now imagine those things that will bring a particular variety of satisfaction or a particular mode of expending libidinal energy.

It is important to recognize that the primary process is a rather chaotic, irrational mode of thought that does not distinguish between reasonable and unreasonable need-fulfilling images. The concern of the id and its primary process thinking is to gain satisfaction, regardless of whether or not the method of satisfaction is practical or will be tolerated by the environment. What the personality next requires, then, is a component that recognizes the nature of the environment, as well as the demands of the id, and can, therefore, provide realistic methods of investing energy. This second component of the psychic apparatus is called the *ego*. Freud postulated that the ego arises from, or separates out of, the id and is fueled by libidinal energy from the id. In effect, the id's primary process develops images of things that fulfill needs, but the image is only an initial, incomplete step toward satisfaction. Another agent, the ego, is required to bring the dream into reality. Freud explained that "the ego is that part of the id which has been modified by the direct influence of the external world through the medium" of conscious perception (Freud, 1923, p. 15). Furthermore, he proposed:

> It is to this ego that consciousness is attached; the ego controls the . . . discharge of excitations into the external world; it is the mental agency which supervises all its own constituent processes, and which goes to sleep at night, though even then it exercises the censorship on dreams (1923, p. 7).

Hence the ego serves as a decision maker that tries to negotiate a satisfactory solution to the conflicting demands that come on the one side from the id (which says "I want") and on the other side from the environment or "real world" (which says "You'll get it with a minimum of cost or pain only under these conditions"). Whereas the id works on the pleasure principle, the ego operates on the *reality principle,* which can be stated as: Recognize the conditions and demands of the real world and then seek methods of fulfilling the id's needs that are acceptable in such a world.

To play its role of negotiator, the ego is constantly assessing the kinds and strengths of needs arising from the id and at the same time assessing the conditions of the environment. From this assessment, the ego attempts to devise behaviors that represent the best compromise between the id and the outside world. Or, as is sometimes the case, the ego must negotiate a compromise among several demands coming simultaneously from the id, such as the demands of hunger and fatigue arising at the same moment.

We noted that the id, by means of the primary process, associates certain objects with need fulfillment. These associations are stored as memory images. It is now up to the ego to turn the images into reality. This problem-solving act is called the *secondary process.* The individual's skills of perceiving, remembering, analyzing, and taking action develop from this constant interaction among (1) the id's needs, (2) the maturing bodily organs, such as eyes and ears, and (3) the ego's increasing awareness of the complexities of the world.

The Superego's Role

Our next concern is with the third component of the psychic apparatus, the *superego*. Early in a child's life the rules of the world—the rules of *do* and *don't*—are enforced by the environment. The infant, in Freud's system, has no inborn inner voice telling her what is right and what is wrong. In effect, the child is born neither moral nor immoral, but *amoral*. She has no knowledge of good or bad. Her morality is simply that of getting pleasure (as demanded by the id) in a manner that will avoid punishment or pain (a manner arranged by the ego). The very young child, therefore, does not automatically feel bad or guilty or ashamed when she transgresses one of society's expectations. She feels bad only when the consequences of her behavior are either the withholding of rewards or the application of punishment. It is usually the child's parents who produce her good and bad feelings by manipulating the system of rewards and punishments she will experience.

Although children are not born with knowledge of what is good and what is evil, they are born with a capacity for two things: (1) to develop internal values and (2) to feel good (pleased and proud) when they abide by these values and to feel bad (sad, ashamed, and guilty) when transgressing them. Over the years of childhood and adolescence this capacity acquires contents in the form of moral values the child adopts from the environment. It is this third component of the growing personality that Freud labeled *superego*. How and why the superego appears and grows are matters intimately involved in the psychosexual stages of development and will be discussed in connection with them. For the present we will restrict our attention to the role the superego plays in the mental life of the older child and adolescent.

Just as Freud pictured the ego as developing out of the id, so he saw the superego arising from the ego (Freud, 1923, pp. 18–29). He explained:

> This new psychical agency continues to carry on the functions which have hitherto been performed by the people in the external world: It observes the ego, gives it orders, judges it and threatens it with punishments, exactly like the parents whose place it has taken (1938, p. 62).

Freud conceived of the superego as having two aspects, the *conscience* and the *ego ideal*. The conscience represents the "should-nots" of the child's world, the things for which he has been punished. The ego ideal represents the "shoulds," the positive moral values the child has been taught. Whereas the very young child must be punished for transgressions and rewarded for good behavior by his parents, the maturing child gradually does not need outside sanctions. His superego plays the punishing and rewarding roles for him. For disobeying the values he has now accepted as his own, the child's conscience punishes him with guilt, shame, and fear. For abiding by his moral values, his ego ideal rewards him with feelings of self-righteousness, self-praise, and pride.

With the addition of the superego to the id and ego, the apparatus of the mind is complete. The behavior of older children and adolescents is thus a result of the way the ego has negotiated a settlement among three conflicting sources of demands: (1) the id, which insists on immediate fulfillment of wishes, (2) the environment, which sets conditions under which wishes can be satisfied without punishment, and (3) the superego, which presses the youth to live up to a set of moral values he has incorporated from his parents and from other significant people in his world.

Mechanisms of Defense

As the ego develops over the years, it evolves techniques or habits for accommodating the conflicting demands made on it. A strong, mature ego uses direct means to accomplish this. It frankly admits the nature of instinctual demands, environmental forces, and the superego's commands. Then it proposes forthright, reasoned ways to effect a solution that satisfies each source of demand to an acceptable degree. But an ego that is weak, still childish and immature, slips into using more devious techniques of adjustment, techniques that Freud called *defense mechanisms*. The ego, in effect, seeks to fool itself and others concerning the state of affairs it faces, for it feels inadequate to solve the conflict among the demands that confront it.

The most significant defense technique, *repression*, has already been described. It is the automatic, nonconscious process of pushing distressing matters out of consciousness and into the unconscious. Although repression clears the conscious mind of worries, the repressed material continues to foment distress in the unconscious and produce the sorts of neurotic symptoms that Freud met in his medical practice.

A second mechanism is *sublimation*, the substitution of a culturally higher, socially more acceptable mode of expressing sexual or aggressive energy. Such altruistic acts as caring for children or aiding the sick, or such artistic endeavors as writing poetry or performing a ballet, are viewed by Freudians as substitutes for direct sexual behavior.

A third defense technique is *regression,* which consists of returning to an earlier, more primitive mode of adjusting to problems. A person may turn to this device when facing a new or distressing situation. As a simple example, a twelve-year-old girl feels frustrated when her mother criticizes her in public, so the girl begins sucking her thumb or the corner of her handkerchief as she did when she sought solace as an infant.

A mechanism that has been readily adopted into commonsense understanding is that of *projection.* When a child senses within his own personality a motive of which he is ashamed or which he fears, he may not admit its existence consciously to himself, but instead he may constantly see this motive in other people. He attributes to others those unacceptable acts and feelings that his own id urges him to express. Thus the child who harbors hate in his own unconscious will accuse others of hating him, claiming at the same time that he himself bears no malice. Likewise, a person who is repressing strong sexual desires of which he is ashamed will assume that others are trying to seduce or assault him sexually.

The device called *reaction formation* has been particularly useful to psychoanalysts, for it enables them to explain behavior that would otherwise appear to refute typical predictions that derive from the theory. Reaction formation consists of a child's adopting behavior that is just the opposite of an instinctual urge. For instance, a child may act compulsively clean, avoiding dirt and frequently washing her hands and changing her clothes. The direct interpretation of such behavior is that the child desires to be clean— cleanliness is her basic need. But Freudians would suspect something different. Since in their theory the basic drives involve such sensuous pleasure as sexual stimulation and bowel and urinary functions, they would propose that the child is not motivated by a basic cleanliness need. Instead, she really wants to become soiled, to mess around in dirt and feces, but she has been punished by her parents for expressing such desires so now she feels her basic urges are wicked. To control them, she represses the original desires and in her conscious life adopts the opposite sort of behavior as a desperate means of mastering the urges of which she is ashamed. In short, her behavior represents a reaction against her instinctual drives.

Three more defense mechanisms can be briefly described. *Compensation* is a device by which the child seeks to overcome a personal or environmental barrier by substituting success in some other realm of life than the one in which he suffers the weakness. *Rationalization* consists of giving a socially acceptable reason for a behavior that actually was motivated by a less honorable reason. *Escape* is leaving the scene of a distressing experience. The escape can be either physical, such as a girl's running away from home, or psychological, such as a youth's retreating into daydreams in school when the lesson is confusing.

These defense mechanisms, which are only some of those identified by Freud and his followers, illustrate the kinds of strategies the ego employs to satisfy, as well as possible, the conflicting demands made on it.

Now that we have identified the main components of the psyche and their functions, we can look at the psychosexual growth stages involved in the development of these components.

THE PSYCHOSEXUAL STAGES OF DEVELOPMENT

To account for the sorts of dreams and memories of childhood that his patients described, Freud produced a model of child development that featured a series of growth stages. The current neuroses of his patients, he thought, were the result of inadequate solutions to the problems the individual had faced as a child at one or more of these stages. He labeled these growth steps *psychosexual phases* because he believed the development of the personality—the *psyche*—was crucially influenced by the manner in which the child learned to expend sex energy (libido) from one period of life to the next. In other words, Freud proposed that the most significant emotional experiences during childhood and adolescence are those associated with expending libido in relation to a series of particularly sensitive zones of the body on which children's attention focuses at different points of development. These *erogenous zones,* in chronological sequence, are the mouth, the anus, and the genital organs. At the time a particular zone is the chief focus for the release of libido, the child not only derives sensuous (sexual, in a broad meaning of the term) pleasure from use of the zone, but her relationships with other people are heavily influenced by the way they respond to her attention to the zone. In essence, Freud proposed that the personal-social relationships the child develops—her feelings about herself and others, and her ways of treating herself and others—are founded in the experiences the child has at each psychosexual stage. Personality problems that arise as the child seeks to work her way through a stage may go unresolved, be repressed by the frantic ego, and continue to agitate within the unconscious and cause neuroses for years afterwards.

Although the number of developmental periods identified between birth and adulthood may vary slightly from one psychoanalytic theorist to another, all of them cite at least five major stages: oral (ages 0–1), anal (ages 2–3), infantile-genital (ages 3–4 or so), latency (ages 4 or 5 to puberty), mature-genital (from midteens to adulthood). We will examine these stages and the substages involved in several of them.

Birth: The Traumatic Beginning

Birth is not a stage of growth, but it is a highly significant event in psychoanalytic theory because it is regarded as the first great shock of the child's life. In the Freudian view, the newborn is overwhelmed with stimulation from the environment into which he or she emerges from the womb. The reaction is intense fear, for the undeveloped ego has no means to cope adequately with such a flood of stimuli. The birth trauma, then, is the prototype of all subsequent fear-producing situations the child will meet as he grows to old age. When later in life he is confronted by extreme stimuli, either extreme instinctual demands or extreme pressures from the environment, and his existing ego techniques are ineffective for mastering the stimuli, the original fear occasioned by the birth trauma will be reactivated, and he will revert to infantile behavior. Consequently, according to Freudian theory, an easier birth, involving less shock upon entering the world, can be expected to build less fear into the unconscious of the growing child, and he may be able to face frustrating experiences later in life with greater emotional control.

Stage 1: The Oral Period (Ages 0–1)

The psychoanalytic model of the child pictures the newborn not as a passive slab of damp clay on which environmental experiences will engrave a personality structure but as a dynamic energy system pressing to expend its energy. Or more precisely, the id of the neonate is seeking to invest libidinal energy in images of objects that will satisfy the instinctual needs and bring the pleasure of release. This act of investment (the primary process of the id) is called *cathexis*. When the id channels energy into an image of an object, it is said to be *cathecting* that object.

Following birth, the natural initial object for cathexis is the mother's breast or a suitable substitute because it is through the mouth that the newborn must now obtain life-sustaining nourishment. She must also use her mouth and nose for breathing. The nerve endings in the lips and mouth are particularly sensitive and offer the infant special pleasure. Freud wrote:

> The baby's obstinate persistence in sucking gives evidence at an early stage of a need for satisfaction which, though it originates from and is instigated by the taking of nourishment, nevertheless strives to obtain pleasure independently of nourishment and for that reason may and should be termed *sexual* (1938, p. 11).

The adequacy with which the child satisfies the need for food, drink, and breath gives him his first impressions of the world and of his relation to it. Not only is his personality influenced by how soon and how completely the pent-up libidinal energy is released, but the atmosphere associated with how these needs for release are either met or neglected affects him also. If his mother holds him affectionately and soothingly during the feeding process, the child will pass through the oral period in a happier, more confident state than if he is never cuddled and if there are distressing sounds and sights bombarding him while feeding.

In addition to taking in food and drink, the oral zone is used by the infant to investigate the parts of the world she can reach. She examines most objects by putting them to her lips or into her mouth. Freud suggested that the basic reason the child mouths objects is that she wishes to *incorporate* them and thus to control and master them.

The infant's personality, being mostly pleasure-seeking id, begins to distinguish *me* from *not-me* (evidence of a growing ego) by regarding pleasure-giving objects as *self* and non-pleasure-giving objects as *non-self*.

Some psychoanalysts divide the oral period into two substages, the early or *receptive stage* and the late or *biting stage*.

The receptive stage covers the first few months of life when erotic pleasure is derived from sucking, swallowing, and mouthing. At this time the infant is rather passive and plays an extremely dependent role. If his feeding and other dependency needs are not adequately met or if great conflict is associated with them, a residue of unfulfillment and conflict is repressed into the unconscious to reveal itself in subsequent years, often as neurotic overdependency or a compulsive habit of trying to "take in" other people and objects. In essence, Freudian theory sees the experience the child has with satisfying instinctual drives at a particular psychosexual stage as forming a model for attitudes or relationships that may be carried over to later life.

The biting stage occurs during the latter portion of infancy when teeth are erupting and gums are harder. The dominant zone of gratification is still the mouth, but at this point the act of touching things with the lips or of swallowing is not as satisfying as biting or chewing. As the infant's perceptual skills mature, she begins to recognize the features of outside objects more clearly. She now recognizes that one object, such as mother, can have both pleasure-giving and pain-giving functions. Mother gratifies hunger when the baby cries. But mother also has to carry out other activities in her life, so she cannot satisfy the baby's demands immediately all the time, and the baby finds this postponement painful.

As a result, the infant develops his first *ambivalent* feelings. He both loves and hates the same object. Freudian theory proposes that the child's early ambivalent feelings and sadistic tendencies are expressed in biting—biting his mother's breast, people's fingers, toys, and the like. If progress through this stage is incomplete, so that the infant experiences insufficient satisfaction of biting needs and has inadequate opportunities to express ambivalence without unduly painful repercussions, then a residue of conflict remains in the unconscious to disturb the individual in later life. If the child's progress through the latter oral stage is arrested—that is, if he becomes *fixated* at this point in psychosexual growth—then he may evidence such fixation as an adult through a pattern of "biting" criticism of others or by frequently "chewing out" people around him.

This phenomenon of fixation can occur at any of the psychosexual stages. Freudians hold that fixation—carrying into later life those modes of libidinal gratification suited to an earlier stage—can be the result of either too little or too much satisfaction at the stage in question. If the child's attempts at libidinal investment in an erogenous zone are frustrated, so there remains pent-up energy and inadequate satisfaction, then fixation may occur in the form of a constant seeking to gain the satisfaction in symbolic ways in subsequent years. In contrast, if so much satisfaction with a given erogenous zone is experienced so that the child does not wish to abandon this pleasure by moving ahead to mature forms of libidinal expression, then fixation may again be the result. At each psychosexual stage, the child progresses most satisfactorily if she gains enough pleasure to move ahead without dragging along a residue of unfulfilled needs, yet does not gain so much satisfaction that she is unwilling to advance.

Stage 2: The Anal Period (Ages 2–3)

During the second and third years of life, much of the attention of child and parents typically focuses on establishing proper control of the bowels. This time of life is usually called the anal period because the prime concern is with expelling and retaining feces. However, it is sometimes referred to as the *anal-urethral period* because control of urinary functions is also involved. Thus the dominant zones of gratification or libido investment become the anal cavity, the sphincter muscles of the lower bowel, and the muscles of the urinary system.

The shift of the child's attention to the anal area does not mean that the expression of instinctual energy via the oral zone has stopped. It means, rather, that anal activities usually become of major concern for both child and parent. In response to questions about the sequence of the oral, anal, and genital stages, Freud wrote:

It would be a mistake to suppose that these three phases succeed one another in a clear-cut fashion. One may appear in addition to another; they may overlap one another, may be present along side of one another (1938, p. 12).

In the anal period, much of the child's important contact with adults and much of the emotion adults express toward him are related to toilet training. Like the oral stage, the anal period can be divided into two sub-periods, the first concerned with pleasure in expelling feces and urine and the second with retaining these materials.

During the *expulsion stage* the child meets her first serious experience with an external barrier (parents' coercion to have the child control the bowels) to an instinctual cathexis (wishing to defecate). If the child is to accomplish bowel and bladder control, the ego must apply resistance to the child's urge to eliminate at the moment she feels the need. Thus the ego must borrow libido from the id to energize the resistance. Such a use of libidinal force by the ego—or at a later stage, by the superego—is called *countercathexis* or *anticathexis*. In short, the cathexis or energy investment of the id in the pleasurable release of defecation must be countered by an opposing cathexis of the ego if the child is to meet the parents' demands for cleanliness and thus retain their love.

This is a crucial time for the child to learn to earn love, praise, and approval. If the period is not handled properly by parents—if they harshly impose cleanliness standards before the child is physiologically prepared to control the bowels and bladder, for example—then the child's personality will retain vestiges of fear, guilt, and defiance. The repressed conflict may produce an adult who is compulsively regular and clean or, in contrast, one who is bitter and, in a symbolic sense, voids and urinates on others in his social interaction. The frequent use of the words *crap, shit,* and *bullshit* among adults is said to reflect a measure of fixation at the anal stage.

In the second half of the anal period, the child has learned to *retain* feces and urine at will. She now gains sensuous satisfaction by holding in, that is, by keeping the product she values. Freudians suggest that the child's idea of things having value comes from this period, and inadequate passage through the stage may show up later in life in acts of hoarding and collecting things.

Stage 3: The Infantile-Genital Period (Ages 3–4 or so)

The boy's penis and the girl's clitoris and vulva become the key objects of erotic pleasure during the third major psychosexual period. It, too, can be divided into two phases.

During the first phase, called the *phallic stage,* the child discovers that fondling the genitals, titillation, and masturbation (but without orgasm) give erotic pleasure. The child next associates fondling the genitals with a love object with whom he or she wishes to have some sort of sexual relations. For the boy, Freud says:

> The object that has been found turns out to be almost identical with the first object of the oral pleasure-instinct, which was reached by attachment (to the nutritional instinct). Though it is not actually the mother's breast, at least it is the mother. We call the mother the first *love*-object (1917, p. 329).

While the boy is viewing his mother as the desired object, he is at the same time recognizing that he cannot have her all to himself, for his father is the successful competitor for her affections. The resulting psychological conflict—wanting to possess mother but prevented from doing so by the powerful father—has been labeled the *Oedipus complex* or *Oedipus conflict.* The girl is in the opposite situation, wanting her father as her love partner but being defeated in this contest by her mother. The resulting conflict for the girl has been called the *Electra complex,* but both the boy's and girl's problems are usually subsumed under the Oedipus label.

During this period the child experiences strong ambivalent feelings, seeking the parent of the opposite sex as a lover, but at the same time both fearing and loving the parent of the same sex. An adequate resolution of the Oedipus situation occurs when the child rejects the sexual feelings toward the taboo object, the opposite-sex parent, and, at the same time, identifies with the parent of the same sex. By identifying with the same-sex parent, the child both assuages feelings of fear of reprisal and incorporates the traits of the same-sex parent, the traits that made that parent win the love of the other. In effect, the boy identifies with his father and seeks to adopt his father's characteristics. The girl does the same with her mother. This is the way Freudian theory accounts for the development of masculine and feminine characteristics that fit the mode of the society into which the child is raised.

It is during this process of solving the Oedipus conflict by repressing sexual desires and adopting parental characteristics that the superego evolves. To control what he now considers his dangerous sexual urges, the child incorporates parental values into his personality. These values, in the form of a superego that separates out of the ego, enable the child to reward and punish himself and thus control his own behavior in the absence of outside authority figures.

If the Oedipus conflict is not adequately resolved through repression of sexual impulses and identification with the like-sex parent, remnants of the conflict remain in the unconscious to distort the personality of the adolescent and adult. For instance, homosexuality sometimes has been explained as the child's identifying with the other-sex parent and thus modeling his or her subsequent living habits and sexual tastes after the opposite-sex parent rather than the same-sex one.

The resolution of the Oedipus complex leads into the second portion of the infantile-genital stage, called the *latency period*. Since this time of latent eroticism is so different in its manifestations from the early infantile-genital stage, we will treat it as a major period by itself.

Stage 4: The Latency Period (from Ages 4 or 5 to Puberty at Ages 11–13)

During this period, the dominant zone of gratification is still the genital area, but this is usually not displayed in the child's behavior, for both the boy and girl are repressing expressions of sex in order to solve the Oedipus conflict. The child has cathected or adopted both the gratifying and punishing parts of the parents and thus considers talk and displays of sex to be "nasty." The boy stops masturbating because he is afraid of being punished by having his penis cut off, and the girl stops because she is afraid of losing parental love. According to Freud (1938, p. 10), the child falls "victim to *infantile amnesia*" and "forgets" (by use of repression) the sex urges and activities of the first five years of life.

Throughout the years of latency the child's interests in working and playing primarily with children of his or her own sex is a manifestation of efforts to control sexual thoughts. This period has sometimes been called the *gang age* because children seldom voluntarily form groups that include the opposite sex. Because of this same-sex tendency in social relationships, the period is also referred to as the *homosexual phase*, although the homosexual relationships often do not involve any overt sexual acts. Indeed, the rejection of "sex" which the child so strongly evidences at this time in order to control Oedipal tendencies can preclude even thinking about physical displays that might be construed as sexual, whether the object of these displays is a same-sex or opposite-sex peer. In effect, the superego serves as a strong, moralistic internal representative of parental, and thus societal, rules. Playing by the rules both in games and in other daily activities becomes a matter of great importance to children in this phase of growth.

Solving the Oedipus conflict and working through the latency phase successfully is a difficult, stressful task, and often children fail to complete it successfully. Some become fixated at this stage, so that in adult life they never feel comfortable around the opposite sex, and they may avoid sexual relations with the opposite sex or else perform sexual activities in an emotionally detached or aggressive manner.

Stage 5: The Mature Genital Period (from Ages 14–16 to 18 or 21)

The maturing of sexual functions at puberty and beyond is signaled in girls by menstruation and such secondary bodily changes as the rounding of the breasts and the growth of underarm and pubic hair. The parallel maturation in boys is shown by growth of the genital organs, the appearance of sperm cells, nocturnal emissions of semen (often accompanied by erotic dreams), lowering of the voice pitch, and the growth of underarm, facial, and pubic hair.

The primary zone of erotic pleasure or libidinal cathexis is still the penis in the boy and the vaginal area in the girl, but now the gratification involves sexual orgasm. Whereas during the latent period the child was interested primarily in peers of the same sex, now the attention turns to the opposite sex. In mature sexuality the dominant erotic activity becomes copulation with a partner of the opposite sex. To make the transition from the rejection of sex at the latency phase to the wholehearted pursuit of heterosexual activity is typically a psychologically demanding challenge, particularly in societies that have erected moral barriers against intercourse between unmarried people, especially between adolescents. And such was the case in the late nineteenth-century Viennese society from which Freud drew so many of his patients on whose psychoanalytic histories he erected his theory.

The process of working through the problems of this transition successfully not only enables the youth to gratify sexual instincts in a mature fashion but also gives her or him a less egocentric, more objective perspective of the world in general. The superego has been well formed, with its appropriate conscience and ego ideal. The ego operates on the reality principle, having developed direct modes of solving life's problems and not depending unduly on defense mechanisms.

However, it is during this final stage of psychosexual development that society's rules about the conditions under which sexual intercourse is permissible often press youths to adopt sublimation as a defense mechanism. That is, the adolescent abstains from copulation and substitutes instead artistic or philanthropic activities to express sexual drives indirectly. The substitute may be writing poetry, reading literature, singing or playing a musical instrument, caring for children, aiding the handicapped, engaging in sports, or the like. (The question of whether such sublimation actually does satisfy sexual urges is an unsettled issue, still debated among psychoanalysts and among psychiatrists of other persuasions.)

The Stages and Therapy

Freud's concept of stages is the key to the practice of psychoanalysis as a method of aiding both children and adults who suffer neuroses, with *neuroses* meaning psychic disorders which are distressing but do not cause the person to view the world in a seriously distorted way, as is the case in psychoses. The task of the therapist is to use free association and dream interpretation to search back through the patient's psychosexual history to locate the stage at which unresolved conflicts were repressed. Through analysis the therapist hopes to reveal to the patient the original causes of the repressed problem and, by consciously reviewing the original conflicts, to help the patient recognize them for what they are and to integrate this new understanding into the personality. In short, the conflict is dug up and relived both intellectually and emotionally. When this process is complete, the neurotic symptoms that brought the patient to the psychoanalyst are expected to disappear. Thus psychoanalysts do not attempt to change neurotic symptoms directly, which they believe is folly but, rather, to find the repressed conflict that is causing the symptom. They believe that when the conflict is resolved and psychologically integrated, the symptoms will evaporate. Treating a symptom directly, they say, does not solve the problem but at best only causes the patient to substitute a different symptom for the one that has been treated. The underlying cause, they insist, must be found and relived realistically. (As we will see in Part Six behaviorists believe quite the opposite.)

TWO FACETS OF DEVELOPMENT

Now that the main features of Freud's model have been described, we will consider two aspects of it in more detail. The discussion will illustrate something of the complexity of Freud's speculation about development and also show how these aspects—the development of consciousness and of ego strength—fit into the overall framework.

The Development of Consciousness

In Freud's system, the conscious aspect of mental life does not burst forth in its mature, ultimate state at the time of birth or during infancy. Instead, both consciousness and the preconscious develop over the years as the personality is influenced by increasing internal maturation and by ever-widening experiences with the world. This development is perhaps best explained in terms of the relationship that evolves among the levels of awareness (con-

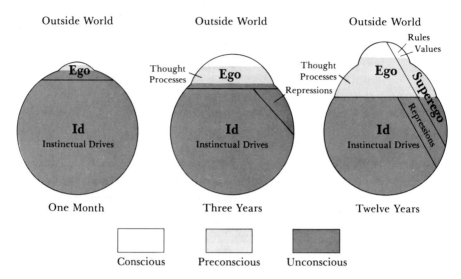

Figure 8.1 Developmental Trends in the Structure of the Mind

scious, preconscious, unconscious) and the apparatus of mental life (id, ego, superego).

One of the major challenges Freud faced over the last two or three decades of his life was that of describing clearly the way levels of consciousness interacted with the id, ego, and superego as the child grew up. As he admitted, his attempts at solving this riddle met with only partial success because of the difficulty of penetrating such tangled and clouded territories as the preconscious and unconscious. "And the profound obscurity of the background of our ignorance is scarcely illuminated by a few glimmers of insight" (Freud, 1938, p. 20). Nevertheless, he did depict something of what he saw with the aid of such glimmers, and Figure 8.1 attempts to diagram this. (For Freud's sketches of the adult mind, see 1923, p.14; 1933, p.111.)

The diagrams, based on Freud's opinions about the course of personality development in the Western industrialized society he knew best, sketch the anatomy of the mind at three age levels—one month, three years, and twelve years.

Shortly after birth the mind of the newborn in Freud's system is nearly all unconscious, with the unconscious dominated by the instinctual urges arising from the core of the id. Indeed, throughout life the commanding functionary in the unconscious is the id, operating on the pleasure principle without regard for the rules of the outside world. At this beginning stage of life the ego, as arbitrator between instinctual demands and the realities of the outside world, is as yet very small and weak. Only a tiny part of the ego can properly be called conscious, for the young infant has but an embryonic, vague awareness of its existence.

When we identify the ego as the operative of the personality that takes action in the real world to expend instinctual energy from the id, then it is reasonable to assume that the predominant portion of the ego shortly after birth must be preconscious and/or unconscious. This assumption is based on the observation that most—or perhaps all—behavior of the newborn is performed without conscious intent. The neonate does not have to decide to make the heart beat, the lungs breathe, the lips suck, the eyelids close under strong light, or the arms and legs wiggle. These are all done automatically. But as time passes, the internal maturation of the neural system and sensations from the outside world press the infant to become increasingly aware of what possible actions may fulfill needs arising from the unconscious sources. The child also becomes more skilled in choosing from among these possibilities those acts that are likely to bring the greatest satisfaction at the least expense in terms of pain. In short, the reality principle on which the ego operates begins to guide more of the infant's behavior.

By age 3 the child's transactions with the world have improved the clarity of consciousness and greatly expanded the area of the preconscious. At this point we can identify more precisely the characteristics of the conscious and the preconscious and describe their interactions.

The conscious—sometimes called the *system perceptual conscious*—is what the individual is attending to at the moment. It is what we are presently aware of seeing, hearing, feeling, or thinking about. The conscious is the outermost surface of the mental apparatus, the part in immediate contact with the outside world. The conscious is the nucleus of the ego (Freud, 1923, pp. 9, 18).

The images or ideas on which our attention is focused at the moment are limited in number and scope. We cannot keep many things in consciousness at one time. Rather, the images are like a sequence of individual pictures; each appears momentarily, then shifts in form or passes by to make way for the next. This notion of the kaleidoscopic nature of the conscious is reflected in the phrase *stream of consciousness*. However, once the images pass, they are not gone forever. Either we can purposely bring them to mind again by recalling them to the stage of consciousness, or else they may intrude from without (as sense impressions on the eyes and ears from sources in the environment) or extrude from within (as thoughts and feelings that rise into our awareness from we know not where). However, whether from an outside or an inside source, these things that catch our attention must have one characteristic: They must be *perceptible*. They must assume a recognizable form as an image or a verbal symbol or word construction. In other words, amorphous, raw sensations from one's unconscious cannot be perceived until they are cast either as *mental images* (pictorial or auditory forms as in dreams) or as *verbal symbols* or *word presentations* (words, phrases, and sentences that have been attached to sensations recorded from the outside world).

Functions of the Preconscious   With this logic in mind, let us consider the reasons why Freud postulated the existence of a *preconscious* as an intermediary between the conscious and the unconscious. Freud envisioned the unconscious (chiefly the domain of the id) as the receptacle for instinctual energy, for ill-defined needs and urges. But he also needed a receptacle for material that was not in the mind at the moment but that could be recalled at will. So, as the storage area for memory traces of conscious perceptions from the past, for material not at the moment "conscious" but yet available to be retrieved if desired, he created the preconscious. Whereas the unconscious was pictured mainly as the operating arena for the id, the preconscious was described as basically under control of the ego.

In addition to being the storage area for retrievable memory traces, the preconscious was pictured as the processing chamber in which the ego receives amorphous urges from the id and recasts them into the image or verbal form required for their perception by the conscious ego. Recall that before the conscious ego can find ways to satisfy inner needs through trafficking in the real world, the needs must be put into perceptible shape. Freud proposed that this act of translating was performed by preconscious molding procedures that "we may—roughly and inexactly—sum up under the name of thought-processes" (Freud, 1923, pp. 9–10). It seems likely that what he meant by *thought-processes* are those mental acts known as analyzing, synthesizing, denoting, identifying, evaluating, and such.

In speaking of things arising from the unconscious and seeking expression, Freud distinguished between the route taken by ideas and the route taken by feelings. While ideas need to be processed by the preconscious, clothed by it in the recognizable raiment of familiar images or word presentations before they can appear in consciousness, feelings do not. Rather, they are emitted directly into consciousness from the unconscious (Freud, 1923, pp. 12–13).

Having identified the conscious and preconscious roles performed by the ego, we can now understand more clearly the differences between the mental maps for the one-month-old and three-year-old in Figure 8.1. The neonate's preconscious barely, if at all, exists, and the conscious is very limited in scope and clarity. But by age 3 the conscious is more extensive and acute, and the preconscious is far larger, in the sense of containing rapidly increasing numbers of memory traces drawn from experiences in the world. Furthermore, the preconscious has acquired certain of its contents—particularly its thought processes—from the unconscious. As the hypothetical twelve-year-old mind also illustrates, this trend of the preconscious becoming more complex over the years continues throughout the period of child and adolescent development. Greater internal maturation of the neural system interacts with more and more experiences in the outside world to produce more memory traces and more sophisticated thought processes.

The Dynamics of Repression   A comparison of the diagrams of the one-month-old and three-year-old minds also shows that the ego has now added something of its own to the unconscious. This something consists of psychologically painful thoughts that have been repressed into an unconscious condition by the ego because it found them too unbearable to maintain in consciousness or preconsciousness but did not know how to eliminate or solve them in a satisfactory conscious manner. We assume that these repressed materials at age 3 are seated in anxieties that arose during the oral and anal stages (from birth through about ages 2–3) from conflicts with the parents. For example, in Freud's view parents' unreasonable and often harsh demands for bowel and bladder control when the child is not yet ready for such control can cause the child to feel inadequate and to fear the loss of parental love. Since the child's weak ego cannot solve the conflict on the conscious level, the ego frantically relegates the painful events to the unconscious. And, as the diagram of the twelve-year-old mind suggests, we can assume that the amount of repressed material will increase by that age due to the psychic conflicts experienced during the Oedipal period around ages 3 to 5 and thereafter.

In summary, then, throughout the early years of life, the child's conscious grows in clarity, and the ego builds up a supply center of recallable memories from past perceptions, memories deposited in an expanding preconscious. At the same time, particularly painful problems that the immature ego is ill prepared to master are pushed out of consciousness to be actively held in the unconscious by means of energy borrowed from the id. The supply of psychic energy available for conducting conscious and preconscious affairs is thus depleted by this diverting of energy for purposes of repression. Furthermore, as noted earlier, such repressed problems are really postponed rather than solved, for they continue to seethe and to express themselves out of the unconscious in deviant ways, such as neuroses.

The third diagram, the hypothetical twelve-year-old mind, also shows the new functionary, the superego, which has grown out of the ego during the Oedipal period of middle childhood. Freud proposed that the superego starts developing around age 3, or perhaps slightly earlier, in which case a sliver of its influence could have been included in the diagram of the three-year-old mind. The superego at the conscious and preconscious levels appears as the set of conscious values or rules of living that guide the older child's behavior even when parents, teachers, and police are not present. But the existence in the adolescent's psyche of free-floating anxiety and of vague feelings of guilt and shame that are not attached to any particular event suggests that the superego has an unconscious aspect as well. In effect, the older child or adolescent can "feel bad" without knowing why. This means, in Freud's scheme, that the youth has incorporated into her personality certain parental expectations that she does not consciously recognize. Apparently these expectations or standards are ones associated with traumatic early experiences that have since been repressed.

Thus, as the child grows up, the relationships among levels of consciousness and the psychic operatives (id, ego, and superego) shift so that the child gains increasing control over his fate. At the same time, he is victimized by repressions that sap his psychic energy, divert his attention from reasonable conscious action, and cause distressing, illogical thoughts and behavior.

Developing Ego Strength

Closely tied to the processes we have just discussed is the matter of developing a strong ego. Although Freud did not describe ego strength in exactly the terms used here, it seems reasonable to assume, from all he wrote about the ego, that the following definition faithfully reflects his opinion: A strong ego is one that has at its command sufficient adjustment techniques to: (1) fulfill the id's instinctual needs without neglecting or unduly postponing any need and, at the same time, (2) satisfy the expectations imposed on the individual by both (a) the physical and social environments and (b) the individual's superego.

A weak ego, in contrast, is one that lacks sufficient conscious methods of expending instinctual energy that are acceptable to the environment and superego. A weak ego, faced by conflicting demands that it cannot consciously satisfy, reverts to its emergency technique of repression. Consequently, the weaker a person's ego, the more repressions we can expect to accumulate in the unconscious to plague him—unless, of course, some outside agent, such as a parent or other caretaker, intervenes to reduce the number of demands pressed upon the ego from the environment. It is in this matter of intervention that Freud's concept of ego strength bears important implications for child-raising practices.

The newborn's ego is very weak. It has only a few, simplistic methods for

arbitrating the conflict between id demands and environmental requirements. The child will require far greater neural maturation and experience
with the world to develop the broad array of sophisticated adjustment
methods that mark the strong ego. If the neonate is to survive and is to avoid
storing up a dangerous cargo of repressions to bear through life, she requires a lot of outside help from parents and others. Although there is
nothing these outside agents can do to control the instinctual drives arising
from the id, they can do something about the environment. Their aid in
reducing the weak ego's burden of decisions can take two general forms.
First, parents can provide the infant with certain things that she cannot
obtain by herself, such as food and warmth. They can also furnish, in
gradual steps, opportunities for the child to exercise her body and her
perceptual system so that she learns to comprehend and act on her world in
increasingly effective ways. Second, parents can protect the infant from
intense stimuli that could overwhelm her perceptual capacities, stimuli that
frighten her because she cannot understand or control them. Examples of
such stimuli are loud noises, flashes of light, loss of support so the child
suddenly drops, angry arguments and fights, and the like. But perhaps even
more important is the parental role of protecting the young child from
societal expectations that are beyond the child's capacity to fulfill. It was in
relation to this role that Freud particularly criticized European child-rearing
practices of his day. He felt that since nothing could be done to lessen the
instinctual-drive demands on the weak ego, it was necessary for society to
permit these drives freer direct expression in the early years of life instead of
strictly censoring such expression.

> From a biological standpoint the ego comes to grief over the task of
> mastering the excitations of the early sexual period, at a time when its
> immaturity makes it incompetent to do so. It is in this lagging of ego
> development behind libidinal development that we see the essential pre-
> condition of neurosis; and we cannot escape the conclusion that neuroses
> could be avoided if the childish ego were spared this task — if, that is to say,
> the child's sexual life were allowed free play, as happens among many
> primitive peoples (Freud, 1938, p. 57).

While Freud proposed that fewer repressions and subsequent neuroses
would develop if sexual urges (including sucking and biting in the oral stage
and bowel and urinary activities in the anal stage) were allowed "free play,"
he proposed as well that civilization as we know it would not have developed
under such free-expression conditions. He believed that the early "dam-
ming up" of the sexual instinct forced the growing child and subsequently
the adult to redirect at least a portion of this energy into other channels

through the adjustment technique of sublimation. This redirecting or sub-limating process, he felt, caused many of the developments of our culture, since diverted libido was put to the task of fueling inventions, art works, literary creations, social service, and the like (Freud, 1938, p. 58). So in this sense, the variegated culture that we enjoy has been paid for, at least partially, by repressions by a weak ego early in life.

What, then, does all this mean for parents and other caretakers who wish to guide child growth in ways that promote the development of a strong ego and keep at a minimum repressions that will cause distressing neurotic symptoms? The answer, from a psychoanalytic viewpoint, consists of five principles. Both actual parents and surrogate parents should:

1. Recognize the nature of instinctual urges and accept the desirability of permitting expression of the urges.

2. Recognize the normal psychosexual stages of development and the sorts of conflicts the child faces at each stage.

3. Provide at each developmental stage enough opportunities for the child to satisfy instinctual drives within an atmosphere of under-standing, but not furnish so much satisfaction that the child becomes fixated at that point and is unwilling to move ahead to the next stage.

4. Furnish plenty of nurture and protection to the infant in the early years so that the child's weak ego is not overwhelmed by the physical environment and societal standards.

5. As time passes, provide increasing amounts of guidance (teaching) in problem solving so that the ego develops an ever-expanding repertoire of conscious adjustment techniques to fill all kinds of instinctual demands under all sorts of environmental conditions.

In summary, the theory Freud devised to explain the origins of adult neuroses yielded, as a by-product, a number of general principles for guiding the normal personality development of children at all stages of the growth process, including the development of a strong ego.

Now that we have considered key elements of Freud's model of child development, we will look briefly at the sorts of contributions his daughter Anna made to his work.

ANNA FREUD'S PSYCHOANALYSIS OF CHILDREN

Sigmund Freud's model of child development was not constructed from direct observations of children. It was fashioned from the free associations and dreams of the neurotic adults he treated. However, Freud's daughter Anna (born 1895) spent a major part of her adult life as a psychoanalyst working directly with children. She was a rather strict adherent of her father's theory, but she found it desirable to clarify and embellish certain aspects of it on the basis of her experience treating childhood neuroses. Her additions to Freudian theory were not published as a single, comprehensive treatise, but appeared instead as occasional articles and speeches over a period of forty years, from the 1920s to the mid-1960s. These scattered works have now been brought together in five volumes as *The Writings of Anna Freud* (1974).

The kinds of contributions she made can be illustrated with three examples; these concern: (1) the psychoanalytic treatment of a child while his or her superego is still being formed, (2) the value of direct observations of children, and (3) implications of psychoanalysis for raising the normal child.

Status of the Superego

Like her father, Anna Freud explained that many adult neuroses result from an overly punitive superego. It is the task of the psychoanalyst to help the patient reorganize the contents of the superego so they fit reality more adequately and do not pose unreasonable standards to which the individual is forced to aspire. In the adult neurotic, this rebuilding task is long and painful, for the superego has, since the time of early adolescence, become a powerful component of the personality, highly resistant to alterations. But in the older child or early adolescent, the superego is yet in the process of formation. The child is still in a state of transition between (1) receiving orders or values from her or his parents or parent figures and (2) receiving orders from the evolving superego, which has not yet separated from either the ego or its external sources (parents, peers, teachers).

Adult psychoanalysis need involve only the patient and the analyst. However, in Anna Freud's opinion, childhood neuroses are best treated by the analyst working both with the child and with such important agents of his environment as parents and teachers. By changing parents' expectations for, and treatment of, the child, the analyst hopes to influence the contents of the as-yet-dependent superego and cure the neurosis with greater speed than would be possible in an adult, whose overly demanding superego has already solidified. Thus the analyst who works with children manipulates the environment in addition to re-forming the relationships within the child's personality among the id, ego, and superego (A. Freud, 1974, vol. I, pp. 57–58).

Direct Observations of Children

In adult psychoanalysis, the source of the therapist's information is almost exclusively the patient's talk about herself. However, children are not as adept at explaining, upon command, their past history, worries, and fantasies. Thus Anna Freud recommended that in child analysis dream interpretation should be supplemented with information provided by the child's family and by the therapist's observations of the child's actions. By noting patterns of feeding, sleep, illness, play, and the like, the analyst can select aspects of behavior that, according to psychoanalytic theory, grew out of the earlier oral, anal, and infantile-genital periods. Therefore, in child analysis certain types of observations can serve as substitutes for the free-association data on which the analysis of adults' psychological problems is usually founded (A. Freud, 1974, vol. V, pp. 95–101).

Psychoanalysis and Child-Rearing Practices

In 1956 Anna Freud stated, "While we are unable to alter the innate givens of a human being, we may be in the position to relieve some of the external pressures which interact with them" (1974, vol. V, pp. 265–266). She believed that psychoanalytic theory could make a major contribution toward the relief of such external pressures by helping parents gain "insight into the potential harm done to young children during the critical years of their development by the manner in which their needs, drives, wishes, and emotional dependencies are met" (1974, vol. V, p. 266). She then explained that the types of help psychoanalysis had already provided included: (1) the sexual enlightenment of children, (2) recognition of the role of conflict, conscience, and anxiety in the development of the child—a recognition that resulted in parents' limiting their authority over the child, (3) freedom for the child to express aggression, (4) recognition of the importance of the mother-infant relationship, and (5) an understanding of the mother's role as an auxiliary ego for the growing child.

In summary, Anna Freud extended psychoanalytic theory by adding to it a variety of conclusions she extracted from her direct observations of, and therapy sessions with, children at several stages of their development.

PRACTICAL APPLICATIONS

Freudian theory has been applied to the treatment of children in at least three major ways—in general child-rearing practices, in schooling at the early childhood level, and in modes of therapy.

Over the past few decades, psychoanalytic suggestions have exerted substantial influence on the child-rearing views of "concerned and well-read" adults, especially in Europe and America. These suggestions have focused on children's emotional needs, particularly in the areas of sex and aggression, and on such concepts as unconscious motivation. For instance, from the Freudian proposals about the oral stage comes the recommendation that infants be given plenty of opportunities to be cuddled and to satisfy their sucking needs, especially at feeding times. From beliefs about the anal phase comes the recommendation that toilet training should not be attempted too early, nor should it be enforced in a punitive fashion. Furthermore, toilet training should not be accompanied by distressing emotional outbursts from parents or even by half-disguised expressions of disgust, which the child interprets as threats of the withdrawal of parents' love if the child does not perform how, when, and where the parents desire. There are also suggestions about how adults can best react to children's sexual curiosity during the years of childhood and adolescence. And from Freud's proposals about unconscious motivation, parents have increasingly come to expect that a child may not be aware of the true reasons he acts as he does because the stimuli for the acts may be repressed intentions. Thus, when the child is asked to explain why he has acted in a given manner, the reasons he offers may simply be rationalizations, that is, socially acceptable explanations for behavior that actually derives from ignoble motives.

In the realm of formal education, nursery school and kindergarten practice in particular has been influenced by Freudian beliefs about sexual curiosity, nontraumatic toilet training, the symbolic meaning of children's play with water and such messy substances as mud and finger paints, children's needs for such physical contact as hugging and stroking, their inquisitiveness about the usually hidden body parts of the opposite sex, and the importance of teachers as role models with whom the child may identify.

Techniques of psychotherapy for disturbed children have also been strongly affected by psychoanalytic theory. In order to understand the dynamics of interaction among members of the child's family, therapists provide dolls that can represent family members and then interpret in psychoanalytic terms the child's dramatic play with the dolls. In other cases the child is asked to draw a picture of her family and to talk about the relationships among the members and how she feels about them. Furthermore, children's use of such play materials as punching bags and wet clay has been interpreted as revealing the sources of a disturbed child's shame, hate, distrust, or fear. Use of such materials has also been judged of cathartic value, relieving in socially acceptable ways the child's pent-up distress.

RESEARCH CHALLENGES

The number of child development researchers turning to psychoanalytic sources for topics to investigate appears to have diminished over the past three decades or so. This shift is partly due to the attractiveness of more recent sources of ideas, such as Piaget's work, social learning models, the humanistic movement, and information-processing theory. And it is due as well to the fact that certain issues first popularized by Freud, such as the mind's levels of consciousness, have become so incorporated into the mainstream of psychology that they no longer are identified specifically as Freudian notions.

Yet research from a Freudian perspective does continue because there remain in psychoanalytic theory a good many unresolved matters—at least unresolved for people who are not doctrinaire Freudian disciples. Here is a sampling of such issues.

To what extent do objects and events in people's dreams have the same symbolic meaning in one person's life as they do in another's (a question inspired by Freud's contending that projectile shapes in dreams are to be interpreted universally as male phallic symbols while receptacle shapes are to be interpreted as female sex symbols)? Do dream objects and events have universal meanings only within a given culture? Or does an object have an idiosyncratic meaning for each person so that it is improper to interpret one person's dream contents as having the same meaning as another's?

To what degree do interpretations of children's doll play represent extensions of the therapist's own personality conflicts and obsessions rather than accurate descriptions of the child's inner life?

Is is true that too little or too much satisfaction at a psychosexual stage of development will lead to personality disorders in later life? And if so, how does one judge at the time the child is in a stage what constitutes too little or too much satisfaction? From the viewpoint of healthy development, is it ever desirable for a child to use such ego defense mechanisms as regression and projection? If so, how does one judge when their use is desirable and when it is not?

To cure a child of distressing fears or compulsive acts, is it necessary to unearth events in the child's earlier life that ostensibly created the fear or compulsion, or is it sufficient to work directly on dispelling the distressing symptoms by retraining and reassuring the child? And if a symptom is dispelled by direct retraining, will a different undesirable symptom inevitably arise to take its place?

FREUDIAN THEORY: AN ASSESSMENT

My assessment of psychoanalytic theory in terms of the nine appraisal standards is given on the accompanying rating scale. My explanation for these ratings begins with the item I rated the highest and then moves to those I rated lower.

There can be little doubt that Freudian theory deserves high marks for its success in stimulating new discoveries (item 8). It has been the basis for hundreds of articles reporting clinical studies of children's development, usually in the form of analyses of deviant types of development. It has also motivated investigators to launch new journals dedicated entirely to psychoanalytic topics and to write scores of books that offer extensions,

Freudian Theory

How well do I think the theory meets the standards?

The Standards	Very Well	Moderately Well	Very Poorly
1. Reflects the real world of children		X	
2. Is clearly understandable		X	
3. Explains the past and predicts the future	Specificity X	Accuracy ?	
4. Guides child rearing	X		
5. Is internally consistent		X	
6. Is economical		X	
7. Is falsifiable			X
8. Stimulates new discoveries	X		
9. Is self-satisfying		X	

embellishments, or revisions of the theory. Furthermore, the Freudian model has furnished ideas that have become the focus of investigations by experimental psychologists, including such prominent behaviorists as Dollard and Miller (1950) and Sears, Rau, and Alpert (1965).*

The second highest rating, on item 4, is my estimate of the substantial influence psychoanalytic suggestions have exerted on the child-rearing views as summarized above under practical applications. Frequently, specific beliefs about child raising derived from Freudian theory appear as topics in both professional and popular publications and in the mass media.

However, although psychoanalytic theory offers guidance for handling children's emotional growth, it offers little or no help for directing children's academic (cognitive) development or physical growth, except in cases of physical ailments suspected of having a psychological origin. The rating on item 4, therefore, is a balance between Freudian suggestions about emotional development and a lack of suggestions about cognitive and physical growth.

As for the theory's clarity (item 2), I estimate that it deserves a mark slightly above the middle of the scale. Freudians explain the system's main components rather clearly, I feel, at least in general. And Freud's practice of illustrating these components with examples from cases of people undergoing psychoanalysis helps communicate what he intends. But when we move beyond the basic outline of the theory's structure, many puzzles appear, calling for greater clarification. As one illustration of confusion, E. Nagel has complained that the Freudian:

> Sometimes describes the main theoretical components of the mental apparatus as "units of functions," and suggests that unconscious drives are like dispositions. But he also declares that these components possess energies and conflict with one another—though without explaining in what sense functions can be charged with energies or dispositions can be engaged in conflicts (1959, p. 46).

In short, when we inspect the psychoanalytic model of child development in detail, we find it can profit from a good deal of additional clarification.

The issue of clarity is also related to item 1 (reflects real world of children), which I have rated slightly below the center. I believe that in Freud's favor are his (1) bringing to public view the importance and commonality of sexual interests in childhood and adolescence, (2) identifying defense mechanisms children develop, (3) describing children's ambivalent

---

*For summaries of experimental studies, see Frenkel-Brunswik (1954), Hilgard (1952), Kris (1947), and Sears (1943).

feelings—hate combined with love—toward parents and others close to them, and similar proposals. Observations of children's behavior would appear to substantiate these findings as phenomena in real children's lives (Hilgard, 1952).

But balanced against such items, which are confirmable by direct observation or assessment, is a large portion of Freudian theory that has not been substantiated in such an open or public manner. Some critics have been particularly blunt in their charges that psychoanalysts have failed to conduct the investigations that will convincingly test the theory's proposals. M. Scriven has written that:

> As a set of hypotheses it was a great achievement 50 years ago; as no more than a set of hypotheses it is a great disgrace today. . . . It is in fact the most sophisticated form of metaphysics ever to enjoy support as a scientific theory (1959, pp. 226–227).

Part of the difficulty with Freud's model as an accurate reflector of real children's development lies in the source of data on which he founded his theory. He did not directly observe, test, or measure children during their years of growth, as did many other theorists. Actually, there were at least four somewhat "slippery" steps between his data and the growing child. That is, his process of collecting data during therapy sessions with neurotic adults involved: (step 1) the analyst's *interpreting* from his viewpoint or through his "lens" (step 2) ostensibly *symbolic* material derived from (step 3) reported *dreams* and *memories* of neurotics about (step 4) *ostensible experiences* from their childhood one or more decades earlier. In view of this mode of gathering information, the theory's data base might be a distortion of typical children's actions, thoughts, and emotions during each phase of growing up. I am skeptical about how well it represents real children's development, and I share the opinion of those critics who ask that the Freudian model be supported more adequately with publicly verifiable evidence.

Probably the main reason psychoanalytic theory has been difficult either to verify or to refute is not that its adherents are stubbornly defensive or are inept researchers (though in some instances this may be the case), but that many of its key elements, including the unconscious, repression, reaction formation, and symbolism, seem to render it nonfalsifiable. These elements have caused critics to harbor "the suspicion that Freudian theory can always be so manipulated that it escapes refutation no matter what the well-established facts may be" (Nagel, 1959, p. 44). Since I share this suspicion, I have rated psychoanalysis at the bottom on item 7 (falsifiability).

Imagine that we wish to check the validity of the concept of the Oedipus conflict, and will do so by interviewing adolescents about the sexual ideas they had during their earlier childhood years. If the adolescents' answers corroborate the notion that the father–daughter, mother–son "family romance" is widely spread, we might consider these answers as evidence supporting the Oedipus-complex concept. But let us say that we get just the opposite results from our interviews. The adolescents, seeking to be as truthful as possible, rarely have any memories of Oedipal strivings. Can we then interpret this as evidence against the notion of a universal Oedipus conflict? Freudians would say no. They would contend, instead, that the negative responses show that the earlier sexual urges have been repressed into the unconscious, so the adolescents' denial of such thoughts is proof of both the Oedipus complex and of the defense mechanism of repression. Under these conditions, there is no way to test the validity of the Oedipus concept through the retrospective interview that Freudians use as the source of evidence about how children develop.

The concept of reaction formation poses the same problem for assessing the theory. Reaction formation is the defense mechanism that occurs when a person is driven by an urge or wish (id) that conflicts with her moral values (superego), and to solve the conflict she (ego) represses the urge and behaves as if her motives were just the opposite. A child's overt sex play is seen as direct evidence of the proposed libidinal energy. But the opposite behavior—puritanical avoidance of sex—is interpreted as an expression of exactly the same libidinal or sexual energy but expressed through the mechanism of *reaction formation*. Likewise, both the child who habitually fights (displaying direct aggression) and the one who is the habitual pacifist (showing reaction formation) are seen as driven by the same aggressive urge (death instinct). Once more, an appraiser of the theory is at a loss in deciding how to handle a model that derives identical conclusions from diametrically opposed data.

The role of symbols in Freud's scheme presents other puzzles. Freud proposed that a person's ego, in cooperation with the superego, censors repressed material that seeks to arise from the unconscious into consciousness. But he also said that repressed wishes can sneak past the censor in disguise, that is, in symbolic form. For instance, we noted in Chapter One that Freud considered any elongated, projectile-shaped object that appeared in a dream to be a symbol of the male penis. An open, container-like object symbolized the female vagina (Freud, 1900). In a similar fashion, Freud interpreted many other images from dreams as symbols, rather than as direct descriptions, of events in people's daily lives. So Freudians, with this notion of symbolism in their analytic armory, can interpret all sorts of thoughts that people express as support for their theory.

So, Freud's model of child development and personality structure may be correct, but the game of verification is unmanageable if it must be played with the elastic ground rules permitted by the inclusion of such concepts as the above. The fairly low mark given for item 5 (internal consistency) is also primarily a result of these considerations.

On item 6, whether the theory is economical, I have marked Freud's theory near the middle. While some aspects of his model appear to be direct, economical ways to explain the phenomena on which he focuses, others appear to me unduly complex. There should be simpler ways to account for the phenomena in question. For instance, there should be less confusing and simpler ways to account for fixations than to claim that they are caused by both over- and undersatisfaction of needs at a given psychosexual stage. Furthermore, there should be simpler ways to account for the prepuberal child's personal-social behavior than the Oedipus complex that Freud proposed. This is not to say Freud is wrong, but the same phenomena can be attributed to simpler sets of factors.

The difficulty experienced in giving a reasonable rating on item 3 (explains the past and predicts the future) is reflected by the two marks on the line. The mark for specificity is at the high end of the scale, principally because Freudian explanations of what psychosexual events occurred earlier in an individual's life, and why they occurred, are quite specific. Psychoanalysis emphasizes the past history of development as uncovered through free association and dream interpretation. But psychoanalytic predictions of the future are usually sketched in a more general way, often in terms of possible deviant development that might occur if the child's needs during upcoming psychosexual stages are not dealt with wisely by the adults who most affect the child's life. In consideration of the theory's very specific explanations of the past and more general predictions of the future, I have marked it relatively high for *specificity*.

However, *accuracy* of explanation and prediction is quite a different matter. For the sorts of reasons given in the discussion of falsifiability I am skeptical about the validity of explanations founded on the theory. On the basis of this skepticism, I have used a question mark as a rating in the lower range of item 3. The theory needs better validation.

Finally we come to the self-satisfying quality of Freud's model (item 9). In the case of psychoanalytic theory, this ninth standard is of particular importance because Freud's proposals have depended so heavily on personal affirmation for their acceptance. By *personal affirmation* I mean the "feeling" that psychoanalytic theory does indeed describe the way one's personality evolves and functions. Or as S. Hook has noted (1959, p. 213), some Freudians' response to criticism has been that "psychoanalysis may be unscientific, but it is true." And to some degree I must admit to sharing such a feeling. Despite the shortcomings of Freudian theory when judged against common scientific criteria like the foregoing standards, much of the theory makes a kind of existential sense to me. I believe in the unconscious, in repression, in our use of defense mechanisms, and in many other concepts the theory includes. But I remain skeptical about still other aspects of the model. For these reasons, I have rated it in the middle of the scale for item 9.

FOR FURTHER READING

The first two books are paperbacks offering concise, simplified, and accurate accounts of psychoanalytic theory.

Hall, Calvin S. (1954) *A Primer of Freudian Psychology*. New York: World. This is a systematic description of psychoanalysis as a theory of personality development. Hall has based his account on material drawn from a variety of Freud's writings.

Stafford-Clark, David. (1967) *What Freud Really Said*. London: Penguin. A description of the evolution of Freud's ideas, including summaries of several of his most significant publications.

The next two items are translations of Freud's own writings. The first of these is a seventy-five-page summary of psychoanalytic theory written near the close of his career. The second is a thirty-volume edition of his complete works, useful for its detail and for the picture it offers of Freud's revisions over a period of nearly five decades.

Freud, Sigmund. (1938) *An Outline of Psychoanalysis*. London: Hogarth, 1973.

Freud, Sigmund. (1964) *The Standard Edition of the Complete Psychological Works of Sigmund Freud*. James Strachey, translator and editor. London: Hogarth. In thirty volumes.

The most complete source of Anna Freud's works is the following collection:

Freud, Anna. (1974) *The Writings of Anna Freud*. New York: International Universities Press. In five volumes.

CHAPTER NINE

Erikson's Variation on Freud's Theme

Erik Homburger Erikson (born 1902) is a German-born psychoanalyst whose self-imposed mission has been to extend and refine Freud's notions of personality development, with particular attention to child development.

Three of the most significant features of Erikson's refinement have been his proposals regarding:

1. The development of the *healthy personality,* in contrast to Freud's emphasis on the growth and cure of neurotic behavior.

2. The process of socializing the child into a particular culture by passage through a series of innately determined *psychosocial stages* that parallel Freud's psychosexual stages.

3. The individual's task of achieving *ego identity* by means of solving specified identity crises at each psychosocial stage of growth.

Erikson's professional career began in Vienna, where he graduated from the Vienna Psychoanalytic Institute before coming to the United States in 1933. He entered clinical practice in the United States, became a citizen in 1939, and over a period of four decades made significant contributions to the literature on psychoanalysis, personality theory, educational practice, and social anthropology.

Much of Freud's theory—the existence and nature of the unconscious, the tripartite composition of the mind (id, ego, superego), psychosexual stages, and more—was accepted by Erikson as valid. Since he accepted these concepts, Erikson wrote relatively little about them. Instead, he focused his work on those facets of psychoanalytic theory he believed required extension and, to some degree, revision. In discussing Erikson's contributions, I focus on the key additions he proposed, not on his entire system of beliefs. These additions are: (1) the nature of a healthy personality and of ego identity, (2) the epigenetic principle, and (3) stages of psychosocial growth and the identity crises. Finally, there is an assessment of Erikson's ideas from the viewpoint of someone who works with children and is interested in theory construction.

EGO IDENTITY AND THE HEALTHY PERSONALITY

Erikson agreed with those critics of Freud who claimed that Freud had focused only on neurotic personalities and, in consequence, had neglected to define the nature of healthy personalities or to trace their pattern of development. Erikson sought to right this imbalance, and he began by identifying the characteristics of the healthy personality. These characteristics would be the goals and signs of desirable human development.

One statement of such characteristics that Erikson found suitable was that of Marie Jahoda, an American psychologist who believed that a healthy personality *actively masters* the environment, shows a certain *unity of personality,* and is able to *perceive* the world and self *correctly* (Erikson, 1968, p. 92). The newborn child displays none of these characteristics. The healthiest adult personality displays them all. Thus, in Erikson's view, "childhood is defined by [the characteristics'] initial absence and by their gradual development in complex steps of increasing differentiation" (1968, p. 92).

Phrased in a different way, "growing up" is a process of achieving *ego identity.* In Erikson's system, ego identity has two aspects. The first or inner-focused aspect is the person's recognition of his own unified "selfsameness and continuity in time" (Erikson, 1959, p. 23). It is knowing and accepting oneself. The second or outer-focused aspect is the individual's recognition of and identification with the ideals and essential pattern of his culture; it includes sharing "some kind of essential character with others" (Erikson, 1968, p. 104). The person who has attained ego identity has a clear picture and an acceptance of both his inner essence and the group culture in which he lives.

Since, in Erikson's view, human development consists of moving from nonego identity to ego identity, his picture of the developmental process features a description of "conflicts, inner and outer, which the vital personality weathers, re-emerging from each crisis with an increased sense of inner unity, with an increase of good judgment, and an increase in the capacity 'to do well' according to his own standards and to the standards of those who are significant to him" (Erikson, 1968, p. 92).

THE EPIGENETIC PRINCIPLE

Studies of the development of the human organism while it is still in the mother's womb have suggested that it develops from a single fertilized cell and follows the same general stages as all human organisms, until, after about nine months, a highly complex, multicellular baby with many differentiated but coordinated parts is born. The entire pattern of development, it is believed, is governed by a genetic structure common to all humans. In other words, the genes establish a construction plan and timetable for the development of each part.

Studies of physical development after birth suggest that the genetic plan does not stop with birth. Rather, the sequence of development of such skills as crawling and walking and such characteristics as adolescent breast growth in girls and facial hair in boys has been established by the genetic plan. These characteristics arise at a particular time in life according to a preestablished time schedule that is little affected by environmental influences.

The term *epigenetic principle* has been given to this belief that everything that grows is governed by a preset construction plan: "Out of this ground plan the parts arise, each part having its time of special ascendency, until all parts have arisen to form a functioning whole" (Erikson, 1968, p. 92).

Many people have accepted the principle as a guide to understanding physical growth. But Erikson extended the principle to social and psychological growth as well, proposing that personality appears to develop also according to steps "predetermined in the human organism's readiness to be driven toward, to be aware of, and to interact with a widening radius of significant individuals and institutions" (1968, p. 93). He recognized that this interaction would be somewhat different from one culture to another since the different cultures in which children grow up can vary in many significant ways. However, he held that personality growth follows a sequence of "inner laws" that set the potentialities for the kinds of significant interactions the child will achieve with the people and institutions she does meet in her particular culture.

In short, Erikson proposed that it is the nature of the human species to pass through an identifiable series of psychosocial stages as the individual grows up, stages determined genetically, regardless of the culture in which the growth occurs. The social environment, however, does have a significant effect on the nature of the crises arising at each stage and on the success with which the child and adolescent will master the stage.

✳ THE GRID OF PSYCHOSOCIAL STAGES

Erikson accepted Freud's set of psychosexual stages as a basically valid description of the key concerns of personality development from infancy to adulthood. However, Erikson felt that the Freudian formulation was incomplete in at least four respects.

✓First, he thought Freud gave too little recognition to the socialization of the child, particularly to the various patterns of behavior that different cultures consider desirable—patterns the child needs to adopt or adapt if he is to be given the approval of the group within which he grows up.

✓Second, Erikson believed there are stages of development after adolescence that Freud failed to recognize. Thus Erikson defined more clearly four additional levels from puberty and beyond.

✓Third, Erikson believed the interaction of the individual with her social environment produces a series of eight major *psychosocial crises* the individual must work through in order to achieve eventual ego identity and psychological health. Since Freud had not defined crises in a clear fashion, Erikson did so.

Finally, Erikson believed that the concepts of development could be better understood if they were cast in the form of a grid or matrix; such a grid had not been employed by Freud. Erikson produced a number of such grids to clarify the interaction and correlation among various aspects of development. One of these "worksheets," as he called them, is produced in an adapted form as Table 9.1.

Among Erikson's most significant additions to child development theory is his proposal that an individual undergoes eight psychosocial crises during development. These are listed in column A of Table 9.1. Each crisis or stage is phrased as a struggle between two opposite or conflicting personality characteristics. The trait of *trust* vies for dominance over *mistrust* in the infant's personality. At the next stage, the trait of *autonomy* struggles for ascendancy over *shame* and *doubt*. Six subsequent crises mark the next six stages of psychosocial growth to full ego identity or psychological maturity in the adult.

Although these conflicting traits or tendencies are cast in the form of absolutes, such as "absolute trust" versus "absolute mistrust," in reality they form graduated scales in the personality. Complete trust appears at one end of the scale line and complete mistrust at the other. Between these extremes are gradations that the individual may attain. In reality, no one reaches either extreme. Each personality represents some mixture of self-trust and mistrust, as well as some combination of trusting and mistrusting other people and the world in general. Consequently one way of describing the configuration of a given child's or adolescent's personality within Erikson's system would be to identify where, along each of these scale lines, the individual stands at any particular time.

Before we consider each of the stages in more detail, let's examine the other columns in Table 9.1 so the relationship between this material and the psychosocial crises is clear.

Column B of Table 9.1 lists the expanding circle of significant people with whom the growing child interacts. The particular crisis the child or adolescent faces at a given stage is worked out through interaction with the people or the social setting identified in column B as appropriate to the crisis.

Column C suggests those acts on which the growing child's attention concentrates at each crisis stage, and column D indicates which psychosexual step correlates with each act. Thus, during Freud's oral stage of earliest infancy, the baby concentrates on the acts (psychosocial modalities) of getting and giving in return. At the psychosexual stage of puberty, stage V, the young person concentrates on the acts of being oneself and sharing being oneself.

Keeping this worksheet in mind, we will consider in more detail the nature of Erikson's eight successive psychosocial crises or phases (Erikson, 1959, pp. 65–98).

Basic Trust versus Basic Mistrust

Erikson proposed that a sense of *trust*—being able to predict and depend upon one's own behavior and the behavior of others—is derived primarily from the experiences of the first year of life. In other words, a child's fundamental attitude about the dependability of the world is built chiefly on the relationship established as an infant during the oral or incorporative stage when feeding and mouthing objects is of prime importance. The most important person in the infant's life at this juncture is the mother or mother substitute. The particular point on the trust–mistrust scale that the child ultimately reaches will depend to a great extent on the quality of his relationship to the maternal figure during this first year out of the womb. If the infant's need for food, for exercising the lips and gums and the sucking mechanism, is frequently frustrated, the infant will begin life more toward the mistrust end of the scale. If the quality of affectional relationships at this time is poor, with the mother emotionally rejecting the baby while tending to its physical needs, the sense of trust will be damaged. This sets a poor foundation for the trust–mistrust ratio on which the child is to build the rest of his or her life.

Table 9.1 A Psychosocial Development "Worksheet"

Stage Number	Column A *Psychosocial Crisis*	Column B *Radius of Significant Relations*	Column C *Psychosocial Modalities*	Column D *Freud's Psychosexual Stages*	Column E *Approximate Ages in Years*
I	Trust versus Mistrust	Maternal person	To get To give in return	Oral-Respiratory, Sensory-Kinesthetic (Incorporative Modes)	0–1
II	Autonomy versus Shame, Doubt	Parental persons	To hold on To let go	Anal-Urethral, Muscular (Retentive-Eliminative)	2–3
III	Initiative versus Guilt	Basic family	To make (going after) To "make like" (playing)	Infantile-Genital, Locomotor (Intrusive, Inclusive)	3–6
IV	Industry versus Inferiority	"Neighborhood" and school	To make things (completing) To make things together	Latency	7–12 or so

Stage Number	Column A *Psychosocial Crisis*	Column B *Radius of Significant Relations*	Column C *Psychosocial Modalities*	Column D *Freud's Psycho-sexual Stages*	Column E *Approximate Ages in Years*
V	Identity and Repudiation versus Identity Diffusion	Peer groups and outgroups; models of leadership	To be oneself (or not to be) To share being oneself	Puberty and Adolescence	12–18 or so
VI	Intimacy and Solidarity versus Isolation	Partners in friendship, sex, competition, cooperation	To lose and find oneself in another	Mature Genitality	The 20s
VII	Generativity versus Self-Absorption	Divided labor and shared household	To make be To take care of		Late 20s to 50s
VIII	Integrity versus Despair	"Humankind" "My kind"	To be, through having been To face not being		50s and beyond

Adapted from Erikson, 1959, p. 166.

As to how permanent the damage done at this early stage will be, Erikson said that the manner in which this first crisis, like the succeeding ones, is settled at the crisis period is not necessarily unalterable for the rest of the person's life. Damage to the sense of trust that occurs by an unsatisfactory infant-mother relationship during the first year of life can be repaired somewhat in later years by the child's enjoying a particularly trustworthy social environment. However, the damage will not be completely undone by later positive experiences. In like manner, an infant who establishes a secure attitude of trust during the first year may have this attitude shaken in later years by experience with undependable people who are significant to him. But he will still retain a measure of self-trust and feel a trust of others founded on his success in passing through the trust–mistrust crisis of infancy. This principle of the permanence of influences during a crisis period is valid as well for the other crises faced at subsequent stages of growth.

Autonomy versus Shame and Doubt

In parallel with Freud's psychosexual anal stage during the second year of life, Erikson proposed a second psychosocial crisis. This second stage is influenced by the child's maturing muscle system, with an increased ability to expel or retain things, particularly bodily wastes. Evacuating the bowels and bladder not only causes the child to feel good but gives her a growing sense of power through control over the evacuation system.

In Erikson's opinion, the child's new sense of power is the basis for his developing a sense of autonomy, of being able to do things for himself. At the same time he runs the risk of trying too much too soon and thereby attracting the censure of those around him. Thus during this period the child requires a delicate balance between (1) parental firmness that lets the child know he has a trustworthy world that will prevent him from overstepping the bounds and (2) parental flexibility and patience that allows him gradually to gain bowel and bladder control at a pace commensurate with his understanding and the conscious control of his sphincter muscles. If outer control is too rigid or too early, demanding he control bowel and bladder before he is able, the child will be faced with "a double rebellion and a double defeat" (Erikson, 1959, p. 68). He is powerless to manage his bowels and powerless to control his parents' actions. So he either seeks satisfaction by regressing to oral activities — sucking his thumb, whining, and demanding attention — or he fakes progression by becoming hostile and willful. He may pretend that he has achieved control by rejecting others' aid, even though he really lacks the ability to be so independent.

Erikson proposed that parents who impose strict bowel training on the two-year-old may influence the child to become an overcompulsive adult who is stingy and meticulous with love, energy, time, and money. This overcompulsive behavior is accompanied by a lasting sense of doubt and shame. In contrast, firm but gradual and kindly bowel training can aid the child in developing a sense of *self-control without loss of self-esteem* and produce an adult with a strong but socially acceptable sense of autonomy (Erikson, 1959, p. 68).

Initiative versus Guilt

During the fourth and fifth years of life, the child gains more skill in using language, in moving about, and in handling things. As a result, his imagination expands to encompass "so many things that he cannot avoid frightening himself with what he has dreamed and thought up. Nevertheless, out of all this he must emerge with a sense of *unbroken initiative* as a basis for a high and yet realistic sense of ambition and independence" (Erikson, 1959, p. 75).

This is the time of the Oedipus conflict, when the conscience develops and serves as a control on initiative. Fear of sexual impulses toward the opposite-sex parent causes feelings of guilt. In order to navigate through this period successfully, the child needs the guidance of parents and teachers who understand the trials the child is facing. Through such understanding, the important adults in the child's life can alleviate the hatred and guilt the child may feel. This permits the "peaceful cultivation of initiative, a truly free sense of enterprise" (Erikson, 1959, p. 82). The child's mental and physical skills, unfettered by overbearing guilt, permit her to go after life in a self-confident way.

Industry versus Inferiority

Throughout the Freudian latency period, in the years before puberty, the child wants to get busy with activities worth his attention and to pursue these activities with his peers. In Erikson's opinion, children during the elementary school years need and enjoy hours of make-believe games and play, but they become dissatisfied with too much of this and want to do something worthwhile. They want to earn recognition by producing something, to gain the satisfaction of completing work by perseverance.

If adults pose tasks for children that they can accomplish and that they recognize as interesting and worthy, and if the adults furnish the guidance needed for completing the tasks, then the children have a better chance to come through the latency period with a sound sense of industry. However, if the child has not solved the Oedipal conflict or if family life has not prepared him or her well for school life, the period can produce just the opposite—a sense of inadequacy and inferiority. Feelings of inferiority may also occur if the things the child has already learned to do well are considered insignificant by the teacher and classmates. Furthermore, in Erikson's opinion, the child may have potential abilities that, if not evoked and nurtured during latency, may "develop late or never" (1959, p. 87).

Identity versus Identity Diffusion

Of all the growth stages, the one on which Erikson focused the greatest attention in his writings is the period of adolescence, particularly the onset of adolescence. During the early teens, with the arrival of puberty, the body grows rapidly and changes in curious ways. These changes are disturbing to both girls and boys. Their social roles take on new form, and the views they held of themselves in childhood no longer fit their new appearance and their new feelings for the opposite sex. In addition, adults and peers adopt new expectations for them as they move from childhood into youth. The confusion this creates for the incipient adolescent has been labeled the *identity crisis* by Erikson.

During this period the results of earlier years' experiences should lead to a successful integration of the individual's basic drives with her or his physical and intellectual endowment and opportunities in life. In effect, the child's development over the first dozen or so years should now synthesize to give a sense of *ego identity* or self-definition.

> The sense of ego identity, then, is the accrued confidence that one's ability to maintain inner sameness and continuity is matched by the sameness and continuity of one's meaning for others. Thus, self-esteem . . . grows to be a conviction that one is learning effective steps toward a tangible future, that one is developing a defined personality within a social reality which one understands (Erikson, 1959, p. 89).

Furthermore, the young adolescent should gain an increasing strength of purpose and understanding of reality as she recognizes that her own way of dealing with life—her way of mastering reality—is a proper variant of the ways in which other people successfully deal with their lives.

The great danger of this period has been termed either *role confusion* or *identity diffusion* by Erikson (1963, p. 261; 1959, p. 92). The youth does not know who he is to himself or to others. As a defense against a sense of identity diffusion, adolescents may overidentify with heroes or cliques and with crowds and causes; they can temporarily lose their own individuality. They help one another during these years of confusion and of unclear occupational direction by clustering together, by stereotyping themselves in their clothes and speech, in their ideals, and in their idols and enemies. They are frequently intolerant of others outside their clique. In search of self, they often come into conflict with parents, siblings, and others close to them while refighting "many of the battles of earlier years, even though to do so they must artificially appoint perfectly well-meaning people to play the roles of adversaries" (Erikson, 1963, p. 261).

Youths who solve the problems of the adolescent years come through with a strong sense of their own individuality and a recognition that they are acceptable to their society. Those who fail to work their way through the identity crisis continue to display in later life such marks of immaturity as intolerance, clannishness, cruel treatment of people who are "different," blind identification or loyalty to heroes and idols, and the like.

Three Adult Stages

With his description of the adolescent identity crisis, Erikson carried the narrative of psychosocial development through the second decade of life. However, unlike Freud, he did not stop at this point in describing personality growth. Rather, he added three more stages, depicting key conflicts faced by adults in their early, middle, and later years. Since our chief concern in this book is with growth through the teenage years, I will not dwell on the three adult stages but will simply mention the nature of the crises faced at those levels.

The transition from adolescence to adulthood is accompanied by the crisis of *intimacy and distantiation versus self-absorption.* Or, phrased another way, it is a crisis of intimacy and solidarity versus isolation. In Erikson's view, the youth who emerges from adolescence with a reasonable sense of her own identity is then prepared to establish a nonexploitative intimacy, sexually and intellectually, with a companion of the opposite sex. The youth whose identity is secure is also prepared to defend his or her rights and individuality against attackers. This ability to defend oneself is termed *distantiation* by Erikson. In his words, distantiation is the readiness to "repudiate, to isolate, and if necessary to destroy those forces and people whose essence seems dangerous to one's own" (1959, p. 95). Youths who fail at this stage are unable to establish intimate relations with a companion, so they retreat into self-absorption.

During the second adult stage, the psychosocial conflict involves *generativity versus stagnation* (or generativity versus self-absorption). Sexual partners who find true genitality (capacity for orgasmic potency with a love partner of the opposite sex) wish to combine their personalities in producing and caring for offspring, a condition that Erikson labeled *generativity*. Such partners are not simply absorbed in their own welfare.

In later years of adulthood the crisis involves *integrity versus despair and disgust*. The older person who achieves integrity is one who accepts his own life cycle and "is ready to defend the dignity of his own life style against all physical and economic threats" (Erikson, 1959, p. 98).

These, then, are the eight stages of development as conceived by Erikson in his theory of psychosocial periods. Since he introduced this scheme in 1959, he has periodically embellished it with additional propositions. For instance, in *Insight and Responsibility* (Erikson, 1964) he expanded his picture of positive ego development by describing a series of human *virtues*, which he identified as "qualities of strength."

> I . . . speak of Hope, Will, Purpose, and Competence as the rudiments of virtue developed in childhood; of Fidelity as the adolescent virtue; and of Love, Care, and Wisdom as the central virtues of adulthood (Erikson, 1964, pp. 113, 115).

These virtues, he said, are an expression of the integration of the psychosexual and psychosocial growth schedules. Each virtue has its particular time of arousal and emphasis in the hierarchy of epigenetic growth stages. For example, Erikson has postulated that the virtue of *hope* arises during early infancy, that of *will* around ages 2 and 3, and that of *purpose* in the preschool years of age 3 to 6. Furthermore, each virtue builds upon those that have developed before it. "Will cannot be trained until hope is secure, nor can love become reciprocal until fidelity has proven reliable" (Erikson, 1964, p. 115). The meanings assigned to these virtues by Erikson and their relationship to the psychosexual and psychosocial stages are displayed in Table 9.2.

Roles of Heredity and Environment   When a theorist suggests that such traits as hope, fidelity, and wisdom trace their essential development to specified age periods that are universal for all children, two questions arise about the theorist's beliefs concerning the roles of heredity and environment. First, does the theorist mean that all children inherit a time-schedule mechanism that preordains the sequence in which character traits evolve and the time when each trait becomes of primary developmental import? Second, does he mean that the actual form each trait assumes is inherited, and that, consequently, the child's social environment has little or no effect on the nature of the hope, fidelity, and wisdom that the child will display in her personality?

In response to these queries, Erikson would say yes to the first and no to the second. Yes, he does mean that the epigenetic principle establishes the sequence and the general time when particular psychosexual and psychosocial concerns appear in center stage, demanding primary attention. But no, the form that a given trait assumes is not determined by the child's genetic nature. Instead, the way a psychosocial concern is resolved and the way the personality characteristics that the child or youth comes to display are formed depend on the way she or he interacts with the social institutions of the particular culture. So while Erikson postulates that the crucial time for the development of hope arises during infancy for all people, he says that the degree of hope or optimism the individual child achieves is determined by the way that child is treated during the first year of life. And such treatment varies greatly from one society to another and from one family to another. In effect, Erikson accords a very prominent role to the culture as an influence on the form that psychosocial traits assume as children grow up.

Toys and Reasons   The importance of social institutions in the sculpturing of the child's personality has also been emphasized in another, more recent extension of Erikson's theory described in *Toys and Reasons* (Erikson, 1977). The general subject of Erikson's attention in this book is human play, with the term *play* used in a very broad sense. According to Erikson children are engaging in their play when they use imagination to devise mental models of their place in their expanding world. These models are visions designed by children to make sense out of their feelings and skills in relation to the array of puzzling stimuli that impinge on them from without. At each stage of development such play or the creation of such visions functions as a tool to help the individual solve the psychosocial conflict on which she or he is focusing at that stage.

Three aspects of Erikson's conception of play are of particular note. First, play in this sense is not an activity limited to the period of childhood, but rather is pursued throughout the entire life span. Nor are these imaginative, playful acts simply pastimes—something nonserious to do when we are not engaged in the work of life. Instead, such acts, during either working time or leisure time, are marks of the lifelong "human propensity to create model situations in which aspects of the past are re-lived, the present represented and renewed, and the future anticipated" (Erikson, 1977, p. 44). Therefore, the child is playing when he builds a structure of blocks or dramatizes with dolls an encounter in the life of a family, but the physicist is

Table 9.2 Stages in the Development of Virtues

Stage Number	Column A *Freud's Psychosexual Stages*	Column B *Erikson's Psychosocial Crises*	Column C *Erikson's Virtues or Qualities of Strength*	Column D *Approximate Ages in Years*
I	Oral-Respiratory	Trust versus Mistrust	*Hope:* The enduring belief that fervent wishes can be fulfilled despite "the dark urges and rages which mark the beginning of existence"	0–1
II	Anal-Urethral	Autonomy versus Shame, Doubt	*Will:* The constant determination to exercise both free choice and self-restraint, despite the shame and doubt experienced during infancy	2–3
III	Infantile-Genital	Initiative versus Guilt	*Purpose:* The "courage to envisage and pursue valued goals uninhibited by the defeat of infantile fantasies, by guilt and by the foiling fear of punishment"	3–6
IV	Latency	Industry versus Inferiority	*Competence:* The free use of skill and intelligence in completing tasks, "unimpaired by infantile inferiority"	7–12 or so

Stage Number	Column A Freud's Psychosexual Stages	Column B Erikson's Psychosocial Crises	Column C Erikson's Virtues or Qualities of Strength	Column D Approximate Ages in Years
V	Puberty and Adolescence	Identity and Repudiation versus Identity Diffusion	*Fidelity*: Sustaining freely pledged loyalties despite contradictions in value systems	12–18 or so
VI	Mature Genitality	Intimacy and Solidarity versus Isolation	*Love*: "Mutuality of devotion forever subduing the antagonisms inherent in divided function"	The 20s
VII		Generativity versus Self-Absorption	*Care*: Concern for obligations "generated by love, necessity, or accident"	Late 20s to 50s
VIII		Integrity versus Despair	*Wisdom*: "Detached concern with life itself, in the face of death itself"	50s and beyond

Adapted from Erikson, 1964, pp. 115–134.

also playing when she fashions a model of the universe, and the army general is playing when devising a battle strategy and conducting war according to the "rules of the game."

Second, although the psychological purpose of play is to enable the individual to organize and master her own existence, play cannot fulfill this purpose if conducted only in a solitary setting. There is an essential social quality to much if not all play. In Erikson's view, the individual's imaginative models or mental pictures of herself in her world need to be shared with and affirmed by others. The growing child does not achieve identity or self-concept in isolation but through the interplay of her imaginative creations with those of significant people in her environment. For the preschooler, this interplay can be the child's producing a visual construction with toys and blocks in the presence of an understanding observer. In spontaneous dramatic play with peers, the child has her model situation affirmed and clarified by other children participating in the drama in a way that makes sense to them all—they have produced a shared vision of their world. The games of school-age children are also microcosms—miniature, imagined worlds with defined roles, goals, boundaries of time and space, and rules that define the right way to do things. So also are the games of adults, whether in the form of sporting events and parlor pastimes or in the form of maneuvers in national politics and war (Erikson, 1977, pp. 53–64).

Third, within any society, as time passes, the dominant shared visions or world views assume rather permanent form. Each individual or each generation does not create entirely new ones. The dominant models become traditional and ritualized, and people who share these ways of viewing themselves within their world become convinced that theirs are the right ways or best ways. To perpetuate such models, the institutions of the society—the family, church, school, social club, mass communication media, judiciary, business organizations, and government—teach the viewpoints and rituals to the young. In this way one group of people perpetuates a culture or pattern of rituals and world views that differs from the patterns perpetuated by other groups.

Whereas the biologically inherited genes differentiate the human species from such other species as chimpanzees and hummingbirds, it is the set of socializing institutions within a given culture that causes differences between the people in that society and the people in another society. These resulting groups of people, each marked by the attitudinal and ritual signs of its own culture, are what Erikson has called *pseudo-species*:

> By pseudo-speciation, then, we mean a sense of irreversible difference
> between one's own and other "kinds," which can attach itself to evolved
> major differences among human populations or, indeed, to smaller and

smaller differences which have come to loom large. In the form of man's "in"-group loyalties, such a specific sense of being elect—as a tribe or nation, creed, class, or ideology—can contribute to the highest achievements in citizenship, courage, and workmanship and can, in fact, weld together in new loyalties (*civis Romanus*, Christian love) previously inimical entities. In the form of new "out"-group enmities, on the other hand, it can express itself most variably—in mortal hatred as well as in phobic avoidance, or in sheer clannishness (Erikson, 1977, pp. 76–77).

Of the various aspects of play, as Erikson has used the term, the one facet on which he centers particular attention in *Toys and Reasons* is that of *ritualization*. He has fitted various forms of ritualization into his stages of the life cycle, tracing each form from its beginnings in childhood and adolescence to its form in the adult world. Erikson's chart of the ontogeny of ritualization is shown in Figure 9.1. As the chart suggests, the evolution of ritualization according to the epigenetic schedule proceeds as follows.

The earliest beginning of ritual in infancy has been labeled *mutuality of recognition* by Erikson, for the first social interaction in the infant's life involves the infant's needs being cared for by parents, particularly by the mother. By means of the child-care ritual—the mother's touch, her smile, the name she gives the child—a mutual mode of recognizing each other and of affirming their identities and relationship develops. This initial ritual serves as the foundation for subsequent rituals of mutual recognition and bonding that will mark later stages of life: the relationship between teacher and pupil, club or gang leader and group member, chieftain and warrior, political figure and citizen, God and believer. Erikson proposes that people are born with the need for such "regular and mutual affirmation and certification" and that its absence can radically harm an infant (Erikson, 1977, p. 88). He has called this aspect of ritualization the *numinous*, for it represents reassurance for the individual through familiarity and mutuality in relation to an object or personage of devotion. Among the institutions of adult society, that of organized religion most obviously represents the numinous:

> The believer, by appropriate gestures, confesses his dependence and his childlike faith and seeks, by appropriate offerings, to secure the privilege of being lifted up to the very bosom of the divine which, indeed, may be seen to graciously respond, with the faint smile of an inclined face (Erikson, 1977, pp. 89–90).

This first aspect of ritualization, the numinous, develops throughout life and combines with subsequently developed rituals to form the complex that makes up the cultural patterns the child's personality acquires.

The second aspect, arising at age 2 or 3 in relation to the toilet-training

Infancy Age 0-1	Early Childhood Age 2-3	Play Age 3-6	School Age 6-12	Adolescence Age 12-18	Elements in Adult Rituals	Principal Societal Institutions in Adult Life*
Mutuality of recognition					Numinous	Church, family
	Discrimination of good and bad				Judicious	Court of law
		Dramatic elaboration			Dramatic	Stage, movies, television, literature
			Rules of performance		Formal	School, craft training agency, licensing agency for vocations
				Solidarity of conviction	Ideological	Political group, church, military
					Generational sanction	Marriage, guardianship, professional training and licensing agencies (for teachers, physicians, clergy, etc.)

*The institutions in adult life are partly quoted directly from Erikson and partly the present author's extrapolations from the general tenor of Erikson's analyses.

Figure 9.1   Stages in the Development of Ritualization (Adapted from Erikson, 1977, pp. 85–114)

stage, is that of discriminating good from bad. From these early years the rituals involved with making judgments develop until they reach their most formal version in the procedures of judicial courts. Hence Erikson has applied the word *judicious* to this second sequence of imaginative models of a culture.

The third sort of ritualization is seated in the dramatic play of the preschool years, ages 3 through 6, when the child's new sense of guilt at the time of the Oedipus conflict motivates the child to seek a resolution of the conflict through imagined dramas. For example, in his clinical experience with children, Erikson has observed them use toys as elements in creating a narrative with a plot that includes conflicts that are finally resolved. These are the elements—plot, conflict, resolution—that make up the sophisticated adult versions of ritualization performed on the stage, in motion pictures, and on radio and television. Effective drama is a vision of reality condensed in space and time and experienced by the audience as "unbearably personal and yet miraculously shared" (Erikson, 1977, p. 102).

A fourth element of ritualization, emphasized during the elementary school years (ages 6–12), is that of *methodological performance*. During this stage the child is assigned a series of tasks that prepare him to master the skills and work habits that will enable him to participate in the economic and technological life of the society, be it agricultural, industrial, commercial, or literary. This stage is the beginning of the child's learning to gain satisfaction through competently performing the formal tasks of the society. This "work role which we begin to envisage for ourselves at the end of childhood is, under favorable conditions, the most reassuring role of all, just because it confirms us in skills and permits us to recognize ourselves in visible works" (Erikson, 1977, p. 106).

A fifth element that enters at the time of adolescence is the adoption by the growing youth of a set of convictions that tie together in a coherent manner (1) the psychosocial identity she has achieved up to this point and (2) the structure and expectations of the adult culture. Erikson has identified two varieties of ritual prominent during these years. First are the *spontaneous "rites"* by which adolescents ritualize relations with their peers and mark their subculture as distinct from childhood and adulthood. Second are the *formal rites,* such as school graduation and joining the church, that represent the passage into, and adoption of, adult status and values. The solidifying of convictions during adolescence leads to the development of the mature ideologies of adult life.

The final stage in the evolution of ritualization is *generational sanction* because as the youth achieves adult status he is officially authorized through such rituals as marriage and guardianship to take on the teaching, productive, and curative roles for a new generation of children. Whereas the child and adolescent are the objects of rituals supervised by adults, the new adult now becomes the ritualizer for the young. The evolution of ritualization for the growing years is now complete.

Erikson's unflagging desire to enrich the psychoanalytic model prompted him at the end of the eighth decade of his own life to publish yet another view of growth, this time a retrospective account from the vantage point of old age, an unraveling of the stages of development from the final phase of life back to birth (Erikson, 1982). In this recent work he reiterates his confidence in psychoanalytic inquiry as the most profitable method for depicting how human personality develops.

PRACTICAL APPLICATIONS AND RESEARCH CHALLENGES

In the main, the applications described in Chapter Eight for Freudian theory are the same as those for Erikson's extension of psychoanalysis. Like Freud's model, Erikson's variation has guided general child rearing, influenced early childhood education, and generated techniques of therapy for disturbed children. In particular, Erikson's description of an adolescent identity crisis has influenced parents' treatment of adolescents and has encouraged school personnel to help students master the crisis by means of life-adjustment courses and study units on self-understanding in social studies and literature classes. Techniques of therapy for disturbed adolescents have also been affected by Erikson's attention to youths' struggle for identity.

Research challenges described for the psychoanalytic model apply as well to Erikson's theory. In addition, we are able to discover further research questions in the new territory Erikson opened beyond the boundaries of Freud's theory. The following are a few such possibilities.

Are the crises Erikson identified at each stage of child growth actually the central concerns for all children at those stages, or may the types and order of crises differ from one society to another or from one particular child to another?

To what extent is the dominant kind of play Erikson identifies for each stage of life found in all cultures? If this dominant kind is indeed found, are there likenesses and differences among cultures or among individuals within a given culture in the typical form of such play? If so, what causes these likenesses and differences? Or, stated another way, what are the usual or normative ways children in various cultures play during a given stage? Do the norms differ from one society to another, and if so, why?

In regard to each of Erikson's dimensions of growth—psychosexual, psychosocial, and the special variety of psychosocial defined as play—how much deviation from the norm is found among children in various cultures and in various families? What attitudes are held within each culture or family toward such deviations? In various societies, what sanctions are applied to children or what help is given to them when they deviate from the norm, and why are such sanctions and help applied? As the generations have passed, what changes have taken place in the typical attitudes in a given society regarding both the norms and deviations, and what factors have caused such changes? What problems between generations (grandparents, parents, children) are caused by these changes?

ERIKSON'S VERSION OF PSYCHOANALYSIS: AN ASSESSMENT

Since Erikson's theory is an extension of the psychoanalytic model and is in essential agreement with it, the evaluation of Freudian theory at the end of Chapter Eight is also applicable to Erikson's theory in most respects. Therefore, rather than repeat the assessment from Chapter Eight, I will confine my appraisal in the following paragraphs to ways in which Erikson's views and contributions differ from Freud's.

Not only has Erikson been acclaimed for his detailed definitions of psychosocial stages and the proposed identity crisis of adolescence, but he has been credited as well with significant contributions to psychoanalytic research methodology. Among the complaints that critics have lodged against Freud is the charge that he was anthropologically naive. By this they mean that he based his theory on a very narrow range of personalities, assuming that the themes of neurotic behavior and thought he found in his patients were an accurate reflection of the modes found in the rest of humanity. In effect, critics have questioned how accurately the patients met in a late-nineteenth-century Viennese psychiatric practice, which were mainly women of upper-middle-class Jewish society, represent people in general. Erikson, in contrast, drew the cases on which he based his speculations from a far wider geographical sampling than Freud. Erikson was a psychoanalyst in Europe, but he also participated in intensive studies of cases at the Harvard Psychological Clinic, of infants suffering neuroses at the Yale University Department of Psychiatry, of normal adolescents in northern California, of Sioux and Yurok Indians, and of numerous other Americans. Furthermore, he focused more attention on normal development than did Freud, particularly the normal development of the healthy self or ego in personal and social relations.

Erikson also furthered the development of *psychohistory*, which is the analysis of the psychological development of individuals by the use of what they have written and said and by reports of their actions. Perhaps the most notable of his analyses of world figures have been those of Martin Luther (1958) and Gandhi (1969). His purpose in these endeavors was to identify significant relationships between the life histories of great leaders and "the historical moment of their emergence" (Erikson, 1975, p. 10). In particular, he concentrated on "the powers of recovery inherent in the young ego" (Erikson, 1958, p. 8).

This same concern for the influence of the broad social setting on personality development caused Erikson to seek ways for elucidating and verifying impressions derived from the psychoanalytic interview. He saw sociological and anthropological research techniques as serving to help clinicians recognize the importance of the social environment in which their data are obtained.

> Clinical evidence, finally, will be decisively clarified, but not changed in nature, by a sharpened awareness (such as now emanates from sociological studies) of the psychotherapist's as well as the patient's position in society and history (Erikson, 1964, p. 80).

All of the foregoing points I would put on the credit side of the assessment ledger. On the debit side I find the same basic problems of scientific validation described in the assessment of Freud's theory. For example, not everyone has found the evidence cited in support of Erikson's proposed psychosocial crises to be convincing. Some of the difficulties with the evidence are reflected in the following questions: Isn't the major evidence in favor of Erikson's scheme mainly in the form of his interpretation of selected, illustrative clinical cases—cases of individuals in therapy, of such figures as Luther and Hitler, and of such groups as Sioux Indians? And couldn't another theorist find as convincing a variety of illustrations as these to suggest that psychosocial crises come in quite a different order than that suggested by Erikson? For example, why is the crisis of autonomy versus shame necessarily set in the second year of life? Couldn't we easily find behaviors at other ages that could reasonably be interpreted as symptoms of an autonomy crisis, behavior such as the striving for independence that appears to mark the years of adolescence?

These questions and the ones noted under "Research Challenges" are the kinds that have not yet been answered adequately by the investigative methods Erikson used. Like Freud's system, and for somewhat the same reasons, Erikson's model has been difficult to translate into a form that permits experimentation or controlled observations that produce convincing evidence about the validity of the theory's components and principles.

In conclusion, Erikson's writings about development have generated much discussion in psychological circles and have attracted the admiration of many readers who have found his insights true in their own experience. But many of his proposals, like Freud's, must be accepted on faith, faith in the theorist's interpretive skills and in his authority rather than on experimental and observational evidence that would more clearly compel readers to arrive at the same conclusions. Of course, this charge can be made against many other theories of development as well.

FOR FURTHER READING

The two books by Erikson that most directly describe his overall theory of development are:

(1963) *Childhood and Society.* 2d ed. New York: Norton.

(1968) *Identity: Youth and Crisis.* New York: Norton.

Recent volumes illustrating the manner in which Erikson embellishes his basic theory with further proposals are:

(1977) *Toys and Reasons.* New York: Norton.

(1982) *The Life Cycle Completed.* New York: Norton.

For a biographical study of the theorist, see:

Coles, Robert. (1970) *Erik H. Erikson: The Growth of His Work.* New York: Little, Brown.

PART FIVE

THE GROWTH OF THOUGHT AND LANGUAGE

A search for patterns of development in children's cognitive and verbal skills, and for the mechanisms that bring these patterns about

The four chapters of Part Five treat (1) Jean Piaget's psychology of the child, (2) Soviet development models, particularly as guided by Lev Semenovich Vygotsky, (3) a child development version of information-processing theory, and (4) Lawrence Kohlberg's proposal about the growth of moral reasoning. Such diverse bedfellows are billeted together in Part Five because the four not only focus on thought-and-language issues, but the latter three are all linked in one way or another with Piaget's work. Vygotsky offered an alternative interpretation to Piaget's analysis of children's early speech, information-processing theorists simulated certain Piagetian mental-growth stages with computer programs, and Kohlberg founded his moral-reasoning stages on Piaget's studies of children's moral judgments.

The title of Part Five—The Growth of Thought and Language—is not meant to suggest that other theorists in this book have ignored mental development or verbal communication. Rather, the title simply highlights the fact that a major emphasis in the four models included in this section has been the growth of children's cognitive and verbal abilities.

The first of the four, Jean Piaget (1896–1980), was a Swiss who has often been acclaimed the most influential researcher in the field of child development in the twentieth century. He gained this distinction for proposing a novel model of children's mental development, a model founded on a great quantity of ingenious research on children from the time of birth to adolescence. Beginning in 1921 and continuing for nearly sixty years, he published hundreds of journal articles and books on all sorts of questions related to children's thought processes: how dreams and play evolve, how symbols develop, how moral judgments grow, how perceptions change, how intelligence improves, how numbers are conceived, what causes physical events, and many more. The diverse topics on which Piaget wrote are all connected to his basic model of intellectual growth. The view of Piaget offered in Chapter Ten focuses on the most fundamental elements of that model.

The second theoretical persuasion examined (Chapter Eleven) is one that has dominated developmental psychology in the Soviet Union for more than half a century. The Soviet perspective has been included for two main reasons. First, it illustrates a development theory that, out of political necessity, conforms to the tenets of the Marxist sociopolitical philosophy on which the Soviet state is founded. Second, Soviet developmentalists have displayed noteworthy inventiveness in research methodology and analysis while producing a large quantity of empirical studies on childhood and adolescence.

The third model of development (Chapter Twelve) derives from a general information-processing paradigm that in recent years has attracted great attention among psychologists. Developmentalists' recent enthusiasm for information-processing theory as a useful model of how children's minds operate has been stimulated to a considerable extent by the rapid advances of computer technology during the past two decades.

As an example of a development theory that focuses on a particular realm of thought rather than on thinking processes in general, Chapter Thirteen reviews a theory of the growth of children's expressed moral values. The model, formulated by the American psychologist Lawrence Kohlberg, seeks to explain how children's ways of defending value judgments change systematically over time.

CHAPTER TEN

Piaget's Cognitive Development Theory

Jean Piaget (1896–1980) was a precocious boy who, in his teens, had already developed an intense interest in biology, particularly in the biological bases of knowledge. By age 21 he had earned a doctorate at the university in his hometown of Neuchatel, Switzerland, and had published more than two dozen professional papers on biological studies, most of them concerning mollusks. This early specialization in biology had a lasting influence on his conceptions of the development of the mind.

Upon finishing his doctorate, he shifted his attention to psychology, which he studied in Swiss psychological clinics and at the Sorbonne in Paris. While in Paris (1919–1921), Piaget worked on standardizing tests of children's abilities in the laboratory school of the French expert on intelligence measurement, Alfred Binet. During this time Piaget was not as interested in whether children got the test items correct as he was in the thinking processes that led children to produce the answers they gave, especially the incorrect answers. This interest set the focus for his research during the rest of his career.

Although Piaget is commonly referred to as a child psychologist, the research task he set for himself was that of a *genetic epistemologist*. This means that the central question guiding his investigations was not, What are children like? but, How does knowledge develop in humans? Or more precisely, How does the relationship between the *knower* and the *known* change with the passing of time? So the term *genetic* (meaning the genesis or the mode of development) and *epistemology* (the theory of knowledge) does indeed describe the field of his endeavors. Children of different age levels just happened to be the instruments by which his investigations in this field were carried out.

In the following review of Piaget's work, we will consider: (1) his methods of research, (2) his conception of knowledge, (3) his conception of the process by which children's knowledge grows, (4) his definition of the stages of intellectual growth, (5) four of his key concepts, (6) the practical applications of his theory in education, (7) research challenges, and, finally, (8) an assessment of his theory.

PIAGET'S CLINICAL METHOD

While working at Binet's test-construction laboratory, Piaget devised the basic technique of studying children that would become the mainstay of his methodology during the next fifty years. His approach, known as a *clinical method,* involved a researcher posing problems for children and then observing how the children went about finding a solution. For children who had not yet reached puberty, the problems usually involved objects the child could see and manipulate, such as two lumps of clay that could be formed into different shapes or two glasses of water of different sizes. By the time the child could use language at age 3 or 4, the experimenter asked questions about solutions to the problems being posed. During the adolescent years, children were more often given verbal problems and asked how they arrived at their solution.

Unlike some other experimenters, Piaget did not limit himself to asking each child a preconceived set of questions. Rather, after beginning an interview with a standard question or two, he felt free to create, on the spot, additional questions designed to probe the thought processes that produced the child's initial answer. Piaget defended this deviation from a single, standard set of questions by explaining that all children do not interpret a given question in the same way. Thus the experimenter probes the child's understanding and may then cast the problem in a different form to help ensure that the problem situation is the same for each child, even though the wording of it may not be identical each time (Phillips, 1975, pp. 4–5).

A typical interview is illustrated in the following passage in which eight-year-old Per is being questioned about some flowers—primulas and other varieties—that the woman interviewer placed before the child. The interviewer's purpose was to discover how Per classifies objects into a general set (flowers) and into subsets within the general set (primulas, violets, tulips). At the point we enter the discussion, Per has already devised three levels of classes: yellow primulas, primulas, and flowers (adapted from Inhelder & Piaget, 1964, p. 107).

Interviewer: Can one put a primula in the box of flowers (without changing the label)?
Per: Yes, a primula is also a flower.
Interviewer: Can I put one of these flowers (a tulip) in the box of primulas?
Per: Yes, it's a flower like the primula.

When the experimenter does so, Per changes her mind and puts it back with the other flowers.

Interviewer: Can one make a bigger bunch with all the flowers or with all the primulas?
Per: It's the same thing, primulas are flowers, aren't they?
Interviewer: Suppose I pick all the primulas, will there be any flowers left?
Per: Oh, yes, there will still be violets, tulips, and other flowers.
Interviewer: Well, suppose I pick all the flowers, will there be any primulas left?
Per: No, primulas are flowers, you're picking them too.
Interviewer: Are there more flowers or more primulas?
Per: The same number, primulas are flowers.
Interviewer: Count the primulas.
Per: Four.
Interviewer: And the flowers?
Per: Seven.
Interviewer: Are they the same number?
Per *(astonished):* The flowers are more.

In effect, then, Piaget's research methodology consisted of his first observing children's reactions to their surroundings. Then, on the basis of these observations, he composed hypotheses about the sorts of biological and mental structures that underlie their reactions. Finally, he cast the hypotheses in the form of problems or questions that he posed to children in order to reveal their thinking processes and thus test the hypotheses. Over the years he produced many problem situations that were subsequently used by researchers in many parts of the world to investigate matters that Piaget studied, as well as other aspects of development.

PIAGET'S CONCEPTION OF KNOWLEDGE

A useful step toward understanding Piaget's theory is to learn how he defined *knowledge* because his conception differs from most popular beliefs.

We can perhaps best see this difference by beginning with a review of four commonsense ideas about knowledge and how it is acquired.

First, common sense holds that knowledge is a body of information or beliefs a person has acquired, either through instruction or through direct experience with the world. This idea of a collection of information is reflected in such everyday phrases as "She's a storehouse of knowledge" and "I wish I had all his knowledge."

Second, it is also a commonsense conviction that a person's knowledge is a fairly faithful representation of what the person has been taught or has witnessed. It is assumed that if two people, both with good eyesight, observe an event from the same vantage point, their knowledge of the event will be essentially identical. The great dependence on witnesses in court cases is founded on this conviction.

Third, common sense indicates that our storehouse of knowledge is increased as we add item upon item from our daily experiences. That is, we take in bits of information and pile them onto the proper heap in the storehouse, with each heap related to a different aspect of life.

Fourth, common sense tells us that whenever we need to recall an item of knowledge from the storehouse of memory, the item can be recovered in essentially the same condition as it was when first acquired. Of course, some details of the item may now be a bit vague, but if we can recall the item at all, it will be basically in its original form.

How did Piaget's views differ from such commonsense notions? To begin, he did not agree that knowledge is a body of acquired information or a state of possessing such information. Instead, he conceived of knowledge as a *process*. To *know* something means to *act* on that thing, with the action being either physical or mental or both. The two-year-old child's knowledge of a ball consists of his picking it up, pressing it with his fingers, tossing it, and observing it bounce away. As children grow up, they gain more experience with such direct, physical knowing, and they mature internally so that they are increasingly freed from having to carry out direct physical behavior in order to know something. They become able to produce mental images and *symbols* (words, mathematical figures) that represent objects and relationships. Hence the older child's knowledge increasingly becomes mental activity. She "thinks about" things by carrying out *interiorized actions* on symbolic objects (Piaget, Apostel, & Mandelbrot, 1957, pp. 44–45). So to Piaget, knowledge was a process or repertoire of actions rather than an inventory of stored information.

Piaget also disagreed with the commonsense idea of *perception,* that is, with the way objects or events are recorded in the child's mind. In Piaget's opinion, the child does not take in a picture of objective reality. Instead, as the child perceives or takes in the world, the picture is biased by the condition of the child's perceptual mechanism. If we adopt the analogy of viewing the world through glass, then in the Piagetian model the child does not record events through a clear window. Rather, he views events through a colored lens that is given its present focus and tint by both (1) the child's past experiences and (2) his current stage of internal maturation. The way that two children know (act on) the same object will not be identical, for the lens of one will have a somewhat different focus and tint than the other's.

But if knowledge is a process of acting on percepts rather than a collection of information, then what is *memory* and how does it operate? Piaget agreed that the results of a person's past actions can be stored as memories to be retrieved when needed. He also agreed that the quantity of memories increases with maturation and experience. But he did not believe that the act of remembering is simply a matter of summoning images of past events from memory and placing them in the showcase of consciousness so that, like museum pieces, they can be viewed in their passive, original condition. Rather, retrieving stored vestiges of the past, which he labeled *active memory*, is "interiorized recitation" or "a reconstitution of the past" (Piaget, 1946, pp. 5, 261). Remembering is a reenacting of the original process of knowing. However, it cannot simply be a repetition of the original knowing because the child's mind has subsequently been altered by additional experiences and further internal maturation. So the interiorized recitation or rehearsal of the stored event is, as it were, now performed on a somewhat altered mental stage according to revised stage directions.

To summarize, in Piaget's system, knowledge is a process of acting—physically and/or mentally—on objects, images, and symbols that the child's perceptual lens has cast into patterns that are somewhat familiar to her or him. The objects are found in the world of direct experience, while the images and symbols can be derived not only from the "real world" but from memory as well.

One way to conceive of mental growth or the development of intelligence is to picture it as a constant effort on the part of the child to expand and refine her knowledge, her repertoire of mental actions. Or, in different terms, "All knowledge is continually in a course of development and of passing from a state of lesser knowledge to one which is more complete and effective" (Piaget, 1972, p. 5).

This idea that a child's knowledge improves with age is hardly a noteworthy discovery. Everyone knows that already. But what everyone does not know is the specific ways knowledge changes, at what times it changes, and for what likely reasons. These are the things Piaget provided. Table 10.1 illustrates five categories of behavior he treated. In the description, I am

Table 10.1 Growth in Sample Aspects of Knowledge: Infancy to Adolescence

From Infancy	Through Early and Middle Childhood	To Adolescence
Egocentrism versus Objectivity		
Not distinguishing between self and the environment	Partially distinguishing between self and the environment	Clearly differentiating self from objects of the environment
Object Permanence (Conservation)		
Not recognizing (not constructing) the permanence of objects whose location is changed	Recognizing (constructing) object permanence when location is changed, but failing to recognize (to construct) which characteristics of objects are unchanged (or are conserved) when objects are transformed	Recognizing (constructing) which aspects of objects are unchanged (are conserved) when the objects are transformed
Symbolic Functioning		
Not recognizing (not constructing) that one thing can represent something else	Recognizing (constructing) symbolization through such acts of imitation as gesture, play, drawing, and oral echoing	Recognizing (constructing) complex written and spoken symbols and signs
Internalization of Action		
Adapting to the environment solely by physical acts	Beginning to act internally on objects (manipulate them mentally) while observing them	Accomplishing faster, more complete adaptation by internally (mentally) manipulating objects of the environment, their classifications, and their relationships
Classes and Relationships		
Not recognizing (not constructing) classifications of objects or relationships among objects	Recognizing (constructing) classes and relationships among objects that are directly touched, seen, or heard	Not only recognizing (constructing) classifications of and relationships among objects directly perceived but also (1) of imagined objects and events and (2) of classification and relationship systems themselves

using the verbs *recognizing* and *constructing* as synonyms, believing that the more passive *recognizing* is the familiar way people refer to such mental behavior but that *constructing* more accurately reflects Piaget's conception of knowledge as a process of active production on the child's part.

These, then, are some of the directions of intellectual development that Piaget's theory depicts and explains (Piaget & Inhelder, 1969). Our next task is to identify the mechanisms that, in Piaget's opinion, bring about these kinds of development.

THE MECHANISMS OF DEVELOPMENT

The purpose of all behavior or all thought, according to Piaget's system, is to enable the organism—the child—to adapt to the environment in ever more satisfactory ways. Piaget called the techniques of adaptation *schemes* or, in older translations of his writings from the original French, *schemas* or *schemata*. A scheme or technique of adjustment can be biological or mental or both. In Piaget's words:

> A scheme is the structure or organization of actions as they are transferred or generalized by repetition in similar or analogous circumstances (Piaget & Inhelder, 1969, p. 4).

The *grasping* movement of the infant's hand is such a scheme, a physical organization of actions that the infant can generalize to grasp a bottle, a rattle, or the edge of the crib. On the intellectual level, an adolescent's concept of a *series* is also a scheme, a mental organization of actions. He can apply it in constructing a series of numbers, arranging a series of sweaters according to shades of color, or arranging a series of young girls by height or attractiveness.

A scheme can be very simple, such as the action pattern involved by a child putting her thumb into her mouth. Or it can be complex, comprising physical and mental subschemes, as in the chain of acts required for starting a car and driving it down the street or in the mental chain needed for solving quadratic equations.

Schemes always include accompanying feeling tones. When Piaget talked of *affective schemes,* he did not mean schemes distinct from mental structures but "simply the affective aspect of schemes which are otherwise also intellectual" (Piaget, 1962, p. 207).

The newborn's schemes are very limited in number, consisting of reflex action patterns—sucking, crying out, sneezing, flexing limbs, and the like. But as the days pass, other sensorimotor actions build out of these beginnings. Then, still within the first year of life, identifiable intellectual schemes evolve and over the following years multiply enormously. Thus, when we conceptualize child development in terms of schemes, we should picture it as the child's acquiring ever greater quantities of schemes that become interlinked in ever more sophisticated patterns.

How does this process of evolving schemes come about? To understand the process, we need to learn the meanings Piaget assigned to the words *assimilation* and *accommodation*. To help explain these matters, I would liken schemes to musical themes or tunes, for tunes are organizations of sounds just as schemes are organizations of sensorimotor and mental actions.

The Function of Assimilation

At every point in his life, the child's adaptation to the environment in order to satisfy his needs is accomplished by means of schemes. The child's repertoire of schemes at any given time is like a collection of melodies he already knows. When he faces the problem of satisfying needs, he inspects the environment to perceive how its apparent structure seems to fit schemes currently in his armory. It's as if he listens to the sounds coming from his surroundings to determine if they match, or nearly match, a tune he knows. When he finds what he considers a good match, he has achieved his adaptation. When the infant in the crib drops her doll onto the floor, she inspects the scene to decide if the conditions of her problem match any scheme or strategy in her repertoire of solutions. A twelve-year-old boy assigned to draw a map of the route from home to school must likewise search his available action structures to find ones appropriate to the task. A high school student listening to her English teacher lecture about the plot structure in Hamlet must incorporate the ideas from the lecture into suitable schemes already in her mind if she is to comprehend, or mentally construct, the meanings intended by the teacher.

This process of matching environmental stimuli to existing mental patterns is not simply a matter of ingesting objective reality from the world. Rather, the child reshapes the events of the world somewhat to fit the pattern of his or her existing schemes. It's as if the child hears several tones, and decides that they sound enough like a familiar melody to indeed be that melody.

Piaget applied the label *assimilation* to this process of taking in or understanding events of the world by matching the perceived features of those events to one's existing schemes. As Piaget put it: "To assimilate an object to a schema means conferring to that object one or several meanings" (Piaget, Jonckheere, & Mandelbrot, 1958, p. 59).

The Function of Accommodation

However, often the perceived structure of events does not readily fit the child's available schemes, even with some perceptual bending or shaping of that structure. When this occurs, one of two consequences can be expected. The first is that the event is not assimilated at all. It is ignored or passed by, like a person's rejecting several sounds as meaningless noise instead of recognizing them as a familiar tune. The encounter with the environment simply does not register on the child. Such is the case when a father tries to teach his young son to draw with proper visual perspective but finally concludes, "He can't do it at all. He just doesn't catch on."

The second possible consequence of a poor match between the perceived environment and available schemes is not outright rejection but dissatisfaction and continued efforts to achieve a match.

> New objects which present themselves to consciousness do not have their own qualities which can be isolated . . . they are vague, nebulous, because unassimilable, and thus they create a discomfort from which there emerges sooner or later a new differentiation of the schemas of assimilation (Piaget, 1963, p. 141).

So it is that schemes, under pressures from perceived realities of the environment, are altered in form or multiplied to accommodate for the lack of an adequate match. In effect, a tune from the child's existing store of melodies is revised to become a variation of the original theme, a variation that better fits the sounds of the world. Piaget used the term *accommodation* to identify this process of altering existing schemes to permit the assimilation of events that otherwise would be incomprehensible.

Since no new event is perfectly identical with those past events that were used in the formation of schemes, there is always some degree of mismatch of schemes with new events. But this is cared for by the balancing counter-play between assimilation and accommodation, which are two of the basic innate acts Piaget called *functional invariants*. Assimilation reshapes the environmental input to fit existing schemes, whereas accommodation revises or adds to the schemes to readjust for environmental features that cannot conveniently be ignored or distorted.

Just as adaptation to the world is achieved by the functions of assimilation and accommodation, so within the child's biological-mental self a process of *organization* operates to ensure that all schemes are properly interrelated, properly adjusted to each other to form an integrated person.

> It is sufficiently well known that every intellectual operation is always related to all the others and that its own elements are controlled by the

same law. Every schema is thus coordinated with all the other schemata and itself constitutes a totality with differentiated parts. Every act of intelligence presupposes a system of mutual implications and interconnected meanings (Piaget, 1963, p. 7).

Therefore a child's development, according to Piagetian theory, seems somewhat like a progressively complex symphony. Its multiple melodies are the schemes formed from the balanced counterpoint of assimilation against accommodation. And the interweaving of themes produces a coordinated whole.

All these matters can be summarized in three quotations from Piaget:

The filtering or modification of the input is called *assimilation;* the modification of internal schemas to fit reality is called *accommodation* (Piaget & Inhelder, 1969, p. 6).

Adaptation is an equilibrium between assimilation and accommodation (Piaget, 1963, p. 6).

The "accord of thought with things" (adaptation) and the "accord of thought with itself" (organization) express this dual functional invariant of adaptation and organization. These two aspects of thought are indissociable: It is by adapting to things that thought organizes itself and it is by organizing itself that it structures things (Piaget, 1963, p. 8).

Four Causal Factors

We next face the question of what factors or forces determine how this adaptation-organization system will operate in a given child's development. What causes a child to acquire her particular schemes and at what times in her growing up? How does environment as compared to heredity influence the kinds and rate of scheme formation?

In responding to such questions, Piaget proposed four underlying causal factors: (1) heredity (internal maturation), (2) physical experience with the world of objects, (3) social transmission (education), and (4) equilibrium.

1. **Heredity**   In the continuing debate among developmentalists over the roles of nature and nurture, Piaget has been classified by most writers as an interactionist, and certainly he considered himself so. He did not accord either heredity or environment greater power in determining development. Instead, he saw each playing a distinct and necessary part to complement the part of the other.

What role did Piaget see nature playing? He said that not only does heredity provide the newborn with the initial equipment to cope with problems she or he will meet in the world, but heredity also establishes a time schedule for new development possibilities to open up at periodic points throughout the child's growing years. This is the internal-maturation factor in heredity. It functions rather like a legislative body, which from time to time passes a new act of *enabling* legislation. Each such act, or maturational change, creates possibilities for new schemes to be created that could not have been generated earlier, but this action neither requires nor guarantees that the potential schemes will materialize. The extent to which the potentialities are actually realized is determined by the sorts of experiences the child has with his or her environment. So internal maturation is a necessary but not sufficient condition for development to proceed.

Much of the practical use of Piaget's findings for educators and parents lies in his identification of approximate age levels at which the maturation needed for developing particular schemes or intellectual operations occurs. If suitable maturation has not yet taken place, it is futile to try to teach the child a particular skill. The probable reason the father failed to teach his young son proper visual perspective was that the maturation necessary for developing the required schemes had not yet occurred.

Piaget (1973, p. 27) viewed as folly the efforts of some psychologists to dissociate the effect of heredity from that of the heredity—environment amalgam in seeking to decide which of the two is more important for development: "If a maturation effect intervenes everywhere, it remains dissociable from the effects of the exercise of learning or of experience."

2. Physical Experience It is essential to recognize that Piaget, unlike most theorists, separated the child's trafficking with the environment into two varieties: (a) direct and generally unguided experience with objects in the world—called *physical experience*—and (b) the guided transmission of knowledge, that is, education in a broad sense—called *social transmission*. We will consider direct experience first, for it is the type on which Piaget has focused the greater part of his attention.

In this case, the child directly manipulates, observes, listens to, and smells objects to see what occurs when they are acted upon. From such investigations the child generates a logic or knowledge of the properties of things and how they work. Piaget stressed that it is not observation of the passive objects themselves that develops the child's logic or intelligence, but the set of conclusions the child draws from those actions that bring about events and influence objects. So simply seeing a feather or brick or lump of clay is not enough for intellectual development to take place. Such development depends on the *experience* derived when physically or mentally participating in such events as the following:

A chicken feather and a metal bolt are simultaneously dropped from the same height.

A brick is put into a bucket full of water, and a pine block the size of the brick is put into a second bucket of water.

Three lumps of clay are rolled into shapes: the first into a ball, the second into a sausage, the third into a long snake.

The child tries to cut a board—first with scissors, next with a knife, and then with a saw.

These sorts of experiences contribute to the aspect of intellectual development that Piaget (1973, p. 2) called *spontaneous* or *psychological:* "the development of the intelligence itself—what the child learns by himself, what none can teach him and he must discover alone."

Although physical experience with the action of objects is essential to mental growth, by itself it is, like maturation, insufficient to bring about development.

3. Social Transmission   This is education in a broad sense—the transmission of knowledge to the child from without. Like the first two factors, this one is important but is insufficient by itself to effect mental growth, for it depends upon both maturation and direct experience to prepare the schemes that permit assimilation of what parents, the school, and the general social milieu seek to teach the child. This factor contributes what Piaget called the *psychosocial* aspect of cognitive development (1973, p. 2).

4. Equilibrium   This last force is the one that maintains a balance among the other three, fitting the maturational, direct experience, and social transmission influences together harmoniously. Piaget (1973, p. 29) felt the need for such a factor because "a whole play of regulation and of compensation is required to result in a coherence."

In summary, then, the sorts of knowledge the child acquires in terms of mental schemes, and the time at which they are acquired, depend upon such factors as maturation, physical experience, social transmission, and equilibrium. These factors regulate the stages of cognitive growth through which, in Piaget's system, all children normally develop. It is to this series of levels or stages that we now turn.

LEVELS AND STAGES OF DEVELOPMENT

As noted in Chapter 2, one of the traditional issues in the field of child development is whether growth proceeds continuously—by imperceptibly small increments—or advances by stages. And if a theorist proposes that it does indeed move by stages, then what criteria does she or he apply in identifying a stage?

Piaget, like apparently all developmentalists, recognized that from day to day, growth is continuous, with no major leaps ahead from one day to the next and no extended plateaus of dormancy in growth. At the same time, when he viewed the entire span of the growth years, Piaget was able to distinguish breaks in the process. These breaks suggested to him that the child has at each such point completed one phase of development and is now engaged in a further one.

To say that Piaget proposed *a* series of developmental stages would be oversimplifying his work. Actually, he identified a number of different series, each related to a different aspect of personality or mental life. For example, one series concerns steps in understanding physical causality (1930), another the steps in imitation and play (1951), still another in the conception of moral principles and justice (1948), and others in understanding number (1952), space (1956), and movement (1969). But underlying these and other specific series of stages there appears to be a basic set that provides the framework for overall sensorimotor-intellectual development. Let's look at this underlying set.

There is some confusion in the writings of Piaget and his followers about how many major stages, and their constituent substages, best reflect the growth process. Some authors picture three major levels, others four, and some even five. In the following discussion I have cast the scheme into one of its most familiar forms, with four major levels or periods, each divided into subperiods designated as stages. In this fourfold division, the levels are called (1) the sensorimotor period, (2) the preoperational thought period, (3) the concrete operations period, and (4) the formal operations period. As we trace the child's progress through the stages, we will see her grow from being (a) an entirely self-centered infant with no realistic knowledge of her environment to become (b) an adolescent who employs logic and language with facility to intellectually manipulate the environment and thus comprehend, ever more realistically, how the world functions.

Although age designations are attached to each of the four periods in the following discussion, they should be regarded as only approximations, as rough averages, for as Piaget pointed out:

> They are not stages which can be given a constant chronological date. On the contrary, the ages can vary from one society to another.... But there is a constant order of succession ... that is, in order to reach a certain stage, previous steps must be taken. The prestructures ... which make for further advance must be constructed.

Thus we reach a hierarchy of (mental) structures which are built in a certain order of integration and . . . appear at senescence to disintegrate in the reverse order (1973, pp. 10–11).

Level 1: The Sensorimotor Period (Birth to Age 2)

During the first two years, infants are unable to verbalize very well any thoughts they may have, so it is necessary to estimate their intellectual growth by the manner in which they sense (see, hear, feel, taste, smell) their environment and by the manner in which they subsequently act upon it (motor behavior). Piaget's observations of children in this age period enabled him to distinguish six stages through which they develop (Piaget & Inhelder, 1969, pp. 4–12).

The first stage (0–1 month) features the baby's adapting to his environment by means of his inherited, ready-to-operate, unlearned *reflexes*. It is by reflex activity that the baby sucks, cries, breathes, coughs, urinates, defecates, and makes gross bodily movements.

The second stage (1–4 months) is marked by the infant's gradually acquiring adaptive actions as the result of experience. During the first stage there was no distinction between the functions of assimilation and accommodation. But during the second, assimilation and accommodation can be distinguished as the infant starts to alter her sensorimotor action patterns (her schemes) on the basis of the responses of her environment. She accommodates or alters schemes somewhat on the basis of the reactions of the environment to her acting upon it. "For instance, when the child systematically sucks his thumb, no longer due to chance contacts but through coordination between hand and mouth, this may be called acquired accommodation" (Piaget, 1963, p. 48).

During this second stage the child engages in a great deal of repetitive activity, such as grasping and letting go of something over and over again. These actions, labeled *primary circular reactions,* were interpreted by Piaget as evidence that learning new associations or acquiring knowledge is not accomplished by the environment's imposing them on the child's mind. Rather, as noted in our earlier discussion of Piaget's concept of knowledge, intellectual development even during the sensorimotor period involves understandings "discovered and even created in the course of the child's own searchings" (Piaget, 1963, p. 55). So the repetitious activity of the infant is purposive, designed either to preserve or rediscover an act or skill. In other words, it functions as practice.

The third stage (4–8 months) marks the beginning of the infant's distinguishing between self and outside objects. It also marks the start of intentional acts, of consciously acting to attain a goal. The intention, however, is of a transitional type. The child does not foresee a goal, then attempt an act designed to achieve the goal. That sort of "true" intention comes at the fourth stage. But during the third stage the child will repeat an act that he happens to have performed with satisfaction. The primary circular reactions of the second stage were not movements designed to produce a particular result in the environment; they were simply self-centered acts showing no apparent awareness of an environment. However, at this third stage, the repetitive behavior that occurs—the *secondary circular reactions*—suggests a beginning awareness of the environment, for the acts seem directed toward reproducing a result that, by chance, has just been effected. For example, when the infant happens to hit a rattle hanging within reach in his crib, he may enjoy the sound. Then by gradually moving his hands and occasionally hitting the rattle, he begins to distinguish between his hand, the rattle, and other objects, so he comes purposely to grasp or hit the rattle directly and not by chance.

The fourth stage (8–12 months) signifies the emergence of clear acts of intelligence. The infant anticipates people and objects. She searches for objects that are out of sight, thus showing that objects have now attained a quality of permanence for her. Prior to this time, if a toy was moved from one location to another, she apparently felt that it had dissolved into the nothingness around her and that a new toy had appeared from the nothingness at the second location, even though the toy had been shifted from the first spot to the second within the baby's presence. Along with this initial step in recognizing qualities of permanence of objects, the infant also begins to comprehend cause and effect, that certain acts will bring about predicted results. Consequently, she can conceive of an end result ahead of time, then fashion an act to bring the result about. Her behavior now can be called truly intentional and thus qualifies as the beginning of *practical intelligence,* which consists of envisioning goals or desired ends and then employing existing schemes as means for achieving the ends (Piaget & Inhelder, 1969, pp. 10–11).

The fifth stage (12–18 months) involves the child in *tertiary circular reactions.* Recall that primary circular reactions (1–4 months) were events repeated over and over simply to preserve them, a kind of practice. Secondary circular reactions (4–8 months) were the purposive repetition of acts the infant found satisfying the first time, and so chose to repeat again and again, even in new settings—a kind of application of known means to new situations. In contrast, tertiary reactions are not exact repetitions of the original act. Rather, they consist of reproducing the original event in modified form—a kind of variation on the original theme. The one-year-old, according to Piaget (1963, p. 266), tries, "through a sort of experimentation, to find out in which respect the object or the event is new. In other words, he will not only submit to but even provoke new results instead of being satisfied merely to reproduce them once they have been revealed fortuitously."

Prior to the fifth period, acts of intelligence involved only an application of existing schemes to new situations, that is, assimilating new events into already acquired schemes by attending only to the features of the object or event that were similar to existing schemes. But now, in the fifth period, the child pays greater heed to the ways the new object or event differs from his present mental constructs, and he employs the process of accommodation to differentiate existing schemes and construct more suitable new ones. So tertiary circular reactions involve "reproductory assimilation with differentiated and intentional accommodation" (Piaget, 1950, p. 104).

The sort of "discovery of new means through active experimentation" (Piaget, 1963, p. 267) that marks this fifth stage was illustrated by Piaget with the case of a child who, sitting on the floor, seeks a toy that is out of reach. During his grasping, he pulls the edge of the small rug on which the toy lies, an act that is either an accident or a substitute for getting the toy. When he notices how his tug on the rug made the toy move toward him, he then intentionally pulls the rug as the instrument for obtaining the object (Piaget & Inhelder, 1969, p. 11).

Object Relations   Up to this point in our discussion of mental growth stages, we have implied but not addressed directly one of the most important dimensions of development in Piaget's system. It is that of *object relations*, meaning the way the child conceives of herself in relation to the objects of the world as well as the way she sees the objects' relationships to each other. In the beginning, the infant's universe is centered entirely on her own body and actions. There are no objects but only a world of what Piaget called "unsubstantial tableaux" that vaguely appear and then dissolve, never to reappear, or else they come back in some altered form (Piaget & Inhelder, 1969, p. 14). Nor is there a single space and time within which sensations of sight, sound, touch, temperature, taste, and smell are coordinated. Being lifted into mother's arms and fed is, in Piaget's estimation, sensed by the baby as separate impressions of postural change, pressures on various parts of the body, the touch of the lips to the nipple, voice sounds, shifting light patterns, and the ingesting of milk—none of which has any connection with the others. When the infant's mental organization of the universe is so unstructured, she does not—indeed could not—conceive of cause and effect relationships among objects. Even during the advance of infancy, as she begins to differentiate objects from herself and invest them with some permanence in time and space, her conception of cause remains egocentric: Nothing happens in the world except as a result of her own wishes and actions. But by gradual steps over the coming years she recognizes more accurately objective causality in the world.

In summary, an important perspective from which to view child development is that of object relations. Among researchers, Piaget was particularly noted for his contributions in tracing developmental changes in children's conceptions of the permanence of objects, the objects' positions in space and time, and causal relations among them. In our continuing discussion of mental stages, this should become readily apparent.

At the sixth and final stage (18–24 months) of the sensorimotor period, the child no longer has to experiment with objects themselves to solve problems, but can represent them mentally and can cognitively combine and manipulate them. In effect, he is now mentally inventive. For example, a child at this stage sees a toy outside his playpen out of reach. He also sees a stick within arm's reach. He decides that he can use the stick as a tool for pulling the toy to the playpen, and he then uses the stick for this purpose. Prior to the sixth stage he might have gotten the toy if the stick had already been in his hand and he had groped for some time and happened to touch the toy. But he would not have preplanned the act by mentally combining the stick and the toy's distance before picking the stick up. Attainment of this new inventiveness makes intelligence now "capable of entering the framework of language to be transformed, with the aid of the social group, into reflective intelligence" (Piaget, 1963, p. 356).

Level 2: The Preoperational Thought Period (about Age 2 to Age 7)

In our review of this level of preoperational thought, we need to understand what Piaget meant by *operations*. Such understanding will make clear what sorts of "operational thought" this level 2 thinking precedes, that is, what sort it prepares the child to perform at a later level of growth.

Operations, in Piaget's system, are ways of manipulating objects in relation to each other, such as arranging them in a series according to size or putting them in classes according to color. If the objects are actually before us, like actual colored blocks or ponies, the manipulations we perform on them, either by physically moving them or by observing how we might move them, are called *concrete operations*. We will meet these operations when we come to the third major period of development, which follows the preoperational level. When concrete operations are transposed into verbal propositions about the relationships that exist or might exist among objects, and these propositions are mentally manipulated, the intellectual actions are called *formal operations* (Piaget, 1969, p. 206). These we will meet at the fourth level of intellectual growth.

An operation, however, is not just any manipulation of objects. Indeed, as the term *preoperational thought* indicates, the mental activities of most children under age 7 do not yet qualify as operational. To be classified as operations, actions must be internalizable, reversible, and coordinated into systems that have laws that apply to the entire system and not just to the single operation itself. As Piaget explained, operations:

> are actions, since they are carried out on objects before being performed on symbols. They are internalizable, since they can also be carried out in thought without losing their original character of actions. They are reversible as against simple actions which are irreversible. . . . Finally, since operations do not exist in isolation they are connected in the form of structured wholes (1972, p. 8).

The characteristics of operations should become clear when we review the third and fourth periods of intellectual growth, for then we will discuss in some detail illustrations of children displaying operational thinking. For the present we will review the preoperational thought period knowing that it leads to children's performing concrete and formal operations.

This preoperational period can be divided into two stages. The first extends from age 2 to about 4 and is characterized by egocentric use of language and heavy dependence on perception in problem solving. The second lasts from about age 5 to around 7 and is marked by more social or communicative speech and greater dependence on intuitive thinking rather than just on perception.

Before inspecting these two stages in detail, we need to be aware of the great importance Piaget attributed to language in the development of intelligence during this period. Language, he said, performs three roles: (1) It enables the child to communicate with other people, thus opening the opportunity for socialization of action; (2) it enables the child to internalize words in the form of thoughts and a system of signs; and most important, (3) it internalizes action so the child does not have to depend on manipulating things physically to solve problems. Instead, she can represent them by mental images with which she conducts experiments. She becomes less bound by time and space. She can increasingly imagine things that are out of sight, far distant, and in the past. She can experiment with these things in different mental combinations far quicker than she could manipulate them physically.

Egocentric Speech   During the years 2–4, the child learns an increasing variety of words. He begins to talk a lot, and the talk is two varieties. Some of his talk is *social communication*—asking parents to reach a toy he cannot get, telling his sister he wants the doll back, or telling mother he wants to go to the toilet.

But a far larger proportion of the child's talking and listening is *egocentric,* a running oral commentary that accompanies what the child is doing at the moment and is not intended to communicate anything to anyone else. Since this kind of talk often appears in social situations, such as in a group of children at play, it can at first glance be mistaken for social communication. However, on closer inspection it becomes apparent that everyone is talking to herself or himself without listening to the others. For this reason, Piaget labeled such speech *collective monologues.* An important causal factor behind this discourse, in Piaget's opinion, is the child's lingering self-centeredness. The child still views life from her own perspective and has difficulty seeing things from the perspectives of others. Hence she does not try to comprehend what others say so she can respond from the viewpoint they express.

To check this hypothesis, Piaget observed preoperational children in situations requiring them to explain something to another child, and then noted, from the other child's behavior, how well the explanation or directions had been understood. The observations revealed a systematic egocentricity in the sense that the child giving directions had great difficulty adopting the other's viewpoint, casting the explanation in a form readily comprehended from the second child's perspective (Piaget & Inhelder, 1969, pp. 120–122).

While children's growing language skills aid their mental development, they do not free reasoning abilities from the influence of immediate perception. Children of age 2 through 4 or 5 base their problem solving heavily on what they see or hear directly rather than on what they recall about objects and events. What they perceive about an object is what dominates their conclusions, not what they conceive about the object based on memories of the object's permanent characteristics. Children at this age suffer from the limitations of what Piaget called *centration.* Presented with a visual stimulus, a child centers on one aspect and believes that this aspect completely characterizes the stimulus. The child cannot consider two dimensions, such as height and width, at the same time. For instance, if there is the same amount of water in two glasses of identical size and shape, the four-year-old will agree that both contain the same amount of water. But if the child sees the water from one glass poured into a taller and thinner glass, he will center on the height dimension only and conclude that the taller glass contains more water. It may be apparent that centration is not the only factor involved in the child's error of judgment. Other characteristics of immature logic also contribute to the error. For example, the preoperational child fails as well to comprehend the principle of *compensation,* that is, that the dimensions of an object can operate in coordination so that one dimension compensates for another. The greater width of the original glass compensates for its lack of height.

Intuitive Thought   By the time the child reaches age 5 or 6 or so, she enters the stage Piaget labeled *intuitive thought.* It is a transition period between depending solely on perception and depending on truly logical thinking. An experiment with beads illustrates the characteristics of such transitional thinking. Six red beads are lined up on a table, and the child is told to put as many blue beads on the table as there are red ones. At age 4 or 5 the typical child makes a row of blue beads about the same length as the red row, without bothering to make sure there are six blue ones. But a child a year or two older lines up six blue beads opposite the red ones, thus displaying progress toward recognizing equivalent quantities. But there are still short-comings in his logic, for if the experimenter then spreads out the red beads to form a longer line, the six-year-old thinks the number of red and blue beads is no longer equivalent (Figure 10.1). He is still unduly influenced by perception of line length rather than the logic of quantity. In the terminology used by Piaget, the child has not recognized that the number of beads has

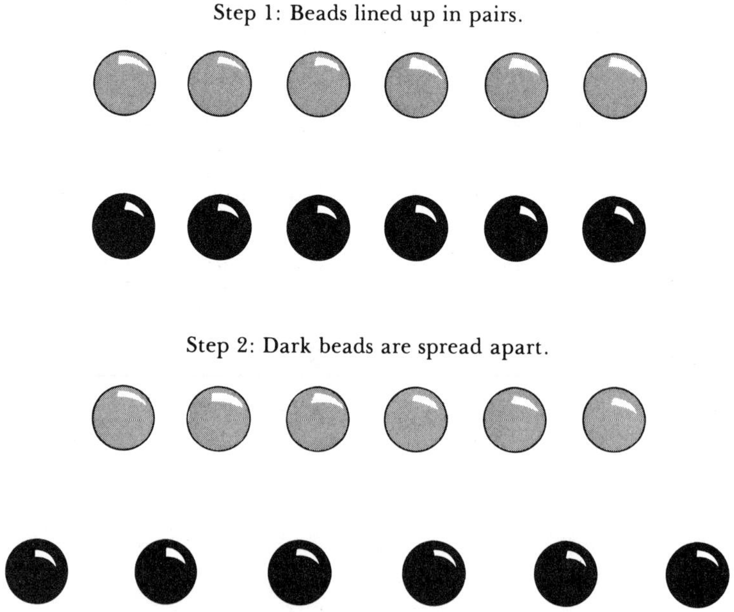

Step 1: Beads lined up in pairs.

Step 2: Dark beads are spread apart.

Figure 10.1   A Piagetian Experiment in Conservation

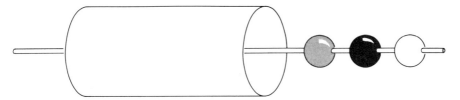

Figure 10.2   Piaget's Beads and Tube Task

been *conserved* or is *invariant* even though the length of the two lines has been altered (Piaget, 1950, p. 132).

Another Piagetian experiment also illustrates the transitional—between dependence on perception (on how things look) and on logic (on what principles govern their operation)—nature of the child's thinking during this stage of intuitive understanding. Three beads—one red, one blue, one yellow—are on a string that passes through a cardboard tube (Figure 10.2). A child is asked to observe the order of the beads before they are slipped into the cardboard tube where they cannot be seen. Then the child is asked to predict the order in which the beads will emerge from the other end of the tube. All children can predict correctly. But if asked to tell in what order they will emerge if poured back out through the same end they entered, the child under age 4 or 5 will be confused. She fails to see that they will emerge in the opposite sequence if they are backed out of the tube. Furthermore, while the beads are in the tube, if the apparatus is turned 180 degrees and the child is asked the order in which the beads will emerge, the child from about age 4 to about age 7 will fail to see that half a turn will change the order of emergence from red–blue–yellow to yellow–blue–red. She then is given a chance to try it and see what happens. Intuitively she comes to recognize what the half turn will do. By experimenting further, she finally admits that if given two half turns, the order of emergence will be the same as it was originally. She intuitively gets the idea, yet still does not understand the principle that an even number of half turns keeps the emergence as it was originally, but an odd number reverses the order of emergence. This is shown by the fact that even after the experiments, the child is no better able to predict the effect of three half turns than she was originally (Piaget, 1950, pp. 135–136).

In short, the intuitive stage marks a movement toward greater *decentration.* The child is better able to see more than one factor at a time that influences an event. He is on the verge of a major advance in logical thought.

To summarize, children make several important growth gains during the preoperational thought level between ages 2 and 7. They acquire facility in spoken language as a tool for communicating with others and for helping themselves think aloud. By age 7 their communicative language greatly increases as collective monologues decrease. They also gain skill in solving problems intuitively when the objects involved in the problems are in front of them. They become less self-centered in that they recognize that objects have an existence and permanence of their own that does not depend on the child's wishes or actions. Specifically, children recognize the permanence of an object's substance when its location or shape is changed. Water poured from a bowl into a tall glass is still water. A ball of clay rolled into a sausage shape remains the same clay. But preoperational children are still in the process of transition toward decentering, for they do not yet recognize that volume, weight, and mass are also conserved in the acts of pouring and rolling. Even though they have made great advances by age 7 in comprehending how the universe of things operates, they are still strongly dependent on perception (how events seem to the eye) rather than on logic (what principles govern events).

Level 3: The Concrete Operations Period (about Age 7 to Age 11)

At the concrete operations stage, children become capable of performing operations that are directly related to objects. In the formal operations period, which comes later, they will learn to perform operations on verbally stated hypotheses and propositions that are not limited to particular objects (Piaget & Inhelder, 1969, p. 100). The term *concrete* does not mean children must see or touch actual objects as they work through a problem. Rather, "concrete" means that the problems involve identifiable objects that are either directly perceived or imagined. In the later formal operations period children are able to move ahead to deal with problems that do not concern particular objects. To illustrate this difference, we can consider the following two items, the first suitable for the concrete operations child, the second for the more advanced formal operations child or adolescent:

Concrete: If Alice has two apples and Caroline gives her three more, how many apples will Alice have altogether?

Formal: Imagine that there are two quantities which together make up a whole. If we increase the first quantity but the whole remains the same, what has happened to the second quantity?

It may be apparent that even though children do not need to see the objects in order to carry out the operations, in the early transitional phase toward learning and mastering such operations, they will be aided by viewing the actual objects or pictures of them.

In the earlier brief introduction to the term *operations*, I defined it but did not illustrate its several characteristics. I will do so now. Piaget said that for an action of the child to qualify as an operation, it had to be internalizable, reversible, and coordinated into overall systems. Furthermore, operations are not unique to an individual child but are common to all people of the same intelligence level. Finally, an operation assists the child not only in his private reasoning but also in his "cognitive exchanges," which bring together information and combine it in various ways (Piaget, 1953, p. 8; Piaget & Inhelder, 1969, pp. 96–97).

By *internalizable* Piaget meant the actions can be carried out in thought "without losing their original character of actions" (1953, p. 8).

By *reversible* he meant they can be readily inverted into their opposite. For example, two groups of apples that have been combined (added together) to form a whole group can as easily be reduced (subtracted from the whole) to their original status. Hence adding is an operation. In contrast, Piaget said, writing from left to right is only a simple action and not an operation, for it cannot be inverted into writing from right to left without the child's having to develop an entirely new set of actions (1953, p. 8).

Reversible transformations may be of two varieties: *inversions*, where $+A$ is reversed by $-A$ (addition reversed by subtraction, multiplication reversed by division) and *reciprocity*, where $A < B$ is reciprocated by $B > A$ (the width of the bowl of water compensates for its lack of height, and the height of the glass of water compensates for its lack of width). When an object is moved or transformed in some way, in a transformation that qualifies as operatory, not everything about the system changes. Some features remain constant. As we have seen, Piaget gave the label *conservation* to this feature of constancy or invariance of objects. So we can say that a child's scheme or idea of a permanent object consists of that combination of features of the object that do not change when the object is moved or acted on. How adequately the child's scheme matches that of adult logic or "reality" can be judged if we assess which aspects of objects the child believes have been conserved during the transformation. Many of the problem situations Piaget contrived for children to solve are designed to test children's notions of conservation. And his investigations have shown that the particular aspects a child sees as being conserved depend on the child's age, or more accurately, on the child's developmental level.

For example, when two lumps of clay the same size and shape are shown to a child and then one lump is rolled into a sausage form, the child of age 7 or 8 discovers that the substance has been conserved. But not until age 9 or 10 does she discover that the weight has been conserved as well. And not until age 11 or 12 does she discover the conservation of volume that occurs when an object is immersed in water and the displacement measured (Piaget & Inhelder, 1969, p. 99).

Thus during the concrete operations period, from age 7 to around 11 or so, children gradually discover more of the properties of objects and transformations and master mental operations that can be applied to their concrete world.

The concrete operations child not only gains greater command of the notions of conservation and reversibility but also becomes capable of decentering his attention, of recognizing the way two or more dimensions of an event interact to produce a given result. He no longer centers his attention solely on the height of the water glass or only on its width but considers both dimensions simultaneously and recognizes their interaction. When presented with twelve wooden beads (nine red, three white), the child no longer will say there are more red beads than wooden beads when asked to compare red ones with wooden ones. At the concrete operations level he now recognizes that color and construction material are two different classifications, and he is not stuck by centering on only color or material. He also can now order things in a series according to a stated criterion, such as size or number.

Whereas the preoperational child focused on the static beginning state and final state of an object in a transformation, the concrete operations child can comprehend the transformation as a process. For example, typical preoperational children at age 3 or 4 think there is more clay in five small balls than in the original large ball from which the five were made. Even when the transformation, and its reverse of recombining the five into one, is performed before their eyes, three- and four-year-olds still say that the five contain more clay than the one. But by age 6 or 8, children agree that the quantity remains the same in the change from one to five balls and back again.

The egocentrism that caused the younger child to see things only from her own viewpoint changes as the older child achieves the aspects of cognitive growth mentioned above and as her increased facility with language leads to greater socialization. The child in the concrete operations period now has a more objective view of the universe and better understands how others see things.

Children's concepts of causation also mature during this period. For instance, a comparison of a child aged 6 years and 8 months and a child aged 10 years and 3 months illustrates the development of the concept of displacement of volume. The experiment involves dropping a small stone into a container of water (Piaget, 1930, pp. 169–172).

When the experimenter asks the six-year-old what will happen if the stone is dropped into the water, the child says the water will rise *"because it is heavy in the water."* The experimenter says, "You see the pebble hanging on this thread: if I put it in the water as far as this (half-way), will it make the water rise?" *"No, because it is not heavy enough."*

In contrast, the ten-year-old says the water will rise *"because the pebble takes up space."* The experimenter asks, "If I put this wood in, what will happen?" *"It will lie on the water."* "And what will the water do?" *"It will rise because the wood also takes up space."* "Which is the heavier, this pebble (small) or this wood (large)?" *"The pebble."* "Which will make the water rise the most?" *"The pebble takes up less space, it will make the water rise less."*

So the child arrives at the early teen years with increased skill in accounting for the cause of physical events and is ready to solve not only problems that involve objects, but also problems concerning hypotheses and propositions about relationships.

Level 4: The Formal Operations Period (about Age 11 to Age 15)

In adolescence children are no longer limited by what they directly see or hear, nor are they restricted to the problem at hand. They can now imagine the conditions of a problem—past, present, or future—and develop hypotheses about what might logically occur under different combinations of factors. For example, if we begin a problem with "Imagine that water in the river ran up hill . . . ," children younger than 12 will claim that the subsequent problem cannot be solved because water does not run up hill. But by the close of the formal operations period teenagers can accept the hypothetical condition of upward flow and can apply it in solving the posed problem.

Another of Piaget's favorite examples further illustrates the difference between the concrete operations child and the one who has attained formal operations ability. This is a problem involving *transitivity*, meaning that a relationship between two elements or objects is carried over to other elements logically related to the first two. For example, the child has solved the problem of transitivity if he recognizes that when $A = B$ and $B = C$, then $A = C$. Or if $A < B$ and $B < C$, then $A < C$. So the question posed to the child is this: "Edith is fairer than Susan; Edith is darker than Lily; who is the darkest of the three?" Piaget (1950, p. 149) found that before age 12 children rarely could solve this. Instead, they engaged in such reasoning as: "Edith and Susan are fair, Edith and Lily are dark, therefore Lily is darkest, Susan is the fairest, and Edith is in between." However, the adolescent in his midteens can solve the problem accurately, for he comprehends the transitivity it involves.

Prior to early and middle adolescence, therefore, children are still bound by their perceptions. But during the formal operations period they are able to engage in "*pure* thought which is independent of action" that they see or carry out themselves (Piaget, 1950, 149). Adolescents can hypothesize and draw deductions from the hypotheses. They can understand general theories and can combine them to solve assumed problems. In effect, by age 15, the framework of the average youth's thinking has evolved into its mature state. The types of thought of which the adult is capable are now all within the youth's repertoire of mental functions.

Does this mean, then, that there is no intellectual growth beyond mid-adolescence in Piaget's model of the mind? No, it does not. It means that the framework of thought is complete, but the framework is not all filled in. Further experiences during the years of youth and adulthood fill in the outline with additional, more complex schemes or greater knowledge, so the adult *does* know more than the adolescent. However, the adolescent is capable of all the forms of logic that the adult commands.

According to Piaget, the most obvious distinction between adolescent and adult thought is the greater lingering egocentrism displayed by adolescents. The teenage youth, with her newly acquired skills of logical thought, is an idealist who expects the world to be logical. She fails to recognize or accept the reality that people do not operate solely on the basis of logic, and she becomes a reformer and critic of the older generation, foreseeing a glorious future in which she and her peers will right today's wrongs. In Piaget's opinion, this egocentrism and idealism is rendered more realistic and social by the youth's entering the occupational world or by her taking on serious professional training.

> The adolescent becomes an adult when he undertakes a real job. It is then that he is transformed from an idealistic reformer into an achiever. In other words, the job leads thinking away from the dangers of formalism back into reality (Inhelder & Piaget, 1958, p. 346).

This move from adolescence into adulthood, then, completes the sequence of stages through which the intellect develops during the first two decades of life.

FOUR CONCEPTS: A CLOSER LOOK

The foregoing introduction to Piaget's system serves as a backdrop to a more detailed examination of four concepts mentioned earlier, those of genetic epistemology, stages or periods of development, functional invariants, and equilibrium.

Genetic Epistemology

At the beginning of this chapter genetic epistemology was defined as the study of changes in the relationship between the knower and the known with the passing of time. We noted as well that Piaget's investigations of children's cognitive development were stimulated by his interest in clarifying issues of genetic epistemology rather than by his desire to catalogue ways children at different age levels think about the world around them. And because this epistemological intention led to Piaget's publishing findings about how children's minds operate, some people have inferred that genetic epistemology and Piaget's proposals are one and the same. To correct this impression, Jacques Vonéche, who occupies the Piaget professorial chair at the University of Geneva, has suggested that the general discipline of genetic epistemology should be:

> disembarrassed from the unhappy fusion it has undergone, in recent times, with Piaget's specific attempt to orient that discipline along certain lines. . . . [Furthermore] besides limiting genetic epistemology to the sole attempts of Jean Piaget, there is another confusion generally made by philosophers and scientists alike, that of fusing Piaget's epistemology with his psychology. Numerous examples can be given of people who sincerely think that genetic epistemology is the title Piaget bestowed upon his theory of intellectual development in human ontogeny, although it should have seemed unlikely that a person of Piaget's considerable historical erudition and critical acumen would conflate individual developmental psychology with genetic epistemology (1985).

Piaget's approach represents only one of a variety of solutions scholars have attempted for studying "the mechanisms of the growth of knowledge" ever since James Mark Baldwin coined the term *genetic epistemology* in 1906 (Baldwin, 1906, 1908, 1911). And as Vonéche has implied, *genetic epistemology* and *genetic psychology* are not the same thing, even though there is a connection between them. Genetic psychology can be defined as the study of how the intelligence or the behavior of a typical member of a species changes over a lifetime. However, genetic epistemology involves not only this question of how intelligence develops but also such philosophical issues as the nature of being (ontology), the way knowledge should be defined, and the kind of evidence admissible for establishing the validity of knowledge.

The theory we have reviewed in the foregoing pages has been Piaget's psychology of cognitive development, not his complete version of genetic epistemology. However, it is useful to note ways in which certain of his assumptions about epistemology influenced his research methods and theoretical conclusions. For example, Piaget did not assume, as philosophical solipsists do, that the "real world" is simply what the individual's experience tells him is real. Rather, Piaget assumed that there is a "real world" outside of the individual "knower"; as children develop they achieve an increasingly accurate match between what is most adults' conception of a real world and the child's own conception. And, as noted earlier, Piaget also defined knowledge in a particular way—as physically or mentally acting on things, rather than as a fund of beliefs shared by members of a given society or as an individual's own storehouse of information. Furthermore, Piaget held that evidence obtained by the methods of modern science constitutes genetic epistemology's proper way of knowing. Finally, he viewed genetic epistemology as an interdisciplinary undertaking in which developmental psychologists participated with other scientists.

The first rule of genetic epistemology is therefore one of collaboration. Since its problem is to study how knowledge grows, it is a matter then, in each particular question, of having the cooperation of psychologists who study the development as such, of logicians who formalize the stages or states of momentary equilibrium of this development, and of scientific specialists who show interest in the domain in question [such as physics, biology, sociology]. Naturally we must add mathematicians, who assure the connection between logic and the field in question, and cyberneticians, who assure the connection between psychology and logic (Piaget, 1972, p. 8).

Stages of Development

Among scholars of Piagetian theory, the terms *stages, steps, levels, periods,* and *phases* of development are sometimes employed interchangeably. Or, as found earlier in this chapter, a major plateau in development may be called a *level* or *phase* and a subplateau called a *step* or *stage* or *substage*. But whatever the term used, the idea behind all such designations is that children's development is marked by times of noticeable change that are interspersed with times of stability.

Although all stage theorists agree that stages involve alternating times of change and of stability, few believe that change-and-stability is the *only* quality that defines a stage theory. Instead, most theorists propose additional factors they believe a growth pattern should exhibit in order to qualify its stable times as *stages*. As for Piaget, he contended that stages should have five further qualities—they must be universal, invariant in sequence, transforming and irreversible, gradually evolved, and ultimately in equilibrium.

1. *Universality.* The quality of universality means that stages are the same for all members of the species. A pattern of behavior that is found only in some children does not qualify as a stage. The pattern must be found in all children.

2. *Invariant Sequence.* In Piaget's view, as well as in the opinion of most developmentalists, sets of behaviors do not compose a hierarchy of stages unless everyone goes through the sets in exactly the same sequence. For example, if some children exhibited formal operational thinking directly after the sensorimotor phase, whereas other children moved from sensorimotor to preoperational thought, then Piaget's sets of sensorimotor, preoperational, and formal operational thinking would not be stages. All children must pass through all the stage gates in the same order.

3. *Transformation and Irreversibility.* When children enter a new stage, they not only interpret all future experiences through the lens of the new stage, but problems solved in the past by the methods of the previous stage are all now transformed, seen through the conceptual lens of the new stage. In effect, the child who has thoroughly progressed into formal operational thinking will seldom if ever go back to thinking in concrete or preoperational terms. This means that the naivete of early childhood is "spoiled" by progress into the more sophisticated thought of middle childhood. In short, stage progression is irreversible. For instance, after children in the concrete-operations stage discover the principle of compensation (that the width of a glass bowl compensates for its lack of height, enabling the bowl to hold as much water as does a tall glass), they no longer limit their attention to only one dimension of containers whenever they are asked about the quantities and weights of a substance that might fit into various containers. With this discovery, children are never again amazed by the kinds of results that surprised them at an earlier age when they saw liquid poured from one vessel into another of a different shape.

4. *Gradual Evolution.* Elevation to a new level or stage does not occur all of a sudden, or even within a period of a month, a few months, or a year. Instead, in Piaget's system movement to a new stage occurs gradually, a bit here and a bit there until finally enough of a child's behavior exhibits the traits of the new stage to say that the

transformation to the next level is complete. For example, children do not grasp the conservation of substance, quantity, mass, or volume of objects all at the same time but accomplish it only over a period of years.

5. *Equilibrium.* Once a child consolidates his thinking patterns into a coherent way of acting in the world, this new stage of cognitive development is said to have reached a state of stability and balance. The stage is now in equilibrium.

Piagetian stage theory does not require that children pass through the stages at the same speed nor that all children eventually reach the highest level. Piaget expected individual differences in the rate of progress, and he noted that some children would fall short of the formal operations level or, in the case of severe mental retardation, might not even get past the sensorimotor or preoperational levels.

However, while the five attributes of stages may seem clear at a conceptual level, some of them have posed awkward problems about child nature as observed in daily life. For example, when a child's thought processes about a variety of aspects of her life are compared, it is clear that there is considerable unevenness in the kinds of thinking she exhibits in solving different types of problems. For example, in mathematics it is typical for children to conceive of the conservation of number and length before that of area and volume. And the differences in the stages of children's thought processes in one domain, such as mathematics, and another, such as that of moral reasoning, are even greater. This brings up the question of whether the general stages of mental growth Piaget postulated really do form a valid description of how children's thinking develops. Perhaps there are only special stages for different aspects of life that cannot legitimately be compounded into a single general system.

One way that Piaget accounted for this lack of coordination of children's thinking processes was the notion of gradual evolution, described under item 4. He gave the term *horizontal décalage* to the apparent lag in a child's applying in all aspects of life a mode of thinking that Piaget proposed was characteristic of a single stage. For example, during the concrete-operations phase of development, when children see a ball of plasticine clay divided to become five smaller balls, they do not simultaneously discover that both the substance and the weight have been conserved as the number of balls has changed from one to five. Instead, children comprehend the conservation of substance (clay remains clay) at an earlier age than they comprehend that the weight also remains unchanged. In effect, there is some horizontal *décalage* (meaning *displacement*) between the time a child applies a new stage of thinking to one facet of life and the time she applies that same stage to other facets. However, we may ask: Does labeling this phenomenon *horizontal décalage* really explain the apparent unevenness in the way children apply a particular level of thought to different aspects of life, including different subject-matter areas in school? We will examine this further in the assessment of the theory at the end of the chapter.

Piaget called *vertical décalage* a child's applying increasingly complex modes of thought to the same phenomenon or problem in life. For example, in the beads-and-tube task pictured earlier a kindergarten child may physically reverse the tube and thereby be able to tell the order in which the colored beads will emerge from the tube, although she cannot explain why she knows. In contrast, a primary-grade child not only can predict the order of the beads without physically turning the tube but also can explain how her mental image of the tube has enabled her to solve the problem. Subsequently, a youth who has achieved formal-operations thought patterns can even explain the abstract principle which enables her to accurately predict the order of the beads, no matter how many times the tube is turned. Thus, *vertical décalage* refers to the displacement of one mode of thought by a sequence of more sophisticated modes as the child matures. Although the notion of horizontal décalage seems somewhat at odds with Piaget's theory of broadly encompassing stages of mental development, the idea of vertical décalage fits quite logically into his stage model.

Functional Invariants

It is apparent that Piaget's model accounts for the ways in which children's thought structures vary from one stage of development to the next. He also points out that, as children grow up, their schemes change by increasing in number, in precision, and in interconnections. But not everything about development changes as the years pass. Certain aspects continue unaltered over the entire life span. Piaget called these aspects *functional invariants* to signify not only that they are stable but also that they are *processes* or *functions* rather than structures.

Two such functions are *adaptation* and *organization*. Throughout life, people adapt to their environment and reorganize their schemes in ways that promote survival. Three other invariant functions—*assimilation, accommodation,* and *equilibrium*—serve as the chief instruments for promoting adaptation and organization. The lifetime process of adapting and organizing consists of a never-ending cycle of assimilation, of accommodation, and of the achievement of a temporary state of equilibrium which is soon disturbed by events that stimulate further assimilation, which starts the cycle over again.

Among these invariants, the one whose meaning seems most elusive is equilibrium, so let's inspect it in more detail.

Equilibrium

At least part of the reason people have difficulty comprehending *equilibrium,* or the companion term *equilibration,* is that Piaget seems to have used it to mean different things at different times. In general, *equilibration* seems to mean a process of movement toward a state of *equilibrium* or of balance, a state in which an organism remains until conditions upset the balance. In this sense, "a state of equilibrium is not a state of final rest, but constitutes a new point of departure" (Piaget in Battro, 1973, p. 57). However, these rather gross meanings seem insufficient to clarify Piaget's diverse applications of the term; as the following excerpts from English translations of his publications suggest.

> [We may] (a) conceive of equilibrium as characterized by *maximum* entropy, (b) or as due to the intervention of coordinations which introduce from outside an order diminishing the entropy, (c) or else as due to a sequence of "strategies" of which each one will be oriented by the results of the preceding one up to the moment when the actions become reversible through the very coordination of these preceding strategies that would have been freed from the earlier historic process in order to reach equilibrium.
>
> Equilibrium [is the] place of specific junction between the possible and the real.
>
> The structures can be interpreted as . . . the result of an autonomous process of equilibration.
>
> The best equilibrated states . . . correspond to a maximum of activities and a maximum of opening up of exchanges.
>
> The system is in equilibrium when the operations of which the subject is capable constitute a structure such that the operations can unfold in two directions (either by strict inversion or negation, or by reciprocity). It is therefore because the totality of possible operations constitutes a system of potential transformations which compensate each other — and which compensate each other as far as obeying the laws of reversibility — that the system is in equilibrium.
>
> We shall say that a structure has . . . a permanent equilibrium if, when the initial field C is modified to C' the substructure of the elements corresponding to C conserves the same equilibrium as before (Piaget in Battro, 1973, pp. 49, 56–58).

In addition, Piaget modified his basic conception of equilibrium by attaching to it such adjectives as *momentary, semipermanent, permanent,* and *operational.* However, these adjectives seem to have been of limited help to his reading audience.

P. H. Miller (1983, pp. 75–76) has attempted to clarify Piaget's usage by proposing that Piaget differentiated the use of equilibrium according to at least three spans of time: (1) the moment-to-moment encounters a child has with the environment as the child attempts to master the encounters by assimilating, accommodating, and finally achieving the state of satisfactory resolution called equilibrium; (2) the final step in a child's moving gradually out of one stage and establishing himself securely in the next higher stage; and (3) the process of achieving ever better adaptation and organization over the entire series of growth periods, birth through adolescence.

Finally, there are frequent passages in which equilibration seems to mean the unexplainable coordinating power that makes all parts of the developmental system work together in harmony.

EDUCATIONAL APPLICATIONS OF THE THEORY

During the past two decades Piaget's writings have exerted a growing influence on the conduct of education in many parts of the world. Piaget himself pointed out the educational implications of his model. To illustrate some of these implications, we will inspect the Piagetian model's application to questions of: (1) the choice of learning objectives, (2) curriculum sequencing, (3) grade placement of topics, (4) the assessment of children's intellectual functioning, and (5) teaching methodology.

The Choice of Learning Objectives

As educators have selected learning goals for pupils to pursue, they usually have based their choices on tradition or on analyses of what children need to learn in order to succeed in the culture in which they are growing up.

The word *tradition* in this context refers to the curriculum of the past. That is, members of the adult generation recall what they were taught in school and assume that this same pattern of facts, concepts, skills, and values will be equally proper for the coming generation of children. This might be called the conservative approach to selecting objectives since it emphasizes the conservation or retention of traditional goals.

The phrase *analyses of what children need to learn in order to succeed* identifies the practice of educators who inspect present-day society and predict changes that will likely occur in that society over the coming decades. On the basis of such analyses, they estimate the knowledge, skills, and values that will best equip the growing child or youth to become a happy, constructive member of that society. This could be called the *personal-social adjustment* approach to establishing objectives, for it emphasizes the achievement of objectives that enable the individual to fulfill personal needs within a culture that is continually evolving. A curriculum produced by such a process of analysis can be expected to retain some of the goals of the past, but it also will offer new objectives that result from changes in the society.

There is also a third tack, which derives from Piagetian theory and might be called the *cognitive development* approach. To understand the main focus of this approach, we need to consider once again (1) the distinction Piaget made between *spontaneous* or *psychological* development and *psychosocial* development and (2) his ideas about the interaction of nature and nurture.

As explained earlier, several factors determine when a child will develop through the levels of sensorimotor reactions, of concrete operations, and of formal operations. The first factor is the internal maturation of the neural system. The time at which the maturational steps needed for a given level of cognitive functioning occur is established by nature, by the child's genetic time schedule. But the developmental potential that this maturation provides cannot be realized unless the child obtains suitable direct experiences in life, experiences that bring the potential to fruition. Piaget called these unguided experiences (the second factor) *psychological* or *spontaneous* development. The third factor is that of more formal instruction, the sort that goes on in school. It needs to be preceded by the first two, maturation and psychological development, if it is to be successful. Piaget called this third factor *psychosocial* development.

This Piagetian view of intellectual growth is the foundation for the cognitive development approach to selecting instructional goals. From such a perspective, the central goal of the school is not to teach particular facts and concepts, nor is it to teach solutions to personal and social adjustment problems. Instead, the purpose of schooling is to promote the optimal development of thinking skills appropriate to each level of growth. As a result of such schooling, by the time the child reaches adolescence she should be able to efficiently apply formal operational thinking in understanding life and in solving whatever problems she faces. In such a curriculum the child does indeed learn facts and concepts. However, these are not selected for any inherent value they might have but rather for their worth in fostering the development of the particular level of cognitive growth that the child is currently working toward.

Curriculum Sequencing

Piagetian theory not only furnishes a vantage point from which to select objectives, it suggests as well the sequence in which these objectives and their associated learning tasks should appear in the curriculum. For example, in reasoning about scientific and mathematical phenomena, children at the preoperational level can consider only one dimension at a time, such as only the height or only the width of an object. At the concrete operations level they can comprehend the interaction of two dimensions, such as height and width, simultaneously. Not until they reach the formal operations level can they consider the interaction of more than two variables. A similar sequence has been identified in the realm of moral or ethical judgments.

> At the egocentric stage in the logic of feeling, the self becomes the single dimension around which feelings and social interaction revolve. The second, sociocentric stage corresponds to concrete operations, in interacting with peer-group norms as the other dimension. The allocentric stage is multidimensional like formal operations: the individual can construe himself as a dimension in a matrix, including abstract principle and social norms as other dimensions (Biggs, 1976, p. 157).

A further example of a sequence is that of understanding the conservation aspects of physical objects. The child's comprehension moves from that of understanding the conservation of the quantity of substance (the space an object appears to take up) to that of the weight of the substance and then to that of the volume of the substance.

These sequences, along with a variety of other more specific ones, can suggest to curriculum developers a psychologically sound order in which to confront children with different learning tasks. In the traditional school curriculum, children are often expected to acquire concepts of mass, weight, volume, space, time, causality, geometry, speed, and movement in a sequence that is at odds with the child's natural pattern of comprehending such concepts (Elkind, 1976, p. 196). A curriculum plan founded on Piagetian theory and empirical studies would seek to correct such incoordination between development and school learning activities.

Grade Placement of Topics

Piaget's results also suggest at what general age level each step in a given sequence is likely to occur. For instance, understanding of conservation of substance seems to come around age 7 for most children, of weight around age 9, and of volume around age 11 or 12 (J. L. Phillips, 1975, p. 100).

These age points are similar, but not identical, from one child to another and from one ethnic or socioeconomic group to another. Differences among children in the age at which they achieve a particular new level are apparently due to differences in those primary causal factors that Piaget said underlie development: the genetic time schedule for internal maturation, self-directed experience with the world, and instruction or training. Some children are genetically equipped to advance earlier than others. Some have better opportunities to engage in profitable direct experiences and to receive more useful instruction. What these differences in influence mean for curriculum developers is that some flexibility is needed in the grade placement of learning goals founded on Piagetian theory. Not every child will be ready at the same time to accomplish the next step in a cognitive development sequence. However, the general placement of a given objective in the school's grade hierarchy can be estimated. Curriculum developers know whether a particular cognitive skill is more suitable for the preschool years than the primary grades (1 through 3) or for the upper elementary grades (4 through 6). They also know whether a particular understanding is more likely achieved in the junior high (grades 7 through 9) than the senior high years (10 through 12).

As already noted, Piaget, besides outlining the stages of development described earlier for general cognitive development, also identified within the general structure a variety of separate sequences, such as one for the understanding of number, another for causality, a third for conservation of physical aspects, a fourth for moral reasoning, and so on. Although the pattern of one such sequence is much like the pattern of another, the timing of steps within different sequences does not always coincide. In other words, there is some unevenness in progress between sequences.

This lack of coordination between sequences can be illustrated by noting that the logic children use to explain their moral or ethical judgments usually lags a couple of years behind the level of logic they use to explain physical phenomena. It is not yet known whether this lag is due entirely to the greater amount of experience and instruction children have with physical events as compared to moral issues or whether some maturational factor also contributes its influence. Piaget's most frequent collaborator, Barbel Inhelder, believed:

> The general succession of stages seems to be confirmed by all authors, but the relationship between different tasks and substructures, apparently requiring the same mental structure, is still far from adequately explored; what is more, the experimental findings on this point are difficult to interpret (1968, p. vii).

However, the implications of such a finding for curriculum developers seem clear. It is not sufficient to use only Piaget's *general* developmental stages as guides to the placement of learning activities in the school's grade structure. Rather, it is important to assign activities according to the various types of sequences that are involved. For example, activities to promote a given level of moral judgment should be assigned a grade or two later in the school program than activities to promote a similar level of mathematics and science knowledge.

It is possible, though, to use the same general topic or problem situation at both a lower and an upper grade level. For instance, E. A. Peel, a British educational psychologist, (1976, p. 181) recommended that a spiral plan for teaching both physical science and social science can be adopted for adolescents. In such a program, students in an upper secondary grade can return to topics they studied three or four years earlier. The virtue of this approach from a Piagetian viewpoint is that the pupils are thereby not simply reviewing or repeating their earlier experience since during the intervening years the *quality* of the students' intelligence has changed. Whereas a child at the beginning of the secondary school could offer only partial and single explanations of a phenomenon, the youth in high school is able to apply "a greater conceptual repertoire and more mature form of intellectual enquiry" (Peel, 1976, p. 181) to the same phenomenon. In effect, the second time the youth studies the topic she or he does so by means of a new, more complex cognitive lens—in other words, a more complex schema.

The Assessment of Intellectual Functioning

Piagetians are critical of the use of traditional intelligence tests for estimating children's cognitive development and readiness for another step in a learning sequence. Their chief complaint is that the typical intelligence test determines whether the child can give a correct answer to questions; it does not reveal the child's thinking processes. Thus the test fails to indicate a pupil's current level of cognitive development. As a result, Piagetians prefer to base their judgements of children's cognitive styles on: (1) how children solve the problems posed in the tasks Piaget used in his research studies and (2) teachers' observations of the level of children's reasoning during the regular activities of the classroom (Elkind, 1976, pp. 171–194).

Dissatisfaction with standard intelligence tests has stimulated a pair of researchers at the University of Montreal, Monique Laurendeau and Adrien Pinard, to devise a new scale of mental development, a test that represents "an attempt to combine the advantages of Piaget's method (thoroughness and flexibility of questioning) with those of traditional psychometric methods (standardization of questioning)" (J. L. Phillips, 1975, p. 162). Unlike such tests as the Stanford-Binet or Wechsler Intelligence Scale for Children, the Montreal scale does not involve each child's being asked to answer exactly the same questions. Instead, the way a child responds to one question influences the nature of the succeeding questions the child is asked. Furthermore, the tester is not only interested in the number of right answers the child gives, but is equally interested in "wrong" answers since they too are valuable in revealing the child's mode of thinking. In sum, the Montreal project represents an extension of Piagetian theory into the realm of formal intelligence testing.

Teaching Methodology

A common way to conceive of teaching methodology within a Piagetian-based curriculum is to define the two most basic responsibilities of the teacher as those of:

1.   Diagnosing the current stage of a child's development in the various growth sequences the curriculum is designed to promote, and

2.   Offering learning activities that challenge the child to advance to the next higher step of the particular type of sensorimotor-cognitive development that the sequence involves.

In other words, the teacher is not viewed as being a fount of knowledge from which the pupils are expected to fill their minds. Nor is the teacher's job simply that of a pleasant clerk who displays equipment and materials in the classroom and then stands back while children explore the objects on their own. Instead, the teacher is expected to achieve a proper balance between actively guiding or directing children's thinking patterns and providing opportunities for children to explore by themselves.

Not all educators have come up with exactly the same picture of teacher behavior for achieving this balance between active guidance and passive permission. H. G. Furth and W. Wachs, who describe their experimental Piagetian-type school in their book *Thinking Goes to School* (1975), recommend that the teacher offer a sequence of activities that will enable pupils to achieve their next developmental steps efficiently. The activities give a structure or direction to pupils' work, but each child is free to pursue each activity in his own manner or is free not to participate in the activity at all if he so chooses.

The teacher in our school knows that he can do no more than provide the occasion and leave the child free to use it well. He can coach and facilitate and encourage; but in the final analysis it is the child himself who initiates intellectual growth (Furth & Wachs, 1975, p. 46).

A somewhat different version of the teacher's role within a Piagetian-based curriculum is given by D. Elkind (1976), who identified three modes of learning, each featuring a different combination of the assimilation and accommodation processes.

The first mode Elkind called *operative learning*. It is most prominent when the child's intelligence "is actively engaged by the materials she is interacting with" (Elkind, 1976, p. 113). Working with the materials, the child may face contradictions in the way she supposes they will respond, and the contradictions will force her to abstract new understandings from her actions on the materials.

> Operative learning, in addition to facilitating the development of mental operations, also gives rise to *practical intelligence*. Practical intelligence consists of the operations and knowledge the child requires to get about in the everyday world. Much of it . . . is unconscious (Elkind, 1976, p. 114).

The second mode Elkind called *figurative learning*. It involves the child acquiring "aspects of reality" that cannot be reconstructed or rediscovered by the child on his own but "must be largely copied" (Elkind, 1976, p. 114). Perhaps the prime example of this mode is the learning of language—the vocabulary, syntax, pronunciation, and gesture that make the speech of one culture different from that of another. For such aspects of reality, the teacher adopts a more active instructional role, more "teaching" in its traditional sense.

The third mode is *connotative learning*. It is the "conscious conceptualization of one's own mental processes, what has been called *reflective intelligence*." It is most prominent during the years of adolescence (Elkind, 1976, pp. 115–116). "Connotative learning is expressly concerned with the construction of meanings, with establishing connections between concepts and figurative symbols. It is no less than the child's efforts to make sense out of her world" (Elkind, 1976, p. 116).

In promoting operative learning, the teacher may bring objects—a bird, a telescope, a toy boat—to the classroom and may pose questions that stimulate pupils to discover aspects of the item. However, to a great extent the pupils are left on their own to explore the objects. For the figurative mode, the teacher furnishes models and gives demonstrations and explanations, such as showing how to carry out arithmetic computation efficiently or how to use phonics to discover the pronunciation of new words met in a reading passage. With connotative learning, the teacher still encourages pupils to make discoveries and use the communication skills they have acquired, but the "teacher's most important role in connotative learning is to help children do work of the quality that they are really capable of doing" (Elkind, 1976, p. 231). In other words, the teacher stimulates them to produce to the best of their ability.

Whether teachers adopt a Furth and Wachs version or an Elkind version of a Piagetian-based instructional style, they need to carry out their teaching in a setting that is conducive to a substantial amount of small-group and individual activities. Tables, desks, and chairs need to be movable. Different interest centers around the classroom need to be available for use by pupils who are at a given developmental level and can most profitably pursue activities and use materials suited to promoting progress to the next level.

In summary, Piaget's theory and his empirical research findings suggest guidelines about how children's sensorimotor-cognitive development can best be nurtured.

RESEARCH CHALLENGES

A worldwide review of psychology books and journals for the past two decades will show that Piaget's model has exceeded all others in stimulating research. This high degree of research fertility appears to have resulted from a variety of factors.

For one, Piaget's interests ranged over a great many facets of child life, furnishing topics for a diversity of research appetites. He also devised a large number of innovative tasks for children to perform, tasks that permitted trained observers to draw inferences about how children's minds operated at different stages of growth. He thus added to researchers' armory of investigative techniques. And his new approach to assessing intelligence stimulated others to pursue such questions as: How does children's success on traditional intelligence tests compare with their success on Piagetian tasks? And what do such results imply for defining intelligence?

Two other aspects of Piaget's work have kindled scores of studies—his limited sample of European children as the basis for his early speculations and his identifying rather definite age levels for the stages of children's intellectual growth. As a consequence, other researchers have tried to learn the extent to which such results are true also for children in different cultures. His discovery of the growth of conservation in children's thinking has been particularly fruitful in exciting the study of conservation among diverse kinds of children.

Furthermore, a variety of Piaget's beliefs about mental growth have been investigated by other developmentalists. For example, is it true that children must engage in unguided experience with natural phenomena before they can profitably be instructed in such matters? And can instruction hasten the child's arrival at a new stage of mental growth?

In addition to these issues, another array of research challenges has been inspired by the sorts of puzzles mentioned in our inspection of Piaget's key concepts. For instance, precisely what are the characteristics of *equilibrium* in the varied ways Piaget used the term, and how can we identify these characteristics in children's behavior? Exactly how does the process of equilibration operate? Since there is an obvious lack of coordination among the different aspects of mental growth, how is a child's final attainment of a new growth stage properly assessed? And is the application of a simple label, such as *décalage*, sufficient explanation for the lack of coordination? Furthermore, how can we tell when a child is *assimilating* and when *accommodating*? If these two concepts are to help us understand children and guide their development, how can they be distinguished in daily child behavior?

Piaget's theory has also motivated other theorists to extend his model beyond the borders within which he operated. As an example, Klaus Riegel (1973, pp. 346–370), who styled his own theory of development as *dialectical*, criticized Piaget for ending the stages of intellectual growth with the formal operations period of adolescence. Riegel accepted the Piagetian stages as being reasonable as far as they went, but then proposed a dialectical scheme of his own whereby one set of psychological forces struggled against other sets to produce development beyond the middle teen years.

PIAGET'S THEORY: AN ASSESSMENT

Once again, the nine standards of judgment from Chapter One provide my framework for evaluating Piaget's model of development.

Piaget's theory comes off with rather high marks in all categories. Certainly he has been the single most important stimulator of research studies, so I feel he deserves a top rating on item 8. E. R. Hilgard and G. H. Bower, in appraising Piaget's work from the viewpoint of learning theory, have written that:

> One of the problems that have beset psychology as a science is that there are so few discoveries of genuinely new phenomena. . . . Consequently, it is worth noting that the facts of conservation, as pointed out by Piaget and his associates, represent one of the genuine "discoveries" within his experimental observations (1975, p. 327).

Furthermore, I can find no fault with the internal consistency (item 5) or economy of explanation (item 6) of the theory.

In terms of reflecting the real world of children (item 1), the theory gains great strength from the host of empirical studies on which the author based his speculations. My only reservation on this score relates to the matter of individual differences among children. Piaget's great emphasis was on what the average child does. And though he gave some recognition to individual differences, he paid only slight attention to the factors that cause such differences. It is true that he stated that the social milieu within which a child is reared will affect the rate with which the child moves through the developmental stages, but Piaget did not make any careful analysis that I know of of how different factors or agents in the social setting influence the attainment of mental skills. E. Zigler (1965, pp. 361–362) charged that "nothing in Piaget allows one to assess the effects of either the state of the organism or of differences in the environment that give rise to individual differences in development."

Piaget's Theory

How well do I think the theory meets the standards?

The Standards	Very Well	Moderately Well	Very Poorly
1. Reflects the real world of children		X	
2. Is clearly understandable		X	
3. Explains the past and predicts the future		X	
4. Guides child rearing		X	
5. Is internally consistent	X		
6. Is economical	X		
7. Is falsifiable		X	
8. Stimulates new discoveries	X		
9. Is self-satisfying		X	

As for the theory's value in explaining the past and predicting the future (item 3), it does rather well both (1) for the sorts of cognitive behavior on which the model focuses and (2) for the average child. Piaget claimed that the sequence of the changes plotted in his stages of mental growth is invariant from one child or one society to another. And there have been empirical investigations conducted in many nations that support this claim (Piaget, 1973, p. 7; Sigel & Hooper, 1968). He further noted that the rate of passage through stages may vary by as much as two years between the average children of one culture and those of another (Piaget, 1973, pp. 25–27). So he predicted accurately the types and sequence of cognitive behaviors children can be expected to exhibit, but he did not furnish adequate explanations of deviations from the average.

I have found Piaget's works that are in English translation relatively clear (item 2) when studied carefully. Certainly the frequent examples of children's answers to problems posed for them, examples with which Piaget's writings are liberally illustrated, enhance the clarity of his exposition. However, some competent readers have found some of his concepts and explanations quite difficult to grasp. For example, in an early attempt to replicate Piaget's studies of children's ideas of causality, J. M. Deutsch (1943, pp. 129–145) was unable to understand the distinctions Piaget proposed among a number of causal explanation categories.

I also find an unsatisfying circularity in some of Piaget's explanations, as when he suggested in publication *A* that equilibrium explains reversibility ("The equilibrium finally reached between assimilation and accommodation explains then the reversibility of the operational grouping.") and in publication *B* that reversibility explains equilibrium ("Equilibrium will thus be defined by reversibility.") (Piaget in Battro, 1973, pp. 56–57). Hence I have rated the theory between the "very" and "moderately well" designations on clarity.

In terms of guidance for child rearing (item 4), the theory has proven of great interest to educators, who have been making increasing use of Piaget's description of developmental stages to determine the sequence and grade placement of cognitive skills to be learned, particularly skills in mathematics and the physical sciences. Educators are also using Piagetian tasks—the test problems from his clinical method—both for assessing children's developmental status and for providing them with opportunities to try the thought processes represented in the developmental stages of the theory (Furth & Wachs, 1975; Tronick & Greenfield, 1973; Piaget, 1970b). Thus the Piagetian model offers a good deal of guidance for child rearing in cognitive areas.

The model does not, however, furnish guidance for a variety of other problems for which parents, teachers, pediatricians, and social workers often seek aid. The problems I refer to are ones reflected in such phrases as *poor self-concept, lack of friends, easily frustrated, too heavily influenced by undesirable peers,* and *lacks significant goals or purpose in life.* For coping with such matters, Piaget is of little help. But, as he frequently pointed out, his area of concern was genetic epistemology; and the above problems are not central to that concern. Nevertheless, I balanced the foregoing positive points against the negative and rated the theory between "very" and "moderately well."

Next, how falsifiable is the theory (item 7)? Many aspects of Piaget's model are in forms that make determining their validity very testable. Such is true of the developmental stages, both their sequence and their age placement. However, several of the concepts at the core of the theory are not, I believe, susceptible to confirmation or disconfirmation. Included are the concepts of schemes, assimilation, and accommodation. I see no way of testing their validity. Hence I balanced the many falsifiable aspects of the Piagetian model against the apparently few that must be accepted on faith and marked item 7 somewhat above the center.

Finally, I find the theory to be overall quite satisfying (item 9). Despite the reservations mentioned above, I am convinced that the greater part of Piaget's writings is valuable and accurate. After studying his works, I feel that I understand the development of children's thinking processes far better than before. And as a consequence, I believe I can work more effectively with children and youths. I feel the theory rates a high mark.

FOR FURTHER READING

Piaget, Jean, and Barbel Inhelder. (1969) *The Psychology of the Child.* New York: Basic Books. Although any of the books listed under Piaget's name in the bibliography at the end of this volume offers useful insights into his many-sided theorizing, this volume by Piaget and his long-time colleague, Inhelder, is particularly helpful in reviewing not only the principal aspects of basic cognitive development but also the associated social and affective interactions, including moral feelings and judgments.

Battro, Antonio M. (1973) *Piaget: Dictionary of Terms.* New York: Pergamon Press. People who have had difficulty with the meaning Piaget intended for the specialized terms he used will find this book useful. Battro lists Piagetian terms alphabetically and then under each he gives one or more definitions in the form of quotes from Piaget's writings.

Campbell, Sarah F. (1976) *Piaget Sampler.* New York: Wiley. An autobiography by Piaget (covering the years 1896–1966) appears as Chapter 10 in this potpourri of articles by the theorist.

Many books published in recent years have been designed to offer a condensed version of Piagetian theory, that is more readily understandable than Piaget's original writings. The following two small volumes, one by Phillips and the other by Sigel and Cocking, are among the more readable and up-to-date books of this type.

Phillips, John L., Jr. (1975) *The Origins of Intellect: Piaget's Theory.* 2d ed. San Francisco: Freeman.

Sigel, Irving E., and Rodney R. Cocking. (1977) *Cognitive Development from Childhood to Adolescence: A Constructivist Perspective.* New York: Holt, Rinehart & Winston.

CHAPTER ELEVEN

Vygotsky and the Soviet Tradition

During the years following the Russian revolution near the close of World War I, psychologists under the new Soviet Union government struggled with the problem of devising a theory of human development compatible with the Marxist political tenets on which the new state was founded. By the mid-1920s the most successful solution to this problem was that created by Lev Semenovich Vygotsky (1896–1934), a teacher of literature whose first research as a young scholar between 1915 and 1922 focused on artistic creation (Vygotsky, 1971). In 1924 Vygotsky began serious work in the areas of developmental psychology, education, and psychopathology, pursuing these interests at a highly productive pace until he died of tuberculosis in 1934 at the age of thirty-eight.

Although his career as a psychologist was brief, Vygotsky earned high regard in the Soviet Union for establishing an acceptable sociopolitical foundation for much psychological investigation. He did this by casting in suitable research form "the Marxist-Leninist thesis that all fundamental human cognitive activities take shape in a matrix of social history and form the products of sociohistorical development" (Luria, 1976, p. v).

In other words, according to this doctrine, the intellectual skills or patterns of thinking that a person displays are not primarily determined by innate factors, that is, inherited intelligence or mental abilities. Instead, patterns and levels of thinking are products of the activities practiced in the social institutions of the culture in which the individual grows up. In keeping with this thesis,

> It follows that practical thinking will predominate in societies that are characterized by practical manipulations of objects, and more "abstract"

forms of "theoretical" activity in technological societies will induce more abstract, theoretical thinking. The parallel between individual and social development produces a strong proclivity to interpret all behavioral differences in developmental terms (Luria, 1976, p. xiv).

From this viewpoint, the history of the society in which a child is reared, and the child's own developmental history in terms of her experiences in that society, are both extremely important in fashioning the ways the child will be able to think. Furthermore, advanced modes of thought—conceptual thinking—must be transmitted to the child by means of words, so language becomes a crucial tool for deciding how children learn to think.

It was in an atmosphere of these assumptions that Vygotsky wrote *Thought and Language* shortly before his death. In 1936, two years after its publication, the volume was suppressed in the Soviet Union because of disputes within the nation's psychological community. But when the disputes ended, the book was distributed once again. However it wasn't translated into English until 1962, so it is only in recent years that Vygotsky's theory has become widely understood and discussed in English-speaking countries. During the 1970s further works by Vygotsky and his followers were translated into English, providing ample evidence of his talent as a theoretician and practitioner who was skilled in applying research findings to the improvement of child rearing and schooling (Cole, 1977; Luria, 1976; Vygotsky, 1978).

This chapter is divided into six sections: (1) a description of the main features of Vygotsky's theory of the relationship of thought to language, (2) an explanation of a series of key generalizations that he proposed about human development, (3) a brief review of general trends in Soviet developmental psychology from the 1920s into the early 1980s, (4) practical applications of Vygotsky's theory, (5) research challenges it has stimulated, and (6) an assessment of the theory.

The chapter focuses on Vygotsky's theorizing, not simply because he was the chief architect of Soviet developmental psychology in the early years of the Communist regime, but because his proposals contribute to discussions in contemporary psychology. The late Alexander R. Luria (1902–1977), a world-renowned Soviet developmentalist, before his death wrote that:

> Vygotsky was a genius. After more than half a century in science I am unable to name another person who even approaches his incredible analytic ability and foresight. All of my work has been no more than the working out of the psychological theory which he constructed (Vygotsky, 1978, dust jacket).

THE OUTLINES OF VYGOTSKY'S THEORY

Four characteristics that marked Vygotsky's work were: (1) a sincere dedication to Marxist social philosophy and a conviction that psychological development was intimately linked to the tenets of that philosophy, (2) a thorough acquaintance with the work of leading European and American psychologists of his day and of earlier decades, (3) considerable direct experience with children, and (4) great ingenuity in devising methods for gathering and interpreting data.

To understand something of the climate for psychology in Vygotsky's time, we need to recall two antithetical views of human thought that were prominent in the early twentieth century.

The first was a traditional view of the mind that grew out of the faculty psychology of past centuries. Psychologists in the late nineteenth and early twentieth centuries studied mind and its functions by means of introspection. A person carefully looked into his or her own mind to analyze the working of perception, thought, memory, feelings, and the like.

The second movement was in direct opposition to the first. It represented an effort to be scientific and objective about the study of humans, just as physics, chemistry, and biology were objective sciences. In America this movement became known as behaviorism, for its leaders proposed that the proper study of humans involved observable behavior as measured and recorded by scientists outside the people being observed. Behaviorists of the early twentieth century rejected the abstract, unobservable items of past speculation, such items as consciousness, feelings, will, and mind itself. But what about thought and thinking? Everybody knows there are such things as thoughts. Behaviorists of the day said that what people for years had been calling "thinking" was really speech behavior, but it was below the hearing threshold, a kind of "silent speech." So the staunchest behaviorists of Vygotsky's day had eliminated mind and its functions in favor of analyzing only observable acts.

Vygotsky saw shortcomings in both of these schools of theory. He did not trust introspection as a secure methodological base on which to found scientific psychological theory. And as for behaviorists' rejecting mind, he wrote:

> In that psychology ignores the problem of consciousness, it blocks itself off from access to the investigation of complicated problems of human behavior, and the elimination of consciousness from the sphere of scientific psychology has as its major consequence the retention of all the dualism (mind versus body) and spiritualism of earlier subjective psychology (1962, p. vi).

In his own research Vygotsky set about investigating conscious thought processes, but he did so by means of newly created objective measures that did not depend upon introspection or "spiritualism" for testing.

Vygotsky chose to study, in particular, the relationship between thought and language. Was thought identical with language, as Watsonian behaviorists claimed when they said thinking is just silent speaking? Or was thought independent of language, complete in itself, as many introspectionists seemed to believe, with language simply serving as the tool for communicating thought to others—just as a camera is an instrument for communicating visual images. Or, as a third possibility, were thought and language separate functions that could commingle and in so doing modify each other?

To arrive at an answer, Vygotsky (1) analyzed a host of studies of thought and language conducted by psychologists and anthropologists from numerous countries and (2) devised his own investigations of thought and speech as found among children, adolescents, and adults in the Soviet Union. He cast his interpretations of these findings as three sets of conclusions about child development. The first set concerned the development of conceptual thought, the second the development of speech, and the third the connection between the first two. The nature of these conclusions is the subject of the rest of this section. However, we will consider the three sets in reverse order, beginning with Vygotsky's general views on the relationship between the development of thought and the development of language (*language* in this case meaning *speech*).

In general, Vygotsky concluded that the child's thought and speech begin as separate functions with no necessary connection between them. They are like two circles that do not touch. One circle represents nonverbal thought, the other nonconceptual speech. As the child begins to grow up, the circles meet and overlap (Figure 11.1). The juncture of the two represents *verbal thought*, meaning that the child has now begun to acquire concepts that bear word labels. A *concept* here means an abstraction, an idea that does not represent a particular object but rather some common characteristic shared by—or some relationship among—diverse objects.

The two circles never completely overlap. Even though the common portion becomes more prominent as the child develops (particularly in a highly literate cultural setting), there always remains some nonverbal thought and some nonconceptual speech. An example of nonverbal thought in the adult is her skillful use of tools. An example of nonconceptual speech is her singing an old song or reciting a poem or repeating a memorized telephone number. These repetitions by rote are "mental activity" but are not of the conceptual variety that Vygotsky identifies as verbal thought.

Figure 11.1 shows Vygotsky's general idea of the thought–language

SPEECH   THOUGHT

Stages of Development   Stages of Development

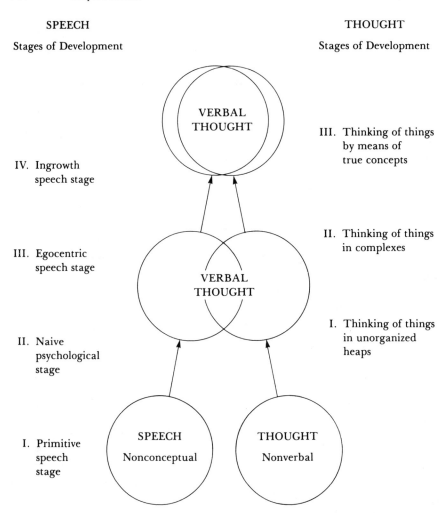

IV. Ingrowth
    speech stage

III. Thinking of things
     by means of
     true concepts

III. Egocentric
     speech stage

II. Thinking of things
    in complexes

II. Naive
    psychological
    stage

I. Thinking of things
   in unorganized
   heaps

I. Primitive
   speech
   stage

Figure 11.1   Vygotsky's View of Speech and Thought Development

relationship during a child's development, but the actual coordination between the two circles is probably far more complex. Vygotsky admitted that the pattern of their interaction was not yet clear. But he did contend that:

> Progress in thought and progress in speech are not parallel. Their two growth curves cross and recross. They may straighten out and run side by side, even merge for a time, but they always diverge again. This applies to both phylogeny and ontogeny (1962, p. 33).

Vygotsky disagreed with theorists who said that children, as a result of internal maturation, can achieve skill in advanced conceptual thought on their own, distinct from what they are taught. While admitting the necessary role of internal maturation in development, Vygotsky believed that children's informal and formal education through the medium of language strongly influences the level of conceptual thinking they reach. If the language climate within which children grow up (direct speech, mass communication media) is dominated by simplistic or "primitive" language, then the children will think only simplistically or primitively. But if the language environment contains varied and complex concepts, then children will learn to think in varied and complex ways, given that their initial biological equipment (sense organs, central nervous system) is not impaired.

In extending the scope of his theorizing beyond children's development, he suggested that the stages through which a child's thought and language evolve are likely the same as those through which mankind's have evolved over eons of time. Thus studying children's ontogenetic development not only helps us understand the child's thought and speech but also serves as the most practical method for estimating the phylogenetic development of our species.

These are the general features of Vygotsky's theory. The model is not a completed theory, with all details filled in and each proposal buttressed with a mass of empirical evidence. Rather, as Jerome S. Bruner (Vygotsky, 1962, p. viii) has written, the book *Thought and Language* "is more programmatic than systematic." It's as if Vygotsky had found only parts of the thought–speech puzzle by the time he wrote the volume, and his theory or "program" represented his assumption that when the rest of the parts were eventually discovered, the final assemblage would take on the general configuration he had outlined in his proposal.

Stages in Speech Development

Vygotsky's studies led him to conclude that speech development proceeds through the same four stages and is governed by the same laws as those relating to other mental operations that employ signs, that is, such other operations as counting and memorizing with the aid of mnemonic devices (Vygotsky, 1962, pp. 46–47).

He called the first of these four stages the *primitive* or *natural stage*. This first period, which represents the time before the circle of language overlaps the circle of conscious thought, lasts from birth until about age 2 in Vygotsky's opinion. The stage is characterized by three nonintellectual speech functions. First are sounds representing *emotional release*—crying with pain or frustration, cooing or babbling with contentment. Next, as early as the second month after birth, these emotional noises are joined by sounds that can be interpreted as *social reactions* to other people's voices or appearance. The noises of social contact include laughter and a variety of inarticulate sounds. The third type of thoughtless speech consists of the child's first words, which are *substitutes for objects and desires*. These are words learned by conditioning, by parents and siblings matching the words frequently to objects, just as some animals can be conditioned to recognize words as labels for things.

Around age 2 the primitive stage ends and the second period begins, that of *naive psychology*. The child discovers that words can have a symbolic function, and he displays this discovery by frequently asking what things are called. He no longer is simply conditioned by others to label objects and actions, but actively seeks this information himself. As a result, his vocabulary increases at a great rate. With the advent of the naive stage, the circles of language and thought begin to merge.

During this second period the child exhibits the beginnings of practical intelligence by recognizing characteristics of her surroundings and by starting to use tools, that is, starting to use objects as means to accomplish desired ends. However, her language is considered naive because she uses grammatical structures properly without recognizing the underlying functions they serve.

The experience the child gains using language in relation to the objects of the world subsequently enables the child to move to a third level, the stage of *egocentric speech*. This kind of talk makes up a large proportion of the preschool and kindergarten child's speech, particularly that occurring in play situations. It takes the form of a running monologue that accompanies the child's activities, whether he works alone or beside others. It requires no response from anyone because it is not directed at anyone but the speaker. This commonly observed phenomenon has been interpreted in various ways by different investigators. Some have viewed egocentric speech as a "running accompaniment" or tune that merely parallels the child's thought and activity as he plays. But Vygotsky arrived at a different conclusion. He saw egocentric speech as an important new tool of thought. Not only does the child think to speak, but what he says to himself influences what he then will think, so the two interact to produce together conceptual or verbal thought.

To test this hypothesis, Vygotsky arranged for problems to arise during the play-work activities of young children. For example, a pencil for the drawing task would be missing or the paper would be too small or too large. The investigators then observed that the amount of egocentric talk on these occasions was double that observed when children did not face such problems (Vygotsky, 1962, pp. 16–17). This Vygotsky interpreted as evidence that egocentric speech is not just a release of tension or an expressive accompaniment to activity but is also a significant tool "of thought in the proper sense—in seeking and planning the solution of a problem" (1962, p. 16).

Nor did Vygotsky agree that egocentric speech simply died out after age 7 or so. Rather, he saw the decline of egocentric speech as a signal of the onset of the fourth stage in his developmental hierarchy, the *ingrowth stage*. The child learns to manipulate language in her head in the form of soundless speech, thinking by means of logical memory that employs inner signs for solving problems. Throughout the rest of her life, the individual will use both inner speech and outer speech as tools in conceptual or verbal thought.

In summary, children's speech grows through four stages between the time of birth and the years of primary school, age 7 or 8. The process begins with nonintellectual or "thoughtless" speech and develops via naive and egocentric language into inner speech that is inextricably interwoven with conceptual thinking. Now that we have traced development from the vantage point of speech, we will trace the development of verbal thinking from the vantage point of thought.

Stages in Conceptual Thought Development

Vygotsky's method of studying the development of conceptual thought involved two steps: (1) devising a test that would reveal the process a person follows when faced with the necessity to create a concept and administering the test to children, adolescents, and adults and then (2) comparing the developmental hierarchy revealed in this testing with reports from other psychologists who had longitudinally followed the conceptual growth of individual children from one year to another. The purpose of this comparison was to determine whether the differences observed in testing cross sections of people of different ages accurately reflected the changes in thought processes that occur in the individual as he or she matures.

To begin we will briefly look at the testing instrument Vygotsky created (now known as the Vygotsky blocks), for it reveals something of his research ingenuity. One of the sticky problems faced in testing children's concept-formation process is that of finding concepts for them to generate in the testing situation that we are sure they did not already know. In particular, we want to ensure they have mastered the concept and have not simply memorized a word that suggests they know the concept when they actually do not.

Vygotsky solved this problem by constructing a set of twenty-two wooden blocks of different colors, shapes, heights, and sizes (*size* meaning overall horizontal area). These characteristics vary in such a manner that no two blocks are alike in all ways. On the bottom surface of each block is written one of four nonsense words: *lag, bik, mur, cev.* Irrespective of the blocks' color or shape, *lag* appears on all tall, large blocks; *bik* on all flat, large ones; *mur* on tall, small ones; and *cev* on short, small ones. Each testing session begins with the examiner spreading the blocks before the child in a random mixture, then turning up a sample block and showing the child the name on the bottom. The child is asked to pick out all the blocks he thinks are the same kind, that is, ones that bear the same name. When the child has done so, the examiner turns up one of the selected blocks he knows is wrong and shows the child that it does not bear the correct word. The child is asked to try again. This process is repeated over and over until the child solves the problem. The solution, of course, requires that the child recognize that the word represents a concept composed of two of the dimensions of the blocks—both height and horizontal size. Since there is no single word in normal language representing this combined concept, the child cannot have known or rote memorized it prior to the testing session (Vygotsky, 1962, pp. 56–57).

Throughout the testing session the examiner carefully watches the combinations the child chooses each time, for the nature of each combination reflects the strategy of thought in which the child has engaged. Using the block problem with several hundred subjects of different ages enabled Vygotsky to identify a hierarchy of three major stages children pass through in achieving true conceptual thought between the preschool years and middle adolescence. Within each stage, children also traverse a series of subphases.

Conceptual thinking is really a mode of organizing one's environment by abstracting and labeling a quality shared by two or more phenomena. The major steps in children's intellectually organizing perceived phenomena are (I) clustering things into unorganized heaps, then (II) putting things together in complexes, and, as puberty arrives, (III) beginning to think in genuine concepts. But even when the adolescent achieves the ability to think conceptually, she does not entirely abandon the two earlier forms of thought; they merely subside in frequency and reappear on certain occasions.

The three major stages and the subphases, based upon children's and adolescents' solutions to the Vygotsky-blocks problem, are as follows (Vygotsky, 1962, pp. 58–81):

Stage I Thinking in *unorganized congeries* or heaps. During this period the child puts things in groups (and may assign the group a label) on the basis of what are only chance links in the child's perception.

Subphase I-A: Trial-and-error grouping. The groups are created at random, blind guess.

Subphase I-B: Visual-field organization. The child applies a grouping label to a collection of things that happen to appear together in space and time.

Subphase I-C: Reformed heaps. The child first produces groupings on the basis of either guess or visual-field organization, then in dissatisfaction tries to reform the heaps by shifting elements in them around, but the items are still not alike in any inherent way.

Stage II Thinking in *complexes.* Individual objects are united in the child's mind not only by subjective impressions but also by bonds that actually exist among the objects. This is a step away from egocentric thinking and in the direction of objectivity. In a complex, the bonds between components are *concrete* and *factual* to some degree rather than abstract and logical. Five types of complexes succeed one another during this stage of thought.

Subphase II-A: Associative complexes. These are based on any bond the child notices, such as color, shape, or nearness of objects to each other.

Subphase II-B: Collection complexes. Items are grouped by contrast rather than by similarity. For example, one block of each color may be put in a group and given a label. (At a dinner table, a knife, fork, spoon, plate, cup, and saucer would make up a set of a collection variety.)

Subphase II-C: Chain complexes. These involve a consecutive joining of individual items with a meaningful bond necessary only between one link and the next (as in the game of dominoes). A *large* green block may be linked to a *large red* block, then a *red* small *round* one followed by a *round* yellow middle-sized one.

Subphase II-D: Diffuse complexes. These are groupings in which there is a fluidity in the attribute that unites the individual elements. The child may put triangles together, then add a trapezoid to the group because the trapezoid's points remind the child of a triangle's points.

Subphase II-E: Pseudoconcept complexes. These at first view appear to be groupings based on true conceptual thinking. But when the label the child has applied is challenged, he shows he is unable to rationalize the grouping condition adequately. If he has put all red blocks together and the experimenter turns two blocks over to show they do not bear the same name (one is *mur* and the other *bik*), the child is unable to give up his first basis for grouping and to seek a different one, a different characteristic that unites the objects. Pseudoconceptual thinking represents a transition from thinking in complexes to thinking in true concepts.

Vygotsky made an important distinction between pseudoconcepts and true concepts: True conceptual thinking requires that the child spontaneously group objects on the basis of abstract characteristics that she perceives and not simply apply ready-made labels that she has been taught to use with other, common groupings. Vygotsky explained this phenomenon, which causes many adults to mistakenly assume that young children think conceptually, in this way:

> Pseudoconcepts predominate over all other complexes in the preschool child's thinking for the simple reason that in real life, complexes corresponding to word meanings are not spontaneously developed by the child: The lines along which a complex develops are predetermined by the meaning a given word already has in the language of adults (1962, p. 67).

Stage III   Thinking in *concepts*. On the threshold of this final major stage, we will pause and inspect two paths of thought development—*synthesizing* and *analyzing*—that have now converged to make conceptual thinking possible.

The first path was through the sequence of complexes. The main function involved in such complex thinking was the *drawing together* or synthesizing of phenomena that share common aspects. The second path leading to conceptual thinking followed the process of *separating* or analyzing phenomena by singling out or abstracting elements from them. In Vygotsky's opinion these two processes, uniting and separating, arise from different sources in the child's development. We have already traced the path of drawing together or synthesizing. We will now move back to find the beginnings of the other, that of abstracting or analyzing.

In his experiments, Vygotsky located the beginnings of abstracting at the point where children identified ways in which objects were *maximally similar*, that is, alike in as many ways as possible. For example, they pick two blocks that are both tall *and* yellow or both short *and* green. But since such pairs of blocks also differ in shape or horizontal size, the child's abstracting process is somewhat in error. However, at this age the child overlooks the discrepancies and overemphasizes the similarities he first identified.

At the next stage of abstraction, the child identifies a *single characteristic* by which to group objects, selecting only green blocks or only tall ones. Vygotsky called these single-characteristic selections *potential concepts.*

The child then takes the final step into conceptual thinking when she makes a new synthesis of accurately abstracted traits, a synthesis that is stable and convincing in her mind, and this synthesis "becomes the main instrument of thought" (Vygotsky, 1962, p. 78). The child—by now an early adolescent—views things in terms of her synthesized and analyzed concepts. But even among adolescents conceptual thinking is somewhat unstable, being more consistent in concrete situations that have objects present than in solely verbal situations. Furthermore, there is no sharp break between one sort of thought and another. As the child begins to achieve conceptual thought, her thinking in complexes continues, although it diminishes in frequency. A person, even as an adult, is never "purely" a conceptual thinker.

Throughout this process of mental development, language has served as a significant tool or mediator for thinking activity. The intellectual operation of forming concepts, according to Vygotsky (1962, p. 81), "is guided by the use of words as the means of actively centering attention, of abstracting certain traits, synthesizing them, and symbolizing them by a sign."

As mentioned earlier, after Vygotsky conducted his experiments with the blocks and identified his hierarchy of mental acts leading to true concept formation, he studied the literature on children's linguistic development, on the thought processes of primitive peoples, and on the nature of languages as such. The comparison of his own experimental results with those from the professional literature convinced him that the stages he had identified were essentially an accurate description of the development of conceptual thought. He apparently felt that a significant portion of the thought-and-language puzzle had been solved.

KEY GENERALIZATIONS ABOUT DEVELOPMENT

Vygotsky also produced a variety of other insights that illustrate other facets of development. The following selections reflect some of these beliefs. Each selection in a sense describes a direction that development takes, since each is cast in a form that pictures the way the condition of the young child changes as the child grows toward adolescence.

Structures and Functions

At each level of development, the child's manner of interacting with the world is determined by the particular *structures* of the personality at that time. A given structure equips the child to function in a particular way. By *function,* Vygotsky appeared to mean the way the child interpreted the world and responded. The first structures displayed by the newborn and young child Vygotsky termed *elementary.* They are seated in the conditioned and unconditioned reflexes, in the basic biological nature of the individual, and their functions "are totally and directly determined by stimulation from the environment" (Vygotsky, 1978, p. 39).

As the child grows up, he periodically arrives at new stages at which new structures are built, thereby creating potentials for new functions. Vygotsky termed these *higher structures,* ones that emerge in the process of cultural development and utilize signs (language) and tools. Whereas the elementary functions consist of the child's reacting directly to stimuli from the environment, for "higher functions, the central feature is self-generated stimulation, that is, the creation and use of artificial stimuli which become the immediate causes of behavior" (Vygotsky, 1978, p. 39). The older child, then, "thinks up" things to do and employs language and tools in pursuit of need fulfillment.

Vygotsky proposed that as a child moves from a more elementary to a higher structure, the process at each step of development involves the same sequence of events. "The initial stage is followed by that first structure's destruction, reconstruction, and transition to structures of the higher type. . . . Higher psychological functions are not superimposed as a second story over the elementary processes; they represent new psychological systems" (Vygotsky, 1978, p. 124). We might note that both Werner (Chapter Seven) and Piaget (Chapter Ten) held similar views.

Memory

In keeping with his lower and higher levels of structure and function, Vygotsky defined two separate types of memory. The lower type, corresponding to elementary structures, he called *natural memory.* This sort dominates the intellectual behavior of both young children and nonliterate peoples. Natural memory consists of a person's retaining mental images of actual experiences and objects. Such "memory traces" resemble pictures and sounds in the mind, revealed in studies of young children's eidetic or photographic records of events. Natural memory is the most basic form of cognition, "the definitive characteristic of the early stages" of mental development (Vygotsky, 1978, p. 51).

In contrast to natural memory is the abstract variety that evolves as the child gains command over signs that form language. Objects and events can be symbolized as words and figures, and these symbols can themselves be manipulated to form new meanings. The older child develops concepts by abstracting a common quality from various events and by comprehending principles that represent relations among the concepts. For the adolescent, remembering is not simply the recall of images. As Luria (1976, p.11) explained, "although the young child thinks by remembering, an adolescent remembers by thinking." An adolescent girl's "memory is so 'logicalized' that remembering is reduced to establishing and finding logical relations; recognizing consists in discovering that element which the task indicates has to be found" (Vygotsky, 1978, p. 51).

Perception

As the child develops, her perception progresses from a natural form to higher forms that are mediated by language. The preverbal infant seems to perceive only immediately present visual and aural fields. Then, as language is gradually acquired, the child gains more control over what she attends to and how she perceives it. Vygotsky concluded that the chief function of speech for the young child is that of applying labels to things, thereby singling out the object from its background for attention and imposing some of her own structure on the natural sensory field. At the same time, the child accompanies her first words with expressive gestures, ostensibly compensating with gesture for her shortcomings in communicating with language.

At a more advanced stage of development, speech functions as an instrument for synthesizing and thereby producing more complex forms of perception. Speech frees the child from the immediate visual field.

> The independent elements in a visual field are simultaneously perceived; in this sense, *visual perception is integral*. Speech, on the other hand, requires sequential processing. Each element is separately labeled and then connected in a sentence structure, *making speech essentially analytical* (Vygotsky, 1978, p. 33).

In summary, then, these examples of the theorist's beliefs about elementary and higher functions, about memory, and about perception illustrate his deep conviction that acquisition of tool use and language is essential for the development of higher cognitive processes. And in keeping with his Marxist views about the significance of the social environment for development, he saw the language environment—the *culture*—in which a child is raised as being crucial in determining the direction and extent of the individual's intellectual growth. The history of that particular culture and the history of the individual child's experience in that culture mold the child's cognitive abilities.

CENTRAL CONCERNS IN SOVIET DEVELOPMENTAL THEORY: 1920s–1980s

In pointing out the chief interests of Soviet developmentalists during the past six decades, V. V. Davidov (1985) emphasized the crucial role played by activity at each stage of child development. An *activity* is a person's goal-oriented, genuinely industrious interaction with the world, with the product of this activity becoming transformed in the structure of the individual's intellect. More specifically, as a child engages in a type of social interaction with others in his or her culture, this activity is accompanied by signs or language that represent the activity. The signs or language are then internalized by the child so that the internalization alters the psychic structures that, in turn, produce new psychic functions by which the child interacts with the world.

At the base of such a theory is the concept of a hierarchy of types of activities, with a dominant or *leading activity* at the top of the hierarchy at each stage of development. Thus each period of human development is motivated by a particular leading activity. The change from one leading activity brings about a change in the person's perception of life and signifies the transition from one stage to the next. A leading activity is marked by three features: (1) it is the chief factor establishing a given period in the child's psychological development, (2) it is within the field of this activity that particular psychic functions emerge, and (3) the climax of the activity forms the foundation for the next leading activity.

Thus successive leading activities signify the focus of development over the passing years and become a series of developmental stages. The best-known version of this series was described by Vygotsky and D. B. Elkonin (Davidov, 1985; Elkonin in Cole, 1977, pp. 538–563). It consists of six levels:

1. *Intuitive and emotional contact between child and adults (birth to age 1).* The basic types of development produced by this contact include feeling a need for interacting with other people, expressing emotional attitudes toward them, learning to grasp things, and displaying a variety of perceptual actions.

2. *Object-manipulation activity (early preschool years, ages 1–3).* Children adopt socially accepted ways of handling things, and through interaction with adults they develop speech and visual-perception thinking (memory images).

3. *Playing-games activity (later preschool years, ages 3–7).** Children engage in symbolic activities and creative play. They now have

---

*Traditionally Soviet children have started elementary school at age 7, some of them having been in preschool programs for two or three years.

some comprehension of how to cooperate together in group endeavors.

4. *Learning activity (elementary school years, ages 7–11).* Children develop theoretical approaches to the world of things, a function that involves their considering objective laws of reality and beginning to comprehend psychological preconditions for abstract theoretical thought (intentional mental operations, mental schemes for problem solving, reflective thinking).

5. *Social-communications activity, (early adolescence, ages 11–15).* Adolescents gain skills in initiating types of communication needed for solving life's problems, in understanding other people's motives, and in consciously submitting to group norms.

6. *Vocational-learning activity (later adolescence, ages 15–17).* Older adolescents develop new cognitive and vocational interests, grasp elements of research work, and attempt life projects.

The transition from one stage of development to another disrupts the stability of the child's ways of thinking and interacting with the world and produces *crises* as the child struggles with the prerequisites for the next activity that is to occupy the leading role. Thus development is composed of cycles of stability interspersed with transitional crises.

Davidov (1985) identified five major concerns that are increasingly engaging the attention of Soviet developmental psychologists: (1) elucidating the basic concepts of development concerning humans in general and the specific ways individuals' intellects evolve, (2) creating a complete theory of intellectual development incorporating the leading activities of the successive stages of child growth, (3) discovering how the historical development of a society relates to its members' intellectual development, (4) determining methods for studying critical periods over the entire life span of development, and (5) studying intellectual development in middle-aged and elderly people.

PRACTICAL APPLICATIONS

In a society whose entire apparatus—scientific, organizational, artistic, educational, social, athletic—is designed to promote such sociopolitical goals as those of Marxist-Leninism, developmental psychologists are necessarily practical people who focus their theories on the solution of problems in the society. Vygotsky and his fellow developmentalists accepted this responsibility with apparent enthusiasm as they applied their studies to aiding the physically and mentally handicapped, spreading literacy throughout the third largest population in the world, improving instructional methods in the schools, raising the level of intellectual functioning of disadvantaged groups in the society (Luria, 1976), and promoting better child-rearing practices in general.

In formulating the theoretical foundations for these practical undertakings, Vygotsky and his colleagues often departed from the dominant views of European and American psychologists. An example from Vygotsky's writings illustrates one of these departures. The issue is that of learning readiness. That is, how does a teacher or parent know when a child is capable of learning to perform a given intellectual function or task? This determination traditionally has been based on aptitude and intelligence test scores. The child's developmental level is determined on the basis of how adequately she or he answers the question or solves the problems posed by the test. Or Piagetian tasks have been used to reveal the present mode of the child's mental functioning. Ostensibly this assessment informs the educator of the base on which instruction might build. If the child's test performance shows that he has mastered the level of thought necessary for a given type of learning, then those learning activities are appropriate for that child at that point. However, if the child's intellectual development appears insufficient for pursuing the proposed learning task, then the task should be postponed until a later date.

However, Vygotsky disagreed with this line of logic and proposed instead that two developmental levels were important for determining whether a given sort of learning could profitably be attempted. The first and lower level, which he called the *actual developmental level,* was the one established by the tests or Piagetian tasks. It showed the stage of development that had already been completed. But Vygotsky contended that this level was not a good indicator of how well a child can learn new material with some hints or help from an instructor. Besides the development that has been completed, there is development that is currently evolving, and this sort of learning potential is not adequately revealed by traditional tests. Rather, it is revealed during the process of teaching a child, by observations of how the child's intellect functions in relation to hints or leading questions or suggestions from a sensitive instructor. Studies conducted by Vygotsky and his associates supported this contention and motivated him to identify a second developmental level that extends above the actual level. He called this the *zone of proximal development.*

> [The zone] is the distance between the actual developmental level as determined by independent problem solving and the level of potential

development as determined through problem solving under adult guidance or in collaboration with more capable peers.

The zone of proximal development defines those functions that have not yet matured but are in the process of maturation, functions that will mature tomorrow but are currently in an embryonic state. These functions could be termed the "buds" or "flowers" of development rather than the "fruits" of development. The actual developmental level characterizes mental development retrospectively, while the zone of proximal development characterizes mental development prospectively (Vygotsky, 1978, pp. 86–87).

Such a notion of learning readiness, when applied to practical teaching situations, significantly influences the teacher's decision about what kinds of learning activities to provide and how to decide whether children are capable of profiting from them. For example, a teacher who knows the sequence in which the zones of proximal development evolve in the field of mathematics can predict the next mathematical skill that a child should be capable of mastering. Equipped with this knowledge, the teacher can design learning activities for the child that will stimulate the early fruition of that skill.

Research Challenges

The extensive pool of research questions generated by Soviet theories of development is the result of the interaction of several factors. One factor has been the fundamental assumptions about human nature and society in Marxist doctrine. The most important of these is the assumption that a person's present state of development has been influenced chiefly by environmental forces rather than heredity. A second assumption derives from the Marxist belief that the evolution of society is produced through the dialectical confrontation of forces. When this notion of dialectical confrontation is applied to individuals, then the growth of human intelligence can be interpreted as resulting from the confrontation of mental tendencies and the subsequent resolution of the conflicts by the child's progressing to a more advanced mode of thought. Soviet psychologists, motivated by such assumptions, have sought to identify the kinds of environmental forces—including child-rearing and teaching techniques—that are most influential in producing these advances in mental development.

A second factor affecting the nature of Soviet research has been the practical goal of using the science of human development for fostering the progress of the Marxist social revolution. This aim of maximizing people's roles in the cause of the revolution has engaged developmentalists in a great many studies of children in varied life situations as well as in laboratory settings.

A third factor has been the marked ingenuity of such scientists as Vygotsky in viewing children's behavior from diverse perspectives and thereby producing new interpretations of behavior. For example, the idea that play involves imaginary situations was not a novel notion in Vygotsky's day, but the way he perceived this imaginary quality in relation to other aspects of play was novel. His studies of children's play convinced him that play is not always pleasurable (as when a child loses a race), that children use play to fulfill needs. He proposed that play is invented by the child when she begins to experience unrealizable tendencies. She is prevented by her immaturity or by social pressures from meeting needs directly, so she creates imaginary situations in which the tendencies can be realized in play form. Vygotsky suggested as well that there is no such thing as play without rules, so that both imagination and rules become the defining characteristics of play. Just as every imaginary situation for the young child contains rules in a concealed form, so also "every game with rules contains an imaginary situation in a concealed form. The development from games with an overt imaginary situation and covert rules to games with overt rules and a covert imaginary situation outlines the evolution of children's play" (Vygotsky, 1978, p. 96).

When a theorist offers such proposals as those about play, he opens the gates to a host of new research issues. Is it true that all forms of what we intuitively call play involve both imaginary conditions and rules? If so, how and why do these vary from one age level to another? What requirements in terms of intellectual functions do various forms of play involve? To what extent do children invent new kinds of play or variations on existing kinds, and why do they create such innovations? Is play actually the *leading activity* of the preschool years in all cultures? And beyond the preschool years, what role does play assume as a subsidiary activity and why? Does play operate differently in one society than in another, depending on the differences between the societies in their levels of historical development—hunter-and-gatherer versus agricultural, agricultural versus industrial, capitalist versus communist?

In like manner, other theoretical proposals from Soviet psychologists have opened additional fields of investigation—proposals regarding the relationship between thought and language, the influence of primitive versus sophisticated tool use on cognitive style, the effect of a society's developmental level on the time children enter puberty and adulthood, and many more.

Since the writings of Soviet psychologists began to enter the international body of psychological literature in the 1960s and 1970s, developmentalists around the world have begun to derive research topics from Soviet theory. It seems likely that this influence on research in nations outside the communist countries will increase in years ahead.

VYGOTSKY'S THEORY: AN ASSESSMENT

As in previous chapters, the nine standards of appraisal from Chapter One provide the framework for evaluating Vygotsky's theory.

Vygotsky's theorizing, warrants a rather high mark for how well it reflects the real world of children (item 1). His speculations were founded on the results of experiments with children of various ages, and he sought to

Vygotsky's Theory

How well do I think the theory meets the standards?

The Standards	Very Well	Moderately Well	Very Poorly
1. Reflects the real world of children		X	
2. Is clearly understandable	X		
3. Explains the past and predicts the future		X	
4. Guides child rearing		X	
5. Is internally consistent	X		
6. Is economical		X	
7. Is falsifiable	X		
8. Stimulates new discoveries	X		
9. Is self-satisfying		X	

check his conclusions with other studies from various nations. I would have rated item 1 even higher if his theory had been further supported with data from studies specifically designed to test his hypotheses (1) by experimental methods in addition to those using such devices as the Vygotsky blocks and (2) with children from more varied cultural environments.

The theory is clearly described (item 2), particularly in its English-language form, which profits from the translators' organizational improvements.

The theory explains the past and predicts the future (item 3) of verbal-thought development for children in general. However, it does not (at least in the form described in *Thought and Language*) provide a means for analyzing the influence of causal factors in a child's life so that the individual child's progress toward conceptual thought can be explained or predicted. Thus I have given it only a moderate rating on item 3.

Implications for child-rearing practices (item 4) in the form of suggestions for teaching scientific concepts have been included in Vygotsky's writings. But as in the case of item 3, I feel the theory's usefulness as a guide to child rearing is limited by the failure to specify how causal factors combine in an individual child's life to determine his or her particular intellectual development. Thus I have rated the theory as moderate on item 4.

I have not located any internal inconsistencies in Vygotsky's model (item 5), and it appears economical (item 6) in that complex theoretical mechanisms are not used to account for phenomena that might be equally well explained by less complex ones. I feel, however, that more elements and a better explanation of their interactions are needed to account for the results he obtained with his block experiments. The theory as it appears in *Thought and Language* is more programmatic than complete and systematic. At the time of Vygotsky's death it was necessarily still in skeletal form. My mark near the center for item 6, therefore, represents my opinion that the theory was somewhat overly economical, barren in detail.

In terms of falsifiability (item 7), I believe all of Vygotsky's hypotheses and proposals, as well as his actual stages of growth, can be tested experimentally to determine whether they are supportable in fact.

As stimulators of new discoveries (item 8), Vygotsky's theoretical proposals are apparently highly regarded in the Soviet Union (Luria, 1976, pp. v, 11–12; Vygotsky, 1962, pp. ix–x). And since his work has been published in the West, it has set off new speculations and investigations that are showing up in English-language publications. Thus I have rated it high on item 8.

Overall, despite some qualifications mentioned earlier, I find Vygotsky's theory of thought and speech quite satisfying (item 9).

FOR FURTHER READING

Vygotsky, Lev S. (1978) *Mind in Society*. Cambridge, Mass.: Harvard University Press.

Vygotsky, Lev S. (1962) *Thought and Language*. Cambridge, Mass.: M.I.T. Press.

For Soviet psychological investigations utilizing Vygotsky's proposal that cognitive development as reflected in speech is heavily influenced by the child's sociohistorical background, see:

Cole, M. (ed.) (1977) *Soviet Developmental Psychology*. White Plains, N.Y.: Sharpe.

Luria, A. R. (1976) *Cognitive Development: Its Cultural and Social Foundations*. Cambridge, Mass.: Harvard University Press.

Luria, A. R., and F. Yudovich. (1971) *Speech and the Development of Mental Processes in the Child*. Harmondsworth, England: Penguin.

For Piaget's reaction to Vygotsky's criticism of an early version of Piagetian theory, see:

Piaget, J. (1962) *Comments on Vygotsky's Critical Remarks Concerning the Language and Thought of the Child and Judgment and Reasoning in the Child*. Cambridge, Mass.: M.I.T. Press, 16 pages.

CHAPTER TWELVE

Information-Processing Theory

As a way of explaining children's behavior, information-processing theory attempts to picture what happens between (1) the moment a child receives impressions from the environment through the senses (mainly through the eyes and ears) and (2) the moment the child visibly responds with such behaviors as speaking, writing, manipulating a toy, catching a ball, or the like. This process has often been compared to the operation of an electronic computer. Data are entered into the computer *(input)*, manipulated within the machine *(throughput)*, and then the results are printed on paper or displayed on a television screen *(output)*. While we can directly witness the first and third steps (input and output), the middle step—the internal operation of the computer—is unseen. Unless we open the computer and have the skill to analyze the inner works while they function, the computer remains a mystery and we must be satisfied with theorizing about what may be going on inside.

The problem of analysis is essentially the same when we view children from an information-processing perspective. Only the input stimuli (observed environment) and the output behavior (observed actions) can be directly witnessed by people outside the child. We are left to speculate about the throughput segment of the process. And although the child can, by introspection, witness this segment and report the way he believes he "thinks," there is a host of evidence to suggest that such introspection leads to incomplete and faulty descriptions. Not only is the immature child's interpretation of his or her thinking process inadequate, adults' analyses of their mental operations appear incomplete and faulty as well because thinking is a highly complex activity whose elements are not readily apparent in our consciousness.

Information-processing theorists speculate about the nature of the throughput portion of the sequence. (This is the portion that, over the decades, has been identified by diverse terms: *mind, self, personality, the inner child, the organism,* and *the mysterious black box.*) They attempt to specify the components of the child's internal mechanisms for manipulating information and to delineate how these components interact to produce the child's behavior.

So far, I have spoken of information-processing theory in the singular, as if it were one unified model consisting of a single set of agreed-upon characteristics. However, this is hardly the case. Within the well-populated camp of information-processing theorists, debates abound about the types of components that compose a person's processing system and about how the components interact. Developmental psychologists Robert Kail and Jeffrey Bisanz (1982, p. 47) propose that information processing, at least in its present state, should properly be dubbed a framework, not a theory, since within this framework are a multitude of different theories that have been created over the past two decades or so. While it is beyond the scope of this chapter to review all these versions, we can look at some of the widely agreed-upon components and can identify the key issues that are debated.

Information-processing models frequently imply that people of all age levels process information the same way. In other words, the developmental dimension is often overlooked. But because our concern throughout this book is with children, our discussion includes material about how information may be processed differently at various stages of children's growth. The topics are presented in the following sequence: (1) interacting components of information processing, (2) modes of investigation, (3) information processing and development, (4) practical applications, (5) research challenges, and (6) a summary assessment.

INTERACTING COMPONENTS OF INFORMATION PROCESSING

The general notion of people functioning as processors of information is nothing new. Historical accounts show that from ancient times people have speculated about how they receive information from the environment, how they think about and remember this information, and how they reach a decision and act on it. What is new is that recent investigations have added greater precision to describing the likely parts of the processing system and their ways of operating.

As typically conceived today, the human processing system consists of four principal elements: (1) *sense organs,* such as eyes, ears, taste buds, pressure and pain nerves in the skin, and others, which receive impressions from the environment, (2) *short-term memory* or working memory, which holds a very limited amount of information for a short period of time, (3) *long-term memory,* which stores large amounts of information perhaps indefinitely, and (4) *muscle systems* energized by nerve impulses to perform all of the motor acts people carry out, such as reading, speaking, running, assembling machines, and the rest. The system also involves functions or processes within each element and the interactions among these elements.

At first glance it might appear that the system operates in the sequence listed above: Sensations from the environment are entered into short-term memory where they are interpreted (perceived), then moved into long-term memory where they are stored until needed for action, at which time they are retrieved to determine what motor acts, if any, to perform. However, because such a sequence is much too simple to account for the way people actually think and behave, theorists have proposed more complex models comprising networks of interaction, with various kinds of information passing instantaneously back and forth among the elements rather than simply traveling in one direction along a single track from the sense organs' input to the muscles' output. The following description is one version of such a processing network.

This version is a model I have assembled from the work of various theorists in order to offer a relatively simple illustration of what can be involved in information-processing explanations of human thinking.* I will illustrate the system with an imagined problem-solving situation faced by an eighteen-year-old who is trying to decide which route to take to a city 300 kilometers away. But before tracing the way the eighteen-year-old would process information according to the theory, I need to describe the system in terms of each component's: (1) function, (2) type of contents, (3) capacity or quantity of contents, (4) processing time, and (5) interactions with other components. The hypothetical system is displayed schematically in Figure 12.1.

The Senses

The open region at the far left in Figure 12.1 represents the world outside the person. The large box enclosed by the bold black line is the person. The individual's intercourse with the environment is mediated by (1) the sense organs as input channels or "windows to the world" and (2) the muscle systems as output channels or actors on the world.

To simplify the explanation, Figure 12.1 shows only three sense

---

*See Anderson, 1983; Broadbent, 1958; Kail & Bisanz, 1982; Klahr & Wallace, 1976; Newell & Simon, 1972; Uttal, 1981.

329

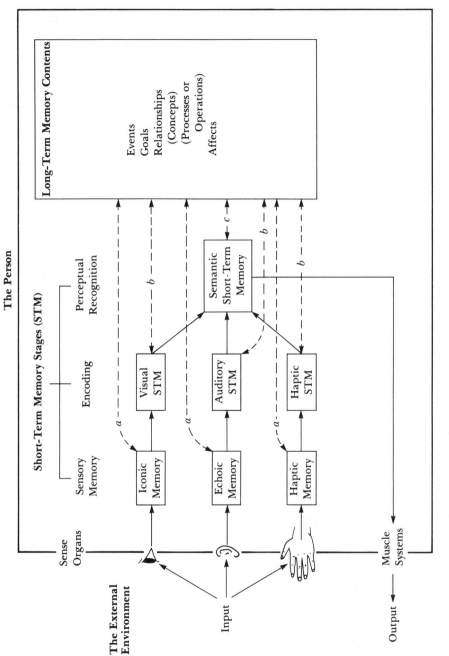

Figure 12.1 A Version of the Human Information-Processing System

modalities—eyes, ears, and the pressure receptors under the skin that people commonly call touch or the tactile sense. Although the organs for detecting smell, taste, temperature, pain, and body position are not pictured, remember that they also feed environmental information into the system.

Each sense organ is obviously a very specialized instrument, attuned to just one kind of stimulation from the environment—the eyes receive only a narrow segment of the wide spectrum of light waves, the ears a narrow range of sound waves, and the tactile receptors only a portion of the impulses that impinge on the skin. Thus, while the sense organs gather information from the environment, they do so in a highly selective way, filtering out far more of the world's potential information than they allow to enter the human processing system.

Short-Term Memory

Stimuli collected by the sense organs are initially processed in what different theorists have variously called *short-term memory, primary memory, active memory,* or *working memory.* Some writers use these terms as synonyms; some make distinctions among them. For example, R. L. Klatzky (1980, p. 87) divides short-term memory into two functions: (1) that of storage, meaning the retention of recognized impressions for a brief time, and (2) that of working memory, meaning "ongoing cognitive activities—for instance, meaningful elaboration of words, symbol manipulation such as that involved in mental arithmetic, and reasoning."

Sensory Memory   In the version of the information-processing approach offered in these pages, short-term memory consists of three stages. The first, *sensory memory,* is apparently located in the sense organ itself and is a stage of momentary image retention. Sensory memory is an unselective form of memory for everything that strikes the particular organ within the range of its receptiveness. The eye's sensory memory holds all receivable light impulses striking the eye, the ear's holds all receivable sound waves striking the ear, and the pressure receptor's holds all tactile sensations on the skin.

Labels applied to memory at this early stage reflect the notion that information is still in a relatively "original" form—*iconic memory* for visual images, *echoic memory* for auditory impressions, and *tactile* or *haptic memory* for touch sensations. The storage of this information is only momentary, perhaps no longer than half a second for visual stimuli before the impression dissipates. Auditory information apparently can last as long as one to two seconds before decaying (Klahr & Wallace, 1976, p. 174). During this momentary retention of stimuli impressions, an interchange occurs between sensory memory and long-term memory (indicated by the lines labeled *a* in Figure 12.1). To clarify the nature of this interchange, we need to take a brief look at the contents of long-term memory.

In this version of information processing, long-term memory is the storage location of ideas or *mental constructions* derived from the person's past experiences. This collection of ideas is the person's *knowledge base*. At each of the three stages of short-term memory, an interchange or transaction (*a, b,* and *c* in Figure 12.1) takes place between the particular short-term stage and long-term memory. The transaction both (1) informs pertinent portions of long-term memory of the nature of the information received at that juncture and (2) permits long-term memory to tell that particular short-term stage which aspects of the stimuli to filter out and which to send along to the next stage. We assume that interchange *a* results in sensory memory identifying certain gross characteristics of the stimuli—such as distinguishing figure from ground—and sending the resulting crudely defined information to the next step along the pathway. An example of distinguishing figure from ground could be separating the outline of a nearby person from the pattern of colors produced by the foliage and buildings behind the person. In the auditory mode it could be separating the sound of a voice from the background sounds of birds chirping, leaves rustling, and a truck rumbling by.

Encoding　The second stage is that of *encoding* or recasting the sensory-memory information into a form that can be used at the third stage. This notion of *encoding* reflects a key assumption made in information-processing theory—that sense impressions are not manipulated or stored in memory in their original form. Instead, impressions are translated into codes, into symbols or *representations* suitable for manipulation by the nervous system. At this second stage of our model, such encoding is accomplished through transaction *b* with long-term memory, in which instructions are issued by long-term memory for how the stimulus information from stage 1 should be symbolized for use at stage 3. As shown in Figure 12.1, stage 2 short-term memory is still divided according to the sense modalities in which the stimuli were originally received. Visual, auditory, and haptic memories are still separated from each other. Stage 2 memory is assumed to last only a brief time and to be of very limited capacity, unable to hold much information, with auditory capacity perhaps greater than visual capacity (Broadbent, 1970).

Semantic Memory　The third stage is called *semantic* short-term memory because at this point the coded materials from the three channels of stage 2 are combined and compared to selected contents of long-term memory to yield meaning (transaction *c*). Stage 3, in effect, is that of *perceptual recognition,* where the person identifies the information for what it represents in terms of her memory (long term) of past experiences. In conscious thought, this is the "Aha!" juncture at which she discovers "So that's what it is!"

Studies of how much information people are able to keep immediately in mind—that is, to maintain in semantic short-term memory—firmly suggest that the average adult can hold seven "chunks" of information at one time, although some people can manage as many as nine chunks while others can manage no more than five or six (Miller, 1956). A *chunk* can be defined as "a portion of a person's knowledge base that is always activated and deactivated as a unit" (Kail & Bisanz, 1982, p. 59). A chunk may be either simple, such as a specific person's name, or it can be complex, such as the concept *television-receiver's-tuning-system* that may, in a single phrase, represent an electronic engineer's entire knowledge of the network of elements that comprise the tuning mechanism of a television receiver.

In speaking of seven chunks, it's important to recognize a distinction between immediate *memory* and immediate *consciousness.* Experiments conducted by S. Sternberg (1969) have suggested that while an individual can immediately recall seven chunks of information, the amount he or she is consciously using in a given instant is more likely to be a single unit or chunk.

Long-Term Memory

I am assuming that long-term memory has two principal functions: (1) directing the operation of the entire information-processing system and (2) storing coded material derived from the person's past experiences. While short-term memory has very limited capacity, long-term memory can apparently accommodate infinite amounts of material. And, as implied in their names, short-term memory retains material very briefly, while long-term memory may retain material indefinitely.

In this version of information processing, I am proposing that coded material stored in memory is of several sorts—single events or episodes, goals, relationships (including concepts and processes), and affects. A *single event* is the memory trace about a specific person or object from a particular incident in the past. E. Tulving (1972) labeled this sort of memory *episodic* to indicate that it is a kind of knowledge specific to a given context, that is, knowledge of how things appeared and when they happened. He contrasted episodic knowledge with what he called *semantic* memories, which consist of more generalized instruments of thought, such as concepts and processes that are not limited to one place or time.

A *goal* is something the individual seeks to accomplish. Goals are the motivational components of information processing. They energize the individual to focus attention on particular facets of the environment and to draw from long-term memory particular contents for interpreting sense impressions.

A *relationship* is a connection between one item in memory and another. Relationships may be of various types. One of the most important is that of concepts, with *concept* being defined as an abstraction of specified characteristics that are shared by individual people, objects, or incidents from the past. Typically a label is attached to the abstraction. For example, *square, red, weather, weaponry, religious,* and *theory* are concept labels. Another relationship is the comparison of one concept with another. For example, the relationship between the concepts *square* and *circle* is defined by the ways in which square and circle are both alike and unalike. (While I define concepts as relationships, some writers prefer to categorize concepts as *associations* rather than relationships and to reserve the term *relationship* for the usages below.)

Some relationships can be called causal because the individual assumes that one concept is the producer of another—as when the idea of heat under a pan of water produces the idea of boiled water. Many causal relationships are complex, with more than one prior condition (the assumed cause) combining to produce a resulting condition (the assumed effect). The idea of how long it will take water to boil can be conditioned by ideas of the amount of water, the water's original temperature, the degree of heat, the heat source, the shape of the pan, atmospheric pressure, and more.

A *process* is a kind of procedural knowledge—a series of steps performed to accomplish some end. Examples of processes are the series of operations required for multiplying 27 by 64, for defining *hypothesis*, for diagraming a sentence, for reading a map, and for driving a car.

Affects are emotions, as suggested by such words as *anger, pity, affection, frustration, attraction,* and *disappointment.* In long-term memory some type of affect or emotional tone is often associated with events, goals, and relationships.

The Structure of Long-Term Memory   Of particular interest to information-processing theorists is the anatomy of long-term memory. What are the structural components of memory and how are they interlinked? One popular suggestion is that long-term memory is organized something like a fishnet, with each node or intersection where the strands are knotted together representing an individual memory trace, such as an event or concept. The multiple strands extending out from the node are the links to other nodes; that is, the strands lead to other events or concepts that the person associates with the memory trace at the original node. The links between some nodes are stronger than between others, meaning that communication across the strong linkages is more frequent and more rapid than between weak linkages. In other words, strong links represent close associations between memories, whereas weak links represent distant associations, ones more difficult to conceive. Obviously such a memory network is infinitely more complex than a simple fishnet in order to account for the intricacies of human thought (Anderson, 1983).

Let us look again at the interactions between long-term memory and the three stages of short-term memory. One of the most important interactions is that of matching the stimuli received from the environment with the contents of long-term memory. In particular, perceptual recognition results when the newly coded material from short-term stage 3 matches identical or similar coded material in the long-term memory network. In this theory, the person "understands" the sensory input or "sees what it means" by accomplishing a satisfactory match. In other words, the person assigns a "meaning" from long-term memory to each new recognizable sensory encounter with the environment.

I am suggesting as well that active decision making and problem solving are carried out through transactions between semantic short-term memory and long-term memory. Not only is information from the environment entered into semantic short-term memory, but material from long-term memory (incidents, goals, relationships, affects) is also inserted into semantic short-term memory and used there. Since short-term memory has such a limited capacity, it is necessary during problem solving for the contents of short-term memory to be constantly changing. Thus there is a great flow of extremely rapid transactions going on all the time, producing the "stream of consciousness" of the person's awareness.

Influences on Long-Term Memory   The source of most, if not all, of the contents of long-term memory is the person's earlier experiences. This is hardly a surprise, for it accords with the commonsense notion that what people remember is what they have learned in the past. But not so apparent is the discovery from experimental studies that the material entered into memory may be distorted during the encoding and storing activities, that is, during the *memory-construction* process. People who hear or read a series of sentences relating to an incident do not simply memorize the sentences. Instead, they tend to abstract the main ideas conveyed in the sentences, and they store this abstracted or more economical version in long-term memory, often omitting some of the original details or the exact phrasing of the incident. Furthermore, ideas already in memory about a given topic will influence how coded traces of a new experience are constructed and stored. For example, hearing about possible dishonesty in public office may well be interpreted and stored differently if the incident is said to involve George Washington or Abraham Lincoln than if it is said to involve some other president whose reputation is less admirable. In effect, new information tends to be coded and stored in ways that make it accord with logic, with one's emotions, and with the contents of one's current knowledge system.

In addition, the coded traces of experiences—called *representations*—may not reside in the long-term state in their original condition but, rather, may be revised in various ways. With the passing of time, or at the moment the memory is retrieved, the memory may be altered by new experiences that have entered the knowledge system since the original memory was recorded, thereby causing one's recollection to differ from the originally stored representation. The new experiences may have distorted the original memory by casting doubt on its logic, by making it more elaborate, by simplifying it so as to fit a stereotyped pattern, or by coloring it with emotions of pleasure or distaste (Dooling & Christiaansen, 1977; Klatzsky, 1980, pp. 301–305; Loftus, 1975).

The combined short-term and long-term memory components make up the human knowledge system. Kail and Bisanz concluded that:

> Despite discrepancies among various theories, most theorists generally agree on the general properties of the human knowledge system. (A) There are, theoretically, no limits on the quantity of knowledge that can be stored. (B) Knowledge is not lost; "forgetting" reflects an inability to access knowledge. (C) Most knowledge can be accessed by multiple routes and multiple cues, reflecting the fact that knowledge is rich in interconnecting links. (D) Knowledge is characterized by a weak form of *cognitive economy:* not all of one's knowledge about concept X need be associated directly with X. . . . Instead, some of this knowledge is available only indirectly, via inference. (E) A process can operate on itself as well on other representations and processes (1982, p. 50).

The System's Behavioral Output

After having described short-term and long-term memory, let's look at the final link in the information-processing chain, that of behavioral output, such as speaking to a classmate, climbing stairs, stepping on the car's brake peddle, writing a homework assignment, and the like. Each decision made in semantic short-term memory elicits from long-term memory coded directions for activating the appropriate muscles. These coded directions are

transmitted through the efferent nerve system to the proper muscle locations to perform the behavior. The action completes the information-
processing cycle.

Although overt action has thus been described as the final link in the
processing chain, it should be apparent that overt action does not have to
occur in order for cognitive development to take place. As our own introspection informs us, we can record events in memory, acquire new concepts,
and attach different emotions to memories simply by "thinking things over"
or "coming to a conclusion" or "changing our mind" without displaying this
in an observable act. However, eventually such development will be reflected
in the ways we act on the world.

The Central Phenomena—Attention, Perception, and Memory

As perhaps can be inferred from the foregoing discussion, information-
processing theories are designed particularly to explain relationships among
a trio of phenomena of traditional interest in psychology, those of attention,
perception, and memory.

In regard to *attention,* theorists have attempted to account for several
factors studied by psychologists for more than a century, from the time of
William James and even earlier (James, 1890, pp. 402–404). James and
others observed that attention is a purposeful operation, so that people
actively seek stimuli rather than only passively record impressions imposed
on them by the environment. Furthermore, people seek selectively. They
focus on certain items for conscious analysis while ignoring others. Such
selectivity is necessary because the human attention-directing mechanism
has limited capacity and apparently can operate on only one item at a time
rather than on several simultaneously. To account for such observations as
these, theorists have proposed that the information-processing mechanism
includes (1) filters to keep the system from being overloaded and (2) special
storage provisions, as suggested at the initial stages of short-term memory, to
extend the time available for extracting information from relatively short-
lived inputs (Horton & Turnage, 1976, p. 205). Theorists have also proposed cycles of interaction between short-term and long-term memory in
order to explain how a person's goals help filter stimuli and how an individual assigns meaning to impressions received from the sense organs.

The phenomenon of *perception,* in which the act of attention is imbed-
ded, typically involves all the steps of the information-processing chain from
the environmental stimuli through the stage of semantic short-term memory
of Figure 12.1. Different theorists have proposed different stages in the
process of perception, with some offering more stages and some fewer than

the ones in the version we are using here. Some theorists have hypothesized that the most significant stage in perception occurs at the sense organ itself—at the eye, the ear, or skin. Others have proposed that the most significant stage is in the brain at the semantic-memory level. In short, a variety of theories of perception exist, with no one of them yet earning general acceptance within the information-processing community (Uttal, 1981, pp. 986–987).

As for *memory,* some writers have sought to explain its complex operations by hypothesizing the existence of such subdivisions as short-term and long-term memory and by identifying a variety of factors affecting the storage and retrieval of information. Others have rejected the notion of such components as short- and long-term memory and speak instead of different depths or levels of processing (Craik & Lockhart, 1972). In effect, there continues to be a diversity of notions about how memory operates.

An Example of the System in Operation

To illustrate how our sample theory can be used to interpret everyday behavior, let's apply the theory's elements to analyze our fictitious eighteen-year-old's trip to a city 300 kilometers away.

As the young woman walks through the business district of her home town, her long-term memory alerts the three stages of her short-term memory to her general goal—to take the trip—as well as to the steps of a process or *strategy* for achieving the goal. This strategy, constructed from her experiences in past years and stored in long-term memory, consists of (1) locating a map of the area, (2) identifying on the map alternative routes to the city, and (3) comparing the desirability of the various routes by testing the alternatives against a series of criteria, including those of distance to travel, road conditions, amount of traffic, safety, attractiveness of the scenery, and others. As she strolls along the street under the influence of this "mental set," she scans the environment for sources of road maps. Her visual attention is caught by a travel agency sign on a store window. For this girl at this moment, that particular sign is a "salient stimulus" in the environment because it matches one of the relationships she has stored in long-term memory (travel agency = maps and road information). Her decision to enter the agency (a decision reached in semantic short-term memory) evokes from long-term memory sequences of operations that cause her efferent nerve system to order the muscular movements that allow her to walk into the shop.

Another process now drawn from long-term into short-term memory starts her scanning the walls to locate sensory stimuli to match the concept of *road map* whose defining features, stored in long-term memory, have now been entered into her short-term memory. By the time she scans half way across the back wall, she finds the desired match. This accomplishment evokes from long-term memory a process that directs her muscles to transport her to the wall to pick up the map. Next, her inspection of the map is guided by a map-analysis process that has just been transferred into short-term memory from long-term memory. The map-analysis process or strategy, constructed in the past from her experiences in reading maps, is composed of a series of steps that include locating the map legend that defines symbols for types of roads, distances, directions of the compass, and cities and towns. As an aid in visually following the alternative routes on the map, the girl adds another modality by tracing each route with her right index finger. At the same time she listens to an employee of the travel agency answer the question she has asked about traffic conditions on the different routes. She is, in effect, simultaneously receiving visual, haptic, and auditory input which is being encoded into semantic short-term memory where it will contribute to her decision about which route to follow.

At this point we leave the young woman, on the assumption that this brief and admittedly simplified analysis has illustrated how incidents from everyday life can be interpreted with one version of the information-processing perspective. We are now prepared to consider the principal methods of inquiry that have led to such theorizing.

MODES OF INVESTIGATION

Present-day information-processing theorists have been employing two modes of investigation for generating and refining their proposals.

The first mode involves using human subjects in experiments designed to answer questions about such matters as how patterns of reflected light stimulate receptor nerves in the eyes, what number of chunks of information can be accommodated in short-term memory, and how material from short-term memory is encoded for storage in long-term memory.

The second mode, which utilizes information from the first mode's experiments, involves employing electronic computers to simulate human mental operations. Theorists working in this rapidly growing field of *artificial intelligence* propose that if they can program a computer to produce the same sorts of solutions to problems that a human would produce, they will have taken a significant step toward understanding human thought processes. In making such a proposal, they are assuming that if a computer program is given the same problem-solving input as a human and the computer produces the same output as the human, then the program may well contain the same sorts of components and processing steps as those operating in the human nervous system.

In applying this same line of logic to explaining children's intellectual development, psychologists face two tasks: (1) devising a series of computer programs so that each program accurately simulates children's thinking processes at a particular stage of mental growth and (2) explaining the means by which the program at one stage can be transformed into the next program in the series. So far, theorists designing computer programs to represent children's thinking processes have been more successful with the first of these tasks than with the second. For example, D. Klahr and J. G. Wallace (1976) managed to prepare what they judged to be rather satisfactory computer simulations of Piagetian preoperational and concrete operations substages for the task areas of class inclusion, conservation, and transitivity. However, the two investigators admitted to being far less successful in fashioning an adequate explanation of how a child makes the transition from preoperational to concrete operations thinking. More experimentation is necessary.

However, by conducting experiments with children at different age levels and by devising computer simulations, investigators are providing a rapidly growing quantity of data about changes that occur in human information processing as people advance in age. Let's now look at examples of the kinds of data being produced by such studies.

INFORMATION PROCESSING AND DEVELOPMENT

We begin by focusing (1) on sensory intake and short-term memory, (2) on long-term memory, and (3) on interactions between components of short- and long-term memory.

Sensory Intake and Short-Term Memory

One notable difference between the infant and the older child concerns elements in the environment to which children attend.

A strong environmental characteristic for attracting attention is that of *novelty*, of things out of the ordinary. The infant, with such a limited store of experience with the world, can be expected to find novelty in events that are quite usual to the more experienced older child. Thus the younger child pays attention to events the older child ignores because such events are so ordinary for the older one.

We see in the behavior of the developing infant that many aspects of attention . . . involve largely automatic reactions to rather simple characteristics. That is, the early responses of infants can be accounted for by assuming the infant is automatically "captured" by sensory input to a greater degree than is an older child or an adult. As the infant develops through childhood to adulthood, he seems to be less and less a "captive" of sensory stimulation and more and more a "capturer" of sensory input (Horton & Turnage, 1976, p. 203).

In brief, the growing child increasingly sets his or her own goals and then purposely seeks out situations in which to invest attention in order to achieve the goals. J. F. Mackworth divided this process of the development of attention into three main stages. At the first stage the very young infant focuses on patterns or objects in his visual and auditory environment, attending to them frequently and at great length, since

His task at this time is to construct internal models of the environment, and everything that he sees is new. Throughout life he will continue to construct such models, but as he grows older his attention is devoted more to comparing new experiences with already stored models. Since the neonate has no such stored models, he must spend a great deal of time on assimilating the stimulus, and therefore he shows little or no habituation (1976, p. 145).

The second of Mackworth's major stages extends from around age 1 until 4 or 5. It consists of the child's beginning to show acquaintance with, or *habituation* to, patterns she has seen or heard before and to select for study those patterns that exhibit novelty. However, at this stage the child may center attention chiefly on a few features on which to base a decision and may overlook other features that would contribute to a more accurate judgment about the significance of the observation. E. Vurpillot (1976, p. 231) noted that the young child's responses to what he observes are often fluctuating and contradictory from one moment to the next "because he focuses his attention first on one detail, then on another. . . . Thus, his greatest weakness lies in an absence of coordination between all the cues he is capable of perceiving and the rules he is capable of using."

At the third stage, the older child or adolescent achieves better cognitive control over attention. She is not so hasty as the young one and can search a display until she acquires all the needed information. She is also better at selecting important details, at altering judgment on the basis of feedback, at abstracting a rule from a sequence of events, and at changing the rule if necessary.

In addition to the matter of how children's ways of attending change with time, another developmental factor in the early phase of processing appears to be the capacity of short-term memory. In discussing the model pictured in Figure 12.1, I proposed that semantic short-term memory in the average adult can accommodate seven chunks of information. Or, stated another way, the average adult has an *apprehension span* of seven chunks, a capacity that apparently was not present at birth but, instead, evolved during the years of childhood. According to some studies, at eighteen months the average child's span is one chunk, a capacity that by age 5 appears to have increased to four chunks, then to five chunks a year or so later, and finally to seven by adolescence. Such changes in short-term memory capacity could help account for the differences in children's thinking and acting at different age levels. For example, observations of children between ages 1 and 2 show that they commonly employ a single word to represent a set of ideas (the phenomenon of *holophrasis*) an older child would describe in several words. Whereas the six-year-old might say, "Mother's bringing the cake out now," the eighteen-month-old is likely to say only "mom" or "cay" in the same situation. S. Farnham-Diggory (1972, p. 62) speculated that "the one chunk span of the eighteen-month-old may be the basic factor in his production of holophrases."

However, not only the number of chunks a child can accommodate but other factors as well contribute to the improved operation of short-term memory with increasing age. One such factor is the structure of the chunks. A chunk that is a concept—such as *transportation*—carries a broader range of meaning by encompassing more of the world's phenomena than does a chunk that represents only a single event or fact—such as *mother's blue dress*. A chunk that represents an entire operation or process, such as the sequence of steps involved in mounting a bicycle and riding it along a winding path, is more encompassing than a chunk that represents only the licking of a postage stamp. Thus, according to one explanation of the contents of short-term memory, a chain consisting of actions that have been practiced so thoroughly that they come to compose an automatic process can be considered a single chunk since when the first action or idea in the chain appears in short-term memory it can trigger the rest of the sequence without the individual having to apprehend—that is, intentionally have to "think about"—the subsequent links in the process. And when an entire chain can be represented as a single chunk, the remaining spaces in short-term memory are available for other chunks of information. According to the theory, this greater complexity of the chunks in the older child's repertoire of memories helps her short-term memory function more efficiently than the younger child's.

The capacity of a child's processing system may also influence what the child attends to in the environment. Infants are attracted by simpler stimuli, such as simpler geometric forms, than are older children because, perhaps, infants lack the capacity to manage complex forms in immediate memory. However, the issue of whether, and how much, the capacity of short-term memory increases with age is neither simple nor settled. Certain investigators have proposed that older children's superiority to younger ones in performance that depends on memory does not result from any larger short-term capacity but rather from the older child's greater fund of knowledge in long-term memory and from his greater facility in using such mnemonic strategies as rehearsal and the clustering of items to be remembered (Chi, 1976, p. 559).

Development of Long-Term Memory

While changes in the sense organs and in short-term memory account for a portion of the age differences in information processing, by far the largest part of the differences is caused by changes in long-term memory. The changes are apparently of two general types: (1) alterations in the nerve structures as determined by genetically timed growth processes and (2) changes in the knowledge base or contents of memory as the result of experience. It is likely that these two types are not independent but that they interact. In other words, the gradual maturation of nerve tissues and changes in their patterning provide increasing potential for the individual to profit from interactions with the environment. And, in turn, as time passes the kinds of memories or knowledge the person accumulates as a result of experiences may hasten or retard the maturation of the electrochemical structures of the nervous system.

Perhaps the most obvious developmental difference between the older and younger child's knowledge base is the quantity of contents stored there, available for interpreting environmental stimuli and for problem solving. The typical older child has compiled a greater number of memory traces (nodes) of events and relationships as the result of more years of experience and a more mature nervous system.

Besides having a greater fund of items in their knowledge base, older children have a greater number of associations between the items or nodes than do younger ones. For example, the typical older child recognizes more ways that the concepts *bucket, string, food, sea,* and *tuna* can be connected than does the younger child. In a sense, the young child's knowledge base is like a small, very loosely woven fabric, knit with only a few strands of memory traces and with the simplest of stitches. In contrast, the adolescent's long-term memory is more like a widespread fabric of intricately interwoven strands forming complex patterns. And it is both the number of items and their patterning of connections that determine how complex a chunk of knowledge will be when it is summoned for action into semantic short-term memory. For instance, a chunk identified by the label *arithmetic* encompasses a great number of items linked in complex patterns in the knowledge base of the typical adolescent, but the chunk *arithmetic* has far fewer items with simple links in the long-term memory of a typical six-year-old.

Furthermore, the processes (sequences of steps for accomplishing a goal) that a child has available in his knowledge base increase in both number and sophistication with advancing age. For instance, if children are asked to memorize a telephone number or a list of street names, the younger ones are likely to depend on only one strategy, such as *rehearsal* (saying the number or list over and over). However, as J. H. Flavell (1977, p. 195) has noted, "rehearsal is by no means the most effective mnemonic strategy available to a sophisticated and resourceful information processor." Adolescents will not only rehearse the items but will *cluster* or *group* them according to some common factor, such as their ordinal or alphabetical sequence. Adolescents may also intentionally *associate* the items with others already in memory, such as comparing the phone number to their own phone number or to a similar number from history, for example, 1492 or 1776 or 1945.

Besides the increase in the variety of mnemonic techniques used, the way a given technique is used also changes as children grow older. For instance, in rehearsing a sequence of items to recall later, children in the lower primary school grades will repeat each new item several times, but they usually do not connect that item with others during the rehearsal process. In contrast, adolescents cluster the items to be memorized into groups, attaching each new item of the sequence to a group, and then practice the group as a whole. In effect, older children are more conscious of their rehearsal technique and more actively fashion their approach in ways that improve the storage and later recall of the information (Ornstein & Naus, 1978). Their superior ability to recall material may thus be caused to a great extent by their imposing some kind of organization on the material when it is first met, whereas younger children do not tend to impose organization.

> Until the age of 7 or 8, children do not ordinarily elaborate and transform stimuli that are to be recalled later. Older children, 11 or 12 years of age, begin to rearrange items and construct additional relationships spontaneously, as adults commonly do (Paris, 1978, p. 153).

Furthermore, older children more readily recognize when a process learned in one setting will be suitable to apply in a different setting.

> There . . . appears to be an identifiable transitional stage during which the child can use a strategy under certain conditions or can learn to use it during a relatively brief training session. However, the strategy is not used spontaneously nor does it show the characteristics of durability or generality. . . . It appears that learning, whether it be through spontaneous experience, informal education, or formal training, is critical in the development of the use of strategies (Hagen, Jongeward, Jr., & Kail, Jr., 1975, p. 73).

In summary, children's mnemonic strategies are not present in long-term memory at birth nor do they automatically appear full-blown at particular times of life; rather they are acquired through experience. The question of whether—and when—they are acquired appears to depend on both the maturity of the child's nervous system and the child's particular foundation of experiences from which to construct the strategies.

Interactions of System Components

As diagramed in Figure 12.1, the human information-processing system includes a constant series of transactions between the contents of long-term memory and the stages of short-term memory. Likewise, the stages of short-term memory constantly interact with each other. The complexity of these interactions is one of the most important factors that render theorizing about information processing so difficult. This assumed complexity can be illustrated by the *verbal-loop hypothesis,* which is an explanation of the changes in children's memory skills with the passing years. In the earlier explanation of Figure 12.1, I proposed that incoming sensations are not perceived or stored in their original form but instead are translated into some sort of code for perception and storage. This encoding likely involves different stages of translation and appears to vary according to the developmental level of a person's cognitive system. In particular, encoding appears related to a person's level of verbal ability, that is, the person's facility in using words. For instance, experiments in which people were asked to reproduce visual forms or to write digits they heard suggest that people perform this task by first translating the visual forms and digit sounds into words and then drawing the forms and digits under the guidance of the verbal descriptions they had stored in memory (Kaufman, 1974, p. 533). The path from input to output was mediated by a *verbal loop* in the middle. If this hypothesis is true, then it may help explain the superiority of older children over younger ones in reproducing visual and auditory stimuli—the older children have greater verbal facility for coding stimuli into words. But while the verbal-loop notion offers some insight into information processing, it is admittedly a crude and very incomplete explanation of the complex relationships that account for people's perceiving and storing and recalling information.

Another facet of the interaction of long-term and short-term memory is speed. Studies of information processing suggest that even when younger and older children both use the same mental procedures in problem solving, the older ones do so more rapidly. The reason is perhaps that the older child's longer experience with the steps of a strategy equips her to manipulate messages through the components of the system with greater facility than can the younger child.

Finally, we may summarize the main developmental characteristics of the human information-processing system by concluding that as age increases, processing increases in speed, in complexity, and in the integration of the system's parts. Furthermore, the data stored in long-term memory grows in quantity, variety, and complexity.

PRACTICAL APPLICATIONS

The most obvious applications of information-processing theory occur in teaching, where the information-processing perspective is helpful in two major ways.

First, information-processing models alert instructors to the stages by which children ingest information from the environment, commit it to memory, and retrieve it to solve problems. By understanding this sequence, a teacher can provide experiences that give learners practice with each stage. Teachers can also help children analyze their own acts of perceiving, storing, and recalling so that they gain greater conscious control over each stage of the process. For instance, children can be taught such memory-enhancing strategies as rehearsal, grouping items, key-word associations, acronyms and rhymes as mnemonic devices, and multiple associations. In other words, teachers help children's metaperception and metamemory, helping them "learn how to learn."

The second application is one I have found particularly valuable, that of using the model as a guide to the diagnosis and treatment of children's learning difficulties. Diagnosis involves first identifying how each component of the model can be assessed through tests, observing the child in learning situations, and interviewing the child. These assessment techniques are used to determine how efficiently each component of the child's information-processing system is operating so that the location of the cause of the child's learning problem may be discovered. Are the child's sense organs faulty, causing either poor eyesight or distorted hearing? Is the child motivated to attend to learning stimuli; that is, does he have the goal of attending to learning stimuli? Was the stimulus encoded inaccurately or not recorded at all during the exchange between short-term and long-term memory (perhaps accounting for the reading disorder of dyslexia or the quantitative-comprehension disorder of dyscalculia)? Or was the stimulus perceived accurately but not stored in a manner that permits ready retrieval, so that when the child needs to recall the memory he cannot? Or have all of the foregoing steps been performed adequately, but a faulty system of sending messages to the muscles has prevented the child from accurately expressing in behavior the results of his learning, as is apparently the case with at least some children who suffer from cerebral palsy?

Once a decision is reached about which components in the system, or which relationships between components, are at fault then methods designed for treating those specific faults are applied. The methods may consist of special training procedures, medical interventions, or both (Thomas, 1981).

In addition, research studies describing the pace at which various components of the information-processing system develop let parents and teachers know what sorts of learning children can reasonably be expected to exhibit at different stages of growth. For example, studies of this sort already suggest at what age children typically can learn a particular mnemonic technique, such as that of creating key words to associate with items to be learned. A growing number of research reports also illustrate ways of teaching such mnemonic techniques and of assessing how well children master them (Brown & DeLoache, 1978; Chi, 1976; Hagen, Jongeward, Jr., & Kail, Jr., 1975).

RESEARCH CHALLENGES

For ambitious researchers, there is no lack of threads of investigation to follow and of tangles to unravel in information-processing theory. W. R. Uttal, after an exhaustive review of studies of visual perception, concluded that "despite the enormous amount of empirical research on perceptual topics, the extent of our ignorance in certain areas . . . is surprising once one delves below the surface of glib superficialities" (1981, pp. 986–987).

To illustrate his point, Uttal has noted that even with modern ultrasophisticated electrophysiological research technology, scientists cannot explain how the action of a network of neurons can be transformed into a person's conscious experience of what she has seen. Nor can they explain how a person imagines a scene that is only suggested, without a stimulus scene in the environment being present. In addition, "we still know very little about the mechanism and processes through which multiple dimensions [such as a side view, a top view, and the object in motion] are integrated to influence collectively the perceptual outcome" (Uttal, 1981, p. 987).

No less intractable than these problems have been developmental issues—those questions about changes in the information-processing system with the passing of time. The following questions suggest a few of the puzzles waiting to be solved.

In regard to the sense organs, are there critical or sensitive periods in the child's development when particular forms of environmental influence (including diet and auditory, visual, and tactile stimuli) foster the optimal accuracy of the organs? If so, when do these periods appear for each sense? What individual differences among children occur in such development, and what are the causes of the differences? If a critical period has been missed, resulting in sensory deficiencies, how can the deficiencies be corrected or at least be minimized? How much filtering of stimuli occurs at the sense organ location in information processing with the passing years?

How does a goal or intention arise in the mind, and how does such intention change as the child develops? At different stages of growth, how much of the child's attention is influenced by the nature of environmental stimuli and how much is determined by motives arising within the child? To what degree do the mechanisms controlling attention vary from one culture to another, and why?

Which of the theories of short-term or working memory is most accurate? At various age levels, what changes occur in the child's way of encoding stimuli to yield meanings and to promote storage in long-term memory? Does the number of chunks that can be accommodated in working memory actually increase with age, or does the improvement in the child's perceptual and memorial strategies account for the child's progress in problem-solving efficiency? Or does a combination of more chunks, better strategies, and a greater store of knowledge produce increased intellectual efficiency?

Which of the theories of long-term memory is most accurate? What is the exact nature of the exchanges between short-term and long-term memory? How do specific training activities at different stages of growth influence the child's present skill at remembering and problem solving? Will such training affect the levels the child will attain as a youth and adult?

These questions, and scores of subquestions derived from them, represent some of the challenges information-processing theory poses for researchers in the field of child development.

INFORMATION-PROCESSING THEORY: AN ASSESSMENT

Once again, my assessment is guided by the nine criteria introduced in Chapter One.

I have rated the theory high on item 1 (the real world of children) because the information-processing model is founded on a growing body of empirical research with children, and computer simulations of child thought and behavior utilize such research for devising the relationships that make up the computer programs.

I have rated the model rather high on clarity (item 2) because those who write about information processing usually are careful to define their terms and illustrate their definitions with examples from research studies or

Information-Processing Theory

How well do I think the theory meets the standards?

The Standards	Very Well	Moderately Well	Very Poorly
1. Reflects the real world of children	X		
2. Is clearly understandable		X	
3. Explains the past and predicts the future		X	
4. Guides child rearing	X		
5. Is internally consistent	X		
6. Is economical	X		
7. Is falsifiable		X	
8. Stimulates new discoveries	X		
9. Is self-satisfying		X	

observations of children. Nevertheless, there are a number of matters that are not clear. Yet the fault, I believe, lies not so much in the theorists' lack of skill in explicating what they believe as in the complexity of the problems they are attempting to solve. They typically admit that they have yet to find satisfactory solutions for numbers of the issues they face. So, to the extent that they have been unable to formulate adequate explanations of observed phenomena, their theorizing necessarily remains unclear. Examples of difficult areas are those of the structure and function of short- and long-term memory, of the process for encoding stimuli sensations, and of the way a person's goals arise to direct attention to selected aspects of the environment.

The theory appears to explain the past and predict the future (item 3) for the elements of child development on which its components focus—the sense organs, attention and perception, and operations of memory. When the present status of these components is assessed, the information-processing theorist is able to propose what has happened in children's past to account for the components' present status. Research studies performed under the guidance of information-processing models provide an expanding pool of information about the development of the sense organs, perception, and memory. As a consequence, predictions about children's future status in relation to these elements can be made with increasing confidence. It is true, however, that predictions about the "average" child of a given age continue to be more reliable than predictions about any particular child. Before more precise judgments can be made about the future of individual children's information-processing systems, more evidence is needed about the causes of children's individual differences in their information-processing components.

I have rated the model high as a guide to child rearing because the results of empirical research provide specific suggestions about what to expect of children at different age levels and about how to promote the development of the information-processing components. Parents and teachers can draw on a growing body of information about care of the eyes and ears, about directing children's attention toward constructive activities, and about strategies for improving memory and for retrieving stored information.

I have not located internal inconsistencies in the versions of information-processing theory I have inspected, so I gave the model a high rating on item 5. Likewise, the components and their interactions as proposed by various theorists have not appeared unduly elaborate to account for the data they intend to explain, so a high rating for economy (item 6) seems warranted as well.

To a great degree both the proposed elements of the information-processing system and the interactions among the elements seem testable, at least potentially (item 7). Some concepts—such as those of short- and long-term memory and the components of each of these hypothetical functions—have not yet been specified precisely enough to determine very well how the concepts can be isolated and their interactions measured, but progress toward this end is being made in empirical studies, particularly with the aid of computer technology. As a consequence, the future of achieving the operational specificity needed for testing the truth of the theory seems to me very promising.

A high rating for the theory's ability to stimulate new discoveries (item 8) appears justified on the basis of the growing quantity of research related to the senses, to the encoding of stimuli from the environment, to the process of memorizing, to problems in the retrieval of stored information, to the mechanisms that guide the muscles to act, and to computer simulations of information-processing functions.

All things considered, I find the information-processing model very satisfactory (item 9). For me, it provides a convincing, integrated structure within which to explain such disparate phenomena as environmental stimuli, the operation of the sense organs, attention and perception, memory, and observable behavior. I rated the theory somewhat below the maximum "very well" level because it generally has not addressed such issues as the role of the emotions, the underlying forces that produce a person's goals, the ways different environments influence mental processes, and the relationship between conscious and unconscious mental operations. These matters I believe need to be formally incorporated into the theory if it is to provide a balanced conception of thought and behavior.

FOR FURTHER READING

Aspects of information-processing theory from a child development perspective are reviewed in the following sources.

Flavell, John H. (1977) *Cognitive Development.* Englewood Cliffs, N.J.: Prentice-Hall.

Kail, Robert, and Jeffrey Bisanz. (1982) "Information Processing and Cognitive Development," in H. W. Reese and L. P. Lipsett (eds.). *Advances in Child Development and Behavior,* Vol. 17. New York: Academic Press.

Klahr, D., and J. G. Wallace. (1976) *Cognitive Development: An Information-Processing View.* Hillsdale, N.J.: Erlbaum.

Miller, Patricia H. (1983) *Theories of Developmental Psychology.* San Francisco: W. H. Freeman, Chap. 4.

CHAPTER THIRTEEN

Kohlberg's Moral Development Theory

So far in this section on cognitive growth and language development we have inspected an overall theory of intellectual growth (Piaget), a theory of the relationship of thought to language (Vygotsky), and a general information-processing theory. To illustrate a different facet of cognitive development, we now consider a theory of how children grow in the ways they defend their moral judgments.

The person whose work I have selected to represent theories of moral judgment is Lawrence Kohlberg (born 1927), a Harvard University psychologist and professor of education. Before outlining his theory, it is important that we understand how the word *moral* will be used throughout the chapter, for the word often means different things to different people.

FACTS, VALUES, AND MORALS

To arrive at a clear definition of *moral,* I will first define a more general term, *value,* of which *moral* is a subcategory. I will also draw on the definition of the term *facts* given in Chapter One and make a distinction between *facts* and *values.*

Earlier I proposed that *facts* are objective information—observations or measurements that are publicly verifiable. In contrast, *values* are opinions about the desirability or propriety or goodness of something. The "something" may be a person, an object, a place, an event, an idea, a kind of behavior, or the like. Statements of fact tell what exists, in what amount, and perhaps in what relation to other facts. Statements of value tell whether something is good or bad, well done or poorly done, suitable or unsuitable. Our focus in the present chapter is on values, not facts, although many of the values discussed will involve the use of facts.

The word *moral* as intended in this chapter is only one subitem under the general term *value*. Many values do not qualify as moral ones. For instance, there are *aesthetic values,* those that involve opinions offered from an artistic viewpoint. Aesthetic values, when applied to a flower garden, a poem, a painting, or a dance performance, are reflected in such phrases as "pleasing to the eye" or "nicely turned metaphor" or "delightfully innovative." Another category is that of *technical values.* These may focus on how efficiently something operates or on how well its parts coordinate. There is also the subgroup of *prudential values* which guide a person's social relations and his investment of time and energy so as to yield him the greatest benefits. A girl finds it prudent not to tell her teacher that the teacher's breath smells sour, and a boy finds it imprudent to wander away to play ball after his father has commissioned him to mow the lawn.

At this point you may ask: How are moral value judgments different from these other sorts? The answer used here is offered by Kohlberg:

> Unlike judgments of prudence or aesthetics, moral judgments tend to be universal, inclusive, consistent, and based on objective, impersonal, or ideal grounds (1968b, p. 490).

According to Kohlberg, it is not a moral judgment when a girl says to her companion, "She's so sensitive about her looks that if you tell her to fix her hair differently and to wear different clothes, she'll never want to be around you again." This is only a prudential judgment, for it is not universal (does not apply to all social situations), nor is it based on impersonal or ideal grounds. In contrast, it is a moral judgment when a girl says, "They should outlaw capital punishment because no one has a right to take another person's life under any circumstances." This judgment is universal, applies in all situations, and is founded on ideal convictions.

Kohlberg's theory of moral development traces the steps by which children grow toward making truly moral judgments. The steps "represent a progressive disentangling or differentiation of moral values and judgments from other types of values and judgments" (Kohlberg, 1968b, p. 410). If the child is successful in advancing to the highest stage of moral judgment, in adolescence he bases his appraisals of moral issues on concepts of justice. In Kohlberg's view, this means that the youth grounds his opinions on the *right of the individual,* and he judges an act wrong if it violates that right. Kohlberg further contends that a *right* in this sense is founded on *equality* and *reciprocity,* so that people are equal in terms of exchange (or contract) and of reward for merit. *Justice* implies that the law is impartial and applies to all equally in its maintenance of the rights of the individual (Kohlberg, 1967, pp. 173, 176).

In order to understand how Kohlberg sees children growing toward the position of basing moral judgments on concepts of justice, we will need to look at (1) the theory's focus and (2) its research methodology. Then I will (3) delineate the moral growth stages, (4) describe how Kohlberg sees children's natures interacting with their environments to determine their stage of moral development, (5) point out several important characteristics of moral growth stages, (6) note what Kohlberg's beliefs imply for moral education, (7) suggest research challenges evoked by the theory, and (8) assess Kohlberg's model in terms of the criteria described in Chapter One.

THE THEORY'S FOCUS

Moral development is usually viewed as one aspect of socialization, with *socialization* meaning the process by which children learn to conform to the expectations of the culture in which they grow up. In the case of moral values, children not only learn to conform, they also *internalize* these standards and thereby accept the standards as correct and as representing their own personal values. A value is considered to be internalized and not just imposed by outsiders when the child conforms in situations (1) that tempt her to transgress and (2) that afford slight chance of her behavior being discovered, punished, or rewarded.

People who have sought to trace the development of morality in children have typically focused on one or more of three aspects of personality: *observed behavior, feelings of guilt,* or *the basis for a moral judgment.*

In the case of *observed behavior,* the question asked by the investigator is, Does the child display greater honesty or integrity or a sense of justice as he grows older? Extensive studies of honesty in children and youths have yielded either inconclusive or negative answers to this question (Hartshorne & May, 1928–1930). Rather than basing their response to temptation only on a growing internal sense of honesty, children and adolescents appear more often to base their actions on prudential judgments (How likely is it that I will be caught?) or on social pressures (Will the group disapprove?). Thus Kohlberg has rejected observed behavior as a profitable criterion for moral development.

A second approach to the study of rule internalization focuses on how the *emotion of guilt* grows as the years advance. This emotion refers to the self-critical and self-punishing acts of anxiety and regret that follow transgression of a rule or cultural standard. Here the assumption is that the child obeys in order to avoid feeling guilty. Kohlberg (1968b, p. 484) says this assumption underlies the concept of conscience in psychoanalysis and in learning theories. He concludes that even though studies of children through projective techniques show a sudden upsurge in such guilt feelings in the years prior to puberty, projective techniques have not been able to predict consistently whether children really will resist temptation. Hence his own theory is not founded on charting the emotion of guilt over the years of childhood and youth. Instead, his work has centered on a third approach, that of tracing the *bases of the child's judgments of moral issues.*

In investigating the *judgmental* side of moral development, the question becomes, Has the child internalized a moral standard, and can she justify that standard to herself and to others? Such an approach was used in the early 1930s by Piaget and has since been refined by other scholars, with Kohlberg being the most prominent researcher in the field during the past two decades. In Kohlberg's opinion the issue is not whether the child acts honestly or whether she feels guilty about transgressing the rules. Instead, the moral-development issue is the judgmental basis the child uses for assessing moral behavior.

KOHLBERG'S RESEARCH METHODS

The studies on which Kohlberg's theoretical proposals are founded consist of describing to children a series of incidents, each involving a moral dilemma. Each child is then asked which solution would be the best or proper one for each dilemma and why that solution would be better than others. For example, here is a typical Kohlberg incident, the one known as the Heinz problem.

> Mrs. Heinz was near death from a special type of cancer. The doctors thought one kind of drug might save her. The druggist who made the medicine she needed was selling it for ten times the amount that it cost him to make it. The sick woman's husband, Heinz, did not have enough money for the medicine, so he went to borrow the money from everyone he knew, but he could collect only about half of what the druggist was charging. Heinz told the druggist his wife was dying and asked him to sell him the medicine cheaper or to let him pay later, but the druggist refused. The druggist said he discovered the drug and he was going to make money from it. So Heinz got desperate and later broke into the drugstore to steal the drug for his wife. The question then is: Should the husband have tried to steal the drug? Why or why not? (Adapted from Kohlberg, 1971, p. 156.)

Responses to such moral dilemmas are then analyzed by Kohlberg and his colleagues to determine which of six developmental stages of moral judgment are reflected in the child's or youth's answers. The task of analyzing and grading children's answers does not involve simply comparing an objective answer sheet to children's responses. Rather, the grading scheme requires training and involves some measure of subjective judgment on the part of the analyst.

Kohlberg began using his moral incidents with a sample of seventy-five young American adolescents in the mid-1950s, and he subsequently tested the same subjects as they grew into adulthood in order to discover the pattern of changes in judgments that might have occurred with the passing years. Furthermore, he and his co-workers have tried to discover what influence cultural factors have on the growth of moral judgments. To accomplish this, they have used the test incidents with both middle-class and lower-class adolescents in the United States and with youths in such diverse locations as Mexico, Thailand, kibbutz communities in Israel, a primitive Malaysian village, Turkey, Taiwan, and others. On the basis of these studies, Kohlberg has concluded that the six stages of moral development he identified are universal—found in all cultures—but that the percentage of youths of different age levels who are at a given stage will vary from one society to another. The nature of these variations will be discussed after I explain the characteristics of the stages.

THE LEVELS AND STAGES OF MORAL GROWTH

In Kohlberg's system, growing up in moral judgment consists of advancing through three levels of development, from a *premoral* or *preconventional* level to one that involves conforming to *society's conventions* and finally to a top level that transcends convention and is based on personal, *self-accepted moral principles*. This top level is sometimes called *postconventional* or *autonomous*. Each level contains two stages, as defined in Table 13.1.

Besides identifying six steps or stages, Kohlberg described thirty or more aspects of life about which people make moral judgments. A person will reveal his dominant stage of moral judgment each time he expresses opinions about any of these aspects. It is Kohlberg's conviction, based on administering his moral judgment incidents to children and youths, that there is a high correlation between a person's stage in regard to one aspect and his stage in regard to others. For example, a young woman's judgment about the value of human life, about telling the truth, and about people's duties and obligations will all tend to reveal the same level of moral development.

The thirty or more aspects of life are divided into three varieties: (1) modes of judgment of obligation and value, (2) elements of obligation and value, and (3) issues or social institutions about which judgments are made. The principal aspects falling within each of these categories are universal,

Table 13.1   Description of Moral Judgment Stages

I. *Preconventional Level (Premoral Level).* A person follows society's rules of right and wrong but in terms of the physical or hedonistic consequences (punishment, reward, exchange of favors) and in view of the power of the authority who imposes the rules.

Stage 1. *Punishment and obedience orientation.* Whether an action is good or bad depends on whether it results in punishment or reward. If the individual is going to get punished for it, it's bad so he shouldn't do it. If he won't get punished, he can do it, regardless of the human meaning or value of the act.

Stage 2. *Naive instrumental orientation.* Proper action instrumentally satisfies the individual's needs and occasionally the needs of others. As in the marketplace, human relations are based on getting a fair return for one's investment. Reciprocity or fairness involves "you scratch my back and I'll scratch yours," but not out of loyalty, gratitude, or justice.

II. *Conventional Level.* A person conforms to the expectations of her family, group, or nation. She actively supports and justifies the existing social order.

Stage 3. *Good-boy, nice-girl orientation.* A person acts in ways that please or help others and are approved by them. For the first time, the individual's intention becomes important ("she means well"). Approval is earned by being "nice."

Stage 4. *Law-and-order orientation.* A person is doing the right thing when he does his duty, shows respect for authority, and maintains the existing social order for its own sake.

III. *Postconventional, Principled, or Autonomous Level.* A person tries to identify universal moral values that are valid, regardless of what authority or group subscribes to the values and despite the individual's own connection or lack of connection with such authorities or groups.

Stage 5. *Social-contract orientation.* This usually involves legalistic and utilitarian overtones. Moral behavior is defined in terms of general individual rights and according to standards that have been critically examined and to which the whole society has given its consent. This is the "official" morality of the American Constitution and the U.S. government. There is a clear recognition that personal values and opinions are relative, and thus there are procedures for reaching consensus and for changing laws for social utility reasons (rather than freezing laws because they are inviolate, as under stage 4's law-and-order orientation).

Stage 6. *Universal ethical principle orientation.* A person's moral judgments are based on universal principles of justice, on the reciprocity and equality of human rights, and on respect for the dignity of humans as individual persons. *Right* is defined by the individual's conscience in accord with self-chosen, general ethical convictions.

Recast and simplified from Kohlberg, 1967, p. 171.

for they are found in all cultures according to Kohlberg. Here is one version of the aspects:

Modes of Judgment of Obligation and Value: Judgments of (a) right, (b) having a right, (c) duty or obligation, (d) responsibility, (e) praise or blame, (f) punishability and reward, and (g) nonmoral value or goodness. Also (h) justification and explanation.

Elements of Obligation and Value: (a) prudence (consequences desirable or undesirable to *oneself*), (b) social welfare (consequences desirable or undesirable to *others*), (c) love, (d) respect, (e) justice as liberty, (f) justice as equality, and (g) justice as reciprocity and contract.

Issues or Institutions: (a) social norms, (b) personal conscience, (c) roles and issues of affection, (d) roles and issues of authority and democracy (division of labor between roles related to social control), (e) civil liberties (rights to liberty and equality as humans, citizens, or members of groups), (f) justice of actions apart from fixed rights (trust, reciprocity, contract in actions of one person), (g) punitive justice, (h) life, (i) property, (j) truth, and (k) sex (1971, p. 166).

To show how one of these aspects can be interpreted in terms of the stages, consider a moral judgment incident focusing on the issue of life (item *h* in the issues list) and see how three boys reacted to the incident. The event posed to the boys involved a doctor who had to decide whether to "mercy kill" a woman requesting death because she was suffering intense pain.

13-year-old boy: "Maybe it would be good to put her out of her pain, she'd be better off that way. But the husband wouldn't want it, it's not like an animal. If a pet dies you can get along without it — it isn't something you really need. Well, you can get a new wife, but it's not really the same." (Scored as stage 2 — the value of life is instrumental to satisfying the needs of its possessor or others.)

16-year-old boy: "No, he shouldn't [kill her]. The husband loves her and wants to see her. He couldn't want her to die sooner, he loves her too much." (Scored as stage 3 — the value of life is based on empathy and affection of family members toward its possessor.)

16-year-old boy: "The doctor wouldn't have the right to take a life, no human has the right. He can't create life, he shouldn't destroy it." (Scored as stage 4 — life is sacred according to a categorical or religious order of rights and duties.) (Kohlberg, 1967, pp. 174–175.)

To summarize, note that Kohlberg's six stages represent a movement from lower levels of moral decision, where moral decisions are entangled with other value judgments and the rules are changed as the facts in the case change, to higher levels that separate moral values (justice and reciprocity) from other sorts and that utilize universal principles that apply to anyone in any situation. To illustrate this movement from the particular to the universal rule, consider three of the stages as they relate to the value of life. At stage

1, only important people's lives are valued, at stage 3 only family members', but at stage 6 all life is valued morally equally (Kohlberg, 1971, p. 185).

THE INTERACTION OF NATURE AND NURTURE

In response to the question of which moral stages a given child will pass through and when she or he will do it, Kohlberg adopted an interactionist position. He does not believe a child's moral stages are produced entirely by genetic inheritance or entirely by factors in the environment. Rather, he proposes that four principal factors interact to determine how high in the six-stage hierarchy a person will progress and when he or she will arrive at each stage. The first factor, and the one with the greatest genetic or inherited component, is the individual's *level of logical reasoning* as identified in Piaget's cognitive growth system. The second, a personal factor that probably has both genetic and environmental elements, is the child's desire or *motivation*, sometimes referred to as the child's *needs*. The remaining two factors are entirely environmental: (1) the child's opportunities to learn *social roles* and (2) the *form of justice* in the social institutions with which the child is familiar. To understand how these factors interact, we need to inspect each in more detail.

The Level of Cognitive and Logical Development

In the realm of children's logical thinking, Kohlberg identifies himself as a disciple of Piaget. First, he is convinced that it is the child's nature to pass through the cognitive development stages identified by Piaget. He further believes that the achievement of a particular cognitive level in Piaget's scheme is a necessary prerequisite to the child's achieving a particular moral-reasoning stage.

To substantiate his belief, Kohlberg administered both Piagetian logical thinking tasks and his own moral-incident tests to the same group of subjects. He discovered that children who did not succeed on a given level of Piaget's tasks almost never showed the moral reasoning level that paralleled the Piagetian tasks. In contrast, children who were in the upper levels of moral reasoning could almost always complete the parallel and the lower-level Piagetian tasks. Consequently, Kohlberg concluded that the sort of logical thinking represented by Piaget's hierarchy forms the necessary foundation for the kinds of moral reasoning measured by his own moral-decision situations. This logical thinking component, then, is the maturational or "natural growth" factor—and perhaps the most powerful of the four factors that Kohlberg believes determine a child's level of moral reasoning.

If the child's cognitive stage were the only component of moral judgment, then as soon as the child reached a given cognitive level, her moral judgments would likewise be at the same level. But such is not the case. There is often a gap between the two, with moral reasoning lagging behind cognitive skill in various degrees. The cause of this lag, according to Kohlberg, is the condition of the other three factors that interact with mental maturity.

The Factor of Will or Desire

While it is always in our own interests to reason at the highest level of which we are capable, it may not be in our best interests to make moral judgments at the highest level. Some people who are capable of judging morally at stage 6 may not do so because they do not wish to end up as martyrs as did Socrates, Lincoln, and Martin Luther King, Jr. So a youth may have the concepts of stages 5 or 6 but not use them habitually because they do not seem worth the trouble or the risk in his particular social setting. Thus a portion of the slippage between cognitive level and moral stage may be accounted for by the operation of a girl's or boy's emotions, desires, or "will power." However, Kohlberg feels that this factor of *will* plays only a minor part in determining judgment stages. The other three factors in the quartet of influences are far more important (Kohlberg, 1971, pp. 188–190).

Social Role-Taking

Kohlberg agrees with many social psychologists that children become socialized by learning to take the roles of people around them. As children interact with others, they imagine themselves in the others' shoes and see life from others' perspectives. Children also learn to see themselves as others see them. Hence *role-taking* or identifying and empathizing with other people enables the child to become an effective social being.

Within the broad sphere of socialization, the development of the more specific area of moral judgment "is based on sympathy for others, as well as on the notion that the moral judge must adopt the perspective of the 'impartial spectator' or the 'generalized other' " (Kohlberg, 1971, p. 190). How well a child learns to adopt others' roles depends to a great extent on the conditions of her social environment. Some environments encourage role-taking and thus hasten children's advance up the moral judgment hierarchy. Other environments limit opportunities to learn role-taking and thus slow children's advances in moral growth and may prevent them from ever reaching stages 4, 5, or 6.

Kohlberg has suggested that it is this difference in role-taking opportunities among cultures or social-class levels that apparently accounts for the marked differences in moral judgment development among societies and between middle and lower socioeconomic classes within a society.

> In four different cultures, middle-class children were found to be more advanced in moral judgment than matched lower-class children. This was not because the middle-class children heavily favored a certain type of thought which corresponded to the prevailing middle-class pattern. Instead, middle-class and working-class children seemed to move through the same sequences, but the middle-class children seemed to move faster and farther (1971, p. 190).

Other studies by Kohlberg's group have shown that popular children who participated a great deal with their peers were far more advanced in moral judgment than unpopular or nonparticipating children. At least part of the cause of this difference seems to be differences in role-taking opportunities in the children's families. Greater role adoption was promoted by families that encouraged sharing in decisions, awarded responsibility to the child, pointed out consequences of action to others, communicated within the family group, and exhibited emotional warmth.

Some people have assumed that the most crucial of these home elements for furthering moral development is the degree to which the atmosphere is warm, loving, and identification-inducing. However, Kohlberg says this is not so. Apparently some minimum level of warmth in her personal contacts with others is necessary for a child or adolescent to feel she is an accepted participant in the social circle. However, what is far more important is that the environment furnish many role-taking opportunities, not that the child receive maximum affection from the group (Kohlberg, 1971, p. 191).

The Justice Structure

The fourth variable that contributes to the growth of moral judgment is the justice structure of the social groups or institutions with which the child interacts. Such social entities include the family, the neighborhood gang or play group, the school, the church, the community, the nation, and those media that provide vicarious opportunities for role-taking—television, radio, books, magazines, and the like.

At all six stages of moral development, the individual has some sort of concern for the welfare of others. But only at stages 5 and 6 is this concern based on what Kohlberg regards as principles of true justice, those of *equality* and *reciprocity*. The principle of equality means that we "treat every man's claim equally, regardless of the man" (Kohlberg, 1967, p. 169). The principle of reciprocity means equality of exchange. It means "punishment for something bad, reward for something good, and contractual exchange" or fulfilling one's bargain.

Within a given society the groups or institutions with which the growing child is intimately involved vary in their justice structures. A public school that the child is forced to attend under compulsory education laws is different from a university that the youth attends voluntarily. A neighborhood play group is different from a reformatory. A Girl Scout troop differs from a family. A family dominated by an autocratic father differs from one in which children are encouraged to make decisions, take responsibility, and be rewarded in accordance with how they carry out their self-imposed commitments.

In effect, Kohlberg proposes that children who participate in social groups that operate on a high level of equality and reciprocity will move to higher levels of moral judgment than children whose main participation is in groups that have lower sorts of justice structures.

So the dominant level of moral judgment a child or youth uses results from the interaction of four determinants: her level of cognitive and logical maturation, her will or desire, her opportunities for role-taking, and the dominant modes of justice in the main social groups of which she is a part.

THE THREE CHARACTERISTICS OF THE STAGES

A large proportion of modern social scientists as well as the "culturally enlightened" laity are what Kohlberg labels *ethical relativists*. They believe that moral principles vary from one culture to another and that there is no logical way to explain or reconcile these differences among cultures. Such a line of thought can easily lead to the conviction that one culture's moral values are as good as another's since each culture has as much right to its own value system as does any other culture. On the basis of this assumption, we would conclude that a person is morally developed or well adjusted when he abides by the dominant values of his society. But it is not necessary for an ethical relativist to stop the extension of this line of logic at the societal level. If he chooses, he can carry it on to individuals within a society. In such a case, he can conclude that it is each individual's right to adopt his own code of ethics, since there is no logical way to judge one person's code better than another's. (Of course, it is clear that extending ethical relativism to the individual will have important consequences for the individual's fate because if he deviates markedly from the group's norms he can be dubbed odd or possibly locked up by the dominant group as a criminal or lunatic.)

However, Kohlberg is not an ethical relativist. He contends that moral development does not depend on the particular society's dominant ideas of justice. Instead, he says that the developmental stages he has identified are universal, integrated, and invariant.

By *universal* he means that he believes the stages are true of all societies. Originally Kohlberg believed that in every culture there are people at all six stages. But more recently he questioned whether stage 6 is ever actually achieved (Colby, Kohlberg, Gibbs & Lieberman, 1983, p. 5). It is true, however, that the dominant moral stage for the society as a whole, or for a given age level, will differ from one culture to another. One culture may operate mostly on stage 2 reasoning, another on stage 4 reasoning. But this does not mean that the patterns of moral thought are quite different in the two cultures. Rather, the discrepancies result from the children in one society advancing up the six-stage hierarchy at a different rate than the children in the other society. The differences in rate might be due partially to genetic differences between the two groups but more likely result from differences in the role-taking opportunities and justice structures of the two cultures. Kohlberg has said that the same stages of moral reasoning are found in all societies, although the number of persons at each stage may differ, as illustrated in Figure 13.1. The graphs compare the moral judgments of boys in middle-class U.S. and Mexican communities with those in an isolated village in Turkey. The age levels charted are 10, 13, and 16. As the graphs indicate, by age 16 some boys in each of the cultures were at each of the six levels of moral growth. However, a larger percentage of U.S. and Mexican boys than of Turkish boys were at higher stages at each age level.

By *integrated* Kohlberg means that in various aspects of life a person's moral decisions will reflect a similar level of development. It would be rare indeed for a person to operate at stage 1 when judging honesty, at stage 3 when judging freedom, and stage 6 when judging responsibility. Rather, judgments in all realms will tend to cluster around the same level—around 1 and 2, around 3 and 4, or the like.

By *invariant* Kohlberg means that a youth cannot skip a stage or two while advancing to a higher level. People must pass through each stage in sequence. A key reason for this invariance, in Kohlberg's opinion, is that each successive stage consists of components of the prior stage plus a new component or two.

These principles of universality, integration, and invariance, and the

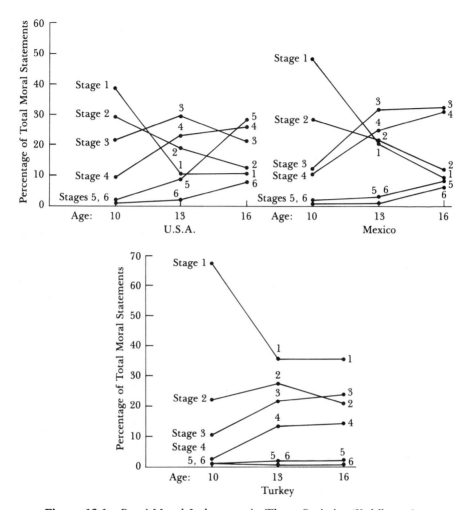

Figure 13.1   Boys' Moral Judgments in Three Societies (Kohlberg & Kramer, 1969, p. 104)

four proposed determinants of moral growth, have important implications for how Kohlberg's theory can be put to practical use.

PRACTICAL APPLICATIONS: FASHIONING A PROGRAM OF MORAL EDUCATION

If Kohlberg's theory is correct, what should be the form of moral education? Before applying our foregoing discussion to answering this question, we need to consider one more concept that Kohlberg adopted from Piaget's

theory of cognitive development, that of *equilibration* or of seeking equilibrium. In Piaget's system, a child continued to be satisfied with simplistic,
unsophisticated answers to questions of relationships among things until (1)
she reached a particular age of internal maturation and (2) had engaged in
enough activities related to the question. At this point she began to feel
dissatisfied and a bit disordered, for she felt an incongruence between her
existing schemes (or conception of reality) and a newly perceived reality.
This dissonance threw her out of cognitive equilibrium and served as a
motive to "change her mind" or to accommodate in order to set things
right—in order to attain equilibrium once more.

Kohlberg has applied this same principle of equilibration to growth in
moral judgment. When the child is cognitively mature enough and has had
enough role-taking experiences in relation to groups that have suitable
justice structures, then he can be stimulated toward upward movement in
the moral judgment stages by being confronted with problems of moral
conflict. In other words, moral education properly consists of confronting
the child or adolescent with moral dilemmas at the same time that the child is
maturationally and socially ready to take a step ahead.

With this use of equilibration in mind, let's now review the components
of a moral education system as conceived within Kohlberg's scheme. First,
the goal of moral education is not to inculcate a particular set of values that
are dominant or at least common in a given society. Instead, the goal is to
stimulate the child's growth through the six stages that are considered
universally valid for all cultures. The teacher's expectation for where the
child or youth should be in moral growth at a particular time is governed by
the teacher's recognition of the level of the child's cognitive development
(per Piaget) and of the opportunities the child enjoys to adopt roles in social
groups. The expectation is also influenced by the sorts of justice found in the
groups in which the child participates and by the child's motivation—that is,
will it seem worthwhile to the child to think at a higher moral level?

The methodology the teacher adopts consists primarily of posing moral
decision problems for the students and having various students give their
arguments to support their decisions. In this process, some students will
argue from the viewpoint of a higher stage than will others. Or the teacher
may argue from a higher stage. This conflict of arguments is intended to
produce a feeling of disequilibrium in young people who are approaching
the threshold of a new stage, so that the basis for their thinking begins to
change and they are hoisted to the new level.

In summary, Kohlberg objects to a pair of commonly practiced systems
of moral education: (1) the "thoughtless system of moralizing by individual

teachers and principals when children deviate from minor administrative regulations" and (2) "the effort to inculcate the majority values, particularly as reflected in vague stereotypes about moral character" (Kohlberg, 1967, p. 169). In place of these he recommends a system that stimulates "the 'natural' development of the individual child's own moral judgment and of the capacities allowing him to use his own moral judgment to control his behavior." The purpose is to aid the child "to take the next step in a direction toward which he is already tending, rather than imposing an alien pattern on him" (Kohlberg, 1967, p. 169).

RESEARCH CHALLENGES

During the quarter century since Kohlberg introduced his theory in 1958, a large number of research studies have attempted to replicate his investigations with children of different ages and in different cultural settings. In some cases his stage structure has been corroborated in cross-sectional research, but inconsistent results in other investigations have cast doubt on the ostensible universal, integrated, and invariant characteristics of the stages he proposed (Kurtines & Greif, 1974). Several longitudinal studies in which different groups of children have been interviewed over a series of years have also revealed anomalies in the originally postulated order of the stages (Holstein, 1976; White, Bushnell, & Regnemer, 1978). A question arises, then, about whether Kohlberg was in error when he concluded that his model truly contained universal stages or whether the anomalies found in the replication studies resulted from the unreliability of his interviewing and scoring methods. To help solve this puzzle, Kohlberg and his co-workers in recent years have changed his original interview techniques and have revised the scoring system. The revision issued in the early 1980s has been built on a substantially revised account of his original six stages. For instance, stage 6 has been omitted from the new manual because in the twenty-year follow-up study of fifty-eight boys who had participated in Kohlberg's original study:

> None of the interviews in the longitudinal sample seemed intuitively to be stage 6, partly because the standard dilemmas are not ideal for differentiating between stages 5 and 6. The question of whether stage 6 should be included as a natural psychological stage in the moral development sequence will remain unresolved until research (using more appropriate moral dilemmas and interviewing techniques) is conducted with a special sample of people likely to have developed beyond stage 5 (Colby, Kohlberg, Gibbs & Lieberman, 1983, p. 5).

The twenty-year longitudinal study, utilizing the new Standard Issue Scoring, yielded results supporting Kohlberg's stage scheme. The subjects, who were in their teens in the original study and in their thirties in the final follow-up investigation, displayed moral reasoning that was consistent across different moral incidents and "developed in a regular sequence of stages, neither skipping a stage nor reverting to use of a prior stage" (Colby, Kohlberg, Gibbs & Lieberman, 1983, p. ii).

Kohlberg's scheme has stimulated a continuing series of investigations, leading not only to refinements of his original theory but also to alternative models. For example, E. Turiel (1977) conducted a series of studies that caused him to conclude that beliefs about *moral* matters (intrinsic effects of actions on persons) develop according to Kohlberg stages, but beliefs about *social conventions* (alterable social interaction features of a particular society, such as matters of etiquette) develop by an entirely different hierarchy of stages. Turiel's proposal, further supported in additional studies, led L. P. Nucci (1982) to recommend different educational procedures for promoting children's growth in moral reasoning than those procedures for fostering social convention reasoning.

In addition, many other questions bearing on Kohlberg's field of concern await investigation. For example, what stages of moral development might be found if a researcher did not start, as Kohlberg did, with equality and contractual agreement as the highest moral value? What if the value selected as the highest level of morality were compassion, self-sacrifice, or nonviolence? Do children grow toward these virtues in the same manner as they seem to grow toward Kohlberg's notion of equality and justice?

Do ordinary people in their everyday lives define moral issues in the same way Kohlberg has in his theorizing? To what extent are moral dilemmas in one society the same as those in another, and why? Do the principal moral dilemmas for children in their daily lives differ from one age level to another, and why or why not?

These are some of the questions evoked by Kohlberg and others' theorizing about how children's values evolve with the passing years.

KOHLBERG'S THEORY: AN ASSESSMENT

When Kohlberg's model of moral development is appraised according to the standards proposed in Chapter One, his theory shows up well in several respects.

The theory provides both for explaining children's past moral judgment behavior and for predicting their future behavior (item 3). Not only does it permit predictions for the average child, but by proposing four

Kohlberg's Theory

How well do I think the theory meets the standards?

The Standards	Very Well	Moderately Well	Very Poorly
1. Reflects the real world of children		X	
2. Is clearly understandable		X	
3. Explains the past and predicts the future	X		
4. Guides child rearing	X		
5. Is internally consistent	X		
6. Is economical	X		
7. Is falsifiable		X	
8. Stimulates new discoveries	X		
9. Is self-satisfying		X	

interacting determinants of moral judgment development, it offers the possibility of doing so for individuals as well (if proper measures of the four variables and their interaction are made available).

The moral education scheme Kohlberg founded on his theory offers clear guidance for child rearing (item 4). Likewise, the theory appears to be internally consistent (item 5) and economical (item 6). It has also stimulated a variety of new investigations and discoveries, particularly in the way moral judgment develops in different cultures (item 8). Kohlberg has been credited with opening a number of new perspectives on moral growth and for doing "some very hard and very unfashionable thinking on moral thought" along with "producing evidence that should force psychologists to take the

cognitive aspects of morality seriously as an important influence on behavior" (Alston, 1971, p. 284).

On the scale of clarity (item 2), the theory deserves a mixed score. On
the positive side are the many specific examples Kohlberg cites from children's moral dilemma responses that clarify terms and differentiate one
stage from another. Such phrases as *instrumental relativist orientation* and
social-contract legalistic orientation are illustrated with examples from children's responses. However, in the opinions of informed scholars in the field,
other key terms have not been distinguished clearly. R. S. Peters (1971, pp.
246–248) has taken Kohlberg to task for being vague and unsophisticated in
comparing *character traits* (honesty, courage, determination) unfavorably
with *principles* (a sense of *justice*). A similar criticism has been directed at
Kohlberg's distinctions between the *form* and *content* of moral reasoning in a
given culture. Kohlberg has said that the content of moral judgments may
vary from culture to culture, but the more basic form of judgments does not.
Yet, when these two concepts are analyzed in detail, it appears that Kohlberg
has failed to produce adequate criteria for differentiating between them.

On item 1, Kohlberg can be credited with basing his model on data
drawn from a variety of real children. However, there is a question about
how realistic he has been in the scope of moral decisions that he analyzed.
The theory is founded on evidence collected from having children and
youths offer solutions to moral dilemma incidents posed to them. Since
Kohlberg wanted to make the respondents think hard in order to test their
reasoning, he necessarily posed incidents that had no obvious solutions in
terms of the dominant standards of a child's culture. However, as W. P.
Alston (1971, p. 284) has pointed out, these represent only a minor portion of
the daily moral decisions a person makes. Thus, according to Alston, Kohlberg's methodology has necessarily caused him to ignore the host of judgments young people make by *habit*. Habitual judgments are easy ones because the reward and punishment system of the culture has fashioned the
individual's "character" so that the solution to such moral issues is obvious
and no alternative solutions can compete successfully with the habitual one.
Alston believes that this lack in Kohlberg's research method has distorted the
theorist's view of the significance of habit or "character traits" and of emotion in determining moral thought and behavior.

Finally, Kohlberg has been criticized for proclaiming the principle of
justice the sole occupant of the highest stage of moral thought without
having sufficient cause to label it more worthy than several other virtues that
might have been selected—for example, sympathy, concern for others,
courage, integrity, or autonomy. As Peters has written, Kohlberg's findings

are of unquestionable importance, but there is a grave danger that they may become exalted into a general theory of moral development. Any such general theory presupposes a general ethical theory, and Kohlberg himself surely would be the first to admit that he has done little to develop the details of such a general ethical theory. Yet without such a theory the notion of "moral development" is pretty unsubstantial (1971, pp. 263–264).

So Kohlberg's theory, like the rest we have considered, has drawn both praise and criticism. But whatever its shortcomings, it remains the most stimulating and potentially fertile model of children's moral growth in current psychological and philosophical circles. For this reason, I have rated it as quite self-satisfying overall (item 9).

FOR FURTHER READING

Colby, Anne, Lawrence Kohlberg, John Gibbs, and Marcus Lieberman. (1983) *A Longitudinal Study of Moral Judgment.* Monographs of the Society for Research in Child Development, Serial No. 200, Vol. 48, Nos. 1–2. Chicago: Society for Research in Child Development.

Kohlberg, Lawrence. (1967) "Moral and Religious Education in the Public Schools: A Developmental View," in Theodore R. Sizer, *Religion and Public Education.* Boston: Houghton Mifflin.

Kohlberg, Lawrence, and R. Kramer. (1976) "Continuities and Discontinuities in Childhood and Adult Moral Development," in Norman S. Endler et al. (eds.), *Contemporary Issues in Developmental Psychology.* 2d ed. New York: Holt, Rinehart & Winston.

PART SIX

BEHAVIORIST APPROACHES TO DEVELOPMENT

A search for the way principles of learning explain development

Some psychologists feel very uneasy about theories that propose *mental elements,* such as soul, ego, or conscience. They are also uneasy about proposed *mental functions*—repression, epigenesis, assimilation, and the like. The trouble, they say, is that they are not convinced that these supposed elements and functions really exist, or at least not in the form that various theorists have proposed. It is clear that no one has ever seen or directly measured such things as mind or the unconscious. Another problem is that one theorist who writes about mind or personality often proposes very different elements and functions than other theorists. And if mind is unavailable for inspection, how do we know which theorist is right?

It was this sort of doubting that in 1914 motivated an American psychologist, John B. Watson (1878–1959), to launch the movement known as *behaviorism* (Watson, 1914, 1919). Watson and his followers felt that it is both misleading and unprofitable to study some speculator's opinions about what the structure of a person's mind or unconscious might be like. They proposed, instead, that it is much more objective and scientific to observe the way people act under different environmental conditions. The observations can then be organized, analyzed, and stated as principles that are intended to explain the behavior. In short, proponents of this point of view claim that the proper business of psychology is to identify the observable conditions that influence human behavior.

Since Watson's early advocacy of behaviorism, the movement has attracted many followers and has spawned several subgroups, particularly in the United States. In Part Six we consider several varieties of behaviorism as they apply to child development. Chapter Fourteen focuses on B. F. Skinner's operant conditioning and on the Bijou-Baer application of this approach to child development. Chapter Fifteen describes social learning theory, principally as found in the writings of Albert Bandura. Social learning theory, in contrast to original Watsonian behaviorism, does recognize cognitive activity while still emphasizing the analysis of overt behavior.

CHAPTER FOURTEEN

Skinner's Operant Conditioning

By the 1980s no American research psychologist was better known than B. F. Skinner (born 1904). The public fame of this Harvard professor resulted from his skillful and often controversial application of his learning theory to the solution of practical educational, personal adjustment, and social problems. In the mid-1950s he refined and popularized such learning devices as teaching machines and programmed texts (Skinner, 1972). In the late 1960s the behavior modification approach to therapy for disturbed people drew heavily on Skinnerian doctrine. In the 1970s his book *Beyond Freedom and Dignity* recommended a plan for social control through operant conditioning that he contended would produce an increasingly peaceful, orderly, cooperative, and efficient society (Skinner, 1971). His theory also has clear implications for the field of child development. In this chapter I will trace the outlines of Skinner's system and describe the principal ways the system can be applied to the understanding of child growth and behavior. Near the end of the chapter I will discuss the work of Sidney W. Bijou and Donald M. Baer, who have been leaders among child psychologists in applying Skinnerian behaviorism to the analysis of child development.

THE NATURE OF OPERANT CONDITIONING

The seeds of Skinner's behaviorism can be traced back to Pavlov's dog. In the early twentieth century the Russian physiologist Ivan Petrovich Pavlov (1849–1936) demonstrated what has become known as *classical conditioning*. He placed meat powder (called an *unconditioned stimulus*) on a dog's tongue, which resulted in the dog automatically salivating (called the *unconditioned response).* Then, on a series of subsequent occasions (called *trials*), he sounded a bell at the same time he gave the food (the meat powder) to the dog. When the food was accompanied by the bell enough times, he found that he could withhold the food and the bell's sound itself would cause the dog to salivate. The bell was now the *conditioned stimulus* that brought about the *conditioned response* of salivating. Classical conditioning, then—which often is called *respondent conditioning*—consists of substituting a new stimulus for an old one by presenting the two at the same time, or nearly the same time, then dropping the old stimulus and allowing the new one to bring about the original response. Pavlov's work inaugurated the era of *S-R* or *stimulus-response* psychology.

American behaviorists adopted the S-R concept as the appropriate model for explaining human behavior without having to speculate about what was possibly going on inside an organism's central nervous system. It was no longer necessary to imagine such things as mind or soul to account for the way people acted. By observing what sorts of stimuli elicited what sorts of responses, psychologists could explain what makes people behave as they do.

One problem that early behaviorists met was that they often could not identify accurately what stimulus was bringing about the responses they observed. Hence they were forced to assume the operation of stimuli they actually could not locate. In the 1930s Skinner suggested a solution to this common problem. He proposed that there was not one kind of conditioning but two. One was the classicial S-R relationship demonstrated by Pavlov. The other, and by far the more frequent in human behavior, Skinner labeled *operant* or *instrumental conditioning.* Instead of the behavior being drawn out or elicited by a stimulus, the behavior (response) was simply *emitted* or expressed without any observable stimulus evoking it.

For example, a pigeon in a cage just naturally does pigeon-like things— walking about and pecking. A baby in a cradle just makes natural baby movements—wiggling its arms and legs in a random way. In Skinner's opinion, it is not important to identify the stimulus that started the pecking and the arm and leg movements. Rather, if we are to understand why behavior occurs, it is far more important to inspect the *consequences* of these movements, for the consequences are what come to control actions. The term *consequences* here refers to whether the pigeon's or infant's movements bring satisfaction to the organism. If the pigeon is hungry and happens to peck a plastic lever that drops food pellets into the cage, then this consequence of the food's satisfying the hunger drive may strengthen the tendency for the pigeon to peck the lever again the next time it is hungry and is in the same cage. After the pigeon has had enough trials at this task, it gradually will become more efficient; that is, it will gradually eliminate the previous random walking and pecking at other things and will peck the lever directly when hungry. So we say the pigeon has *learned* lever pecking, and this learning has been caused or controlled by the consequences of fulfilling the hunger need.

It is Skinner's contention that all or nearly all behavior is a result of either respondent (classical) or operant conditioning, with by far the larger part of human behavior being operant as the child increases in age. If the consequences are rewarding, the actions will more likely be repeated the next time the individual is in a similar situation. If the consequences are either painful or simply useless, the actions will less likely be repeated in the future. Rewarding consequences strengthen tendencies to act; nonrewarding consequences weaken tendencies to act the same way again, so eventually the nonrewarding acts will be dropped or *extinguished* entirely.

This is the general idea of classical (respondent) and operant conditioning. However, in this introduction the theory has been oversimplified, and I have used terms that Skinner and his followers would find imprecise and perhaps misleading. For instance, Skinnerians do not approve of such terms as *hunger need* if such terms require that we assume something inside a person that we cannot observe. They also object to such words as *reward* when its use assumes a feeling state that cannot readily be identified and that is considered to be the cause of some sort of behavior. However, I used these terms, just as Skinner himself used them, because they are familiar and explain the issues more easily than if I had started off with only behaviorist definitions. However, at this point I will begin using more standard behaviorist wording in order to delineate the key features of Skinnerian theory.

To begin, I should point out that Skinner on occasion has denied that he has constructed a theory (Skinner, 1972, pp. 69–71). He claims to be more an empiricist, collecting observable facts of behavior and summarizing them in terms of principles. He proposes that he simply tells it as it is. However, in the broad way that *theory* was defined in Chapter One, his formulations do indeed qualify as theory, as his other writings would attest (Skinner, 1974, pp. 18–20).

He created the concept of *operant* or *instrumental* conditioning to focus prime attention on the importance of consequences in controlling the acts that immediately preceded them. In other words, the act is the operator (operant) or instrument that brings about the consequence.

Types of Consequences

What most people think of as a reward is called a *reinforcer* by behaviorists. A consequence is a *positive reinforcer* if it causes the act to increase in the future when a similar situation arises. For example, if a hungry infant is fed right after he happens to hit a rattle in his crib, the tendency for him to hit the rattle next time he is hungry is increased. This means that feeding has positively reinforced rattle hitting. Likewise, if an affection-hungry school girl picks papers up from around her desk and thus is given a hug by her teacher and told, "You're a great helper, Jenny," then the tendency for Jenny to pick up papers in the future is strengthened. The hug and kind words have positively reinforced the act of tidying up.

Sometimes a child's acts stop an unpleasant condition. For instance, the second-grade teacher is screaming at the children to get into their seats and keep quiet. The unpleasant screaming stops as soon as the children are all in their seats. So the act of sitting down has been instrumental in stopping the unpleasant harangue. The pleasant state of quiet is, for the children, a *negative reinforcer* for sitting down. In effect, a consequence of an action is called a negative reinforcer if the action has caused some unpleasant (*aversive*, in behaviorist terms) condition to stop. Next time the teacher starts ranting at the class, the children can be expected to sit down more promptly because sitting down produced the happy state of quiet the first time.

That is, both positive and negative reinforcement are rewarding. Both increase the likelihood that the child will repeat the same act in similar future circumstances. It is positive reinforcement if it starts a pleasant consequence. It is negative reinforcement if it stops an unpleasant consequence, such as noise or criticism.

A third sort of consequence is *punishment.* Consequences are called punishing or aversive if they reduce the tendency for the child to behave the same way in the future. Punishment, as any parent or teacher knows, is supposed to discourage acts of the same sort on later occasions. Punishment can involve either imposing something unpleasant (spanking, requiring extra homework) or removing something pleasant (taking away privileges).

But punishment is not the only way to eliminate undesired acts. Another way is simply not to reinforce the acts. If a child crosses his eyes in school to get attention but no one pays any attention to this antic, the eye crossing can be expected to stop for it has failed to achieve the desired consequences. In brief, *extinction* of the behavior occurs.

Studies by some behaviorists in the past have caused them to conclude that punishment only temporarily suppresses the expression of undesired behaviors; it does not eliminate or extinguish them. These investigators have claimed that when the punishing agent is not present, the undesired behaviors occur again. However, more recent analyses of the influence of punishment have caused other learning theorists to disagree that punishment is merely a temporary suppressor. They have concluded instead that punishment can be as effective as nonreinforcement in extinguishing undesired acts (Hilgard & Bower, 1975, pp. 223–225).

The foregoing elements, then, represent the basic framework of operant conditioning. If consequences of acts are reinforcing, then the acts will be learned and will appear again when the child is in similar situations. These reinforced actions become habits and form a pattern of behavior that might be called the child's style of life or personality. Consequences that are unrewarding—either punishing or simply nonreinforcing—result in behaviors being dropped from the child's repertoire of actions.

Behaviorists' Notion of Learning

In the discussion so far I have used the word *learning* to refer to a child's coming to the point of habitually showing a particular behavior when in a given situation. However, there is really a more precise way to view learning from the standpoint of operant conditioning. You may recall that in the operant type of conditioning, the focus is not on how we get the child to display a behavior in the first place but on what happens to that behavior as the result of the consequences that follow it. From this perspective, learning is not seen as the process of the child's first displaying the behavior but rather as the process of her displaying it consistently, that is, of her responding at a high rate of frequency when in similar stimulus situations. For example, if a nine-year-old girl comes home from playing with neighborhood friends only one time in ten when her mother calls, "Time to come in, Karin," then we would say that Karin has not learned very well to come when called. Her rate of response is only 10 percent. We do not mean Karin is ignorant of how to return home when her mother calls; her occasional correct response shows that the expected behavior is in her repertoire. But in saying she has not learned very well, we mean she does not respond consistently in this stimulus situation. However, her mother can increase Karin's rate of responding (help her better learn to come when called) by manipulating the consequences. Or, in behaviorist terms, she can rearrange the *reinforcement schedule* to increase her daughter's tendency to come when summoned.

Skinner has made particularly useful contributions to the analysis of the effect on behavior of different kinds of reinforcement schedules. For example, the effects on performance differ when *continuous reinforcement* (rewarding every time the desired act occurs) is used rather than *intermittent reinforcement* (rewarding only certain times the act occurs). Furthermore, different schedules of intermittent reinforcement yield different results. A *fixed-ratio* schedule (such as rewarding every third or every fifth response) has a different effect from a *fixed-interval* schedule (rewarding a response after every two minutes or every five minutes). These sorts of schedules, combined with a variety of others, can produce an array of different behavior results (Hilgard & Bower, 1975, pp. 216–217). For example, when an eight-year-old pupil is in the early stages of learning to raise his hand to speak in class rather than to shout out his opinion, he can profitably be rewarded on each occasion that he raises his hand. But after the habit has been well established, intermittent reward will probably serve to maintain the habit against extinction better than continuous reinforcement.

We can summarize Skinner's viewpoint by saying that from his behaviorist perspective child development is a process of the growing individual's learning increasingly complex and refined ways of acting as a result of the consequences that have followed the behavior she or he has attempted. The role of parents and teachers is therefore twofold: (1) to get children to try desirable acts and (2) to arrange consequences of children's acts so that desirable behavior is reinforced and undesirable behavior is extinguished through nonreinforcement or punishment.

CONDITIONED REINFORCEMENT AND CHAINING

One charge frequently aimed at the operant-conditioning model is that the theory is oversimplified. While critics admit that operant conditioning might account for certain simple acts, they claim it cannot explain complex skills or creative thinking. However, Skinner has proposed several mechanisms that he believes readily account for any sort of behavior that people exhibit, whether the actions are—as nonbehaviorists might say—mental or physical.

The first mechanism is described in the principle of *conditioned reinforcement:* A consequence (called a *stimulus*) that is not originally a reinforcing one can become reinforcing through repeated association with a consequence that is already reinforcing (Keller & Schoenfeld, 1950, p. 232). In other words, if a mother comes to feed her infant son each time he is hungry, and the consequence of the feeding is that it satisfies the infant's hunger, then after enough repetitions of this act the appearance of mother herself—even without food—becomes reinforcing or satisfying. Mother now has the power of being a reinforcer. She has become a *conditioned* or a *secondary* reinforcer. Her appearance and the associated acts that accompanied the original feeding—her smiling and saying, "What a good boy"—can now be used to reinforce or teach other behaviors. For instance, when the growing infant happens to say "mah" during his babblings, the mother's smile and her comment, "What a smart boy—now say Mama," serve to reinforce the utterance of "mah." Consequently, the chance of the child's uttering "mah" again in the mother's presence is increased.

Not only does a growing child soon build up a significant store of conditioned reinforcements that can serve as rewards for actions, but many of these secondary reinforcers become generalized to other actions. That is, the reinforcer not only strengthens its original act but, by being associated with many actions, comes to strengthen any with which it is connected. For adolescents, money is a strong generalized reinforcer and can be used to strengthen or reward all sorts of behavior. For both younger and older children, such phrases as "good girl" and "that's the way to do it" become generalized reinforcers, attached to many behaviors.

F. S. Keller and W. N. Schoenfeld have summarized in the following way the two principles that govern these examples:

> Once established, a secondary reinforcement is independent and non-specific; it not only will strengthen the same response which produced the original reinforcement, but will also condition a new and unrelated response. Moreover, it will do so even in the presence of a different motive.
>
> Through generalization, many stimuli besides the one correlated with reinforcement acquire reinforcing value—positive or negative (1950, p. 260).

Two other conditioning functions that help explain complex behavior are *shaping* and *chaining*. *Shaping* consists of first reinforcing any gross approximation that the child achieves of a desired refined act. Then, after the gross form of the behavior has been well established, it can be shaped by gradual steps into the ultimate refined form by requiring better and better approximations before reinforcement is provided. For instance, in teaching a child to bat a ball, we will first offer praise for her swinging the bat, whether or not she hits the ball. As her swing improves, we no longer praise just any swing, but only those that hit the ball. When she can hit the ball nearly every time, we limit our praise to her hitting the ball into the field in front of her, and we do not praise foul balls that bounce to the side or to the rear. This process of gradually placing more precise limits on the kinds of acts that are reinforced continues, enabling the child to shape her batting skill till she can hit the ball in more precise directions and to specified distances. In a similar fashion, shaping helps expand and refine children's verbal behavior as their utterances are altered by the positive and negative reactions of people with whom they interact.

Chaining enables a person to hook together a sequence of small, individual conditioned acts to compose a complex skill. The process of chaining begins at the final end of the chain rather than at the beginning. Each preceding link of the chain is hooked on by associating it with the link that has already been established through reinforcement. For instance, consider the complex skill known as "having good table manners." We start with a child who yearns for both food and parental approval. Over a sequence of days the child is permitted to eat and is told, "That's fine" and "You're doing a good job" when he uses a fork rather than his fingers for lifting small pieces of meat to his mouth. When the pattern of using the fork is established, we add a new requirement. The child must use a knife and fork to cut large pieces of meat into smaller pieces before he is permitted to eat or is complimented for his actions. When he has learned these two links—eating with the fork after cutting up the pieces—we impose a new requirement, that of tucking a napkin into his shirt before he cuts up the meat, picks up pieces with the fork, eats, and is complimented. By such a process an extended set of habits or conditioned links can be formed into a complicated skill.

In summary, the simple mechanism of reinforcement not only accounts for specific simple acts, but the processes of secondary reinforcement, stimulus generalization, shaping (response discrimination), and chaining can account for all sorts of complex activities, in the opinion of behaviorists. And, they say, it is not necessary for us to fashion these processes consciously; they occur as natural behavior in everyone.

THE SCOPE OF SKINNER'S THEORY

In at least three important ways, Skinner's theory can be called broad in scope. First, it is not limited to any cultural setting; it purports to explain development in all societies. Second, its principles apply to all age levels, from the prenatal period to death. Third, it claims to explain all varieties of behavior—physical, mental, social, emotional. Although the first two claims have not attracted much criticism, the third has been the center of an extended debate, so it warrants close attention.

As noted earlier, behaviorism was originally a reaction against *mentalism*. It was a reaction against saying that human action was caused by ideas or feelings that arose in an unobservable place called *mind* or *soul*. Furthermore, behaviorism was a reaction against mentalists' research methods, which consisted largely of introspection, of a philosopher pondering about the nature of his own thoughts and emotions and then proposing elements or functions of the mind that he thought produced or controlled the thoughts and emotions.

Early behaviorists like Watson and Max Meyer claimed that if psychology is truly to become a science, it must focus solely on objective, publicly witnessed information. Such things as thoughts, mind, and feelings should have no place in this proposed science of human behavior. However, critics of behaviorism said that it is nonsense to deny the existence of such obvious phenomena as thoughts and feelings simply because these things are not directly seen by people outside the skin of the person who is doing the thinking and feeling. In sum, over the past half century behaviorists, including Skinner, have been charged with proposing a simplistic, mindless psychology. But Skinner, while admitting the charges are valid criticisms of early behaviorists, denies that they apply to him. In order to distinguish himself from the others, he has created two labels: (1) *methodological behaviorism* to identify those who would ignore the existence of thoughts and feelings and (2) *radical behaviorism* to identify his own position, which recognizes thoughts and feelings as normal "covert acts" and accepts introspection as a legitimate mode of inquiry (Skinner, 1974, pp. 13–18).

According to Skinner, the sin of mentalism—as practiced by Puritans, Rousseau, Freud, Piaget, and many others—has been to focus exclusively on mental events. This focus has distracted their attention away from an analysis of the external environment's stimuli and consequences that are the elements, he says, that can really account for why people act as they do. But in censuring the mentalists, Skinner has not uncritically embraced the methodological-behaviorist position of Watson and, more recently, of J. R. Kantor. Rather, Skinner has criticized methodological behaviorism for committing the opposite error:

> By dealing exclusively with external antecedent events, it turned away from self-observation and self-knowledge. Radical behaviorism restores some kind of balance. It does not insist upon truth by agreement and can therefore consider events taking place in the private world within the skin. It does not call these events unobservable, and it does not dismiss them as subjective. It simply questions the nature of the object observed and the reliability of the observations (1974, pp. 16–17).

So Skinner accepts thoughts and feelings, but he believes that people's techniques for investigating them are not well developed or very trustworthy. Consequently, he finds it best to depend heavily on an analysis of environmental conditions and people's observable reactions in order to understand a person's genetic and environmental history. He finds it of no explanatory help to create such words as *mind* or *consciousness* to account for a person's inner life. He contends (1974, p. 17) that "what is felt or introspectively observed is not some nonphysical world of consciousness, mind, or mental life but the observer's own body." In other words, Skinner has not divided the person into the traditional opposing aspects of physical and mental. He considers the individual to be an integrated unit. Some actions are observed by people outside the individual's skin (overt behavior) and others are observed only by the individual through introspection (covert behavior).

HEREDITY VERSUS ENVIRONMENT

Behaviorists traditionally have been criticized for underestimating the role of heredity in development. However, Skinner has reacted to such criticism by again distinguishing between the viewpoint of methodological behaviorists and his own. Several decades ago, Watson claimed he could take any healthy infant and raise it to become whatever he chose—doctor, lawyer, artist, beggarman, thief. However, Skinner (1974, p. 221) has dismissed this claim by calling it a "careless remark" and has proposed instead what he considers a more balanced view of the relative contributions of genetic endowment and environmental influences.

To understand Skinner's own position, we should first recognize that he believes the basic drive behind all behavior, human as well as nonhuman, is to survive. All actions are designed to promote the survival of both the individual and the species. Humans, like other species, inherit biological potentials that serve in some ways to enhance and in other ways to limit the chance of surviving in different environments. The potentials that a person inherits have been determined over past eons of time by the survival of the fittest, Darwin's natural selection. People with those traits that promoted survival lived on to produce offspring with these same high-survival characteristics. People lacking such traits died early, so their strains were not reproduced.

For purposes of analysis, it is useful to divide inherited characteristics into two types, although in actual practice the two merge into each other. The first type is well suited to stable environments, and the second to variable, unpredictable environments. That is, some environmental conditions—conditions of climate or the nature of predators and diseases, for example—are relatively permanent over time. In these environments that are stable over a period of centuries, a species can directly inherit traits that arm it for survival, traits like a heavy, white fur coat to match the arctic snow color and instincts or reflexes that give ample warning of approaching predators. But frequently, environmental conditions cannot be directly predicted. Conditions change from year to year, even from day to day. In such settings it is not helpful to inherit a specific, limited reflex or instinct. Rather, it is better to inherit the ability to change behavior on the basis of the environment's reaction. In other words, a species can inherit learning capacity, the ability to profit from the consequences of behavior. This is the second sort of inheritance and the one that Skinner considers the most important thing that humans derive from their genetic endowment. Humans' high level of intelligence or adaptability results from an unusually sensitive genetic potential for operant conditioning.

When Skinner has been pressed to tell exactly which behaviors or personality traits he believes people inherit and which he thinks they learn, he has refrained from identifying specific items, for he claims that not enough research has been done to give clear answers. But he has stated that many of the things that other theorists, such as Gesell and Freud, attribute to heredity are actually learned through conditioning. Skinner concludes that:

> Genetic causes sometimes become a kind of dumping ground: any aspect of behavior which at the moment escapes analysis in terms of contingencies of reinforcement is likely to be assigned to genetic endowment, and we are likely to accept the explanation because we are so accustomed to going no further than a stage of the organism (1974, p. 44).

Skinner, then, would not place himself at either extreme in the nature–nurture controversy. And he rejects the methodological behaviorists' contention that human personality is completely malleable, ready to be formed into whatever pattern the controllers of reinforcement desire. In his novel about a utopian community, *Walden Two* (1948), Skinner described a society in which all children have a highly similar environment until age 10 since they are all raised together in communal centers over the first decade of their lives rather than in individual families. Yet even with this common environment, the children living in Walden Two display a range of intelligence "almost as great as in the population at large. This seems to be true of other abilities and skills as well" (Skinner, 1948, p. 104). In effect, Skinner has proposed that genetic endowment accounts for a significant amount of the variation among children. He is not a thoroughgoing environmentalist. Nevertheless, he appears to assign a more important role to environmental forces than do the other theorists studied so far in this book.

THE STAGES OF CHILD REARING

In several previous chapters we have seen that theories of development are sometimes divided into *stage* and *nonstage* models. A stage model typically pictures the growth of the child as a series of distinct steps or phases. At around a particular age, the child changes noticeably from being one sort of person into being another sort. Then, for some time, the child retains the characteristics of this second sort until once more she or he makes a noticeable change and reaches a new level or phase of growth.

Contrasting with this conception of sudden change from one phase to another is the nonstage model that pictures growth as a very gradual process. Changes occur in miniscule amounts. It is true that in both stage and nonstage theories the child at age 6 will be obviously different from the way she looked and acted at age 3. But to nonstage theorists she has not arrived at 6 by any sudden leaps or insights. Instead, age 6 is just an accumulation of very slight alterations since age 3.

Generally, stage theories have been proposed by investigators who say heredity plays the greater role in development, whereas nonstage models have been devised by those who give more credit to the environment. This linking of stages with hereditarians and gradual growth with environmentalists is not a logical necessity. Gradual growth could reasonably be attributed to a genetic time schedule, and stages might be accounted for by sudden major changes in environmental forces. However, the observed linking has been the dominant trend, and Skinner's theory fits the pattern by being a nonstage model.

Skinner sees development as a continuous, incremental sequence of specific conditioned acts. It is not that he is unable to conceive of behavior being studied in terms of age or the passage of time, "as in the development of a child's verbal behavior or his problem-solving strategies or in the sequence of stages through which a person passes on his way from infancy to maturity" (Skinner, 1972, pp. 567–573). But he feels that (1) it is more accurate to view the developmental steps as very small ones and (2) it is unprofitable to focus only on *what* happens at a particular stage and to ignore the question of *why* it occurs. In other words, he is critical not only of picturing growth as major jumps followed by lengthy plateaus, but also of the developmentalists', or what he refers to as *structuralists'*, failing to explain why these changes occur, other than to state that the cause is an assumed internal maturation whose timing follows a genetic clock. Skinner's interest has been in the management or control of development, not in just describing what it looks like when it takes place.

So in his writings, Skinner makes almost no point of describing the characteristics of children at different age levels. Despite this, he has given some prominent attention to stages, but his stages have been *phases of the environmental treatment of the child,* treatment designed to produce optimal development. In short, he prescribes ways to treat children at different age levels to promote their happiness and well being. To explain what these prescriptions are, I draw upon two of Skinner's publications, which were issued in the middle of his academic career. The first is an article from a

1945 *Ladies Home Journal* describing an air-conditioned, sanitary box in which he and his wife raised their infant daughter (Skinner, 1972, pp. 567–573). The second is the novel *Walden Two* (Skinner, 1948), and particularly the series of chapters detailing child-care methods in the utopian community. I will use child rearing in Walden Two as the focus of the discussion.

Ideal Child Rearing

In the psychologist's ideal child-rearing system, boys and girls are not raised by their individual families but are brought up in communal care centers till they reach puberty. At around age 13, adolescents, individually or in pairs, set up their own living quarters in the apartment complex that houses the adults in the mythical rural American town called Walden Two.

The first two decades of life in Walden Two are divided into five child-raising stages: (1) a lower-nursery stage for infants from birth to age 1, (2) an upper-nursery stage for those ages 1 and 2, (3) a middle-childhood phase for ages 3–6, (4) later childhood for ages 7–13, and (5) adolescence after age 13.

The basic philosophy during this entire two-decade span is that it is important to fulfill children's needs as quickly and as completely as possible in their earliest years. Then, very gradually, the demands and annoyances of normal life are introduced at a scientifically controlled rate that ensures that children can master them without acquiring negative feelings. This system of *behavioral engineering* or controlled operant conditioning is designed to encourage "the productive and strengthening emotions—love and joy. . . . But sorrow and hate—and the high-voltage excitements of anger, fear, and rage—are out of proportion with the needs of modern life, and they're wasteful and dangerous." In Walden Two such emotions, along with jealousy and envy, which "breed unhappiness," are almost unknown (Skinner, 1948, p. 83).

This pattern of providing an initially easy environment that becomes more and more difficult as children acquire the ability to adjust is intended to yield the reward of "escape from the petty emotions which eat the heart out of the unprepared." Children raised in Walden Two not only get the satisfaction of pleasant social relations, they also become far more efficient workers "because they can stick to a job without suffering the aches and pains which soon beset most of us. They get new horizons, for they are spared the emotions characteristic of frustration and failure" (Skinner, 1948, pp. 90–91).

This is the general strategy of child rearing. During the first five years after birth adults see that no important need goes unsatisfied, so the child begins life practically free of anxiety and frustration. But eventually, through the mastery of gradually increasing frustrations, youths in Walden Two experience "the heartache and the thousand natural shocks that flesh is heir to" (Skinner, 1948, p. 93).

With this overall plan in mind, let us now consider some of the ways Walden Two's adults engineer the environment to produce such admirable results.

Birth to Age 1 Infants in Walden Two do not stay at home with their mothers but are collected together in the "lower nursery," each baby in an air-conditioned, enclosed crib like the "baby box" in which the Skinners raised their second daughter for the first year of her life. The purpose of the box is to furnish the infant with a healthful climate, free from the confinement of clothes and blankets and from dust and germs. The baby, clad only in a diaper, lies or sits or crawls about on an easily cleaned plastic mattress, plays with rattles and toys hung from the ceiling of the box, and gazes at the passersby through the large glass window that forms one side of the enclosed crib. The walls of the box are insulated from noise and temperature changes. A shade lowered over the window when the baby is asleep prevents light from disturbing the infant's naps.

After Skinner's own daughter had been in such a box for eleven months, he reported that because of the box's filtered air:

> The baby's eyes, ears, and nostrils remain fresh and clean. A weekly bath is enough, provided the face and diaper region are frequently washed. . . . She has always enjoyed deep and extended sleep, and her feeding and eliminative habits have been extraordinarily regular. . . . Although there have been colds in the family, . . . the baby has completely escaped. She has never had a diaper rash. . . .
>
> One of the commonest objections [of friends] was that we were going to raise a "softie" who would be unprepared for the real world. But instead of becoming hypersensitive, our baby has acquired a surprisingly serene tolerance for annoyances. She is not bothered by the clothes she wears at playtime, she is not frightened by loud or sudden noises, she is not frustrated by toys out of reach. . . . A tolerance for any annoyance can be built up by administering it in controlled dosages, rather than in the usual accidental way. Certainly there is no reason to annoy the child throughout the whole of its infancy, merely to prepare it for later childhood (Skinner, 1972, pp. 570–572).

In Walden Two the parents come each day or so to see the baby, to take it from the box and play with it a while. But this personal attention and display of affection are offered not only by the parents but also by the men and women who are in charge of the nursery. The purpose of sharing the responsibility for infants is to enable a child to imitate numerous desirable models who combine to form "a sort of essential happy adult. He can avoid the idiosyncrasies of a single parent" (Skinner, 1948, p. 119).

Ages 1 and 2   When children are around one year old in Walden Two, they move from their individual cubicles in the lower nursery to the upper nursery. This advanced nursery is composed of several small playrooms furnished with child-size equipment, a dressing room with a locker for each child, and small air-conditioned sleeping rooms. Clad only in diapers, children sleep on easily cleaned plastic mattresses. At playtime they are either naked or in training pants.

Child-raising practices continue to be guided by the principles followed in the lower nursery. Children's needs are met as soon and as completely as possible, with the result that the young child still knows nothing of frustration, anxiety, or fear. This does not mean, however, that the child has no experiences that might bring about frustration. It means, instead, that the behavioral engineers who schedule the child-raising program introduce potentially discouraging experiences "as carefully as we introduce any other emotional situation beginning at about six months" (Skinner, 1948, p. 100). For example, some of the toys children are given are designed to build perseverance.

The personnel of the nursery is balanced between men and women so as to "eliminate all the Freudian problems which arise from the asymmetrical relation to the female parent" (Skinner, 1948, p. 120).

Ages 3 to 6, Middle Childhood   From the standpoint of sleeping accommodations, this period is divided into two segments. At ages 3 and 4 each child is given responsibility for her own cot in a dormitory, and she is introduced to wearing regular clothing. At ages 5 and 6 children move into a complex of alcoves, each furnished like a regular room and holding three or four children with their beds and personal belongings. They are expected to gradually assume increased responsibility for the upkeep of their quarters. A careful schedule of conditioning in ethical behavior is conducted so that the foundations of ethical conduct are virtually complete by age 6.

Ages 7 to 13, Later Childhood   At age 7 children move from the alcoves into a complex of small rooms, each room designed for two children. At frequent intervals roommates are changed so children learn to live with different sorts of age-mates. They no longer eat in a dining room for children but use the adults' cafeteria.

It is impossible to distinguish formal from informal education in Walden Two since children are being taught by designed conditioning schedules wherever they are—in their living quarters, on the playground, and in the community's workshops, laboratories, studios, reading rooms, and fields. Early in their lives, children are given work to do, so they come to have a personal stake in contributing to the community.

Walden Two's behavioral engineers claim that their education system is far superior to that of the typical town because teachers do not waste time duplicating home training or changing the cultural and intellectual habits that children might have acquired outside of school.

From the child's first months after birth, the community depends on his natural curiosity and natural needs to motivate him to learn. The behavioral engineers appeal to humans' "drive to control the environment. . . . We don't need to motivate by creating spurious needs. . . . Promising paradise or threatening hellfire is, we assumed, generally admitted to be unproductive" (Skinner, 1948, pp. 87, 101–102).

The education system has no grade levels since "everyone knows that talents and abilities don't develop at the same rate in different children" (Skinner, 1948, p. 97). Pupils are encouraged to progress as rapidly as they like in any field, and they are not expected to waste time in a classroom being bored by activities they have outgrown. No subjects like English or social studies or science are taught. Rather, children are taught techniques of learning and thinking. Then they are provided chances to learn geography, literature, the sciences, and the like by themselves, based on the firm foundation they have received in ways of thinking: logic, statistics, scientific method, psychology, and mathematics. Children who do not appear to have an aptitude for learning a particular skill or type of knowledge are not required to do so. In other words, Walden Two's educators do not "waste time teaching the unteachable" (Skinner, 1948, p. 97).

Age 13 and Beyond, Adolescence As the child passes puberty and becomes sexually potent, Walden Two does not require that he or she postpone mature forms of sexual gratification until age 20 or older. Instead, the adolescent finds "an immediate and satisfying expression of his natural impulses . . . very different from the secrecy and shame which most of us recall in connection with sex at some time or other" (Skinner, 1948, p. 111). When teenagers fall in love, they become engaged, at which time they consult the Manager of Marriages. He examines their interests, school records, and health status. If there are major discrepancies between the couple in intellectual abilities or temperament, they are advised not to marry or, at least, to postpone marriage for a while. But those who do seem well matched are encouraged to marry and begin having children when they are still age 15 or 16. This early satisfaction of sexual needs, combined with young people's early and gradual introduction to the world of work, makes the period of adolescence "brief and painless."

As for their living accommodations, the young teenagers move, at least temporarily, into rooms in the adult apartment complex, where they usually live in pairs. At the time of marriage, or whenever else he or she chooses, the individual can participate in building a larger room for himself or herself or can refurbish an existing room that has become available.

In effect, during the latter teens the youth gradually achieves adult status without the extended period of stress that adolescence in American society has ostensibly involved.

BIJOU AND BAER'S ADDITIONS TO RADICAL BEHAVIORISM

Perhaps the best known of the child development theorists adhering closely to a Skinnerian behaviorist viewpoint have been Sidney W. Bijou and Donald M. Baer. A significant contribution of these two authors has been their adopting three developmental periods suggested by J. R. Kantor (1959) and their illustrating in detail how traditional behaviorism can account for the changes observed in children at each level of growth. The labels attached to the three successive stages have been *universal, basic,* and *societal.*

The *universal stage,* which extends from the prenatal months until symbolic behavior or language becomes prominent at around age 2, derives its name from the fact that the growth of infants in all societies is much alike during these first years. Although the infant interacts with the environment and thus is influenced by the consequences of his or her actions, the greater determinant of behavior at this time is the child's maturing biological nature. So environmental stimuli play a very limited role in controlling the infant's "simple but self-preserving respondents" and in guiding the development of other behaviors related to "maintaining the biological necessities of life" (Bijou & Baer, 1965, pp. 2–3). The causes of similarities among children in all societies at this stage are primarily the basic biological similarities of the human species, which are the focus of attention in infancy. But, in addition, the social and physical environments are much the same from one culture to another, "not only because of the similarity in limitations imposed by extreme biological immaturity but also because of the extensive uniformity in infant-caring practices" (Bijou & Baer, 1965, p. 179).

The *basic* or second stage of development covers the years between about age 2 and ages 5 or 6. By now the child's biological development is sufficiently stable to meet her basic needs so she is more effective in interacting with the environment and can devote more energy to developing psychological behaviors. The patterns of action acquired during these preschool years depend heavily on the sort of social environment the child's family provides, although part of the child's characteristics are still determined by her biological structure, which results from her genetic inheritance.

During the basic stage, the personality structure is formed through the kinds of opportunities and contingencies the child's parents and other family members habitually provide. In these years the child's basic discriminations and forms of behavior are acquired.

The *societal stage* or third period of development begins around the time the child enters the primary grades and continues throughout the years of schooling. During this period, a myriad of influences from his culture serve to alter and expand the basic pattern of action or personality structure that was fabricated through biological inheritance and the nurturing practices of his family.

In sum, Bijou and Baer demonstrate how respondent and operant conditioning principles can account for the similarities and differences among children at three successive stages of growth.

Responses to Criticism

In addition to applying radical behaviorism to the interpretation of stages of development, Bijou has responded to critics who charge that behaviorism as a learning theory can neither account for child development in general nor explain the causes behind development. He has also answered those who claim that radical behaviorism views the child as only a passive organism and that practical applications of conditioning can harm children.

In reply to the first of these criticisms, Bijou states that while the radical behaviorism model is yet incomplete and therefore is still "on the way to becoming a mature theory," it is nevertheless a "comprehensive approach, including all the essential components of a system" (Bijou, 1979, p. 4). Specifically, modern behaviorism

1. Is founded on a clearly stated philosophy "that the subject matter of psychology is the continuous interaction between a behaving organism and physical and social events that can be observed objectively. . . . Therefore, reductionism, or the analysis of psychological interactions in terms of biological, physical, or chemical processes, is rejected totally" (Bijou, 1979, p. 4).

2. Is a *general* theory whose basic tenets account for (a) the strengthening or weakening of relationships between the child and her environment, (b) changes in abilities and skills, (c) a child's pattern of remembering and forgetting, (d) the transfer of learning from one situation to another, and (e) motivation, emotion, and conflict.

3. Has an established research methodology.

4. Has a precise method for translating basic research into practical applications.

Critics have also claimed that radical behaviorism does not adequately explain the causes underlying children's actions because it fails to identify the events of the past that have contributed to the child's present personality. In reply, Bijou contends that behaviorists are not oblivious to the child's developmental history. However, what is important about this history is not the past events themselves but rather the way such events have shaped the child's skills and attitudes that exist today. Since behaviorists believe that looking to the past cannot inform them accurately of what residue past events have left in the child's present life, they choose instead to observe the child systematically today in order to determine what the present-day consequences are of the child's "interactional history; that is, we learn what the specific events in his or her functional environment mean to him or her" (Bijou, 1979, pp. 5–6).

A further charge frequently leveled at behaviorists is that they view children as passive objects manipulated by environmental forces, objects that "must be stimulated. Hence . . . the person is not seen as playing an active, contributory role in his or her own development" (R. M. Lerner, 1976, p. 279). Bijou says this criticism may be true of Watson's original methodological behaviorism but not of radical behaviorism. The modern behaviorist believes that in every interaction with the environment, the child contributes her own responses and internal stimuli, which have been determined by her genetic structure and personal history. Furthermore, as the child develops, she responds increasingly to stimuli and environmental factors she herself has produced, so that she is engaging in active self-management. But this does not mean the child's behavior is directed toward some inherent goal, such as the goal of self-actualization in humanistic theory (Chapter Sixteen) or of formal operational thought in Piaget's model of cognitive development (Chapter Ten) (Bijou, 1979, pp. 7–8).

Behavior Management

In recent years one of the most popular applications of behaviorism has been in the use of operant conditioning for *behavior management* or *behavior modification*. Such conditioning has been employed by parents for socializing their children, by teachers seeking to control pupils' classroom behavior, and by therapists attempting to alter clients' undesirable habits and phobias. However, objections have been raised in a number of quarters on the grounds that these practices are manipulative, violate human rights, and often harm those who are the objects of the conditioning. Bijou has replied that the principles involved are certainly not inhumane but, rather, are simply the normal ones underlying all behavior, human and nonhuman alike. Therefore utilizing the principles consciously and systematically is not an act of malice or exploitation but is just good sense, for it increases the efficiency in the behavior management that parents, teachers, and therapists all normally attempt. As for potential harm that may result, Bijou states that "this is true for the practical application of any scientific finding when the applier is not adequately trained to the task" (Bijou, 1979, p. 9).

Finally, critics have claimed that behaviorism is useful for analyzing only the simplest stimulus-response learning but fails to account for the complexities of children's language development, problem solving, and creativity. Bijou's answer is that radical behaviorism is yet a new science, still incomplete, but one that displays great potential for explaining all of these phenomena in terms of observable interactions of children with their environment.

PRACTICAL APPLICATIONS

Behaviorism in all its modern varieties has yielded a substantial body of practical implications for child raising, education, and therapy.

Skinner's model served as the foundation for the programmed textbooks and teaching machines that achieved their greatest popularity in the late 1950s and early 1960s. Skinner advocated the preparation of *linear learning programs* consisting of logically ordered small steps of information presented to the learner, who is required to respond at each step (filling in an answer in an incomplete sentence). The learner then receives immediate feedback about how accurate his answer—and thereby his learning—has been at that point. It was Skinner's intention to have the steps arranged so gradually and logically that the learner would be correct nearly every time he answered, with the resultant reinforcement (feedback) strengthening the permanence of each stimulus-response learning bond. Principles from this early model of programmed instruction are observed today in many of the *learning packages* being developed for the microcomputers that are playing a rapidly expanding role in classroom and home instruction. In addition, the international *mastery-learning* instructional movement has drawn on Skinnerian principles for portions of its methodology (Block & Anderson, 1975; Keller & Sherman, 1974).

Skinner's theory has also contributed in a major way to the behavior modification techniques described in Chapter Fifteen, with the effectiveness of such procedures being demonstrated by a growing quantity of empirical research (Kazdin, 1981, pp. 34–57). For example, findings in studies of preschool, elementary school, and special-class pupils "have indicated that when a teacher pays any kind of attention to unruly conduct, such behavior tends to increase (reinforcement); when she directs her attention to desirable personal-social behavior (reinforcement) and totally ignores undesirable behavior, that behavior tends to decrease (extinction)" (Bijou, 1985).

Behaviorism's practical applications in education and therapy have achieved international scope with the establishment of such organizations as the Association for the Advancement of Behavior Therapy and the International Association of Behavior Analysis. Behavioral courses and service programs have been introduced in such diverse nations as the United States, Britain, Brazil, West Germany, Peru, Australia, Colombia, and New Zealand.

RESEARCH CHALLENGES

Two principal lines of research have derived from radical behaviorism and its variants: (1) refinements and applications of behavior management techniques and (2) behavioral analyses of those complex functions that critics claimed cannot be explained adequately within the radical behaviorism paradigm.

Questions about behavior management that continue to stimulate research include: What are the most appropriate incentives or rewards to use with children of different age levels or personality types? What reinforcement schedules are most effective to maintain a desired behavior in children of different age levels or personality types? What are the significant likenesses and differences in two environments that influence how learning achieved in one environment will influence behavior in the other setting (the transfer-of-learning problem)? Exactly what is the nature of punishment as compared with reinforcement? Is withholding a reward a kind of punishment? How effective are different forms of punishment in modifying children's behavior at different age levels, and what desirable and undesirable side effects may result from these forms? If a child has been induced to learn something by being rewarded with a special treat—a toy or snack or privilege—will the child always require such external, material rewards to maintain that learned behavior, or can the material reward later be dropped and the desired behavior continue in a self-sustaining manner?

In the realm of complex human behaviors, a variety of topics have been pursued by researchers operating from the radical behaviorism perspective. Topics include problem solving (Grimm, Bijou & Parsons, 1973; Skinner, 1969), creative behavior (Holman, Goetz, and Baer, 1977), conceptualizing and abstracting (Schilmoeller & Etzel, 1977), early moral development (Bijou, 1976), and self-management (Ballard & Glynn, 1975). Further studies of such topics can be expected in the years ahead.

SKINNER'S OPERANT CONDITIONING: AN ASSESSMENT

I feel that Skinner deserves high scores on nearly all of the criteria proposed in Chapter One.

Skinner's model is clearly described (item 2), enjoying the advantage over mentalist theories of not including in its elements such nonobservable, internal items as ego or conscience, items whose characteristics are difficult to depict to other people.

As attested by *Walden Two* and the programmed learning and behavior modification programs that educators and therapists have adopted in recent years, Skinner's theory offers very detailed guidance for child-rearing practices (item 4).

Since the Skinnerian model is founded on empirical studies of overt behavior, and the mechanisms that account for behavior are rather simple, the theory has the qualities of internal consistency (item 5) and falsifiability (item 7). It has also led to a great deal of research and practical application (item 8). It has helped lead to the extensions of behaviorism found in Chapter Fifteen and to the applications mentioned earlier in the realms of programmed instruction and behavior modification practices.

However, strong criticisms have been raised about the theory's being overly simple, unrealistically economical (item 6). This ostensible oversimplification has caused critics to question how adequately the theory reflects the real world of children (item 1) and how well it explains the past and predicts the future (item 3). In particular, Skinner has been charged with extending conclusions derived from animal experiments—primarily with pigeons and rats—to humans, without accounting properly for differences of intellectual quality among the species. For example, Noam Chomsky (1967), as a leader in the field of psycholinguistics, has argued that Skinner has been imprecise in analyzing such commonsense terms as *want, like,* and *plan* into operant-conditioning elements. Furthermore, Chomsky has assailed Skinner's assumption that children simply repeat the words or phrases they hear, that is, repeat the ones that have brought reinforcement. Chomsky claims that children formulate for themselves, through unseen mental processes, a deeper grammar that undergirds the meaning of the surface appearance of their sentences. This deep grammar structure en-

Skinner's Theory

How well do I think the theory meets the standards?

The Standards	*Very Well*	*Moderately Well*	*Very Poorly*
1. Reflects the real world of children		X	
2. Is clearly understandable	X		
3. Explains the past and predicts the future		X	
4. Guides child rearing	X		
5. Is internally consistent	X		
6. Is economical		X	
7. Is falsifiable	X		
8. Stimulates new discoveries	X		
9. Is self-satisfying		X	

ables children to recognize the equivalent meanings of utterances that are dissimilar in their surface structure *(The girl ate the cake* or *The cake was eaten by the girl* or *The cake was gone, for the girl had eaten it).*

Widespread dissatisfaction has also been expressed over Skinner's explanation of creativity. Many psychologists who admit that reinforcement, nonreinforcement, and punishment can affect whether a person retains or drops a given behavior also feel that Skinner avoids the problem of how the behavior got started in the first place. Where does a new or unique behavior come from? It is proper just to call the pigeon's marching and pecking about the cage *random behavior* without accounting for why the pigeon marches and pecks rather than skates and coughs? How does a brilliant symphony or novel or scientific theory arise? Any psychologist who gives more credit to unobservable thinking behavior—to cognitive activity—can claim that Skinner's few principles of conditioning fail to offer an adequate explanation of innovative or creative acts.

In addition to the foregoing technical objections to radical behaviorism, other critics have, on humane or religious grounds, reacted against Skinner's views. Such criticism is based on a feeling that "it just doesn't seem right" that life operates on the basis of Skinnerian principles. D. B. Stevick, speaking from a Christian perspective, concluded about *Walden Two* that:

> Behavioral engineering rules out the risk and the achievement of freedom, love, self-giving, commitment, self-discipline, loyalty, memory, creativity, and hope. The significance of politics, the integrity of art, the warmth and support of human intimacy—all are lost. . . . The most precious thing about man is his humanity. Walden Two commends its deliberate abandonment (1968, p. 28).

In response to such a charge, Skinner would probably reply that, like it or not, radical behaviorism simply describes the truth about why people act as they do.

Because I believe there is some validity to these criticisms, yet feel the theory still has great virtues, I have marked it slightly above the center on items 1, 3, and 6. And in terms of its overall self-satisfying quality (item 9), I have rated the theory just below the top position.

FOR FURTHER READING

Skinner, B. F. (1974) *About Behaviorism.* New York: Knopf. This is an up-to-date, highly readable overview of radical behaviorism.

Skinner, B. F. (1972) *Cumulative Record: A Selection of Papers.* 3d ed. New York: Appleton-Century-Crofts. Representative articles from various stages of Skinner's career.

For Bijou and Baer's overall scheme, see:

Bijou, Sidney W., and Donald M. Baer. (1961) *Child Development: Vol. I. A Systematic and Empirical Theory.* New York: Appleton-Century-Crofts.

For a detailed analysis of the first stage of development, see:

Bijou, Sidney W., and Donald M. Baer. (1965). *Child Development II: Universal Stage of Infancy.* New York: Appleton-Century-Crofts.

A detailed account of the second stage appears in:

Bijou, Sidney W. (1976) *Child Development: The Basic Stage of Early Childhood.* Englewood Cliffs, N.J.: Prentice-Hall.

CHAPTER FIFTEEN

Social Learning Theory

Some writers have found it useful to distinguish between S-R and S-O-R behaviorists (Woodworth, 1929). The S-R designation identifies behaviorists who focus on observable stimuli (S) and responses (R) without proposing what might be happening inside the person between the S and the R. In contrast, the S-O-R symbol designates behaviorists who are willing to speculate about what occurs within the organism (O) to transpose a stimulus into a response. Different theorists refer to the O function in different ways. Some call it *intervening variables,* some call it *thinking,* and others call it *information processing.*

In terms of these distinctions, both John B. Watson and B. F. Skinner belong in the S-R camp. However, most modern behaviorists better qualify as S-O-R adherents, with many of them belonging in the subgroup of social learning theorists.

Social learning theory gets its name from the emphasis it places on social variables as determinants of behavior and personality. It proposes to correct an overdependence of earlier behaviorism on principles derived mostly from studies of animal learning and of human learning in one-person experiments. Social learning theorists attempt to correct this earlier bias by basing many of their principles on studies of the interaction of two or more people.

The social learning movement has sought to offer both (1) a balanced synthesis of mentalism (which is known today as *cognitive psychology*) and the principles of behavior modification and (2) an analysis of social influences on human development. E. R. Hilgard and G. H. Bower (1975, p. 599) have called this movement "a selective distillation of what is probably a 'consensus' position of moderation on many issues of importance to any theory of learning and behavior modification."

In Chapter Fifteen I include discussions of some important contributions to social learning theory, especially those of Albert Bandura. The models of development proposed are properly considered variants of behaviorism because each theorist subscribes to many of the basic principles found in the formulations of Skinner and other behaviorists. But each also holds some beliefs that can be considered alterations of, or extensions of, the operant conditioning we considered in Chapter Fourteen. Instead of repeating in the present chapter the aspects of agreement among these investigators—such as the nature of operant conditioning and of reinforcement—we will focus only on the variations to behaviorism that they have contributed.

CONTRIBUTIONS BY BANDURA

Although Albert Bandura (born 1925), a Stanford University psychologist, shares many basic convictions with nearly all other behaviorists, he disagrees with traditional S-R theorists on the role of imitation in personality development. Among the areas in which Bandura's position differs from that of such radical behaviorists as Skinner, four are of particular importance: (1) the way a child acquires a new behavior that the child has never attempted before (an area Skinnerians have difficulty explaining), (2) the key steps involved in the process of learning from models, (3) the way that consequences (reinforcement, punishment) influence future actions, and (4) the development of complex behaviors.

The Origin of New Behavior

According to a commonly held S-R view, a child learns such things as language by first babbling a variety of sounds and then having certain of these sounds rewarded by people around her because the sounds approximate words they use. When the child happens to say *dah* or *ee* or *kee*, she is rewarded with smiles and caresses since the sounds have been uttered in the presence of *daddy, eating,* and *kitty.* When such events occur on several occasions, the sounds become conditioned to the objects they represent in the language of that particular culture. Although such a lucky coincidence between sounds and objects might account for children acquiring some simple words, Bandura and other social learning advocates find it inconceivable that this fortuitous process produces the thousands of words and the complex syntax and grammar that the child has mastered by the time she enters school.

In contrast, social learning theorists propose that most of a child's learning comes from his actively *imitating* or *modeling* what he sees and hears other people say and do. Bandura uses the word *modeling*—along with such terms as *observational learning* and *vicarious learning*—to mean that the child adds to his repertoire of actions by seeing or hearing someone else perform the behavior rather than by overtly carrying out the behavior himself (Bandura, 1969, pp. 118–120). So in the social learning theorist's opinion, children's new actions are not simply spontaneous and random hit-or-miss behaviors, with the hits being learned because they are reinforced. Instead, children seek to reproduce what they observe. In some cases this is *one-trial learning*. The first attempt is perfect. In other cases, the first attempt only approximates the desired action, and so requires *shaping* through more refined attempts before the child achieves a level of behavior considered satisfactory by the reinforcing agents in his environment.

Some theorists agree with the importance of imitation but feel that the process only operates when the child's attempts are directly reinforced as she reproduces an observed action. However, Bandura and other social learning investigators have produced evidence to support the belief that a child will also learn when the reinforcement is only vicarious. When six-year-old James observes six-year-old Henry being rewarded for saying "please" in order to get something he wants from the teacher, James learns to say "please" in similar circumstances.

People who have spent much time around children are not likely to consider this idea that children imitate others to be a discovery of cosmic dimensions. It seems to be pretty much common sense. Parents, teachers, coaches, and police commonly use principles of modeling to instruct children in how to add a new learning to their array of skills and knowledge. This sort of instruction is reflected in such phrases as "Try it this way" or "Let me show you" or "I'll tell you how to do it" or "Just read the directions." But more controversial and less obvious than these aspects of imitation is the role of *incidental learning*.

The issue of incidental learning has long been a topic of debate among learning theorists. The question at the center of the debate is this: Can a person learn something he sees or hears if this thing does not fulfill a need he is currently seeking to satisfy or if he is not rewarded for learning it? Many theorists say the answer is no. They claim that a person learns only those things that meet a need he is currently seeking to satisfy. Other things in the environment that are not pertinent to fulfilling the present need are passed by and not learned. And many theorists claim that reinforcement or reward is required for learning. Without reinforcement, either direct or vicarious, the child does not acquire a new skill or knowledge. (See the summary of latent-learning studies in Hilgard & Bower, 1975, pp. 134–136.)

However, Bandura and other social learning advocates have conducted experiments that suggest that the answer to the incidental-learning question is yes, at least in some cases. Children who are not seeking to satisfy any apparent need and who are not rewarded by a current happening may actually learn from the experience, storing in memory the results of their incidental observation for use at some later, appropriate time. According to Bandura, the error made by psychologists who do not admit to such incidental learning has been their confusing learning with performance. Since children who were not reinforced for a given act in experiments did not perform that act, it was assumed that without reinforcement, vicarious or direct, there had been no learning. But Bandura's evidence has supported the belief that people do not overtly display many things they have learned from a model if these things do not appear to yield sufficient rewards in the situation at hand. In other words, social learning theorists assume that for a given life situation, each of us has a series of possible reactions we might display. We have several answers we might give to the question being posed. However, in this multiple-choice situation, all answers are not equally plausible. Some seem better than others, and those better answers are the only ones we exhibit publicly, so other people do not realize that we have learned additional possible answers as well.

Bandura, then, contends that children do not just happen to hit on a new sort of behavior that is then reinforced; instead, he says, children acquire new behaviors by observing models in their environment. But what about the child's *creating* a novel behavior that she has not even seen before? How does this come about? Again, radical behaviorists seem to consider such novel acts accidental or built up in some way from small links of behaviors already carried out. But the social learning theorist of Bandura's persuasion accounts for novel acts by concluding that:

> When exposed to diverse models, observers rarely pattern their behavior exclusively after a single source, nor do they adopt all the attributes even of preferred models. Rather, observers combine aspects of various models into new amalgams that differ from the individual sources. . . . Different observers adopt different combinations of characteristics (Bandura, 1977, p. 48).

So from the social learning viewpoint, novel behavior results from the child's combining different segments of various behaviors he has observed in other people, with the observation including both direct witnessing of events and such indirect modes of securing examples as reading or hearing about ideas and actions.

The Process of Learning from Models

How observational learning takes place is far from completely understood. However, some of the conditions that influence it have been identified. According to Bandura, the main reason a child learns from seeing or hearing a model is that the information she thereby acquires helps her decide how the observed behavior might help or hinder her in fulfilling her needs on some future occasion. This information is stored in the memory in symbolic form, as images or as verbal symbols, for future reference.

This process of learning from models consists of five main functions: (1) paying *attention*, (2) *coding* for memory, (3) *retaining* in memory, and (4) *carrying out motor actions*—and all four of these steps require (5) *motivation* (Bandura, 1977, pp. 22–29).

First, when a child observes a model, the child must *attend to the pertinent clues* in the stimulus situation and ignore the aspects of the model and the environment that are incidental and don't affect the performance that the child seeks to learn. The child's failure to perform the behavior properly later, especially if the behavior has been complex, is often due to his misdirecting his attention at the time the model was observed. Teachers frequently try to prevent this error by eliminating as many of the irrelevant stimuli from the setting as possible and by verbally directing the child's attention to those aspects of the model's performance that are most important.

A second requirement for imitative learning is that the child accurately record in memory a *visual image* or *semantic code* for the act she has witnessed. Without an adequate coding system, the child fails to store what she has seen or heard. There are obvious developmental trends in the ability to profit from models. Older children learn more readily from witnessing others' performances than do younger children. This superiority of older children is due in large part to their more advanced ability to use symbols. Bandura points out (1977, p. 30) that the infant's use of modeling is confined mainly to instantaneous imitation. The very young child will imitate the adult's gesture or word immediately instead of reproducing it after a period of time. But as the child grows up and has more experience in associating words or images with objects and events, she can store these symbols in order to recall and reproduce the events after increasingly extended periods of time. In effect, the development of language and of schemes for coding observations enhances the child's ability to profit from models. Not only must the observations be coded for memory (the input portion), but the codes must be suitable for transforming the perceptions into overt actions (the output portion). Otherwise the child ends up with useless knowledge, symbols that have been stored but cannot be retrieved in a form that leads to action.

A third factor influencing whether the knowledge will be available when needed is that of *memory permanence.* Although the operation of memory is still poorly understood by psychologists, one thing is clear—memories fade or disappear with time. Therefore much that children learn from observing models is forgotten, so that such learning is no longer available when the child needs it to solve some problem in life (Bandura, 1969, p. 202). Such memory-aiding techniques as rehearsal (review or practice) and attaching multiple codes to an event (associating a variety of interlinked words or images with the event) serve to keep the stored information at a level that makes it readily retrieved when needed.

A fourth factor influencing the success of learning from models is that of *reproducing* the observed motor activities accurately. It is not enough that the observer get the *idea* of the actions to perform or that he code and store the idea adequately, it is also necessary for him to get the motor behavior, the muscular *feel* of the behavior. He usually cannot do this perfectly on the first trial. Thus he needs a number of trials in which he approximates the behavior and then receives feedback from this experience to correct the deviations from the ideal that his earlier attempts have involved. It should be apparent that developmental trends in learning efficiency are partially a result of the older child's greater muscular strength and control in comparison to that of the younger child. Even if the younger child could attend properly to the cues of the observed performance and could encode the observations mentally as images or verbal symbols, the younger child still would not perform the modeled activities as well because his muscular development is not as advanced as the older child's.

The fifth requirement in the process of learning from models is that the learner be *motivated* to carry through the several steps of the process. In the behaviorist tradition, this motivational function has been embedded in the crucial role of the *consequences of behavior.* Since the interpretation that Bandura and other present-day social learning theorists place on the function of consequences differs from that of radical behaviorists like Skinner, we need to pay special attention to this aspect of the learning process.

The Role of Consequences

According to Skinner's theory of operant conditioning, in a given stimulus situation a person has a series of likely responses she might give. Which response will actually be given depends upon the comparative strengths of the competing responses in the individual's repertoire of responses. In addition, the strength of a potential response depends on how often that response has been reinforced in the past when the individual has been in a similar situation, that is, when she has faced what she considers a similar problem. In the opinion of radical behaviorists, this strengthening of response tendencies through reinforcement is automatic. When a person's actions are reinforced or rewarded, it is not necessary for her consciously to tell herself, "That worked out well, so I'll try it again in the future." Instead, the strengthening of the response simply comes about without the need for the individual to assess the effect of her behavior. Furthermore, the typical adherent of operant conditioning believes that in order for this automatic strengthening to be most effective, the consequence (reinforcement or reward) must occur as soon as possible after the act so that the two become intimately connected or "conditioned."

However, Bandura disagrees with this interpretation of how consequences influence subsequent behavior.

> Although the issue is not yet completely resolved, there is little evidence that reinforcers function as automatic shapers of human conduct. . . . A vast amount of evidence lends validity to the view that reinforcement serves principally as an informative and motivational operation rather than as a mechanical response strengthener (Bandura, 1977, p. 21).

By *informative* Bandura means that the consequences, rewarding or punishing, tell the child under what circumstances it would seem wise to try a particular behavior in the future. In other words, the consequences improve the child's prediction of whether a given act will likely lead to pleasant or unpleasant outcomes on a later occasion. Bandura does not believe, as radical behaviorists do, that a consequence exerts its influence in reverse chronology, strengthening the behavior that preceded the rewarding consequence. Rather, he contends that the consequence exerts its influence into the future by giving the child information about what effects he can expect if he later acts that same way in a similar stimulus circumstance. By adopting such an interpretation, Bandura feels that he places himself in a better position to account for children learning from models than are the radical behaviorists who propose that consequences automatically reinforce the preceding actions that the individual carried out. That is, Bandura points out that the child can learn from observing others as well as from behaving himself, since watching others can give him the same information he gets from his own behavior consequences if he attends to the significant elements of the observed action.

When Bandura speaks of the *motivational* role of consequences, he means that children will more likely try to learn modeled behavior if they value the consequences the behavior seems to produce. If a pupil yearns for the teacher's approval and observes that the teacher gives such approval to children who spell well, then she is motivated to pay attention to the week's spelling words and to rehearse them so they are well stored in memory.

In summary, then, Bandura does not believe that consequences reinforce responses automatically and strengthen the response that immediately preceded the consequences. Instead, he sees consequences as *regulators* of future behavior—they regulate by means of giving the individual information about likely future consequences and by motivating her to act in one way rather than another in order to obtain the results she seeks.

Complex Behaviors

Not only do Bandura's ideas about modeling differ from those of radical or methodological behaviorists, but his beliefs about how complex behaviors are acquired differ as well. Contrary to more traditional behaviorists, he does not believe a child develops complex behaviors by first imitating one small element of the observed pattern and then gradually building up the entire pattern through a step-by-step accrual of successive elements. Rather, he says that:

> Patterns of behavior are typically acquired in large segments or in their entirety rather than through a slow, gradual process based on differential reinforcement. Following demonstrations by a model, or (though to a lesser extent) following verbal descriptions of desired behavior, the learner generally reproduces more or less the entire response pattern, even though he may perform no overt response, and consequently receive no reinforcement, throughout the demonstration period (Bandura & Walters, 1963, p. 106).

However, once the new behavior has been comprehended through observation, the likelihood that it will be displayed in the child's personality is governed chiefly by schedules of reinforcement and punishment.

A final aspect of imitation learning that is important in Bandura's system is *the nature of the models*. Experimental studies support the common-sense notion of hero worship in the following ways: (1) Children are more likely to model their own behavior after the actions of people they regard as prestigious than after actions of people who are not highly regarded. (2) Children are more likely to adopt behavior patterns from models of their own sex than from the opposite sex. (3) Models who receive rewards, such as money, fame, high socioeconomic status, are more often copied than ones who do not. (4) People who are punished for their behavior tend not to be imitated. (5) Children are more influenced by models they perceive to be similar to themselves, such as in age or social status, than by models they see as being quite different from themselves (Bandura & Walters, 1963, pp. 10–11, 50, 84, 94–100).

In summary, imitation is viewed by Bandura as a major device in children's social development, for through the observation of models, children add new options to their repertoire of possible behaviors. Furthermore, models help children decide under what circumstances they can most profitably put these new options into practice.

From Bandura's social learning perspective we can conceive of child development as a process (1) of the child's gradually expanding his repertoire of answers or possible actions by means of both observing others and trying the actions himself and (2) of the child's using information from the observed consequences to guide future decisions about when one response will be more appropriate than another to fulfill needs and attain rewards. Like Skinner, Bandura does not separate development into a series of stages, but he considers the process of cognitive and social growth to be one of gradual accrual of an ever widening array of response possibilities for increasingly differentiated stimulus situations.

With Bandura's views of the importance of observational learning in mind, let us turn to a currently popular application of social learning theory in the treatment of deviant behavior.

Normality and Deviance

In putting his model of development to practical use, Bandura has centered attention on psychotherapy and the correction of antisocial behavior. His technique of treating deviance does not take the form of curing mental disorders or of alleviating the underlying causes of mental disease, as has been the case in traditional psychiatric practice. Instead, he has rejected the medical concept of deviance, the concept that the person exhibiting the undesired behavior is sick and that this mental condition must be treated to make him well. In place of this belief about curing illness, Bandura advocates what has been termed *behavior modification,* because he is convinced that an act that "is harmful to the individual or departs widely from accepted social and ethical norms" is not symptomatic of some disease but is simply "a way that the individual has learned to cope with environmental and self-imposed demands. Treatment then becomes mainly a problem in social learning rather than one in the medical domain" (Bandura, 1969, p. 10).

In keeping with this viewpoint, Bandura would treat a child who displays undesirable social behavior by manipulating the consequences of the child's acts so that the child finds it more rewarding to adopt more acceptable behavior than to continue in the currently unacceptable pattern. By extrapolating principles from Bandura's discussion, we can summarize the process of carrying out behavior modification in four basic steps:

1. Identify the specific behavior you wish to have the child substitute for the presently unacceptable behavior.

2. Arrange for the child to try out this new, desirable behavior. There are several ways this can be done: simply wait for it to occur spontaneously, provide a model, verbally explain what the desired behavior is, shape it through gradual approximations, or use several of these techniques.

3. Determine what sorts of consequences will be strongly reinforcing or rewarding to the child and what sorts will be punishing.

4. Manipulate consequences so that the desired behavior, when it appears, will yield greater reinforcement than does the undesirable behavior. In other words, arrange a schedule of reinforcement and/or punishment that will make it profitable for the child to give up the old behavior in favor of the new.

Although this process is easy to outline, it is often difficult to carry out in practice. However, such behavior modification is conceived by social learning theorists to be the most effective means of correcting a child's deviant acts.

Critics of behavior modification have charged that it is a naive, superficial approach to psychotherapy or personality improvement. They claim that seeking to change the child's overt actions directly fails to get at the underlying cause. Such criticism is based on the view that overt behaviors, such as thumb sucking, temper tantrums, or stealing, are just surface symptoms of an underlying disorder that lies deep in the personality, probably in the unconscious. Bandura, in reacting to such charges, says that both psychodynamic and social learning theorists are seeking underlying causes. However, the two camps differ in where they believe these causes lie.

Psychoanalysts propose that the causes are repressed conflicts left over in the unconscious from the child's failing to solve the conflicts faced during earlier psychosexual stages of development. Therefore the therapist digs into the patient's psyche to identify which events in the past produced the conflicts, and then seeks to help the patient consciously relive these events and put them into a mentally healthy perspective. Such analysis, say the psychodynamic therapists, frees the patient from her symptoms of deviance, and the personality disorder is cured.

In contrast to this psychodynamic view, social learning therapists hunt for "underlying causes" in the child's present environment. For the social learning theorist, the term *cause* refers to the satisfying consequences that the child's deviant behavior continues to bring him. The child's regrettable behavior persists because it pays off or because he does not know any other way to behave that will bring him more satisfactory consequences. The task of the therapist, then, becomes that of carrying out the four steps of behavior modification.

In both psychodynamic and social learning theories it is possible to "simply treat the symptom" without getting at the "real cause." However, the meaning of this phrase is quite different under the two theories. With the typical psychodynamic approach, "simply treating the symptom" usually means punishing or rewarding the child so she will stop sucking her thumb in school or will stop stealing objects from her classmates' desks. Or it could mean giving the child a posthypnotic suggestion to avoid thumb sucking or stealing. However, in the psychodynamic view, such treatment only suppresses the particular symptom on which the treatment has focused. And because the underlying causes—repressed conflicts—have not been touched, other symptoms will arise.

In social learning theory "simply treating the symptom" is a phrase interpreted to mean that the therapist has been too narrow in her perception of the number of different situations in which the child's deviant response is used. For instance, a ten-year-old boy throws temper tantrums at home, around the neighborhood, in the classroom, and on the playground when things do not go his way. According to social learning theorists as well as other behaviorists, this pattern of action is maintained because people ultimately yield to the boy's demands in order to "avoid all that fuss." To solve the problem, the teacher may seek to eliminate the tantrums in class (1) by not reinforcing them, (2) by helping the boy observe models who use such techniques as reasoning or discussion instead of tantrums to get their way, and (3) by rewarding the boy's attempts to use these more mature techniques. However, while the undesirable behavior may be reduced in school, it may persist at home, around the neighborhood, and on the playground because the consequences in these out-of-class settings have not been altered. Critics of the behaviorists' reinforcement and punishment approach may charge that the classroom treatment of the problem was just getting at the symptoms but not the cause. But the social learning theorist can reply that if the consequences in all four environments—classroom, home, neighborhood, and playground—were altered, the tantrums would disappear entirely, and the problem would be cured.

However, another difficulty may arise to cause Freudians and their psychodynamic colleagues to continue to criticize the behaviorists' approach. It is possible that the tantrums will disappear in all settings, but the new behavior that is substituted may also be deviant. For example, the boy, when he fails to get his way by tantrums, may withdraw from the classroom group and sit brooding. The psychodynamic therapist can now claim that this is simply *symptom substitution,* that one sort of deviance has replaced another because the real unconscious cause was not unearthed and resolved. The social learning therapist will disagree. He will likely say that for any given stimulus situation the ten-year-old has learned a hierarchy of possible responses. The most powerful of these at the top of his hierarchy of appropriateness has been the temper tantrum. If the consequences are altered so such behavior does not pay off for the child, then he can be expected to turn to the next most promising option in his strata of habits. By *promising* I mean the response he has observed or personally tried out that he estimates will bring the most satisfying results in such stimulus situations. Often this second most likely response is also considered undesirable by the important people in his life. So if withdrawal and brooding is the second choice among his options, the social behavior problem is not solved. He is still labeled a problem child.

According to social learning theorists, this is not a problem of symptom substitution, however; it is a problem of the child's having a response hierarchy whose most promising options (that is, promising in the boy's estimation) are all undesirable ones for the society in which he lives. Therapy does not consist of hunting for an unconscious cause. Rather, it consists of helping the boy learn a new, socially approved behavior that is so rewarding that it takes priority over all of the undesirable responses in his repertoire of likely reactions to frustration, both in school and out (Bandura, 1969, pp. 48–52).

As implied, Bandura subscribes to a *reference-group* interpretation of normality and deviance. A child is normal or abnormal only in terms of how her behavior compares to the behavior of other members of a designated group. This reference group might be Catholics, American ten-year-olds, upper-class children, Central Elementary School fifth graders, or any other group. It should be apparent that a child might be considered normal when compared to one group but deviant when compared to another. Hence, when the question of normality arises, it is important to identify the reference group to be used in answering the question.

This matter of reference groups is important not only for determining normality or deviance in a child's development but also for understanding why attempts at behavior modification may fail. Consider a junior high school boy who steals money and equipment from his classmates and from the teacher. School authorities consider this behavior undesirable, so they seek to change it by altering its consequences. They punish the boy by keeping him after school, and they offer him special privileges if he will go for a period of one month without stealing anything. But he continues to steal, and this puzzles the teacher and principal, for it is apparently contrary to social learning principles. But, in the eyes of the social learning theorist, they have simply failed to realize that the boy is still being reinforced for stealing. He persists in his deviant act because he continues to be rewarded by his own preferred reference group, by his gang of delinquent peers whose approval he values more than that of school authorities. Consequently, deviant behavior cannot be understood or altered without our recognizing that various groups' norms are often in conflict with each other and that the rewards dispensed by one group are more influential than those dispensed by another because the child values the first group more. This means that we need to identify which reference groups or individuals serve as the most valued ones in the child's life.

Finally, social learning theory discourages the application of such traditional psychiatric labels as *neurosis* and *psychopathic personality* to children exhibiting antisocial behavior. These children are not considered diseased or mentally deranged. The cause of their deviance, whether it appears to be harmful to themselves or to be contrary to social norms, is not to be found by use of special medical terms or principles. Instead, social learning theorists contend that "a single set of social learning principles can account for the development of both prosocial and deviant behavior and for modifications of behavior toward greater conformity or greater deviation" (Bandura & Walters, 1963, p. 221). Thus treatment of the child consists of altering the consequences the environment provides for the undesired behavior. It does not consist of searching in the depths of the child's psyche for psychosexual or psychosocial conflicts.

Conscience and Self-Control

In social learning theory a child's conscience or moral values are not inborn. The infant arrives in the world amoral. Then, by the same modeling and conditioning principles that produce all of her other beliefs, she gradually acquires her values and a capacity for self-control and self-direction. In other words, her character is learned, not inherited.

Investigations cited by Bandura support his contention that the development of self-control or conscience is heavily influenced by the models children observe and by patterns of direct reinforcement that they encounter, such as disciplinary measures used by parents and teachers. The degree to which a child will resist temptations has been most readily affected in experimental situations by how immediately the model in the situation is rewarded or punished. The characteristics of the model also influence how likely it is that the child will adopt the modeled self-control or lack of it, with the greatest influence exerted by models who are capable, successful, and prestigious.

The timing of reward and punishment is also important. Bandura suggests that many parents mold a child's conscience—meaning his guilt feelings or self-punishing tendencies—more successfully by withholding privileges than by applying aversive stimuli such as a spanking or isolation. He believes that the frequent superiority of withholding or withdrawing positive reinforcers over applying aversive measures is to a great extent the result of timing. Typically, the parent withholds the reinforcer until the child expresses guilt or some self-punishment response. Then the privilege or desired object is restored to the child. But "parents on most occasions administer aversive stimuli some time after a deviation has occurred and fail to make its termination contingent on the child's expressing self-punitive responses" (Bandura & Walters, 1963, p. 221). As a result of the postponed punishment and the indefiniteness of the time to remove the punishment, the child is less likely to adopt the self-control standards the parent desires. Studies have also suggested that the withholding of privileges serves most effectively to develop the child's self-control if the agents who withhold the rewards and subsequently reinstate them are warm, affectionate people rather than unaffectionate people or people who hold a grudge (Bandura & Walters, 1963, pp. 197–199).

Next we consider the work of another neobehaviorist or social learning theorist, Robert Sears, whose studies of imitative behavior preceded those of Bandura.

CONTRIBUTIONS BY SEARS

Between 1945 and 1965, several prominent neobehaviorists recast Freudian ideas into behavioristic terms. John Dollard and Neal E. Miller, two Yale University psychologists, first did this in a 1950 volume entitled *Personality and Psychotherapy*. In this work they explained how neobehaviorist learning theory could account for child-growth patterns that had been postulated in Freud's psychosexual stages.

Later, Robert R. Sears (born 1908), a former Yale professor who moved to the University of Iowa, to Harvard, and then to Stanford, directed several major research projects aimed at investigating the role that various Freudian concepts play in child development. Sear's overall theory is complex and tightly argued within a social learning framework, and its entire structure is worthy of study. (See Maier, 1978, for a summary of the theory.) However, for our present purposes we will consider only an aspect that illustrates the manner in which Sears fits a Freudian proposal into a neobehaviorist model of learning. This aspect is the role that the adjustment mechanism of *identification* assumes in the child's social development.

As Sears has explained, his research has not been aimed at verifying psychoanalytic concepts. Instead, it has been designed as

> a testing of a behavioral theory that was suggested by psychoanalytic observations and was then constructed within the framework of an entirely different theoretical structure. The hypotheses we have proposed . . . are independent of and in some instances irrelevant to psychoanalytic formulations of the theories of identification (Sears, Rau, & Alpert, 1965, p. 242).

Like other behaviorists, Sears believes that the consequences of children's behavior determine which characteristics they will acquire from the environment. However, as Sears and others have observed, many, perhaps most, of the ways that children become like their parents have not been the result of conscious, consistent parental instruction. But if parents do not consciously reinforce and punish behaviors in order to mold children's actions into a pattern acceptable to the culture, how then do children acquire such behaviors and traits? One answer is that children do it spontaneously through identification, that is, through following a model. When identification is interpreted according to an S-O-R paradigm, the assumption can be made that identification is an intermediary process between the S and the R that, "very early in life, enables the child to *learn* without the parents having to *teach*, and which creates a *self-reinforcing mechanism* that competes effectively in some instances with external sources of reinforcement" (Sears, Rau, & Alpert, 1965, p. 2).

To account for the idea that the child reinforces herself for patterning her behavior after a parent, Sears proposed that the infant initially depends on the mother for nearly all gratification of needs. Later, other needs may be satisfied by the father and other members of the family. In effect, the child acquires a dependency relationship to her parents. But as the child matures, the busy parents have less time for meeting the child's needs. To make up for this loss, the child, by means of some unexplained process, begins to imitate the parent. As a result of this modeling of the person she has depended on for satisfaction, the child finds that her imitative behavior furnishes some of the same satisfactions or reinforcement earlier supplied by the parent. In this way, identification or imitating the parent enables the child to become self-reinforcing.

Once Sears and his colleagues thus cast Freud's identification into a behavioristic paradigm, they were able to derive a series of hypotheses about how different sorts of parents might affect their children through the models they provided. These hypotheses were then tested through the study of child-rearing practices in several score of American families. At the end of the investigation, Sears concluded that the hypotheses were at least partially supported by the data. However, a number of puzzling questions were still unanswered, leaving the team of psychologists in the typical position of the investigator at the close of any study—the position of concluding that more research is necessary.

THE KENDLERS' DEVELOPMENTAL-MEDIATION THEORY

For more than two decades the husband-and-wife team of Howard H. Kendler (born 1919) and Tracy S. Kendler (born 1918) of the University of California at Santa Barbara have been evolving a theory of how children learn to distinguish likenesses and differences among things in their environment. The Kendlers' work illustrates the way neobehaviorists employ what they call a *hypothetico-deductive* approach to building theory through formulating hypotheses and then experimentally testing them.

The Kendlers began with some discrimination-learning experiments that other psychologists had conducted, experiments that led to conflicting interpretations about how such learning occurs. Over the years the Kendlers have carried out their own experiments in an attempt to resolve this conflict and other puzzles that have continually arisen in their own and others' studies.

Before describing the Kendlers' main conclusions, let's examine what discrimination experiments involve. A typical, simple experiment requires the subjects (rats, monkeys, children, college students) to figure out which of two choices is the correct one. The problem may involve a white rat having to decide which of two alleys of a maze leads to food, when one alley is marked with a black circle and the other with a white circle. By a succession of tries over a series of days, the rat learns that the white-circle alley leads to food, whether the circle is over the left or right alley.

Discrimination problems can be made more complex if two dimensions are included among the stimuli—for example, both brightness and shape. Now the rat must learn that it is brightness (white) and not shape (a circle contrasted to a square) that discriminates between the food alley and the no-food alley.

The task can be made even more difficult if, after the subjects have learned the correct response fairly well, the experimenter shifts the rule in the middle of the game. The correct answer can be reversed *(reversal shift)*, making black the food alley, or the answer can be shifted to the other dimension *(extradimensional shift)*, making the square figure the correct answer, whether the square is white or black.

Psychologists have exposed many facets of such discrimination-learning situations by altering the stimulus characteristics, by shifting the rules, and by using different sorts of subjects (rats, pigeons, monkeys, children, college students). By observing the results of the manipulations, neobehaviorists have been able to create theories to explain what underlies discrimination learning. From their theories, scientists are then able to produce new hypotheses and to estimate (deduce) what should happen if they conduct another experiment designed to test a particular issue that remains unresolved. The scientist reasons, "If my theory is correct, then I should be able to pose this new sort of discrimination task and the subjects should respond in this predicted way." By carrying out the new experiment, the scientist learns whether the prediction has been accurate and thereby confirms the theory, or whether the results are at odds with his expectation so that he needs to readjust the theory. This process is the hypothetico-deductive approach to theory construction.

The Kendlers' work deserves a place in a child development book because their studies have been conducted with children and college students rather than with animals. Children receive rewards for correctly discriminating among pictures of shapes, sizes, and colors or pictures of animals, vehicles, and toys. From their experiments the Kendlers have concluded that very young children learn to discriminate in about the same fashion as nonhumans, that is, rats, pigeons, and monkeys. Young children draw their conclusions directly from the characteristics they see in the stimuli, the size or shape or color. But when they reach kindergarten or the early primary grades, their discriminations begin to be *mediated* by concepts. In general terms this means that the child develops concepts or mental symbols as mediators, which she manipulates in arriving at decisions instead of reacting directly to the discrimination stimuli. This mediator or "idea" may be either verbal (a label for an object—*circle, green, small*) or nonverbal. The Kendlers have concluded that the skill of discriminating likenesses and differences among things in the world develops through two main stages—an early direct-reaction stage and a later mediation stage. (These findings clearly parallel those of Piaget and Vygotsky.)

Theories like the Kendlers' are never complete. They are always tentative estimates of relationships, estimates that continually undergo refinement and expansion through hypothesis and experiment. They often move in new directions. For example, the Kendlers have begun investigating a likely linkage between their results and Feschwind's studies of brain neurology (Kendler & Kendler, 1975, pp. 191–247). Trends of development of the brain from lower species to higher ones (phylogeny) and trends in the maturation of an individual child's brain (ontogeny) parallel the stages of discrimination-learning in the Kendlers' mediation-development model. Thus it appears possible to give a reasonable neurological explanation for the behavioral changes the Kendlers have observed in children's cognitive processes.

PRACTICAL APPLICATIONS

I have already described the basic steps of the behavior modification process as practiced today in many schools and clinics. And, the sorts of educational applications described in Chapter Fourteen for radical behaviorism apply as well to ones deriving from social learning models. There are, though, two examples that illustrate practical applications introduced by psychologists in other parts of the world than North America.

Joseph Wolpe, a South African psychologist, created a method called *reciprocal inhibition,* which is a technique of counterconditioning to eliminate maladaptive fears that interfere with a person's everyday functioning. Wolpe's technique is based on the assumption that a person cannot be relaxed and anxious at the same time because opposite functions of the autonomic nervous and hormonal systems are responsible for these two reactions. Such conflicting functions include lowering versus raising the blood pressure, facilitating versus inhibiting the digestive processes, and preparing the muscles for action versus relaxing the muscles. Wolpe's treatment is designed to induce relaxation while the person is in the presence of the real or imagined fear-producing situation or object (the stimulus). As a consequence, the bond between the stimulus and the habitual anxiety should progressively weaken until the unreasonable fear eventually disappears (Wolpe & Wolpe, 1981).

In England, Hans J. Eysenck became disillusioned with psychoanalysis as a mode of aiding people with psychological problems and developed a form of behavior therapy research derived from learning theory (Eysenck, 1959). His approach, however, contains fewer cognitive components than are typically involved in the recent forms of behavioral therapy.

RESEARCH CHALLENGES

In many ways the research questions evoked by social learning theory are much like those stimulated by behaviorism. But the cognitive elements included in social learning models generate a further array of research questions for developmentalists.

For example, how effective are different types of models in guiding children's behavior at different age levels? What sex differences, if any, exist at different age levels in the kinds of models that most influence children, and what are the causes of such differences? In what ways may parents function as positive models (ones children copy) and negative models (ones children purposely avoid imitating) and why? What is the strength of parents' influence as models as compared to the influence of teachers or peers at different levels of development? How do children at successive age levels differentiate among the models they follow in different facets of life? Or, stated another way, do children at different stages of growth select different models to copy for moral standards or physical appearance than they select for modes of speech, style of social interaction, or vocational and leisure interests, and if so, why? What effect do models have on children's developing creativity (that is, coming up with novel ideas) at successive age levels? How do various forms of modeling effect behavior in different cultures, and why?

In carrying out a behavior modification program in school, what are the best ways to get children at different age levels to try a desired behavior the first time (so the teacher can then reinforce that behavior with a reward)? In other words, what is the comparative effectiveness at different stages of growth of such techniques as (1) the teacher's introducing the desired behavior by means of a demonstration, (2) admired people in films or on television demonstrating the behavior, (3) peers offering a demonstration in class, (4) the teacher giving complete verbal directions, and (5) the child trying out the new behavior after very brief introductory remarks by the teacher?

Among children suffering from psychological adjustment problems, how effective are behavioral therapy approaches as compared with other therapeutic techniques? What are the proper criteria to use in judging whether one technique is superior to another? Is behavior therapy more effective at one age level than another? Is behavior therapy equally effective with intellectually gifted children, with ones of normal abilities, and with ones below average in mental skills, and why or why not?

The above questions, then, indicate a few of the research possibilities the social learning perspective generates.

SOCIAL LEARNING THEORY: AN ASSESSMENT

Since the social learning theorists discussed in this chapter subscribe to many of the same principles considered in Chapter Fourteen, it seems unnecessary to repeat the entire assessment process used to appraise Skinner's radical behaviorism. Instead, I will first discuss the items or scales on which I would give the social learning theorists very similar ratings to those applied to Skinner. Then I will examine those items on which I would rate the social learning theorists somewhat differently than Skinner.

Like Skinner's system, those of the theorists reviewed in the present chapter are clearly described, are falsifiable, lead to suggestions about child-raising practices, and appear to be internally consistent. They also have helped stimulate further discoveries, with Bandura's work perhaps stronger in this respect than that of Sears and the Kendlers.

Compared to Skinner's radical behaviorism, social learning theories are not as subject to the charge of devaluing mental activity. And unlike Skinner, social learning theorists have accorded a prominent place to the function of imitation in personality development. Furthermore, Bandura, Sears, and the Kendlers have conducted their own research on people, particularly on children, rather than on animals, thus avoiding the criticism directed at Skinner that he has drawn simplistic conclusions about human development by founding many of his principles on conditioning experiments with pigeons and rats. For all of these reasons, I would rate the social learning theorists somewhat higher than Skinner on how well they reflect the real world of children and explain the past and predict the future.

I would also give social learning theory a higher rating on economy of explanation (item 6) because the versions of the theory that we have inspected in Chapter Fifteen appear to suffer less from the charge of being overparsimonious than Skinner's behaviorism.

Despite this array of strengths, however, social learning theory has not been universally adopted by people concerned with explaining children's development. Parents and teachers who seek information about what children are like at different age levels receive no aid from the social learning model, for it describes *how* children learn rather than *what they are like* at different stages of their lives. This criticism is more true of Bandura's work than that of Sears and the Kendlers, who have indeed included some description of child characteristics at levels of development.

A developmentalist who sees a child's genetic endowment and the influence of internal maturation as prime factors behind child growth may also find fault with social learning theorists' slighting of hereditary influences on development.

Finally, all behaviorist approaches, social learning theory included, have been criticized for giving too little recognition to how a child thinks and feels about himself. A developing child, critics have claimed, is not just an animated mechanism to be programmed to suit the desires of agents that control his environment. Rather, in the opinion of humanistic critics (Chapter Sixteen), a child is a unique personality with hopes and plans and feelings that make up the essence of his or her humanness. Behavioristic approaches appear to overlook this matter.

While social learning theory has not satisfactorily answered all the questions about development posed by other theorists, parents, and teachers, it has come perhaps the closest of any theory to describing how children acquire the learned, rather than the inherited, aspects of their personalities. In comparing it to other learning models, Hilgard and Bower have concluded that:

> Social learning theory provides the best integrative summary of what modern learning theory has to contribute to solutions of practical problems. It also provides a compatible framework within which to place information-processing theories of language comprehension, memory, imagery, and problem solving. . . . For such reasons, social learning theory would appear to be the "consensus" theoretical framework within which much of learning research (especially on humans) will evolve in the next decade (1975, p. 605).

In regard to its overall self-satisfying quality (item 9), I would rate social learning theory higher than Skinner's radical behaviorism.

FOR FURTHER READING

Bandura, Albert. (1969) *Principles of Behavior Modification.* New York: Holt, Rinehart, & Winston.

Bandura, Albert. (1977) *Social Learning Theory.* Englewood Cliffs, N.J.: Prentice-Hall.

Kendler, Howard H., and Tracy S. Kendler. (1975) "Discrimination and Development," in William K. Estes (ed.), *Handbook of Learning and Cognitive Processes.* New York: Halsted. Pp. 191–247.

Maier, Henry W. (1978) *Three Theories of Child Development: Erik H. Erikson, Jean Piaget, and Robert R. Sears.* 3d ed. New York: Harper & Row.

Sears, Robert R., Lucy Rau, and Richard Alpert. (1965) *Identification and Child Rearing.* Stanford, Calif.: Stanford University Press.

PART SEVEN

THE HUMANISTIC APPROACH

A search for the way the innermost self develops

Humanistic psychology can be compared to two realms, with the smaller inside the larger. The smaller one represents a publicly declared movement launched in the United States in 1962 with the formation of the Association of Humanistic Psychology and the initial publication of the *Journal of Humanistic Psychology*. The larger surrounding realm includes not only people who subscribe to the association's tenets, as illustrated in the early pages of Chapter Sixteen, but also other theorists who differ in certain respects from those of the inner circle. While there actually is no precise borderline separating inhabitants of the inner domain from those in the surrounding territory, for purposes of discussion it is convenient to distinguish between the two. The humanistic version of development offered in Chapter Sixteen reflects convictions typical of theorists from both the inner circle and the outer realm. Other versions of a humanistic approach, from both the inner and outer domains, can be found in the writings of Gordon W. Allport, (1961, 1968), Arthur W. Combs and Donald Snygg (1959), Earl C. Kelley (1962), Rollo May (Reeves, 1977), Frederick S. Perls (1951), Carl Rogers (1961, 1973), and other authors who publish in the *Journal of Humanistic Psychology*.

The humanistic approach, in contrast to the behaviorists' practice of analyzing people from the outside, analyzes them from the inside. Introspection becomes the chief humanistic investigative technique, for humanistic psychologists believe that the essence of an individual is found not in her overt acts but in her thoughts and feelings about her personal experience. This inward view of personality has appeared over the centuries in numerous versions, each bearing its own name—humanism, existentialism, phenomenology, and others. Philosophers of a humanist persuasion have stressed a belief in each person's possessing a free will that permits him or

419

her to make choices and display creative powers as an individual. One variety of this viewpoint, created in nineteenth-century Europe under the name *existentialism,* proposed that the reality of life resides in each individual's interpretation of his personal existence. Existentialists have emphasized the importance of a person's fully experiencing each moment of life. In a similar manner, *phenomenologists* have proposed that the "truth" about life is found in experiencing rather than in objective descriptions of people's behavior as measured and tested by the techniques of natural science. A mid-twentieth-century variant of phenomenology appeared in a book entitled *Individual Behavior* by two U. S. psychologists, Combs and Snygg, who accorded prime attention to the *phenomenal self,* meaning the personally recognized "I" or "me."

Humanistic psychologists in their research methodology "do not claim to be 'objective.' They are intent on the discovery of methods within the highly subjective interchange of a relationship which will garner 'personal knowledge' of another human being" (Buhler & Allen, 1972, p. 24). As a result of this viewpoint, other psychologists who regard experimental methods as the best source of information about child growth often believe that humanistic approaches do not qualify as proper theories of development. However, under the broad definition of *theory* adopted in this book, humanistic views can form theories of development, for they furnish answers to most of the questions posed about development in Chapter Two. The humanistic theory described in Chapter Sixteen is a composite version built mainly around beliefs extracted from the writings of Abraham Maslow, Charlotte Buhler, and Alvin R. Mahrer, with the first two authors representing the inner circle of humanistic psychologists and the third representing a position that differs in several ways from the beliefs of the inner group.

The Humanistic Perspectives of Maslow, Buhler, and Mahrer

The movement represented by the creators of the Association of Humanistic Psychology (AHP) in the early 1960s was primarily an attempt to focus attention on the growth of *self*. At the same time, it was a reaction against two current streams of psychological thought and thus was dubbed "a third force" in psychology by a Brandeis University professor, Abraham Maslow (1908–1970).

The two theoretical positions that humanistic psychology rejected were behaviorism and psychoanalysis. Behaviorism was accused of reducing individuals to a system of observable acts and thereby missing such human aspects as people's values, feelings, hopes for the future, choices, and creativity. Behaviorists were charged with neglecting to picture the human being as a unitary person in pursuit of goals and ideals (Maslow, 1968, 1970). Freudian psychoanalysis was accused of adopting a negative model of humanity, of espousing a morbid emphasis on neurotic behavior and of failing to define the nature and path of positive, healthy personality development.

Humanistic psychology, as reflected in the Associations tenets, is marked by:

1. A centering of attention on the experiencing *person*, and thus a focus on *experience* as the primary phenomenon in the study of man. Both theoretical explanations and overt behavior are considered secondary to experience itself and to its meaning to the person.

2. An emphasis on such distinctively *human qualities* as choice, creativity,

valuation, and self-realization, as opposed to thinking about human beings in mechanistic and reductionist terms.

3. An allegiance to *meaningfulness* in the selection of problems for study and of research procedures and an opposition to a primary emphasis on objectivity at the expense of significance.

4. An ultimate *concern with and valuing of the dignity and worth of man* and an interest in the *development of the potential inherent in every person.* Central in this view is the person as he discovers his own being and relates to other persons and to social groups (the AHP brochure).

In effect, humanistic theorists propose a positive, optimistic picture of humans and believe that life "is to be lived subjectively, as it takes place."

Ideas arising within the humanistic movement have not been molded into one system, nor do the beliefs of one theorist always agree with those of others, as this chapter demonstrates. Furthermore, humanistic theory is not specifically a child development theory, for most of its materials focus on adults or speak about the life span in general without distinguishing very clearly between one age period and another. However, from the writings of certain humanistic psychologists it is possible to derive answers to many questions about child development,

Three theorists whose works are particularly useful as sources of such answers are Abraham Maslow, Charlotte Buhler (1893–1974), and Alvin R. Mahrer (born 1927). Maslow was first trained in experimental psychology and psychoanalysis, but he concluded that both of these traditions failed to give proper attention to what he considered the essence of human personality, that is, to a person's sense of *self* and to the immediate experiencing of life. Buhler was a well-known European psychologist who made her first contributions to the child development literature in Austria before establishing her home in the United States. Mahrer, now a professor of psychology at the University of Ottawa in Canada, was raised in the United States by Czech-immigrant parents. He earned a doctorate at Ohio State University before entering private practice as a psychoanalytic therapist and then gradually moved away from psychoanalysis to an existential-humanistic position, which he refers to as *experiential psychotherapy.* His book *Experiencing: A Humanistic Theory of Psychology and Psychiatry* (1978) offers extensive proposals about the process of development. As will be illustrated, Mahrer's views in several respects differ from those of Maslow and Buhler. Mahrer admits that he "cannot feel very much at home with the typical humanistic psychologists."

The topics on which the following discussion is centered include (1) the original nature of the child, (2) the importance of needs and goals, (3) the nature of the self, (4) the directions and stages of development, (5) healthy growth, disease, and deviance, (6) nature and nurture, (7) practical applications, (8) research challenges, and (9) an assessment of the humanistic approach.

THE ORIGINAL NATURE OF THE CHILD

In most versions of humanistic theory the biologically determined inner nature of the human consists of basic needs, emotions, and capacities that are either neutral or positively good. Such "bad" characteristics as destructiveness, cruelty, and malice are not innate, according to Maslow (1968, pp. 3–4), but are "violent reactions *against* frustration of our intrinsic needs, emotions, and capacities. . . . Since this inner nature is good or neutral rather than bad, it is best to bring it out and to encourage it rather than to suppress it. If it is permitted to guide our life, we grow healthy, fruitful, and happy."

Therefore the goal of guiding child development is to foster the expression of the child's inner nature. This task is difficult because the inner essence of the child's personality is not very hardy but, rather, is delicate and easily damaged by unfavorable experiences. Suppressing or distorting the expression of the inner nature causes some degree of sickness, bodily ailment, or behavior deviation that sometimes shows up immediately but other times may surface months or years after the maltreatment. Nevertheless, even when the inner essence is suppressed, it continues to live in the depths of the unconscious, always striving for expression or, in Maslow's language, for *actualization*.

Although Buhler and many other humanistic theorists would agree with Maslow's conception of the child's original nature, Mahrer has offered a different proposal. He claims that it is a *humanist* rather than a *humanistic* belief that "the infant has a basic nature which is inherently free, spontaneous, creative, loving, active, striving, actualizing" (Mahrer, 1978, p. 634). As an alternative to such a notion of inherent human nature, Mahrer has proposed what he regards as a true humanistic concept of the initial state of infancy, a state he labels *primitive personality*. This concept is reminiscent of Lewin's *life space* or *psychological field*, in that the primitive personality is not simply something inside the newborn but rather is composed of (1) the physical characteristics and inner potentials of the infant, (2) the parents' convictions of what an infant should be like, and (3) the relationships that exist between the infant and parents as a result of the parents' ideas of how to treat such an infant (Mahrer, 1978, p. 619). The interaction of these internal and external forces, Mahrer contends, determines what the infant experiences, so the interaction is properly identified as the *primitive personality* or original state of the child.

In summary, the dominant conception among humanistic theorists—and humanists—is that the child's original nature is one of positive striving to actualize an inner essence that is good and constructive. But there are other theorists, such as Mahrer, who also identify themselves as humanistic but who subscribe to a somewhat different view of the initial condition of the child.

HUMAN NEEDS AND GOALS

A key concept to which humanistic psychologists subscribe is that human behavior is motivated primarily by the individual's seeking to fulfill a series of needs. However, not all theorists use the word *needs* to label the internal force they believe drives people to thought and action. Some theorists prefer such terms as *wishes, drives, goals, impulses,* or *potentials* (Mahrer, 1978, pp. 20–23).

To differentiate a humanistic view from the concept of needs in other theories, Maslow distinguished two types. The first he called *deficiency needs.* Examples of this variety are the needs for food, for drink, for a comfortable temperature, for safety from bodily harm, for close love relationships, for respect, and for prestige. He proposed that deficiency needs can be recognized by five objectively observed characteristics of the person and by two subjectively experienced feelings. Objectively, a need for something exists if (1) its absence breeds illness, (2) its presence prevents illness, (3) its restoration cures illness, (4) under certain free choice situations, it is preferred by the deprived person over other satisfactions, and (5) it is found to be inactive, low, or functionally absent in the healthy person. Subjectively, a deficiency need is felt as (6) a conscious or unconscious yearning and desire and (7) a lack or deficiency (Maslow, 1968, p. 22).

Beyond these deficiency needs, which are included in other theories of child development, humanistic psychologists postulate a second cluster called *growth* or *self-actualization* needs. They have had far more trouble in specifying this second group than in identifying deficiencies. Maslow admitted that:

> Growth, individuation, autonomy, self-actualization, self-development, productiveness, self-realization, are all crudely synonymous, designating a vaguely perceived area rather than a sharply defined concept. . . . We just don't know enough about growth yet to be able to define it well (1968, p. 24).

But in an initial attempt at a general definition, Maslow proposed that the self-actualizing need is a striving to realize one's potentials, capacities, and talents; it is a seeking to fulfill a mission or destiny or vocation; it can be a fuller knowledge and acceptance of one's own personality and "an unceasing trend toward unity, integration, or synergy within the person" (Maslow, 1968, p. 26).

The highest stage of growth in humans, then, is the achievement of such self-actualization. Commenting on this highest stage, Buhler and M. Allen (1972, p. 45) have said, "All humanistic psychologists see the goal of life as that of using it to accomplish something in which one believes."

The human needs in Maslow's system, then, form a hierarchy ranging from the most basic physiological deficiency needs at the foundation to the self-actualization needs at the apex. Maslow proposed that the lower needs must be filled before the upper-level needs receive attention. In descending order from the apex, they can be placed in five clusters (Maslow, 1970, pp. 80–89):

1. *Self-actualization need:* doing what one, *individually,* is fitted for: "What a man *can* be, he *must* be. He must be true to his own nature."

2. *Esteem needs:* for self-respect and self-esteem and for the esteem of others.

3. *Belongingness and love needs:* for family, friends, lover; affection, rootedness, intimacy.

4. *Safety needs:* for security and stability, for freedom from fear, anxiety, and chaos. This includes a need for structure, law, and limits.

5. *Physiological needs:* for air, food, drink, rest, fulfilling the appetites, and for achieving balance or homeostasis within the body.

THE NATURE OF THE SELF

One conviction that all humanistic psychologists hold in common is the importance of the *self* as the central concern in human development. Although the term *self* appears frequently in humanistic literature, it is not always described in the same way by different writers or even in the same way at all times by a single writer.

Arthur Combs and Donald Snygg (1959, p. 124) proposed that the *phenomenal self* "is not a mere conglomeration or addition of isolated concepts of self, but a patterned interrelationship or Gestalt of all these. It is the individual as he seems from his own vantage point."

Rollo May called the self "the organizing function within the individual ... by means of which one human being can relate to another; consciousness of one's identity . . . as a thinking-intuiting-feeling and acting unity; . . . not merely the sum of 'roles,' but the capacity by which one *knows* he plays these roles; it is the center from which one sees and is aware of these 'sides' of himself" (quoted in Reeves, 1977, pp. 286–287).

Gordon Allport (1961, p. 110) described the self as a "kind of core in our being. And yet it is not a constant core. Sometimes the core expands and seems to take command of all our behavior and consciousness, sometimes it seems to go completely offstage, leaving us with no awareness whatsoever of self."

Frederick Perls called the self the integrator, the synthetic unity, and "the artist of life." And while it is "only a small factor in the total organism/environment interaction, . . . it plays the crucial role of finding and making the meanings that we grow by." It is the "system of contacts [with the environment] at any moment" and is "flexibly various, for it varies with the dominant organic needs and the pressing environmental stimuli; it is the system of responses; it diminishes in sleep when there is less need to respond" (Perls, Hefferline, and Goodman, 1951, p. 235).

Although these descriptions view the self as being entirely conscious, such theorists as Earl Kelley include unconscious functions as well:

> The self consists of an organization of accumulated experience over a whole lifetime. It is easy to see, therefore, that a great deal of the self has been relegated to the unconscious, or has been "forgotten." This does not mean that these early experiences have been lost. It merely means that they cannot readily be brought into consciousness (1962, p. 9).

Both Maslow and Buhler, like many other humanistic theorists, accept the principal agents that Freud defined as composing the personality or mind: id, ego, and superego. They also accept the various Freudian instincts, impulses, and defenses, as well as the primary process (seeking immediate pleasure) and the secondary process (the ego's recognizing the real world and fulfilling the id's demands in the light of reality). But for the humanistic psychologist these separate and often conflicting agents and tendencies become increasingly integrated into a compatible unity—into the *essential self*—as the person matures. Thus the individual who is fulfilling all of her or his needs, basic as well as self-actualizing ones, is marked by a smooth working together or *synergy* of the composite elements of personality (Buhler & Massarik, 1968, p. 19).

Likewise, humanistic psychologists often subscribe to the levels of consciousness postulated by Freud, even if they do not always include the unconscious level in their concept of the essential self. They feel that much of human behavior arises from unconscious motives and that "those portions of ourselves that we reject and repress out of fear and shame do not go out of existence" (Maslow, 1971, p. 158) but go underground into the unconscious. However, humanistic writers strongly disagree with Freud's idea that the contents of the unconscious are principally—if not entirely—antisocial, that is, selfish and resistant to moral values. They believe that the contents also include the roots of creativeness, joy, and goodness.

In humanistic belief, conscience differs somewhat from the punitive Freudian superego whose contents derive exclusively from the rules and expectations imposed by the environment, particularly expectations imposed by parents. Maslow proposed that in addition to values that the child ingests from people around her, her conscience also has a genetic source, a kind of intrinsic feeling or knowledge of the right thing to do. This faint voice has its beginnings in the ancient nature of humans and is linked to the instincts of lower forms of life. It is an inner knowledge of one's true self. Maslow said that intrinsic guilt arises when an individual senses he has betrayed his own inner nature and has deviated from the path of self-actualization.

In Maslow's view, intrinsic guilt is a most desirable thing for it warns the child that she is straying from her true destiny. On the other hand, guilt based on unreasonable expectations from the environment is frequently nonconstructive and detracts from the pursuit of one's identity and self-fulfillment.

A question of continuing debate among humanists is whether the self is an entity or a collection of separate selves, each of which comes into play under particular conditions. P. D. Ouspensky suggested that:

> The principal mistake we make about ourselves is that we consider ourselves one; we always speak about ourselves as "I" and we suppose that we refer to the same thing all the time. . . . We do not know that we have not one "I," but many different "I's," connected with our feelings and desires, and have no controlling "I." These "I's" change all the time; one suppresses another, one replaces another, and all this struggle makes up our inner life (1957, p. 3).

In recent years this notion of multiple selves has been expressed in its most popular form by the psychiatrist Eric Berne in such books as *Games People Play* (1967) and *What Do You Say after You Say Hello?* (1972). In Berne's theory, the three selves that contend for attention on different occasions are those expressing (1) vestiges of the person as a young "child," (2) an internal representation of the person's "parent," (3) and the person as a rational "adult."

In summary, then, despite some lack of consensus about the exact features of the self, all humanistic theorists consider the self the focal object of human development.

THE DIRECTIONS AND STAGES OF DEVELOPMENT

As noted earlier, humanistic psychology was not created as a child psychology. It was devised by theorists concerned mainly with helping adults achieve better personal and social adjustment or, in more positive terms, achieve greater self-actualization. Hence the attention of most humanistic psychologists has focused on childhood only in incidental ways. Our picture of the direction of development and stages of growth in childhood must therefore be gleaned from passing comments. In effect, humanistic psychology, as outlined by its best-known proponents, has not been organized as a system of phases of childhood and adolescence as correlated with chronological ages. To some degree Mahrer is an exception, for he has identified what he calls a sequence of *plateaus* in the development of self. This hierarchy of plateaus represents the closest approximation in humanistic theory to the stages of growth identified in such development models as those of Piaget, Freud, Gesell, and Havighurst.

Despite this lack of precisely defined growth steps for the first two decades of life in most humanistic theories, Maslow and Buhler have identified at least two general levels of change, those of *childhood* and *adolescence*. In discussing these levels, Buhler distinguishes biological from psychological development. From a biological standpoint, she divided the first twenty-five years of life at age 15. During childhood, ages 0 to 15, there is progressive physical growth without reproductive ability. During adolescence or youth, ages 15 to 25, there is continued growth following the onset of reproductive ability (Buhler & Massarik, 1968, p. 14).

Psychological development can also be viewed as two general segments, childhood and adolescence, but the distinctions are not nearly as clear as in the biological realm. Psychologically, the child grows toward self-actualization, toward achieving clearer goals in life and better integration of needs and values. This development of *self* is somewhat correlated with biological growth, in that the very young child is not very self-actualized. Time and experience are required for the child to achieve greater self-realization and synergy. But time alone is not enough. Just becoming older does not assure self-actualization. There are many adolescents and adults who still have not achieved psychological maturity. So the passing of childhood and the arrival of adolescence provides *opportunities for becoming* mature, but such maturing is not automatic.

Buhler concluded that the first appearance of a self-conscious ego occurs when the young child is between ages 2 and 4. During this time "I want" behavior is prominent as "the child begins to discover his own self and the possibility of giving himself a direction of his own" (Buhler & Massarik, 1968, pp. 30–31). The way a child expresses this self-consciousness varies greatly from one child to another, with such individuality being both genetic and environmental in origin. "The child with creative potential begins his first attempts toward self-realization when he is between 2 and 4 years" (Buhler & Massarik, 1968, p. 32).

Motivational Trends

Throughout the next eight or ten years the child's personality gradually evolves until the arrival of marked psychological change around age 10 to 12 or so. At this time, according to Buhler, several *motivational trends* appear, trends that extend into the future and mark the child's individuality in rather permanent ways.

One trend concerns a *constructive-destructive* dimension that involves the person's basic attitude toward life, an attitude that is becoming well set during this period of development. The attitude either can be one of building up positive human relationships and optimistic plans for the future, or it can be one of tearing down relationships by attacking others and despairing of the future. Which of these tendencies is dominant is most clearly evidenced in the way children interact with their parents, particularly in the way conflicts between child and parent are either resolved or expanded.

A second trend relates to *achievement motivation*. The extent to which a child will strive to achieve in her adult life and the form of this achievement will show up most clearly after puberty.

Beliefs and values that are based on more than blind acceptance develop in the early adolescent years, along with *love* and other *commitments* to a cause or to other people. Buhler said that the voluntarily chosen bonds of intimacy and commitment in a mutually shared sex and love relationship may result in "the ecstatic experience of unity . . . one of the most, if not *the* most, essential aims of the maturing person." Maslow called this feeling of unity one of the individual's *peak experiences* (Buhler & Massarik, 1968, p. 37). (The term *peak experiences*, frequently found in humanistic literature, identifies the most wonderful experience or experiences of your life, happiest moments, ecstatic moments, moments of rapture [Maslow in R. Wuthnow, 1978, p. 57]. The attainment of increasing numbers of peak experiences is, from a humanistic perspective, an important goal of human development.)

But even with adolescents' new concern for personally adopted values and immediate ambitions, they usually have only vague and tentative life goals. Rarely do they view life as an entirety, as a complete span of years with possibilities of an integration of all its aspects. "It is the exceptional youth who asks what life is all about" (Buhler & Massarik, 1968, p. 42).

Like Buhler, other writers in the humanistic vein consider adolescence to be a time of increased awareness and searching in the realm of values, goals, and commitment for something considered worthwhile. It is also a time of significant confusion. In this sense, the typical humanistic psychologist would agree with Erikson's notion that adolescence is experienced as an identity crisis. Maslow commented that the uncertainty of many adults in the United States about their own values has led many young people to live not by clear adult values but by "adolescent values, which of course are immature, ignorant, and heavily determined by confused adolescent needs" (Maslow, 1968, p. 206).

In summary, while most humanistic psychologists recognize at least prepuberal childhood and postpuberal adolescence as separate stages in personality development, they do not define substages within these periods, nor do they discuss even these two broad periods in any systematic way. Instead, they give only incidental attention to any idea of growth stages being correlated with age.

A Hierarchy of Plateaus

As mentioned earlier, Mahrer has proposed a sequence of five *plateaus* of personality growth and has linked the sequence to age levels, albeit in a rather vague manner. To contrast his system with the typical sets of growth periods postulated in other theories, Mahrer "sets aside the whole framework of biosocial, biopsychological stages of development" since he contends that "there are no intrinsic forces moving the child from one plateau to another, no biological factors, no built-in developmental sequences, no neurophysiological or hereditary or cultural lines of development" (1978, pp. 788, 790). Instead, he proposes that "people are responsible for an individual's staying on one plateau or moving to another. Those people may include the individual himself, his family, the groups in which he lives, significant strangers" (1978, p. 788)

The hierarchy of plateaus begins after birth with the *primitive personality*, which is the condition of the child encompassed within a *primitive field*. This primitive psychological field is created by parents and others in the child's environment who have a concept of what the infant should be like and who base their treatment of the infant on that concept. During this period the child has no sense of self but is dependent for her identity on the way others act toward her. "What I am is a function of how others see me" (Mahrer, 1978, p. 791). Whether the child advances out of this early condition and onto the next plateau depends on how she is treated by the people in charge of her welfare. If not treated constructively, she could remain a primitive personality all her life, forever relying on the external world as a mirror of her identity.

With proper nurturing, the individual advances to the second plateau, where a sense of self is born. Mahrer estimates that for some people this occurs in early childhood, but for most it happens during middle childhood between ages 6 and 12. For still others it does not appear until adolescence or adulthood, or perhaps never. He further proposes that this second state is not achieved suddenly but occurs "in bits and pieces, little juttings and bursts" (1978, p. 799).

On the third plateau the child becomes an active seeker, a constructor of experience, employing his growing potentials to select activities and to organize his world so that particular kinds of experiences occur. Instead of being manipulated by his environment, he actively fashions and utilizes his surroundings for his own purposes.

While the third period witnesses the individual initially developing skills or "operating potentials," on the fourth plateau new and more sophisticated skills are devised, ones that enable the person to experience life in greater depth and complexity.

The fifth, optimal state of being is that of self-integration and self-actualization, a plateau "beyond normal, mature, adjusted, healthy . . . achieved by a very small proportion of individuals. . . . Our concept is like that of a yogi, an individual who has attained the goal of yoga. . . . the union of self with the supreme reality or universal self" (Mahrer, 1978, p. 833).

Mahrer pictures the plateaus as representing a sequence of three struggles, first to acquire selfhood or personal identity during infancy and early childhood, next to preserve one's identity against the pressures of a changing environment, and finally to "lose selfhood" in ultimate self-actualization.

In conclusion, some developmental periods can be extracted from the works of a few humanistic authors. However, humanistic writers generally do not offer a *growth-stage* theory, but rather a *growth-directions* theory, meaning that a person grows gradually out of being one kind of individual toward being a different kind. But, to recognize whether a child is indeed developing in a proper direction, we need a definition of the desired end product or the desired goal that development is to pursue. Maslow defined this *direction of healthy growth* in two ways, one general and the other more specific.

As a general definition, he said that people are motivated in their development toward "ongoing actualization of potentials, capacities and talents, as fulfillment of mission—or call it fate, destiny, or vocation—as a fuller knowledge of, and acceptance of, the person's own intrinsic nature, as an unceasing trend toward unity, integration or synergy within the person" (Maslow, 1968, p. 25).

But many people found this definition unduly vague, so he provided a more specific description of the end condition of healthy development by specifying a series of traits displayed by a self-actualized person. Such a paragon of excellence exhibits (Maslow, 1968, p. 26):

1. Superior perception of reality

2. Increased acceptance of self, of others, and of nature

3. Increased spontaneity

4. Increased problem solving

5. Increased autonomy, and resistance to enculturation

6. Increased detachment and desire for privacy

7. Greater freshness of appreciation, and richness of emotional reaction

8. Higher frequency of peak experiences

9. Increased identification with the human species

10. Changed (the clinician would say, improved) interpersonal relations

11. More democratic character structure

12. Greatly increased creativeness

13. Certain changes in the value system

Other humanistic theorists besides Maslow have proposed their own set of directions in which development should proceed. For example, Combs (1962, pp. 53–62) has contended that the truly adequate personality (1) both gives love to others and feels loved by them, (2) is open to new experiences, (3) closely identifies with others so that she treats them in a highly responsible, trustworthy fashion, and (4) has a "rich and available perceptual field," meaning that she is well enough informed about the world to clearly understand events in which she is enmeshed.

Carl Rogers (1973, p. 12) pictured proper development as proceeding from rigidity toward flexibility, from static living toward "process living," from dependence toward autonomy, from being predictable toward an "unpredictable creativity," and from defensiveness toward self-acceptance.

HEALTHY GROWTH AND DEVIANCE

In place of the terms *normal* and *abnormal,* Maslow spoke of *health* and *illness* or of *mature* and *immature* development. For example, he distinguished between two sorts of immaturity, *chronological* and *unhealthy.* Chronological immaturity is found in the child as he grows up; it is expected, even necessary, for it consists of the healthy process of developing from a state of weakness, ignorance, and lack of direction to an adult state of self-fulfillment. But when the same sorts of symptoms are found in the adult, they are considered unhealthy, for by adulthood the individual should have become strong, wise, well integrated, and clear in his values and goals.

Deviance—that is, being different from others or failing to fit the norms—is not regarded as necessarily unhealthy. Indeed, being deviant in terms of expressing one's own talents and of following the guidance of one's unique inner gyroscope was viewed by Maslow as essential to achieving self-actualization. If a person adopts the typical behavior or norms of a culture that blocks the expression of her inner nature or personality core, then she is not considered to be normal in the sense of developing properly or in a healthy pattern. Instead, she is regarded in Maslow's system as being immature and unhealthy, for "the main source of illness (although not the only one) is seen as frustrations (of the basic needs, . . . of idiosyncratic potentials, of expression of the self, and of the tendency of the person to grow in his own style and at his own pace) especially in the early years of life" (Maslow, 1968, pp. 193–194).

So it is not deviance from the common or typical behavior of a society that is viewed with disapproval in the humanistic model; it is deviance from one's potential. A child who does not "fit in" to his culture or who "stands against the crowd" is a psychologically healthy child by humanistic standards if that culture is a bad one. And by *bad* Maslow meant a culture that is growth-inhibiting rather than growth-fostering. "The 'better' culture gratifies all basic human needs and permits self-actualization. The 'poorer' cultures do not" (Maslow, 1968, p. 211).

NATURE AND NURTURE

The general humanistic position on heredity–environment issues is that the infant is born with inherited potentials—for growth and for self-fulfillment by pursuing constructive missions—but that these potentials will not flower at all unless they are properly nurtured by the people with whom the child interacts during the growing years. As the discussion of Maslow's views has already suggested, he assigned heredity a strong role in personality development. The essence of the sort of person a child should become is established in the genetic structure as a unique self composed of latent talents and interests. The environment then determines how adequately this idiosyncratic self or identity unfolds or becomes actualized. So while humanistic theorists recognize the significance of innate potentials as the seeds of personality, they still place great emphasis on the function of the social environment in producing the actual personality the growing child displays. The self "is built almost entirely, if not entirely, in relationship to others. While the newborn babe has the equipment for the development of the self, there is ample evidence to show that nothing resembling a self can be built in the absense of others" (Kelley, 1962, p. 9). "People discover their self concepts from the kinds of experiences they have had with life—not from telling, but from experience" (Combs, 1962, p. 84).

Curiously, in one way Maslow's concept of the nature–nurture relationship is similar to the Puritans' and in another way to that of Rousseau. Like the Puritans, Maslow believed that each person is innately suited to a *calling* in life, a particular role. According to both Puritan and humanistic theory, a key task of later childhood and adolescence is that of discovering what one's calling is to be—or, in Erikson's terms, of discovering one's proper identity. The Puritan youth was to seek this identity through prayer and meditation. Under modern humanistic psychology, a youth discovers this calling by interacting with a growth-supporting, permissive, but realistic social environment and, at the same time, by trusting her intuition to guide her toward her calling.

But like Rousseau, and unlike the Puritans, humanistic theorists have suggested that the natural instincts of the child are good and should be followed. Thus the environment should furnish opportunities for the good nature to flower rather than restricting the child's expression by imposing Biblical prohibitions to combat an ostensibly devil-devised evil nature.

PRACTICAL APPLICATIONS

Although the most extensive applications of humanistic psychology have been therapeutic and consciousness-raising activities for adults, a substantial body of literature has been produced as well on child-rearing practices and on schooling and therapy during the first two decades of life. Such child-focused literature can be divided into two types. The first consists of general guidelines and warnings about raising children. The second consists of specific activities for promoting humanistic goals of development.

Examples of general guidelines are such observations as:

> A high quality of maternal love and care . . . seem to prepare the child for emotional contacts with other people and to supply enough confidence to encourage the exploration of new situations. . . . Among the greatest benefits of psychoanalysis is the fact that it has disclosed the damaging consequences of extreme parental demands and discipline. . . . On the whole, it may be assumed that warmth and permissiveness facilitate the growth of sociable, yet independent children, and that parental hostility has debilitating effects (Buhler & Massarik, 1968, pp. 174–178).

> Once the infant puts forth a rudimentary nubbin [of individuality], parental figures can develop that behavior by [an] . . . integrative relationship that is expressed in warmth, love, closeness, acceptance. . . . To relate disintegratively is to relate with fear and hate, depression and anger, meaninglessness and menace to the behavior bit put forth by the infant (Mahrer, 1978, pp. 698–699).

> Anytime a pupil's actions suggest that he can profit from expressing and comprehending (emotionally as well as intellectually) his feelings, the teacher should use methods suitable for promoting such expression and comprehension (Thomas & Brubaker, 1971, p. 260).

> We know only too well that a parent cannot make his children into anything. Children make themselves into something. The best we can do and frequently the most effect we can have is by serving as something to react against if the child presses too hard. . . . Schools should be helping children to look within themselves, and from this self-knowledge derive a set of values, . . . spontaneity and . . . naturalness" (Maslow, 1971, pp. 169, 185–186).

Maslow's faith in the correctness of the child's natural inclinations caused him to recommend a *permissive regime,* meaning that parents should begin meeting the child's needs directly and with as little frustration as possible in early infancy. But as the child acquires greater strength and experience, adults should gradually cease gratifying his needs directly. They should now arrange the child's environment so he can gratify his own needs and make his own choices, for "he 'knows' better than anyone else what is good for him" (Maslow, 1968, p. 198).

The intention of Maslow's educational scheme is not to prevent the developing child from ever experiencing frustration, pain, or danger. But, with a good foundation in the early years of safety, love, and respect, the child should increasingly be allowed to face difficulties that enable her to acquire frustration tolerance. Part of self-realization comes as the older child and the youth learn about their strengths and limitations and learn ways to extend their abilities by overcoming difficulties, "by straining . . . to the utmost, by meeting challenge and hardship, even by failing" (Maslow, 1968, p. 200). Curiously, this general pattern of child raising—except for the desirability of failing—sounds much like the pattern found in Skinner's *Walden Two,* illustrating the observation that children may be treated in similar ways from quite different theoretical viewpoints.

Some humanistic writers have gone beyond offering general suggestions and have described specific activities for implementing their suggestions. For example, Mahrer (1978, pp. 766–771) has proposed a regimen for promoting an infant's development out of the condition of primitive personality into an initial sense of self. The routine to be carried out with the six- to nine-month-old child consists of the adult playing with the baby for thirty minutes to an hour each day. However, it is the infant, not the adult, who determines the direction of the play. The adult's role is first to furnish *effectance-promoting objects* that the child can touch, grasp, squeeze, shape, mouth, crumple, push, throw, hit, release, roll, take apart, open, and close. The objects should also make noise, have odors, and be different colors. And all the objects should be started, stopped, and manipulated by the baby himself, not by the adult. With such equipment at hand, the adult's task is to remain within *interactive distance* of the infant, meaning that the adult's face is within two feet of the child. The baby is then allowed to initiate his own behavior, with the adult focusing attention on and commenting about what the baby is doing, being careful all the while not to interfere with or redirect the infant's activity.

For school-age children and youths, a variety of other writers have proposed specific learning activities. These can be illustrated by examples from *confluent education,* which is a variant of the humanistic movement that emphasizes a confluence or compatible flowing together of the cognitive and emotional aspects of experience. For instance, to help children investigate their feelings about communicating with others under unusual circumstances, one set of activities consists of pupils dividing into pairs. Each pair first sit back to back to converse with each other orally, then sit facing each other to communicate only with their eyes, and finally—with eyes closed—to communicate only with their hands. To foster greater "self-awareness and other-awareness," each child is next asked to "close his eyes and with his hands explore his own face very slowly and get in touch with the various textures and parts of his face" and then to explore the face of his partner (G. I. Brown, 1971, pp. 29–32). An opportunity to investigate feelings of trust and distrust is provided by the *blind walk,* which involves one of the pair of children being blindfolded and then led by her partner around the classroom and other areas of the school. An additional activity to promote self-awareness has been labeled a *fantasy body trip.* Students close their eyes, assume comfortable positions, and "move into themselves" by concentrating on different parts of the body, with each student "beginning with his toes, moving gradually up to his head, experiencing any sensations he might feel emanating from that part of the body" (G. I. Brown, 1971, p. 35).

Numerous additional activities devised by proponents of humanistic development demonstrate ways to plumb the experiences of loneliness, affection, responsibility, anxiety, faithfulness, prejudice, social acceptance and rejection, confidence, insecurity, emotional dependence and independence, and more. Over the past two decades an increasing number of such activities have been included in elementary and secondary school curricula and in nonformal educational programs.

RESEARCH CHALLENGES

Any psychological system whose focus is on internal experience and whose chief source of information is introspection will necessarily face problems of communication and of the public validation of its proposals. Obviously, what one person experiences or feels cannot be communicated directly to others but can only be suggested to others through some form of publicly observable behavior, through words or actions that we hope might to some extent convey subjective experience. In this dilemma of trying to explain to others our internal life humanistic psychology finds its most challenging research problems.

For example, one key question to answer is, What is the structure of the *self* or the *selves*? As noted earlier, definitions of self by various authors are both murky and incongruous. One problem, then, becomes that of discovering research techniques appropriate for resolving the conflicts about the nature of the self.

A further problem is the identification of observable elements or behavioral correlates of such humanistic concepts as *peak experience, self-realization,* and *synergy*. Advocates of the humanistic approach have themselves criticized the movement for proposing goals that are:

> vague, poetic, fragmented, groundless, and nonmeasurable: "helping people become more aware of themselves," more "self-actualized," more "open to experience," more "connected, powerful," more "authentic, genuine, joyful, in touch with themselves," and ad infinitum (Alschuler et al., 1977, p. 30).

Some of these critics have set out to remedy the vagueness, first by defining in more specific terms what such constructs can mean and then by devising methods for assessing people's status in relation to the constructs. Perhaps the best known instrument for this purpose is the Personal Orientation Inventory, a test consisting of 150 paired, opposing statements, with a person's task being that of choosing which of the pair is most relevant in his or her life (Shostrum, 1966). The instrument yields scores along ten scales identified as reflecting self-actualizing values, existentiality (sensing the essence of one's individual self), feeling reactivity, spontaneity, self-regard, self-acceptance, human nature, synergy, acceptance of aggression, and capacity for intimacy. A substantial number of research studies utilizing the inventory, conducted mainly in the late 1960s and 1970s, have suggested that the test is a valid measure of the above concepts, although other studies have failed to establish the instrument's validity. S. R. Maddi has concluded that, "Nonetheless, the POI seems a promising lead in investigating broad patterns of functioning closely associated with the positions of Maslow and other humanistic psychologists" (1972, p. 476).

Others in the humanistic camp have devised techniques for measuring two further constructs of humanistic education—self-knowledge and consciousness—by creating an instrument for eliciting people's descriptions of their experiences. Responses scored by an objective rating system are said to reveal the level of the respondents' self-knowledge and their consciousness of their life condition (Alschuler et al., 1977, pp. 29–47).

Thus steps are being taken, although somewhat slowly, toward casting humanistic goals and personality traits in forms that make them more readily communicated and assessed. However, the assessment devices prepared for adults are suitable for use with older adolescents but not with younger children. Therefore the lack of objective measuring techniques appropriate for use with children continues.

In addition to the foregoing general problems with humanistic theory, a multitude of developmental issues await the attention of researchers. For instance, how is self-actualization displayed in children at different age levels? Or, stated differently, how does a parent or teacher recognize whether the child's or adolescent's *self* is developing adequately? How does a child identify her proper *calling* or mission in life, and when can this realization be expected to take place? How can the desirability of a child's goals or dreams of the future be appraised? What environmental forces during a child's growing years exert the strongest influence on the life goals he adopts? Are there recognizable stages in children's goal-setting development; if so, what are the causal factors behind such stages? And although a host of humanistic teaching techniques—including simulation activities and games—have been created and their virtues lauded by practitioners, very little of what could be defended as *research* has yet been conducted to determine the effects of the techniques on children. Hence validation studies of humanistic practices are called for.

One critic has charged that present-day humanistic theory is constructed on assumptions that are true for only one segment of society, so that the humanistic model is only relevant

> to those who "have" (i.e., achieved sufficient economic wealth) and completely irrelevant to those who are the "have-nots" (i.e., in Maslow's terms, 1968, those too busy concerning themselves with lower-level needs rather than higher-level needs such as self-actualization). Herein lies the contradiction in the practice of contemporary "humanistic" psychology—a contradiction which must be resolved in order for "humanistic" psychology to evolve into a truly *humanistic* psychology (Buss, 1976, p. 258).

This observation evokes further questions that warrant research attention. How do humanistic theorists account for the socialization of the child, that is, the changes in children's social characteristics as they grow up in different cultures? What limits do environmental conditions place on self-realization and the attainment of a calling in life?

In summary, for people who wish to have better evidence than personal testimonials to support the contentions of humanistic theory, many research questions remain to be answered.

HUMANISTIC THEORY: AN ASSESSMENT

Three of the greatest strengths of the humanistic approach are its attention to children's feelings and values as part of their real world (item 1), its concern for the individual's hopes and plans for the future (item 3), and its application of a humanistic view to child raising (item 4).

I agree with humanistic psychologists that the world that is most significant to the child or adolescent is the one she feels that she is experiencing at the moment. This attention to the phenomenal self seems to be a proper counterbalance to the heavy dependence on objectively observed actions of behaviorist views. The typical humanistic theory seeks to devise general principles that underlie different facets of growth, not just one aspect such as cognitive development. However, by concerning itself only with general principles, it has failed to trace the specific ways one aspect, such as language usage, develops in comparison to the ways other aspects, such as physical agility, grow. Hence I have rated humanistic psychology high on item 1 but not at the top.

The humanistic approach has also given attention to the role of hopes, expectations, and plans for the future, facets of development that have been unduly neglected in many other theories. I have sought to recognize this contribution by a high rating on item 3. But the manner in which humanistic theory explains the past appears to me to be imprecise, so the rating for item 3 is not the highest.

Two general principles of child rearing that humanistic theorists appear to support are (1) the adult should seek to perceive life from the emotional and cognitive perspectives of the child and, through such empathy, should treat the child in ways that show respect for and understanding of the child's phenomenal self and (2) the adult should respect the child's right to be an individual with interests, talents, and emotions of his own. These principles are proper ones for child raising, so I have rated humanistic theory high on item 4. But again, the rating is not at the top of the scale, for I believe humanistic theory lacks the specificity that parents and teachers look for in their search for ways to treat the growing child. Of course, such a lack of specific directives to parents is perhaps a necessary part of a theory that emphasizes the unique character of each child.

On other dimensions of the rating sheet, I have judged that humanistic theory fares not so well. One problem is the theory's clarity (item 2). Humanistic writers describe their ideas in terms that can carry quite different meanings for different readers. When you speak of your *peak experiences,* of your *self-realization,* and of your *identity,* how am I to know whether I have experienced the same things that cause you to use these words? Likewise, when I seek inner guidance in making a decision, how do I know which of my impulses represents my *true* inner self, the one that directs me toward self-actualization, and which impulses represent values I have learned from my environment, values that may conflict with my innate essence or calling?

Further puzzles have arisen from seemingly self-contradictory principles offered by humanistic writers. For example, Maslow wrote that "for self-actualizing people, there is a strong tendency for selfishness and unselfishness to fuse into a higher, superordinate unity" (1968, p. 207).

In addition, Maslow's system proposes that children are immature because they are at lower levels in the needs-fulfillment hierarchy and at lower levels on the scales of maturity. Yet he stated that "the highest maturity is discovered to include a childlike quality" (1968, p. 207). If such is true, then how it operates requires a clearer explanation than the existing humanistic literature seems to provide.

In effect, one of the very strengths of humanistic theory, its insistence on the importance of unique personal experiences, leads also to one of its serious weaknesses—its imprecision in communicating the essence of one person's experience to another.

The same personal or existential quality of humanistic thought also contributes to the theory's lack of falsifiability (item 7). The difficulty here

Humanistic Theory

How well do I think the theory meets the standards?

The Standards	Very Well	Moderately Well	Very Poorly
1. Reflects the real world of children	X		
2. Is clearly understandable			X
3. Explains the past and predicts the future		X	
4. Guides child rearing	X		
5. Is internally consistent			?
6. Is economical			?
7. Is falsifiable			X
8. Stimulates new discoveries		X	
9. Is self-satisfying		X	

rests to a great degree in humanistic theorists' preference for using introspection as their principal investigative technique. Although Maslow accepted the objective, scientific modes of studying people that have evolved over the past century or so, he criticized the adoption of behaviorism and of logical positivism as the exclusive, or even as the preferred, mode of understanding human development. He claimed that such approaches to studying the growing child result only in verbal, analytic, conceptual rationality and ignore the more significant aspects of personality—the hopes, feelings, fears, and ambitions of the experiencing self. For example, in discussing motivation, Maslow stated that:

> The original criterion of motivation and the one that is still used by all human beings except behavioral psychologists is the subjective one, I am

motivated when I feel a desire or want or yearning or wish or lack. No objectively observable state has yet been found that correlates decently with these subjective reports, i.e., no behavioral definition of motivation has yet been found.

Now of course we ought to keep on seeking for objective correlates or indicators of subjective states. . . . But until we find [them] we ought not make believe that we have. Nor ought we neglect the subjective data that we do have (1968, p. 22).

Not only does humanistic theory draw upon self-reports, but it accords a key position to nonlogical, or even illogical, intuitive impressions or feelings, which it claims are so often expressions of the true inner self.

If our hope is to describe the world fully, a place is necessary for preverbal, ineffable, metaphorical, primary process, concrete experience, intuitive, and esthetic types of cognition, for there are certain aspects of reality which can be cognized in no other way (Maslow, 1968, p. 208).

This attitude about the proper sources of evidence about personality development influences the humanistic view of the way the theory is validated. In earlier chapters I noted that behavioristic theories depend upon the experimental or field-study testing of hypotheses as the appropriate way to determine whether the theory or some part of it is true. But humanistic psychologists trust their own feelings and logic more than many sorts of objective data to validate their theory. To most if not all humanistic psychologists, it appears to be enough to contend that "I know that's the way things are because it makes sense and feels right to me." But such a testimonial would less likely satisfy a behaviorist, a Piagetian, or a psychoanalyst.

In terms of the theory's internal consistency (item 5) and economy of explanation (item 6), I have placed question marks in the lower reaches of the appraisal scales. My puzzlement regarding these matters is occasioned by a lack of precision in the definition of terms and of the relationships among variables. I find myself unable to make a careful estimate of internal consistency and economy of explanation when I fail to understand the elements of the system adequately. To a considerable extent, humanistic writing appears cast in unscientific, literary language. Rhetoric and obvious enthusiasm do not, I feel, sufficiently make up for what seems to be a structural imprecision in the theory.

During the past two decades or so, humanistic views have gained wide public attention and have influenced the way teachers, parents, social workers, and others perceive children (G. I. Brown, 1971, 1976; Fantini & Weinstein, 1968; Leff, 1978). However, this success in attracting people's interest in perceiving children in ostensibly more "humane" ways has not led to a significant number of new discoveries about children. It is true that such proposals as Maslow's hierarchy of needs have been innovative. But in many instances, the matters of which humanistic writers speak have been matters that people of earlier times had sensed intuitively, and the humanistic theorists' contribution has been to stimulate the rediscovery of these insights about the self, about feelings, and about hopes for the future. If you search through current child development textbooks or inspect journals in the field, you will not find many new items of knowledge about child growth contributed by theorists and researchers who have used humanistic approaches. Hence I have marked the theory in the lower ranges of item 8. My purpose in giving such a rating is not to downgrade the significance of the humanistic persuasion but to note that it has not stimulated, at least not up to the present time, significant amounts of new knowledge about development.

Humanistic theory, then, appeals most to people who place a high degree of trust in their intuitive sense of what is true about the development of one's self. The theory is less convincing to people who require a tightly reasoned, logical model whose elements can be verified through experimental or observational approaches. However, humanistic theorists do not claim to have produced a finished, close-knit theory of child development. Instead, they see their proposals as constituting only a beginning toward a model of human nature "as a total, single, comprehensive system of psychology" (Maslow, 1968, p. 189). And they also believe that their approach, with its emphasis on the experiencing self, holds more promise for revealing the essence of human personality than do such systems as psychoanalysis and behaviorism. I find it moderately self-satisfying (item 9).

FOR FURTHER READING

Buhler, Charlotte, and Melanie Allen. (1972) *Introduction to Humanistic Psychology.* Monterey, Calif.: Brooks/Cole.

Mahrer, Alvin R. (1978) *Experiencing: A Humanistic Theory of Psychology and Psychiatry.* New York: Brunner/Mazel.

Maslow, Abraham H. (1968) *Toward a Psychology of Being.* New York: Van Nostrand Reinhold.

Maslow, Abraham H. (1970) *Motivation and Personality.* 2d ed. New York: Harper & Row.

PART EIGHT

SOURCES OF
FURTHER THEORIES

The purpose of Chapter Seventeen is to suggest sources of additional theories or partial theories that you might find of interest. The list is, however, far from definitive. It is merely a sampling from among the scores of theoretical models in the professional literature. Sources of other theories are the bibliographies in child development textbooks and in journals that publish studies of development.

Of the available textbooks treating theories of development, the following six are perhaps the most useful:

Baldwin, A. L. (1967) *Theories of Child Development*. New York: Wiley.

Crain, W. C. (1980) *Theories of Development: Concepts and Applications*. Englewood Cliffs, N.J.: Prentice-Hall.

Langer, J. (1969) *Theories of Development*. New York: Holt, Rinehart, & Winston.

Lerner, R. M. (1976) *Concepts and Theories of Human Development*. Reading, Mass.: Addison-Wesley.

Maier, H. W. (1978) *Three Theories of Child Development: Erik H. Erikson, Jean Piaget, and Robert R. Sears*. 3d ed. New York: Harper & Row.

Miller, P. H. (1983) *Theories of Developmental Psychology*. San Francisco: W. H. Freeman.

445

CHAPTER SEVENTEEN

An Annotated Bibliography

Ausubel, D. P., and E. V. Sullivan. (1970) *Theory and Problems of Child Development.* 2d ed. New York: Grune & Stratton.
In the words of the authors, this is intended to be "a body of relatively doctrine-free theory dealing exclusively with the major kinds of generalizations that can be made about the nature and regulation of development as a process."

Ayres, A. J. (1972) *Sensory Integration and Learning Disorders.* Los Angeles: Western Psychological Services.
Ayres's theory proposes (1) that a child's disordered ability to integrate sensory input (visual, auditory, tactile) accounts for some sorts of learning problems and (2) that special activities that enhance sensory integration as the child develops will make academic learning easier for children.

Baldwin, A. L., C. P. Baldwin, V. Castillo-Vales, and B. Seegmiller. (1971) "Cross-cultural Similarities in the Development of the Concept of Kindness," in W. W. Lambert and R. Weisbrod (eds.), *Comparative Perspectives on Social Psychology.* Boston: Little, Brown.
The authors interpret the development of kindness from the viewpoint of attribution theory. For a further treatment of the same perspective, see: C. P. Baldwin and A. L. Baldwin. (1970) "Children's Judgments of Kindness." *Child Development,* Vol. 41, pp. 29–47.

Barsch, R. H. (1967) *Achieving Perceptual-Motor Efficiency.* Vol. 1. and (1968) *Enriching Perception and Cognition.* Vol. 2. Seattle, Wash.: Special Child Publications.
Barsch's movigenic model (a theory of movement as it relates to learning) proposes that difficulties in learning are associated with the child's inefficient interaction in space.

Bettelheim, B. (1967) *The Empty Fortress: Infantile Autism and the Birth of the Self.* New York: Free Press.
The author contends that autism represents children's failure from early infancy to develop a sense of autonomy. Bettelheim proposes, from a psychoanalytic perspective, that autism is caused by unsatisfactory parent-child relationships.

447

Bloom, L. (1970) *Language Development: Form and Function in Emerging Grammars.* Cambridge, Mass.: M.I.T. Press.

Bloom uses Chomsky's theory of generative transformational grammar to analyze three children's early speech.

Bloom, L. (1973) *One Word at a Time.* The Hague: Mouton.

In Chapter 5 Bloom proposes a theory of two alternative strategies for the way one-year-olds learn syntax as they move from one-word to two-word utterances.

Braine, M. D. S. (1971) "The Acquisition of Language," in C. Reed (ed.), *The Learning of Language.* New York: Appleton-Century-Crofts.

Braine interprets early language development from a pivotal open grammar perspective.

Bridges, K. M. B. (1966) "The Development of Emotions," in R. L. Wrenn (ed.), *Basic Contributions to Psychology: Readings.* Belmont, Calif.: Wadsworth.

Bridges suggests that original diffuse excitement at birth first differentiates into distress and delight, then into seven more specific emotions by age 2, and subsequently into seventeen emotions by age 5.

Brown, R. (1973) *A First Language: The Early Stages.* Cambridge, Mass.: Harvard University Press.

Brown traces steps in children's early language development, thereby illustrating the thesis that young children at successive age levels display the same forms of syntax and grammar.

Chomsky, Noam. (1968) *Language and Mind.* New York: Harcourt Brace Jovanovich.

Chomsky proposes that children have an inherent sense of grammatical form.

Connolly, K., and J. Bruner. (1974) *The Growth of Competence.* London: Academic Press.

These authors describe how early competence and its cultivation may affect the later functioning of the "more mature organism."

Delacato, C. H. (1966) *Neurological Organization and Reading.* Springfield, Ill.: Charles C Thomas.

Believing that ontogeny recapitulates phylogeny, Delcato states that (1) the child's nervous system matures by regular stages from the spinal medula to the cerebral cortex and (2) that different behaviors (from gross body movements to high-level intellectual functions) parallel these functions. Disorders of behavioral development are seen as symptoms of inadequate neurological development.

Froebel, F. W. A. (1889) *The Education of Man* (trans., W. N. Hailmann). New York: Appleton-Century-Crofts.

Froebel (1782–1852), the originator of the kindergarten movement, believed that "the spirit of God . . . lives in nature, produces, fosters, and unfolds everything, as the common life principle. . . . All the child is ever to be and become, lies — however slightly indicated — in the child and can be attained only through development from within outward." He traces development through four main stages.

Frostig, M., and P. Maslow. (1973) *Learning Problems in the Classroom.* New York: Grune & Stratton.

This approach to treating learning difficulties is based on a visual perception theory supplemented by behavior modification, humanistic psychology, psychoanalytic concepts, and cognitive development theory.

Getman, G. N. (1965) "The Visuomotor Complex in the Acquisition of Learning Skills," in J. Hellmuth (ed.), *Learning Disorders, Vol. 1.* Seattle, Wash.: Special Child Publications.

Getman, an optometrist, has constructed a model of perceptual-motor development levels stressing the role of visual perception in determining the efficiency of a child's intellectual functioning.

Gibson, E. J. (1969) *Principles of Perceptual Learning and Development.* New York: Appleton-Century-Crofts.

Gibson conceives of perceptual learning as an active, self-regulating process enabling the child to become increasingly skilled at extracting and differentiating information that is available in the environment. Further refinements in the theory beyond Gibson's original statement appear in E. J. Gibson and N. Rader. (1979) "The Perceiver as Performer," in G. Hale and M. Lewis (eds.), *Attention and Cognitive Development.* New York: Plenum.

Guilford, J. P. (1967) *The Nature of Human Intelligence.* New York: McGraw-Hill. Pp. 413–438.

Guilford proposes that the mature intellect is composed of a multitude of separate abilities. He rejects the theory that as the child develops the various abilities differentiate gradually out of an initial general ability. He supports the idea that abilities are genetically differentiated from the earliest years.

Hall, C. S., and V. J. Nordby. (1973) *A Primer of Jungian Psychology.* New York: Toplinger.

Chapter 4 describes the development of personality from the perspective of Carl Jung, featuring two interwoven strands that contribute to the growth of personality: "*individuation* of the various structures that make up the total psyche, and *integration* of those structures into a unified whole (selfhood)."

Heafford, M. (1967) *Pestalozzi, His Thought and Its Relevance Today.* London: Methuen.

Pestalozzi (1746–1827), a Swiss educator, followed Rousseau's lead in claiming that the child is innately good "and seeks the good; his conscience only allows him to feel secure when he does the good; and if he is evil, it is surely because the way has been blocked, along which he wanted to be good." The trick in child rearing is to discover nature's patterns of growth and to present the child with a sequence of experiences suited to each growth step.

Himmelweit, T., and B. Swift. (1969) "A Model for Understanding of School as a Socializing Agent," in P. H. Mussen, J. Langer, and M. Covington (eds.), *Trends and Issues in Developmental Psychology.* New York: Holt, Rinehart, & Winston.

A model is created for interpreting longitudinal data on the influence of types of schools on socialization.

Hunt, J. McV. (1961) *Intelligence and Experience.* New York: Ronald.

Hunt's theory supports Piaget's view of the nature of intelligence.

Huxley, A. (1932) *Brave New World.* New York: Harper & Row.

Huxley pictures child-raising practices at some vague future time in a society that controls life carefully, eliminating much of today's individuality and opportunities for personal decision.

Janov, A. (1973) *The Feeling Child.* New York: Simon & Schuster.

The growth of children's emotional reactions is pictured from the viewpoint of the primal theory first described in Janov's *The Primal Scream.*

Koppitz, E. M. (1968) *Psychological Evaluation of Children's Human Figure Drawings.* New York: Grune & Stratton.
The author devised a system for estimating children's mental development and certain personality traits from the children's drawings of the human figure, a system focusing on age 5–12.

Lample-DeGroot, J. (1965) *The Development of the Mind.* New York: International Universities Press.
Lample-DeGroot provides a collection of essays on development from the viewpoint of her version of psychoanalysis.

Lowenfeld, V. (1957) *Creative and Mental Growth.* New York: Macmillan.
Lowenfeld describes stages in children's art productions and tells what he believes these productions reflect about mental growth. The 1957 edition is the most authentic statement of Lowenfeld's views before his death; subsequent revisions of the book have been substantially altered by his posthumous co-author.

McNeill, D. (1970) *The Acquisition of Language: The Study of Developmental Psycholinguistics.* New York: Harper & Row.
McNeill's description reflects a belief in an innate sense of language structure in children.

Montessori, M. (1967) *The Absorbent Mind.* New York: Dell.
Montessori describes key features of her model of child development and of educational procedures that derive from that model. An up-to-date review of Montessori theory and teaching methodology is also found in P. P. Lillard. (1972) *Montessori, A Modern Approach.* New York: Schocken.

Neumann, E. (1973) *The Child.* New York: Putnam.
A description of development from the viewpoint of Carl Jung. Chapter 5 depicts stages in the child's ego development.

Schlesinger, I. M. (1971) "Production of Utterances and Language Acquisition," in D. I. Slobin (ed.), *The Ontogenesis of Grammar.* New York: Academic Press.
A model of sentence production based on a child's intention is proposed to replace the grammatical level of deep structure with semantic intentions. The model forms a generative-semantics approach.

Stemmer, N. (1973) *An Empiricist Theory of Language Acquisition.* The Hague: Mouton.
The steps of a child's acquiring an understanding of language are explained chiefly by means of classical conditioning.

Stevenson, H. W. (1972) *Children's Learning.* New York: Appleton-Century-Crofts.
Results of hundreds of experiments are summarized as generalizations about how children learn, with most experiments interpreted from one or more of four theoretical positions: associative-mediational, reinforcement, cognitive, and perceptual.

Strauss, A., and L. Lehtinen. (1947) *Psychopathology and Education of the Brain-Injured Child.* Vol. 1. New York: Grune & Stratton.
On the basis of their theory that perceptual handicaps cause certain learning disorders, the authors suggest remedial measures composed of visual perception activities.

Sullivan, H. S. (1953) *The Interpersonal Theory of Psychiatry.* New York: Norton.
Sullivan's model shows how children's personalities develop in Western societies

by means of the interpersonal relations in which they engage as they pass through six stages of social-psychological growth.

Thomas, A., and S. Chess. (1980) *The Dynamics of Psychological Development*. New York: Brunner/Mazel.
On the basis of long-term longitudinal studies of more than 500 children, including both the normal and the handicapped, Thomas and Chess created what they term "a human rather than an animal model of developmental theory," featuring the goals and structure of behavior and the process of development.

Turiel, E. (1969) "Developmental Processes in the Child's Moral Thinking," in P. H. Mussen, J. Langer, and M. Covington (eds.), *Trends and Issues in Developmental Psychology*. New York: Holt, Rinehart & Winston.
The writer compares interpretations of moral development from several viewpoints, including those of Kohlberg and Piaget.

van der Geest, T., R. Gerstel, R. Appel, and B. T. Tervoort. (1973) *The Child's Communicative Competence*. The Hague: Mouton.
Studies by the writers are used to support the theory that the language of middle-class and lower-class preschool children is different in content but essentially equivalent in structure.

Vaughn, G. M. (1972) "Concept Formation and the Development of Ethnic Awareness," in A. R. Brown (ed.), *Prejudice in Children*. Springfield, Ill.: Charles C Thomas.
On the basis of his research, the author proposes that "where the concept of race is involved, an identification response (meaning that the child identifies with one or more perceived objects or people) preceded ontogenetically the more usual discrimination response."

Wall, C. (1974) *Predication: A Study of Its Development*. The Hague: Mouton.
Wall offers generalizations about what children affirm or assert about the subjects of their sentences.

REFERENCES

Adler, A. (1927) *The Practice and Theory of Individual Psychology.* New York: Harcourt Brace Jovanovich.

Adler, A. (1930) "Individual Psychology," in C. Murchinson (ed.), *Psychologies of 1930.* Worchester, Mass.: Clark University Press.

Alexander, R. D., and P. W. Sherman. (1977) "Local Mate Competition and Parental Investment in Social Insects." *Science,* Vol. 196, pp. 494–500.

Allport, G. W. (1961) *Pattern and Growth in Personality.* New York: Holt, Rinehart, & Winston.

Allport, G. W. (1968) *The Person in Psychology: Selected Essays.* Boston: Beacon Press.

Alschuler, A., G. Weinstein, J. Evans, R. Tamashiro, and W. Smith. (1977) "Education for What? Measuring Self-Knowledge and Levels of Consciousness." *Simulation and Games,* Vol. 8, pp. 29–47.

Alston, W. P. (1971) "Comments on Kohlberg's 'From Is to Ought'," in T. Mischel, *Cognitive Development and Epistemology.* New York: Academic Press.

Anastasi, A. (1958) "Heredity, Environment, and the Question 'How?' " *Psychological Review,* Vol. 65, pp. 197–208.

Anderson, J. (1983) "A Spreading Activation Theory of Memory." *Journal of Verbal Learning and Verbal Behavior,* Vol. 22, pp. 261–295.

Aries, P. (1962) *Centuries of Childhood.* New York: Knopf.

Ausubel, D. P., and E. V. Sullivan. (1970) *Theory and Problems of Child Development.* 2d ed. New York: Grune & Stratton.

Ayres, A. J. (1972) *Sensory Integration and Learning Disorders.* Los Angeles: Western Psychological Services.

Baldwin, A. L. (1967) *Theories of Child Development.* New York: Wiley.

Baldwin, A. L., C. P. Baldwin, F. Castillo-Vales, and B. Seegmiller. (1971) "Cross-cultural Similarities in the Development of the Concept of Kindness," in W. W.

Lambert and R. Weisbrod (eds.). *Comparative Perspectives in Social Psychology.* Boston: Little, Brown.

Baldwin, J. M. (1906, 1908, 1911) *Thoughts and Things or Genetic Logic,* 3 Vols. New York: Macmillan.

Ballard, K. D., and T. Glynn. (1975) "Behavioral Self-Management in Story Writing with Elementary School Children." *Journal of Applied Behavior Analysis,* Vol. 1, pp. 91–97.

Bandura, A. (1969) *Principles of Behavior Modification.* New York: Holt, Rinehart, & Winston.

Bandura, A. (1977) *Social Learning Theory.* Englewood Cliffs, N.J.: Prentice-Hall.

Bandura, A., and R. H. Walters. (1963) *Social Learning and Personality Development.* New York: Holt, Rinehart, & Winston.

Barker, R. G. (1968) *Ecological Psychology.* Stanford, Calif.: Stanford University Press.

Barker, R. G., T. Dembo, and K. Lewin. (1943) "Frustration and Regression," in R. G. Barker, J. S. Kounin, and H. F. Wright, *Child Behavior and Development.* New York: McGraw-Hill.

Barker, R. G., and P. V. Gump. (1964) *Big School, Small School.* Stanford, Calif.: Stanford University Press.

Barker, R. G., et al. (1970) "The Ecological Environment: Student Participation in Non-Class Settings" in M. B. Miles and W. W. Charters, Jr., *Learning in Social Settings.* Boston: Allyn & Bacon.

Barsch, R. H. (1967) *Achieving Perceptual-Motor Efficiency.* Vol. 1. Seattle: Special Child Publications.

Barsch, R. H. (1968) *Enriching Perception and Cognition.* Vol. 2. Seattle: Special Child Publications.

Battro, A. M. (1973) *Piaget: Dictionary of Terms.* New York: Pergamon Press.

Bernard, H. W. (1970) *Human Development in Western Culture.* Boston: Allyn & Bacon.

Berne, E. (1967) *Games People Play.* New York: Grove Press.

Berne, E. (1972) *What Do You Say after You Say Hello?* New York: Grove Press.

Bettelheim, B. (1967) *The Empty Fortress: Infantile Autism and the Birth of the Self.* New York: Free Press.

Biggs, J. B. (1976) "Schooling and Moral Development," in V. P. Varma and P. Williams (eds.), *Piaget, Psychology, and Education.* Itasca, Ill.: F. E. Peacock.

Bijou, S. W. (1976) *Child Development: The Basic Stage of Early Childhood.* Englewood Cliffs, N.J.: Prentice-Hall.

Bijou, S. W. (1979) "Some Clarifications on the Meaning of a Behavior Analysis of Child Development." *Psychological Record,* Vol. 29, pp. 3–13.

Bijou, S. W. (1984) "Behaviorism—History and Educational Applications," in T. Husen and T. N. Postlethwaite (eds.), *International Encyclopedia of Education.* Oxford: Pergamon Press.

Bijou, S. W., and D. M. Baer. (1961) *Child Development: Vol. I. A Systematic and Empirical Theory.* New York: Appleton-Century-Crofts.

Bijou, S. W., and D. M. Baer. (1965) *Child Development II: Universal Stage of Infancy.* New York: Appleton-Century-Crofts.

Bijou, S. W., and D. M. Baer. (1967) "Operant Methods in Child Behavior and Development," in S. W. Bijou and D. M. Baer, *Child Development: Readings in Experimental Analysis.* New York: Appleton-Century-Crofts.

Block, James H., and L. W. Anderson. (1975) *Mastery Learning in Classroom Instruction.* New York: Macmillan.

Bloom, L. (1970) *Language Development: Form and Function in Emerging Grammars.* Cambridge, Mass.: M. I. T. Press.

Bloom, L. (1973) *One Word at a Time.* The Hague: Mouton.

Bowlby, J. (1969) *Attachment and Loss, Vol. 1: Attachment.* New York: Basic Books.

Bowlby, J. (1973) *Attachment and Loss, Vol. 2: Separation: Anxiety and Anger.* New York: Basic Books.

Bowlby, J. (1980) *Attachment and Loss, Vol. 3: Loss.* New York: Basic Books.

Boyd, W. (1963) *The Educational Theory of Jean Jacques Rousseau.* New York: Russell & Russell.

Boyd, W. (ed. and trans.). (1962) *The Minor Educational Writings of Jean Jacques Rousseau.* New York: Columbia University Press.

Braine, M. D. S. (1971) "The Acquisition of Languages," in C. Reed (ed.,), *The Learning of Language.* New York: Appleton-Century-Crofts.

Bridges, K. M. B. (1966) "The Development of Emotions," in R. L. Wrenn (ed.), *Basic Contributions to Psychology: Readings.* Belmont, Calif.: Wadsworth.

Broadbent, D. E. (1958) *Perceptions and Communication.* New York: Macmillan.

Broadbent, D. E. (1970) "Psychological Aspects of Short-Term and Long-Term Memory." *Proceedings of the Royal Society,* London, Series B, Vol. 175, pp. 333–350.

Brown, A. L., and J. S. DeLoache. (1978) "Skills, Plans, and Self-Regulation," in R. Siegler (ed.), *Children's Thinking: What Develops.* Hillsdale, N.J.: Erlbaum.

Brown, G. I. (1971) *Human Teaching for Human Learning: An Introduction to Confluent Education.* New York: Viking Press.

Brown, G. I. (1976) *The Live Classroom.* New York: Viking Press.

Brown, R. (1973) *A First Language: The Early Stages.* Cambridge, Mass.: Harvard University Press.

Brunk, J. W. (1975) *Child and Adolescent Development.* New York: Wiley.

Buhler, C., and M. Allen. (1972) *Introduction to Humanistic Psychology.* Monterey, Calif.: Brooks/Cole.

Buhler, C., and F. Massarik (eds.). (1968) *The Course of Human Life.* New York: Springer.

Burks, B. S. (1928) "The Relative Influence of Nature and Nurture upon Mental Development," in *Nature and Nurture. Part I: Their Influence upon Intelligence* (27th Yearbook of the National Society for the Study of Education). Bloomington, Ill.: Public School Publishing.

Buss, A. R. (1976) "Development of Dialectics and Development of Humanistic Psychology." *Human Development*, Vol. 19, pp. 248–260.

Cairns, R. B. (1977) "Sociobiology: A New Synthesis or an Old Cleavage?" *Contemporary Psychology*, Vol. 22, pp. 1–3.

California State Penal Code. (1975) Sacramento, Calif.: State of California, Title I, Section 26.

Campbell, S. F. (1976) *Piaget Sampler*. New York: Wiley.

Chi, M. T. H. (1976) "Short-Term Memory Limitations in Children: Capacity or Processing Deficits?" *Memory and Cognition*, Vol. 4, pp. 559–572.

Chomsky, N. (1957) *Syntactic Structures*. The Hague: Mouton.

Chomsky, N. (1967) "Review of Skinner's Verbal Behavior," in L. A. Jakobovits and M. S. Morn (eds.), *Readings in the Philosophy of Language*. Englewood Cliffs, N.J.: Prentice-Hall.

Chomsky, N. (1968) *Language and Mind*. New York: Harcourt Brace Jovanovich.

Colby, A., L. Kohlberg, J. Gibbs, and M. Lieberman. (1983) *A Longitudinal Study of Moral Development*. (Monographs of the Society for Research in Child Development), Serial No. 200, Vol. 48, Nos. 1–2.

Cole, M. (ed.) (1977) *Soviet Developmental Psychology*. White Plains, N.Y.: Sharpe.

Coles, R. (1970) *Erik H. Erikson: The Growth of His Work*. Boston: Little, Brown.

Combs, A. W. (1962) "A Perceptual View of the Adequate Personality," in *Perceiving, Behaving, Becoming*. Washington, D.C.: Association for Supervision and Curriculum Development.

Combs, A. W. (1975) "Humanistic Goals of Education," in D. A. Read and S. B. Simon (eds.), *Humanistic Education Sourcebook*. Englewood Cliffs, N.J.: Prentice-Hall.

Combs, A. W., and D. Snygg. (1959) *Individual Behavior*. New York: Harper & Row.

Connolly, K., and J. Bruner. (1974) *The Growth of Competence*. London: Academic Press.

Craik, F. I. M., and R. S. Lockhart. (1972) "Levels of Processing: A Framework for Memory Research." *Journal of Verbal Learning and Verbal Behavior*, Vol. 11, pp. 671–684.

Crain, W. C. (1980) *Theories of Development: Concepts and Applications*. Englewood Cliffs, N.J.: Prentice-Hall.

Davidov, V. V. (1985) "Soviet Theories of Human Development," in T. Husén and T. N. Postlethwaite (eds.), *International Encyclopedia of Education*. Oxford: Pergamon Press.

Davidson, T. (1898) *Rousseau and Education According to Nature*. New York: Scribner's.

Delacato, C. H. (1966) *Neurological Organization and Reading*. Springfield, Ill.: Charles C Thomas.

Deutsch, J. M. (1943) "The Development of Children's Concepts of Causal Relations," in R. G. Barker, J. S. Kounin, and H. F. Wright, *Child Behavior and Development*. New York: McGraw-Hill.

Dollard, J., and N. E. Miller. (1950) *Personality and Psychotherapy*. New York: McGraw-Hill.

Dooling, D. J., and R. E. Christiaansen. (1977) "Episodic and Semantic Aspects of Memory for Prose." *Journal of Experimental Psychology: Human Learning and Memory,* Vol. 3. pp. 428–436.

Durkin, D. (1976) *Teaching Young Children to Read.* 2d ed. Boston: Allyn & Bacon.

Duvall, E. M. (1971) *Family Development.* Philadelphia: Lippincott.

Eby, F. (ed.). (1971) *Early Protestant Educators.* New York: AMS Press.

Eibl-Eibesfeldt, I. (1975) *Ethology. The Biology of Behavior.* 2d ed. New York: Holt, Rinehart, & Winston.

Elkind, D. (1976) *Child Development and Education.* New York: Oxford University Press.

Erikson, E. H. (1958) *Young Man Luther: A Study in Psychoanalysis and History.* New York: Norton.

Erikson, E. H. (1959) *Identity and the Life Cycle* in *Psychological Issues* monograph, Vol. 1, No. 1. New York: International Universities Press.

Erikson, E. H. (1963) *Childhood and Society.* 2d ed. New York: Norton.

Erikson, E. H. (1964) *Insight and Responsibility.* New York: Norton.

Erikson, E. H. (1968) *Identity: Youth and Crisis.* New York: Norton.

Erikson, E. H. (1969) *Gandhi's Truth.* New York: Norton.

Erikson, E. H. (1975) *Life History and the Historical Movement.* New York: Norton.

Erikson, E. H. (1977) *Toys and Reasons.* New York: Norton.

Erikson, E. H. (1982) *The Life Cycle Completed.* New York: Norton.

Eysenck, H. J. (1959) "Learning Theory and Behavior Therapy." *Journal of Consulting Psychology,* Vol. 16, pp. 319–324.

Fantini, M., and G. Weinstein. (1968) *Toward a Contact Curriculum.* New York: Anti-Defamation League of B'nai B'rith.

Farnham-Diggory, S. (1972) *Information Processing in Children.* New York: Academic Press.

Flavell, J. H. (1977) *Cognitive Development.* Englewood Cliffs, N.J.: Prentice-Hall.

Ford, P. L. (1962) *The New England Primer.* New York: Columbia University Press.

Frenkel-Brunswik, E. (1954) *Psychoanalysis and the Unity of Science.* Proceedings of the Academy of Arts and Sciences, Vol. 80.

Freud, A. (1974) *The Writings of Anna Freud.* New York: International Universities Press. In five volumes.

Freud, S. (1900) "The Interpretation of Dreams," in J. Strachey (ed.), *The Standard Edition of the Complete Psychological Works of Sigmund Freud.* Vol. 4. London: Hogarth, 1953.

Freud, S. (1910) "Five Lectures on Psychoanalysis," in J. Strachey (ed.), *The Standard Edition of the Complete Psychological Works of Sigmund Freud.* Vol. 11. London: Hogarth, 1957.

Freud, S. (1917) "Introductory Lectures on Psychoanalysis, Part III," in J. Strachey (ed.), *The Standard Edition of the Complete Psychological Works of Sigmund Freud.* Vol. 16. London: Hogarth, 1957.

Freud, S. (1920) "Beyond the Pleasure Principles," in J. Strachey (ed.), *The Standard Edition of the Complete Psychological Works of Sigmund Freud.* Vol. 18. London: Hogarth, 1957.

Freud, S. (1923) *The Ego and the Id.* London: Hogarth, 1974.

Freud, S. (1933) *New Introductory Lectures on Psychoanalysis.* New York: Norton.

Freud, S. (1938) *An Outline of Psychoanalysis.* London: Hogarth, 1973.

Freud, S. (1964) *The Standard Edition of the Complete Psychological Works of Sigmund Freud.* James Strachey, trans. and ed. London: Hogarth. In thirty volumes.

Froebel, F. (1889) *The Education of Man* (ed. W. N. Hailmann). New York: Appleton-Century-Crofts.

Frostig, M., and P. Maslow. (1973) *Learning Problems in the Classroom.* New York: Grune & Stratton.

Furth, H. G., and W. Wachs. (1975) *Thinking Goes to School.* New York: Oxford University Press.

Gesell, A. (1940) *The First Five Years of Life.* New York: Harper & Row.

Gesell, A., and F. L. Ilg. (1949) *Child Development: An Introduction to the Study of Human Growth.* New York: Harper & Row.

Getman, G. N. (1965) "The Visuomotor Complex in the Acquisition of Learning Skills," in J. Hellmuth (ed.), *Learning Disorders, Vol. 1.* Seattle: Special Child Publications.

Gibson, E. J. (1969) *Principles of Perceptual Learning and Development.* New York: Appleton-Century-Crofts.

Gibson, E. J., and N. Rader. (1979) "The Perceiver as Performer," in G. Hale and M. Lewis (eds.), *Attention and Cognitive Development.* New York: Plenum.

Godin, A. (1971) "Some Developmental Tasks in Christian Education," in M. P. Strommen (ed.), *Research on Religious Development.* New York: Hawthorne.

Greven, Philip. (1977) *The Protestant Temperament: Patterns of Child Rearing, Religious Experience, and the Self in Early America.* New York: Knopf.

Grimm, J. A., S. W. Bijou, and J. A. Parsons. (1973) "A Problem Solving Model in Teaching Remedial Arithmetic to Handicapped Young Children." *Journal of Abnormal Child Psychology,* Vol. 1, pp. 26–39.

Guilford, J. P. (1967) *The Nature of Human Intelligence.* New York: McGraw-Hill.

Hagen, J. W., R. H. Jongeward, Jr., and R. V. Kail, Jr. (1975) "Cognitive Perspectives on the Development of Memory," in H. W. Reese and L. P. Lipsitt (eds.), *Advances in Child Development and Behavior,* Vol. 10. New York: Academic Press.

Hall, C. S. (1954) *Primer of Freudian Psychology.* New York: World.

Hall, C. S., and G. Lindzey. (1970) *Theories of Personality.* 2d ed. New York: Wiley.

Hall, C. S., and G. Lindzey. (1978) *Theories of Personality.* 3d ed. New York: Wiley.

Hall, C. S., and V. J. Nordby. (1973) *A Primer of Jungian Psychology.* New York: Toplinger.

Hall, G. S. (1891) "The Contents of Children's Minds on Entering School." *Pedagogical Seminar,* Vol. 1, pp. 139–173.

Hall, G. S. (1904) *Adolescence.* New York: Appleton-Century-Crofts. In two volumes.

Hamilton, W. D. (1964) "The Genetical Evolution of Social Behavior." *Journal of Theoretical Biology,* Vol. 7, pp. 1–52.

Harris, M. L., and C. H. Harris. (1971) "A Factor Analytic Interpretation Strategy." *Educational and Psychological Measurement,* Vol. 31, pp. 589–606.

Hartmann, H. (1959) "Psychoanalysis as a Scientific Theory," in S. Hook (ed.), *Psychoanalysis, Scientific Method, and Philosophy.* New York: New York University Press.

Hartshorne, H., and M. A. May (1928–1930) *Studies in the Nature of Character.* New York: Macmillan. In three volumes.

Havighurst, R. J. (1953) *Human Development and Education.* New York: Longmans, Green.

Heafford, M. (1967) *Pestalozzi, His Thought and Its Relevance Today.* London: Methuen.

Hebb, D. O. (1949) *The Organization of Behavior.* New York: Wiley.

Hebb, D. O. (1970) "A Return to Jensen and His Social Critics." *American Psychologist,* Vol. 25, p. 568.

Heider, F. (1958) *The Psychology of Interpersonal Relations.* New York: Wiley.

Hilgard, E. R. (1952) "Experimental Approaches to Psychoanalysis," in E. Pumpian-Mindlin, *Psychoanalysis as Science.* Stanford, Calif.: Stanford University Press.

Hilgard, E. R., and G. H. Bower. (1975) *Theories of Learning.* 4th ed. Englewood Cliffs, N.J.: Prentice-Hall.

Himmelweit, T., and B. Swift. (1969) "A Model for Understanding of School as a Socializing Agent," in P. H. Mussen, J. Langer, and M. Covington (eds.), *Trends and Issues in Developmental Psychology.* New York: Holt, Rinehart, & Winston.

Hinde, R. A. (1974) *Biological Bases of Human Social Behaviour.* New York: McGraw-Hill.

Hirsch, J. (1970) "Behaviour-Genetic Analysis and Its Biosocial Consequences." *Seminars in Psychiatry,* Vol. 2, pp. 89–105.

Holman, J., E. M. Goetz, and D. M. Baer. (1977) "The Training of Creativity as an Operant and an Examination of Its Generalization Characteristics," in B. C. Etzel, J. M. LeBlanc, and D. M. Baer (eds.), *New Developments in Behavior Research: Theory, Method, and Application.* Hillsdale, N.J.: Erlbaum.

Holstein, C. (1976) "Irreversible, Stepwise Sequence in the Development of Moral Judgment: A Longitudinal Study of Males and Females." *Child Development,* Vol. 47, pp. 51–61.

Hook, S. (1959) "Science and Mythology in Psychoanalysis," in S. Hook (ed.), *Psychoanalysis, Scientific Method, and Philosophy.* New York: New York University Press.

Horton, D. L., and T. W. Turnage (1976) *Human Learning.* Englewood Cliffs, N.J.: Prentice-Hall.

Hunt, J. McV. (1961) *Intelligence and Experience.* New York: Ronald.

Hurlock, E. B. (1968) *Developmental Psychology.* 3d ed. New York: McGraw-Hill.

Huxley, A. (1932) *Brave New World.* New York: Harper & Row.

Ilg, F. L., and L. B. Ames. (1955) *The Gesell Institute's Child Behavior.* New York: Dell.

Inhelder, B. (1968) "Foreword," in I. E. Sigel and F. H. Hooper (eds.), *Logical Thinking in Children.* New York: Holt, Rinehart & Winston.

Inhelder, B., and J. Piaget. (1958) *The Growth of Logical Thinking from Childhood to Adolescence.* New York: Basic Books.

Inhelder, B., and J. Piaget. (1964) *The Early Growth of Logic in the Child.* London: Routledge & Kegan Paul.

James, W. (1890) *The Principles of Psychology.* New York: Holt, Rinehart & Winston.

Janov, A. (1973) *The Feeling Child.* New York: Simon & Schuster.

Jensen, A. R. (1969) "How Much Can We Boost IQ and Scholastic Achievement?" *Harvard Educational Review,* Vol. 39, pp. 1–123.

Jensen, A. R. (1973) *Educability and Group Differences.* New York: Harper & Row.

Jones, E. (1961) *The Life and Works of Sigmund Freud.* New York: Basic Books.

Jones, E. E., and R. E. Nisbett. (1971) *The Actor and the Observer: Divergent Perceptions of the Causes of Behavior.* Morristown, N.J.: General Learning Press.

Kail, R., and J. Bisanz (1982) "Information Processing and Cognitive Development," in H. W. Reese and L. P. Lipsitt (eds.), *Advances in Child Development and Behavior,* Vol. 17. New York: Academic Press.

Kantor, J. R. (1959) *Interbehavioral Psychology.* 2d rev. ed. Bloomington, Ind.: Principia.

Kaufman, Lloyd. (1974) *Sight and Mind.* New York: Oxford University Press.

Kazdin, A. E. (1981) "Behavior Modification in Education: Contributions and Limitations." *Development Review,* Vol. 1, pp. 34–57.

Kazdin, A. E. (1978) *History of Behavior Modification: Experimental Foundations of Contemporary Research.* Baltimore, Md.: University Park Press.

Keller, F. S., and W. N. Schoenfeld. (1950) *Principles of Psychology.* New York: Appleton-Century-Crofts.

Keller, F. S., and J. G. Sherman. (1974) *The Keller Plan Handbook.* Menlo Park, Calif.: Benjamin/Cummings.

Kelley, E. C. (1962) "The Fully Functioning Self," in *Perceiving, Behaving, Becoming.* Washington, D.C.: Association for Supervision and Curriculum Development.

Kelley, H. H. (1973) "The Process of Causal Attribution." *American Psychologist,* Vol. 28, pp. 107–128.

Kendler, H. H., and T. S. Kendler. (1975) "Discrimination and Development," in W. K. Estes (ed.), *Handbook of Learning and Cognitive Processes.* New York: Halsted.

Kephart, N. C. (1960, 1st ed.; 1971, 2d ed.) *The Slow Learner in the Classroom.* Columbus, Ohio: Merrill.

Kilpatrick, W. H. (1916) *Froebel's Kindergarten Principles Critically Examined.* New York: Macmillan.

Klahr, D., and J. G. Wallace. (1976) *Cognitive Development: An Information-Processing View*. Hillsdale, N.J.: Erlbaum.

Klatzky, R. L. (1980) *Human Memory: Structures and Processes*. San Francisco: W. H. Freeman.

Klaus, M. H., and J. H. Kennell. (1976) *Maternal-Infant Bonding*. St. Louis: Mosby.

Kohlberg, L. (1967) "Moral and Religious Education in the Public Schools: A Developmental View," in T. R. Sizer, *Religion and Public Education*. Boston: Houghton Mifflin.

Kohlberg, L. (1968a) "The Child as a Moral Philosopher." *Psychology Today*, Vol. 2, pp. 25–30.

Kohlberg, L. (1968b) "Moral Development," in *International Encyclopedia of the Social Sciences*. New York: Macmillan.

Kohlberg, L., and R. Kramer. (1969) "Continuities in Childhood and Adult Moral Development." *Human Development*, Vol. 12, pp. 93–120.

Kohlberg, L. (1971) "From Is to Ought," in T. Mischel, *Cognitive Development and Epistemology*. New York: Academic Press.

Koppitz, E. M. (1968) *Psychological Evaluation of Children's Human Figure Drawings*. New York: Grune & Stratton.

Kounin, J. S. (1943) "Intellectual Development and Rigidity," in R. G. Barker, J. S. Kounin, and H. F. Wright, *Child Behavior and Development*. New York: McGraw-Hill.

Kris, E. (1947) "The Nature of Psychoanalytic Propositions and Their Validation," in S. Hook and M. R. Konvitz, *Freedom and Experience*. Ithaca, N.Y.: Cornell University Press.

Kuhn, T. S. (1962) *The Structure of Scientific Revolutions*. Chicago: University of Chicago Press.

Kurtines, W., and E. Greif. (1974) "The Development of Moral Thought: Review and Evaluation of Kohlberg's Approach." *Psychological Bulletin*, Vol. 81, pp. 453–470.

Lample-Degroot, J. (1965) *The Development of the Mind*. New York: International Universities Press.

Langer, J. (1969) *Theories of Development*. New York: Holt, Rinehart, & Winston.

Lashley, K. S. (1960) in F. A. Beach et al. (eds.), *The Neuropsychology of Lashley: Selected Papers*. New York: McGraw-Hill.

Laslett, P. (1970) in D. B. Rutman, *American Puritanism*. Philadelphia: Lippincott.

Layzer, D. (1974) "Heritability Analyses of IQ Scores: Science or Numerology?" *Science*, Vol. 183, pp. 1259–1266.

Leahy, A. M. (1935) "Nature–Nurture and Intelligence." *Genetic Psychology Monographs*, Vol. 17, pp. 236–308.

Leff, H. L. (1978) *Experience, Environment, and Human Potentials*. New York: Oxford University Press.

Lerner, J. (1971) *Children with Learning Disabilities*. Boston: Houghton Mifflin.

Lerner, R. M. (1976) *Concepts and Theories of Human Development.* Reading, Mass.: Addison-Wesley.

Lewin, K. (1939) "The Field Theory Approach to Adolescence." *American Journal of Sociology,* Vol. 44, pp. 868–896.

Lewin, K. (1942) "Field Theory and Learning," in *Forty-First Yearbook, National Society for the Study of Education, Part II.* Bloomington, Ill.: Public School Publishing.

Lewin, K. (1936) *Principles of Topological Psychology.* New York: McGraw-Hill.

Lillard, P. P. (1972) *Montessori, A Modern Approach.* New York: Schocken.

Loftus, E. F. (1975) "Leading Questions and Eyewitness Report." *Cognitive Psychology,* Vol. 7, pp. 560–572.

Lorenz, K. Z. (1952) *King Solomon's Ring.* New York: Macmillan.

Lorenz, K. Z. (1965) *Evolution and Modification of Behavior.* Chicago: University of Chicago Press.

Lorenz, K. Z. (1977) *Behind the Mirror: A Search for a Natural History of Human Knowledge.* New York: Harcourt Brace Jovanovich.

Lowenfeld, V. (1957) *Creative and Mental Growth.* New York: Macmillan.

Luria, A. R. (1976) *Cognitive Development: Its Cultural and Social Foundations.* Cambridge, Mass.: Harvard University Press

Luria, A. R., and R. Yudovich. (1971) *Speech and the Development of Mental Processes in the Child.* Harmondsworth, England: Penguin.

Luther, M. (1519a) "Duties of Parents in Training Children," in F. Eby (ed.), *Early Protestant Educators.* New York: AMS Press, 1971.

Luther, M. (1519b) "Evil of Lax Discipline," in F. Eby (ed.), *Early Protestant Educators.* New York: AMS Press, 1971.

Luther, M. (1523) "Harsh Methods Opposed," in F. Eby (ed.), *Early Protestant Educators.* New York: AMS Press, 1971.

Luther, M. (1529) "A Short Catechism for the Use of Ordinary Pastors and Preachers," in F. Eby (ed.), *Early Protestant Educators.* New York: AMS Press, 1971.

Luther, M. (1530) "About Aesop's Fables," in F. Eby (ed.), *Early Protestant Educators.* New York: AMS Press, 1971.

Mackworth, J. F. (1976) "Development of Attention," in V. Hamilton and M. D. Vernon, *The Development of Cognitive Processes.* New York: Academic Press.

Maddi, S. R. (1972) *Personality Theories: A Comparative Analysis.* Homewood, Ill.: Dorsey Press.

Mahrer, A. R. (1978) *Experiencing: A Humanistic Theory of Psychology and Psychiatry.* New York: Brunner/Mazel.

Maier, H. W. (1978) *Three Theories of Child Development: Erik H. Erikson, Jean Piaget, and Robert R. Sears.* 3d ed. New York: Harper & Row.

Maslow, A. H. (1968) *Toward a Psychology of Being.* Princeton, N.J.: Van Nostrand Reinhold.

Maslow, A. H. (1970) *Motivation and Personality.* 2d ed. New York: Harper & Row.

Maslow, A. H. (1971) *The Farther Reaches of Human Nature.* New York: Viking Press.

McNeill, D. (1970) *The Acquisition of Language: The Study of Developmental Psycholinguistics.* New York: Harper & Row.

Miller, G. A. (1956) "The Magical Number Seven, Plus or Minus Two: Some Limits on Our Capacity for Processing Information." *Psychological Review,* Vol. 63, pp. 81–97.

Miller, P. (1963) *The New England Mind: The Seventeenth Century.* Cambridge, Mass.: Harvard University Press.

Miller, P. H. (1983) *Theories of Developmental Psychology.* San Francisco: W. H. Freeman.

Montagu, A. (1959) *Human Heredity.* New York: Harcourt Brace Jovanovich.

Montessori, M. (1967) *The Absorbant Mind.* New York: Dell.

Morgan, E. S. (1956) *The Puritan Family.* Boston: Trustees of the Public Library.

Morison, S. E. (1936) *The Puritan Pronaos.* New York: New York University Press.

Muller, P. (1969) *The Tasks of Childhood.* New York: McGraw-Hill.

Nagel, E. (1959) "Methodological Issues in Psychoanalytic Theory," in S. Hook (ed.), *Psychoanalysis, Scientific Method, and Philosophy.* New York: New York University Press.

Neumann, E. (1973) *The Child.* New York: Putnam.

Newell, A., and H. A. Simon. (1972) *Human Problem Solving.* Englewood Cliffs, N.J.: Prentice-Hall.

New England Primer: Or An Easy and Pleasant Guide to the Art of Reading. (1836) Boston: Massachusetts Sabbath School Society.

Norton, J. (1963) in P. Miller, *The New England Mind: The Seventeenth Century.* Cambridge, Mass.: Harvard University Press.

Nucci, L. P. (1982) "Conceptual Development in the Moral and Conventional Domains: Implications for Values Education." *Review of Educational Research,* Vol. 52, pp. 93–122.

Ornstein, P. A., and M. J. Naus. (1978) "Rehearsal Processes in Children's Memory," in P. A. Ornstein, *Memory Development in Children.* Hillsdale, N.J.: Erlbaum.

Otto, H., and J. Mann. (1968) *Ways of Growth.* New York: Grossman.

Ouspensky, P. D. (1957) *The Fourth Way.* London: Routledge & Kegan Paul.

Paris, S. G. (1978) "The Development of Inference and Transformation as Memory Operations," in P. A. Ornstein, *Memory Development in Children.* Hillsdale, N.J.: Erlbaum.

Patterson, S. W. (1971) *Rousseau's Emile and Early Children's Literature.* Metuchen, N.Y.: Scarecrow.

Peel, E. A. (1976) "The Thinking and Education of the Adolescent," in V. P. Varma and P. Williams (eds.), *Piaget, Psychology, and Education.* Itasca, Ill.: F. E. Peacock.

Pepper, S. C. (1942) *World Hypotheses: A Study in Evidence.* Berkeley, Calif.: University of California Press.

Perls, F. S., R. F. Hefferline, and P. Goodman. (1951) *Gestalt Therapy*. New York: Julian Press.

Peters, R. S. (1971) "Moral Development: A Plea for Pluralism," in T. Mischel, *Cognitive Development and Epistemology*. New York: Academic Press.

Phillips, D. C., and M. E. Kelly. (1975) "Hierarchical Theories of Development in Education and Psychology." *Harvard Educational Review*, Vol. 45, pp. 351–375.

Phillips, J. L., Jr. (1975) *The Origins of Intellect: Piaget's Theory*. 2d ed. San Francisco: W. H. Freeman.

Piaget, J. (1930) *The Child's Conception of Physical Causality*. London: Routledge & Kegan Paul.

Piaget, J. (1946) *Le Développement de la Notion de Temps chez l'Enfant*. Paris: Presses Universitaires de France.

Piaget, J. (1948) *The Moral Judgment of the Child*. Glencoe, Ill.: Free Press.

Piaget, J. (1950) *The Psychology of Intelligence*. London: Routledge & Kegan Paul.

Piaget, J. (1952) *The Child's Conception of Number*. London: Routledge & Kegan Paul.

Piaget, J. (1953) *Logic and Psychology*. Manchester, England: Manchester University Press.

Piaget, J. (1962) *Play, Dreams, and Imitation in Childhood*. New York: Norton.

Piaget, J. (1963) *The Origins of Intelligence in Children*. 2d ed. New York: Norton.

Piaget, J. (1969) *The Child's Conception of Movement and Speed*. New York: Basic Books.

Piaget, J. (1970a) *Genetic Epistemology*. New York: Columbia University Press.

Piaget, J. (1970b) *Science of Education and the Psychology of the Child*. New York: Viking Press.

Piaget, J. (1972) *Psychology and Epistemology*. London: Penguin.

Piaget, J. (1973) *The Child and Reality*. New York: Viking Press.

Piaget, J., L. Apostel, and B. Mandelbrot. (1957) *Logique et Equilibre*. Paris: Presses Universitaires de France.

Piaget, J., and B. Inhelder. (1956) *The Child's Conception of Space*. London: Routledge & Kegan Paul.

Piaget, J., and B. Inhelder. (1969) *The Psychology of the Child*. New York: Basic Books.

Piaget, J., A. Jonckheere, and B. Mandelbrot. (1958) *La Lecture de l'Expérience* (Etudes d'Epistémologie Génétique V). Paris: Presses Universitaires de France.

Piaget, J., and A. Szeminska. (1952) *The Child's Conception of Number*. Atlantic Highlands, N.J.: Humanities Press.

Reese, H. W., and W. F. Overton. (1970) "Models of Development and Theories of Development," in L. R. Goulet and Paul B. Baltes, *Life-Span Developmental Psychology*. New York: Academic Press.

Reeves, C. (1977) *The Psychology of Rollo May*. San Francisco: Jossey-Bass.

Riegel, K. F. (1973) "Dialectic Operations: The Final Period of Cognitive Development." *Human Development*, Vol. 16, pp. 346–370.

Rogers, C. R. (1961) *On Becoming a Person*. Boston: Houghton Mifflin.

Rogers, C. R. (1973) "My Philosophy of Interpersonal Relationships and How It Grew." *Journal of Humanistic Psychology*, Vol. 13, pp. 13–15.

Rousseau, J. J. (1773) *Emilius; or, A Treatise of Education*. Edinburgh: W. Coke. In three volumes.

Rousseau, J. J. (1955) *Emile* (trans. B. Foxley). New York: Dutton, Everyman's Library.

Royce, J. (1959) "Herbert Spencer," in *Encyclopedia Americana*. Vol. 25. New York: Americana.

Rutman, D. B. (1970) *American Puritanism*. Philadelphia: Lippincott.

Savin-Williams, R. C. (1976) "An Ethological Study of Dominance Formation and Maintenance in a Group of Human Adolescents." *Child Development*, Vol. 47, pp. 972–979.

Schilmoeller, K. J., and B. C. Etzel. (1977) "An Experimental Analysis of Criterion-Related and Noncriterion-Related Cues in 'Errorless' Stimulus Control Procedures," in B. C. Etzel, J. M. LeBlanc, and D. M. Baer (eds.), *New Developments in Behavior Research: Theory, Method, and Application*. Hillsdale, N.J.: Erlbaum.

Schlesinger, I. M. (1971) "Production of Utterances and Language Acquisition," in D. E. Slobin (ed.), *The Ontogenesis of Grammar*. New York: Academic Press.

Schneirla, T. C. (1957) "The Concept of Development in Comparative Psychology," in D. B. Harris (ed.), *The Concept of Development*. Minneapolis: University of Minnesota Press.

Schneirla, T. C., and J. S. Rosenblatt. (1963) " 'Critical Periods' in Behavioral Development." *Science*, Vol. 139, pp. 1110–1114.

Schneirla, T. C. (1972) in L. R. Aronson, E. Tobach, J. S. Rosenblatt, and D. S. Lehrman (eds.), *Selected Writings of T. C. Schneirla*. San Francisco: W. H. Freeman.

Scott, J. P. (1963) "Critical Periods in Behavioral Development." *Science*, Vol. 138, pp. 949–958.

Scriven, M. (1959) "The Experimental Investigation of Psychoanalysis," in S. Hook (ed.), *Psychoanalysis, Scientific Method, and Philosophy*. New York: New York University Press.

Sears, R. R. (1943) "Survey of Objective Studies of Psychoanalytic Concepts." *Bulletin: Social Science Research Council*, p. 51.

Sears, R. R., E. E. Maccoby, and H. Levin. (1957) *Patterns of Child Rearing*. New York: Harper & Row.

Sears, R. R., L. Rau, and R. Alpert. (1965) *Identification and Child Rearing*. Stanford, Calif.: Stanford University Press.

Sheldon, W. H. (1940) *Varieties of Physique*. New York: Harper & Row.

Sheldon, W. H. (1942) *Varieties of Temperament*. New York: Harper & Row.

Sherif, M. (1966) *In Common Predicament: Social Psychology of Intergroup Conflict and Cooperation*. Boston: Houghton Mifflin.

Shostrum, E. (1966) *Manual for the Personal Orientation Inventory (POI)*. San Diego: Educational and Industrial Testing Service.

Shuttleworth, F. K. (1935) "The Nature versus Nurture Problem: II. The Contributions of Nature and Nurture to Individual Differences in Intelligence." *Journal of Educational Psychology,* Vol. 26, pp. 655–681.

Sidgwick, A. (1959) "Recapitulation," in *The Encyclopedia Americana.* Vol. 23. New York: Americana.

Sigel, I. E., and F. H. Hooper. (1968) *Logical Thinking in Children.* New York: Holt, Rinehart & Winston.

Sigel, I. E., and R. C. Cocking. (1977) *Cognitive Development from Childhood to Adolescence: A Constructivist Perspective.* New York: Holt, Rinehart & Winston.

Simonson, H. P. (ed.). (1970) *Selected Writings of Jonathan Edwards.* New York: Ungar.

Skeels, H. M. (1940) "Some Iowa Studies of the Mental Growth of Children in Relation to Differentials of the Environment: A Summary." *Intelligence: Its Nature and Nurture* (39th Yearbook of the National Society for the Study of Education). Bloomington, Ill.: Public School Publishing.

Skinner, B. F. (1945) "Baby in a Box," in B. F. Skinner (ed.), *Cumulative Record: A Selection of Papers.* 3d ed. New York: Appleton-Century-Crofts, 1972.

Skinner, B. F. (1948) *Walden Two.* New York: Macmillan.

Skinner, B. F. (1950) "Are Theories of Learning Necessary?" *Psychological Review,* Vol. 57, pp. 193–216.

Skinner, B. F. (1969) *Contingencies of Reinforcement: A Theoretical Analysis.* Englewood Cliffs, N.J.: Prentice-Hall.

Skinner, B. F. (1971) *Beyond Freedom and Dignity.* New York: Knopf.

Skinner, B. F. (1974) *About Behaviorism.* New York: Knopf.

Skodak, M. (1939) "Children in Foster Homes: A Study of Mental Development." *University of Iowa Studies in Child Welfare,* Vol. 16, No.1.

Smith, J. E. (1959) *The Works of Jonathan Edwards, Volume 2: Religious Affections.* New Haven: Yale University Press.

Spence, K. W. (1963) in Melvin H. Marx (ed.), *Theories in Contemporary Psychology.* New York: Macmillan.

Stafford-Clark, D. (1967) *What Freud Really Said.* London: Penguin.

Stemmer, N. (1973) *An Empiricist Theory of Language Acquisition.* The Hague: Mouton.

Sternberg, S. (1969) "Memory-Scanning: Mental Processes Revealed by Reaction-Time Experiments." *American Scientist,* Vol. 57, pp. 421–457.

Stevenson, H. W. (1972) *Children's Learning.* New York: Appleton-Century-Crofts.

Stevick, D. B. (1968) *B. F. Skinner's Walden Two.* New York: Seabury Press.

Strauss, A., and L. Lehtinen. (1947) *Psychopathology and Education of the Brain-Injured Child.* Vol. 1. New York: Grune & Stratton.

Strayer, F. F., and J. Strayer. (1976) "An Ethological Analysis of Social Agonism and Dominance Relations among Pre-school Children." *Child Development,* Vol. 47, pp. 980–999.

Sullivan, H. S. (1953) *The Interpersonal Theory of Psychiatry.* New York: Norton.

Suppes, P. C. (1969) *Studies in the Methodology and Foundations of Science.* Dordrecht, Holland: R. Reidel.

Thomas, A., and S. Chess. (1980) *The Dynamics of Psychological Development.* New York: Brunner/Mazel.

Thomas, R. M. (1981) "A Model of Diagnostic Evaluation," in A. Lewy and D. Nevo, *Evaluation Roles in Education.* New York: Gordon & Breach.

Thomas, R. M., and S. M. Thomas. (1965) *Individual Differences in the Classroom.* New York: David McKay.

Thomas, R. M., and D. L. Brubaker (1971) *Curriculum Patterns in Elementary Social Studies.* Belmont, Calif.: Wadsworth.

Tinbergen, N. (1973) *The Animal in Its World: Explorations of an Ethologist 1932–1972.* Cambridge, Mass: Harvard University Press.

Travers, J. F. (1977) *The Growing Child.* New York: Wiley.

Trivers, R. L. and H. Hare. (1976) "Haplodipoidy and the Evolution of the Social Insects," *Science,* Vol. 191, pp. 249–263.

Tronick, E., and P. M. Greenfield. (1973) *Infant Curriculum: The Bromley-Heath Guide to the Care of Infants in Groups.* New York: Media Projects.

Tryon, C., and J. Lilienthal. (1950) "Developmental Tasks: I. The Concept and Its Importance," in *Fostering Mental Health in Our Schools.* Washington, D.C.: Association for Supervision and Curriculum Development, National Education Association.

Tulving, E. (1972) "Episodic and Semantic Memory," in E. Tulving and W. Donaldson (eds.), *Organization and Memory.* New York: Academic Press.

Turiel, E. (1969) "Developmental Processes in the Child's Moral Thinking," in P. H. Mussen, J. Langer, and M. Covington (eds.), *Trends and Issues in Developmental Psychology.* New York: Holt, Rinehart, & Winston.

Turiel, E. (1977) "Distinct Conceptual and Developmental Domains: Social Convention and Morality." *Nebraska Symposium on Motivation,* Vol. 25. Lincoln: University of Nebraska Press.

Uttal, W. R. (1981) *A Taxonomy of Visual Processes.* Hillsdale, N.J.: Erlbaum.

van der Geest, T., R. Berstel, R. Appel, and B. T. Tervoort. (1973) *The Child's Communicative Competence.* The Hague: Mouton.

Vaughn, A. T. (1972) *The Puritan Tradition in America, 1620–1730.* Columbia, S.C.: University of South Carolina Press.

Vaughn, G. M. (1972) "Concept Formation and the Development of Ethnic Awareness," in A. R. Brown (ed.), *Prejudice in Children.* Springfield, Ill: Charles C Thomas.

Vonéche, J. J. (1985) "Piaget's Genetic Epistemology," in T. Husen and T. N. Postlethwaite (eds.), *International Encyclopedia of Education.* Oxford: Pergamon Press.

Vurpillot, E. (1976) "Development of Identification of Objects," in V. Hamilton and M. D. Vernon, *The Development of Cognitive Processes.* New York: Academic Press.

Vygotsky, L. S. (1962) *Thought and Language.* Cambridge, Mass.: M.I.T. Press.

Vygotsky, L. S. (1971) *Psychology of Art.* Cambridge, Mass.: M.I.T. Press.

Vygotsky, L. S. (1978) in M. Cole, V. John-Steiner, S. Scribner, and E. Souberman (eds.), *Mind in Society.* Cambridge, Mass.: Harvard University Press.

Wadsworth, B. J. (1971) *Piaget's Theory of Cognitive Development.* New York: David McKay.

Wall, C. (1974) *Predication: A Study of Its Development.* The Hague: Mouton.

Wapner, S., and H. Werner. (1965) *The Body Percept.* New York: Random House.

Watson, J. B. (1914) *Behavior, an Introduction to Comparative Psychology.* New York: Holt, Rinehart, & Winston.

Watson, J. B. (1919) *Psychology from the Standpoint of a Behaviorist.* Philadelphia: Lippincott.

Weiner, B. (1972) *Theories of Motivation.* Chicago: Markham.

Weiner, B. (1974) *Achievement Motivation and Attribution Theory.* Morristown, N.J.: General Learning Press.

Werner, H. (1961) *Comparative Psychology of Mental Development.* New York: Science Editions.

Werner, H., and B. Kaplan. (1963) *Symbol Formation — An Organismic-Developmental Approach to Language and the Expression of Thought.* New York: Wiley.

White, B. L. (1971) *Human Infants: Experience and Psychological Development.* Englewood Cliffs, N.J.: Prentice-Hall.

White, C. B., N. Bushnell, and J. L. Regnemer. (1978) "Moral Development in Bahamian School Children: A Three-Year Examination of Kohlberg's Stages of Moral Development." *Developmental Psychology,* Vol. 14, pp. 58–65.

Wilson, E. O. (1975) *Sociobiology: The New Synthesis.* Cambridge, Mass.: Harvard University Press.

Wilson, E. O. (1978) *On Human Nature.* Cambridge, Mass.: Harvard University Press.

Wohlwill, J. R. (1976) "The Age Variable in Psychological Research," in N. S. Endler, L. R. Boulter, and H. Osser, *Contemporary Issues in Developmental Psychology.* New York: Holt, Rinehart & Winston.

Wolman, B. B. (1968) *The Unconscious Mind.* Englewood Cliffs, N.J.: Prentice-Hall.

Wolpe J., and D. Wolpe. (1981) *Our Useless Fears.* Boston: Houghton Mifflin.

Woodworth, R. S. (1929) *Psychology.* New York: Holt, Rinehart & Winston.

Worchel, S. and J. Cooper. (1979) *Understanding Social Psychology.* Homewood, Ill.: Dorsey Press.

Wright, H. F. (1943) "The Effect of Barriers upon Strength of Motivation," in R. G. Barker, J. S. Kounin, and W. F. Wright, *Child Behavior and Development.* New York: McGraw-Hill.

Wuthnow, R. (1978) "Peak Experiences: Some Empirical Tests." *Journal of Humanistic Psychology,* Vol. 18, No. 3, pp. 57–75.

Zigler, E. (1963) "Metatheoretical Issues in Developmental Psychology," in M. H. Marx (ed.), *Theories in Contemporary Psychology.* New York: Macmillan.

NAME INDEX

This index contains two types of names: (1) those of people whose specific publications are cited in the text and (2) those of people whose ideas are cited but whose specific publications are not.

SUBJECT INDEX

Ability levels, 93–95, 177
Abnormality, 28, 48, 125, 406–410, 433
Achievement motivation, 429
Accommodation, 266–268
Adolescence, 8–10, 16–17, 29–30, 71, 74–75, 99–101, 108, 132, 134, 136–139, 161–164, 213–214, 237– 239, 242–243, 246–247, 260, 264, 283–284, 341, 343, 388–389
Affect, affection, 67, 136, 333, 357
Age levels, 29–30, 41, 46
Allocentric stage, 293
Altruism, 184–186
Ambivalence, 209–210
Anal-urethral period, 207, 210–211, 238–246
Analogue, analogy, defined, 11, 13
Animal spirits, 66–67
Anticathexis, 211
Applications, practical, 80–81, 101– 102, 124–126, 135, 142–143, 169, 188–190, 224–225, 252–253, 291– 298, 319–321, 345–346, 363–365, 392–393, 415–416, 435–437
Apprehension span, 341
Articulation, 159–160
Assimilation, 266–268, 371
Association for Humanistic Psychology, 419
Assumptions, 12, 14–15, 28
Attention, attention span, 336–337, 339–340, 402
Attitudes, 93–95
Attribution theory, 90–109
Autonomy, 236, 238, 240–241, 246
Axiom, defined, 12, 14–15

Behavior: aversive consequences of, 376–377; complex, 405–406; covert, 381; management, 392; modification, 392, 405–410; profile, 120; settings, 170–172; social, 353; therapy, 405–410, 416
Behavioral engineering, 385
Behaviorism, 10–11, 49, 131, 151, 306, 371–418, 421; methodological, 381; radical, 10–11, 81, 381

Birth trauma, 208
Biting stage, 209–210
Body type, 120
Bonding, 183–184
Boundaries, 149, 152–156, 161–164, 171
Breast feeding, 72

Calling, 71, 78, 434
Calvinism, 53–54, 60, 63, 65
Cathexis, 208
Causality, 271
Centration, 277–278
Chaining, defined, 379–380
Chunk, 332, 341
Circular reactions: primary, 272; secondary, 273; tertiary, 273–274
Classification, ability of, 264
Clinical method, 260–261
Coding, 402
Cognitive psychology, 398
Collective monologue, 277
Common sense, 53–57, 63, 67, 73, 90– 109, 262–263
Compensation, 206
Competence, 246
Complexes, thinking in, 308, 313–314
Computers, 326
Conditioning: classical, 373–374; counter, 415; instrumental, 373–375; operant, 373–375; respondent, 374
Confluent education, 436–437
Congeries, thinking in, 313
Conscience, 68, 75, 137, 204–205, 371, 410–411, 427
Conscious, consciousness, 198–200, 215–218, 326, 332, 381
Consequences, role of, 10–11, 374– 380, 389, 403–411
Conservation, 5, 265, 281–282
Continuity-discontinuity issue, 40–44, 383–384
Conversion hysteria, 197, 199–200
Countercathexis, 211
Creativity, 396, 401–402, 433
Crises, psychosocial, 236–244